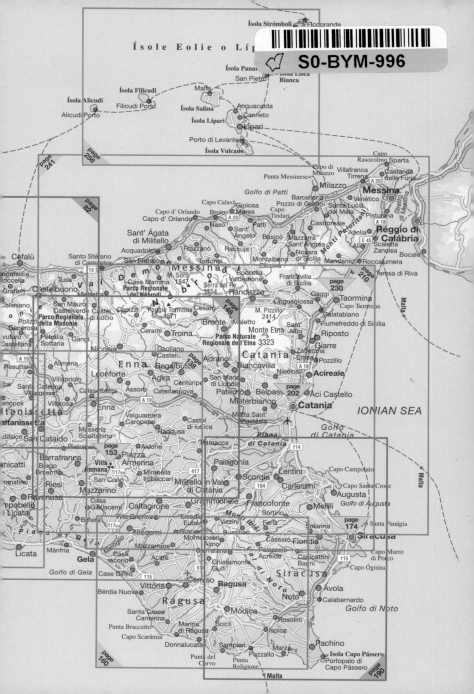

Map Legend

═══╤═══	Autostrada with Junction
═ ═ ═ ═	Autostrada (under construction)
═══════	Dual Carriageway
───────	Main Road
───────	Secondary Road
───────	Minor road
───────	Track
──■─ ■─	International Boundary
─ ─ ─ ─	Province Boundary
_ •_ ▲ _	National Park/Reserve
─ ─ ─ ─	Ferry Route
✈ ✈	Airport
† ⛪	Church (ruins)
†	Monastery
🏰 🏯	Castle (ruins)
⸫	Archaeological Site
Ω	Cave
★	Place of Interest
🏠	Mansion/Stately Home
※	Viewpoint
⚐	Beach
═══════	Autostrada
═══════	Dual Carriageway
───────	Main Roads
───────	Minor Roads
───────	Footpath
▬━▬━▬	Railway
�	Pedestrian Area
▬▬▬	Important Building
▬▬▬	Park
❶	Numbered Sight
🚌	Bus Station
❶	Tourist Information
✉	Post Office
✝	Cathedral/Church
☪	Mosque
✡	Synagogue
𝕴	Statue/Monument
▯	Tower
³⫯ᶜ	Lighthouse

INSIGHT GUIDES

SICILY

APA PUBLICATIONS L

Part of the Langenscheidt Publishing Group

🏛 INSIGHT GUIDE

SICILY

Editor
Brian Bell
Art Director
Klaus Geisler
Picture Editor
Hilary Genin
Production
Kenneth Chan
Cartography Editor
Zoë Goodwin

Distribution

UK & Ireland
GeoCenter International Ltd
Meridian House, Churchill Way West
Basingstoke, Hampshire RG21 6YR
sales@geocenter.co.uk

United States
Langenscheidt Publishers, Inc.
36–36 33rd Street, 4th Floor
Long Island City, NY 11106
orders@langenscheidt.com

Australia
Universal Publishers
1 Waterloo Road
Macquarie Park, NSW 2113
sales@universalpublishers.com.au

New Zealand
Hema Maps New Zealand Ltd (HNZ)
Unit 2, 10 Cryers Road
East Tamaki, Auckland 2013
sales.hema@clear.net.nz

Worldwide
**Apa Publications GmbH & Co.
Verlag KG (Singapore branch)**
7030 Ang Mo Kio Avenue 5
08-65 Northstar @ AMK
Singapore 569880
apasin@singnet.com.sg

Printing
CTPS – China

First Edition 1993
Fourth Edition 2006
Updated 2008
Reprinted 2010

ABOUT THIS BOOK

The first Insight Guide pioneered the use of creative full-colour photography in guidebooks in 1970. Since then, we have expanded our range to cater for our readers' need not only for reliable information about their chosen destination but also for a real understanding of that destination. Now, when the internet can supply inexhaustible (but not always reliable) facts, our books marry text and pictures to provide that much more elusive quality: knowledge. To achieve this, they rely heavily on the authority of locally based writers and photographers.

How to use this book

The book is carefully structured to convey an understanding of Sicily:

◆ To understand the island today, you need to know something of its past. The first section covers its people, history and culture in lively essays written by specialists.

◆ The main Places section provides a full run-down of all the attractions worth seeing. The main places of interest are coordinated by number with full-colour maps. Margin notes provide background information and tips on how to save time and money.

◆ Photographic features illuminate aspects of the island's archaeology, architecture and art.

◆ Photographs are chosen not only to illustrate geography and buildings but also to convey the moods of the city and the life of its people.

◆ The Travel Tips listings section provides a point of reference for information on travel, hotels, shops and festivals. Information may be located quickly by using the index printed on the back cover flap – and the flaps are designed to serve as bookmarks.

The contributors

This edition of *Insight Guide: Sicily* was supervised by **Brian Bell**, Insight Guides' editorial director, whose experience of Sicilian hospitality, food and driving techniques encouraged him to endorse Luigi Barzini's judgment in his classic 1964 book, *The Italians*: "Sicily is the schoolroom model of Italy for beginners, with every Italian quality and defect magnified, exasperated and brightly coloured."

The book was comprehensively revised by **Geoffrey Aquilina Ross**, a journalist and author who is currently based in his native Malta, a 90-minute catamaran ride from Sicily. His knowledge of the island is blended with the expertise of writers who contributed to previous editions, much of whose work survives in this edition.

The principal contributor was **Lisa Gerard-Sharp**, a writer and broadcaster with a special interest in Italy and the principal author of several Insight Guides to the country's cities and regions. In compiling the earlier editions of this book, she found herself intrigued by the clash between the legendary immutability of Sicily and the apparent striving for change, especially among the young.

The History section was the work of **Rowlinson Carter**, a writer with a passion for Classical history. He was fascinated by the Sicilians' early experiments with democracy, but equally intrigued that "the democratic interlude soon gave way to a race of full-blooded tyrants".

The chapters on Food and the Egadi Islands were contributed by **Mary Taylor Simeti**, an American writer who divided her time between Palermo and her farm in Alcamo.

The chapters on the Aeolian Islands and Sicily's Wild Places were written by **Jenny Bennathan**, who combines a love of wildlife with a fondness for the Aeolians. In 1999 she moved to Alicudi, to become the island's 101st resident.

The most recent information update was undertaken by London-based editor and Italy expert, **Natasha Foges**.

This edition was indexed by **Elizabeth Cook**.

CONTACTING THE EDITORS

We would appreciate it if readers would alert us to errors or outdated information by writing to:

Insight Guides, P.O. Box 7910, London SE1 1WE, England. Fax: (44) 20 7403-0290. insight@apaguide.co.uk

NO part of this book may be reproduced, stored in a retrieval system or transmitted in any form or means electronic, mechanical, photocopying, recording or otherwise, without prior written permission of *Apa Publications*. Brief text quotations with use of photographs are exempted for book review purposes only. Information has been obtained from sources believed to be reliable, but its accuracy and completeness, and the opinions based thereon, are not guaranteed.

www.insightguides.com

LEFT: hoping for a catch at Siracusa.

Maps

Map Legend **facing title page**

Travel Tips

TRANSPORT

ACCOMMODATION

ACTIVITIES

A–Z: PRACTICAL INFORMATION

LANGUAGE

THE BEST OF SICILY

Setting priorities, saving money, unique attractions...
here, at a glance, are our recommendations, plus tips
and tricks even Sicilians won't always know

SICILY FOR FAMILIES

These attractions are popular with children,
though not all will suit every age group.

- **Train around the volcano** Dramatic sightseeing. The Circumetnea Railway offers a wonderful ride around the base of Etna through dramatic scenery. Leisurely round trip takes nearly 4 hours with just one stop at Randazzo. Some trains make many stops. From Taormina or Catania. *See page 217.*

- **The Alcántara Gorge Adventure**. *Gola di Alcántara*, near Giardini, is a wild gorge carved by the river, 19 metres (64 ft) deep and sometimes little more than 2.7 metres (9 ft) wide. You can hire boots and wetsuits – the water is freezing. Buses from Taormina and Catania. Avoid Sundays. *See page 217.*

- **To the Islands by Sea** Ferries and hydrofoils sail from Palermo, Cefalù and Milazzo to islands off the Tyrrhenean cost – **Vulcano**, **Lipari** and **Salina** are closest. A great day out in the summer.

(Travel agents can organise links from Catania, Messina and Taormina.) *See page 266.*

- **Puppet theatre** Puppet shows are a Sicilian tradition. Their stories are based on the adventures of the brave knights of Charlemagne (Carlo Magno) with the moral: the importance of honour and chivalry. The best in Palermo are Compagnia Argento, Via Novelli 1 (tel: 091 611 3680). Cuticcio Mimmo, Via Bara all' Olivella 95. (tel: 091 323 400). *See pages 198–9.*

BEST FESTIVALS AND EVENTS

Every city, town and village has days of celebration. Worth making a detour for:

- **Agrigento**: First week of February. The almond blossom and folklore festival in the Valley of the Temples.

- **Catania**: 1–5 February. Celebration of city's patron, St Agata. Giant candles are carried through the streets with a procession of 17th-century carriages and another in which the saint's relics are towed by citizens dressed in traditional white gowns.

- **Piazza Armerina**: 13–14 August. *Palio dei Normanni*. A jousting tournament and processions in medieval costumes celebrate the victory of the Normans over the Arabs.

- **Calascibetta**: 1–3 September. *Sagra di Buon Riposo*, a folk and food festival, with a livestock market, a race *(Corsa dei Berberi)* and much sausage eating.

- **Catania**: 8 September. Festival of Maria SS Bambina. Fisherman's festival with a procession of boats.

- **Zafferana Etnea**. October. *Ottobrata Zafferanese*. Gastronomic feast celebrating the best local produce: grapes, mushrooms, mustard, honey and wine.

BELOW Palermo celebrates Santa Rosalia on 10–16 July.

THE BEST BEACHES

Sicily offers a vast range of beaches, from black volcanic rocks to golden sands. Most beaches in the main resorts charge a fee for which you will get umbrella, beds, showers, *caffè*, depending on the establishment's rating.

● **The islands**: lovely, often volcanic, beaches. Ustica, the Egadi Islands and the Aeolian Islands are ever-popular.

● **Cefalù**, **Mondello** and **Taormina** are extremely clean in the summer season.

● **Siracusa** has beautifully unspoilt beaches to the south and even wild ones near **Capo Passero**.

● **Catania** and **Taormina**: those around **Aci Trezza** and **Aci Castello** tend to be rocky, exciting and well-equipped.

ABOVE: Cefalù's beach, with the Old Town in the background.

ABOVE: bathing in a mud pool on Vulcano in the Aeolian Islands.

THE SWEETEST DESSERTS

● **Cannoli**: crunchy tubes of sweet pastry filled with fresh ricotta studded with pieces of candied fruit and chocolate. Made daily at *pasticcerie*.

● **Cassata**: sweetened ricotta, candied fruit, almond paste, sponge cake. Served as a dessert after a meal.

● **Granita**: sorbet made with fresh fruit. Sometimes a black coffee version. Often served with a brioche.

● **Gelati**: Sicilians say they make the best.

● **Frutta alla Martorana**: invented by nuns. Fruit made, almost realistically, from pure marzipan.

THE FINEST CHURCHES

● **PALERMO**: Of course the **Cappella Palatina** (Palatine Chapel) with its Byzantine and Arab-Norman mosaics. *See Best of Palermo, page 9*.

● **PALERMO: Oratorio del Rosario di San Domenico**, Via dei Bambinai 2, near Vucciria market. Grandiose baroque with wonderful stucco work by Serpotta. *See page 67*.

● **MONREALE**: The **Duomo**. Like the Capella Palatina in Palermo, but much, bigger. Magnificent glittering mosaics adorn every surface. *See pages 81–2*.

● **CATANIA: Cattedrale di Sant'Agata**. Rebuilt after 1094 earthquake using columns from Roman amphitheatre. *See page 203*.

● **SIRACUSA: Duomo**. Temple of Athena converted to Christians. Damaged in 1693 earthquake and remodelled with exuberant baroque style. *See page 183*.

BEST-VALUE SNACKS

● *Lunch*: At a *bar*. Delicious *panini* (rolls), *tramezzini* (sandwiches), *arancini* (deep-fried ball of rice with meat or vegetable filling). Pay first at the *cassa* and then go to counter with the receipt to order. Take out and eat where there is a view.

● *Lunch*: At a *tavola calda*. Simple lunch at self-service buffet with choice of pasta, rice and varieties of grilled vegetables.

● At a *pizza al taglio*. Select freshly-baked slices of pizza to go.

● *Dinner*: At a *pizzeria*. The right one smells of the wood-burning oven. *Pizzerie* open evenings only, maybe on Sundays. They have pasta and meat dishes too.

ONLY IN SICILY...

- **Sicilian baroque** Palaces and churches created with theatrical and extravagant style, with an emphasis on fantasy and ornamentation. There are fine examples everywhere but the best preserved baroque town is golden **Noto**. Look too at its neighbouring towns: Ragusa, Scicli, Comiso, Catania and Acireale, rebuilt after the 1693 earthquake.
- **Superb mosaics** The **Villa Romana** at **Piazza Armerina**, an extraordinary villa with some of the most extensive and beautiful mosaics known. *See page 153.*
- **Thermal spas** Sometimes the smell of the sulphur is strong, but for centuries people have come to wallow in mud baths or take water cures. Especially at **Sciacca** (Palermo province), **Castellammare del Golfo** (Tràpani province). And the bubbling sulphur baths on **Vulcano**.
- **Classical drama** Theatres at Classical sites often return to their original function, Greek drama, from May to July. The best for Teatro Greco are at **Segesta**, **Siracusa** and **Taormina**.
- **Nature reserves** Protected, wild and alive. Outside Palermo is **Lo Zíngaro**, Tràpani has **Lo Stagnone**, outside Catania is **Parco**

dell'Etna. In the mountains, **Parco delle Madonie** and **Parco di Nebrodi**.
- **Caltagirone pottery** Famous for its ceramics since ancient times, Caltagirone *majolica* is unmistakable, painted in blue, green and yellow. Plates, jugs, ornaments and more at a wide variety of prices, depending on the fame of the pottery. Similar pottery from **Santa Stefano di Camastra** (outside Cefalù).

ABOVE: baroque at its best in La Martorana, Palermo.
LEFT: a playful Roman mosaic in the Villa Romana.

THE TOP TEMPLES

Sicily has more ancient Greek temples than Greece. The best:
- **Agrigento**: Ancient Akragas, an opulent city, is now the most significant ancient site in Sicily. In the Valley of the Temples is the world's largest temple. *See pages 118–23.*
- **Segesta**: Tràpani province. Beautiful and lonely setting.

Majestic Doric temple. *See page 98.*
- **Selinunte**: Tràpani province. A once great city founded around 650 BC but ravaged by the Carthaginians. *See pages 102–4.*
- **Mózia**: Tràpani province. Not a temple but site of Carthaginian city on an island in the Stagnone lagoon. *See pages 100–1.*

BELOW: Concord Temple in Valley of the Temples, Agrigento.

THE BEST OF PALERMO

MUST-SEE
- The **Palazzo dei Normanni**, Piazza Indipendenza, houses the Sicilian Parliament, the Royal Apartments, Sala di Re Ruggero (King Roger's Room). The most important must-see here is the **Cappella Palatina** (Palatine Chapel) with Byzantine and Arab-Norman mosaics.

THE MARKETS
- Mornings are best. Great for exploring and finding bargains.

Vucciria (around Piazza Caraccio) is the most established and busy. Others include **Ballarò** (Piazza del Carmine), **Capo** (Via Beati Paoli) and the flea market, **Mercato delle Pulci** (Piazza Domenico Peranni).

CHURCHES
- **The Cathedral**: The *Cattedrale* (Duomo), Corso Vittorio Emanuele. Norman cathedral containing royal tombs and a small museum.
- **La Martorana**: Santa Maria dell'Ammiraglio. Dreamlike Arab-Norman church with Byzantine mosaics.
- **Convento dei Cappuccini**, Via Cappuccini. Gruesome catacombs contain 8,000 mummified Palermitans.

MUSEUMS
- **Museo Archeologico Regionale**, Piazza Olivella. Includes great Classical finds from all over Sicily. One of the richest archaeological collections in Italy and Sicily.
- **Palazzo Abatellis**, Via Alloro 4. The palace dating from 1490 is now the Galleria Regionale della Sicilia, with medieval and Moorish works as well as Renaissance paintings by Antonello da Messina.

OPERA
- **Teatro Massimo**, Piazza Verdi. A neoclassical theatre that is one of the largest opera houses in Europe.

GARDENS
- **Orto Botánico**, Via Lincoln 2. One of the leading botanic gardens in Europe. Over 10,000 different species representative of all areas of the world's vegetation.
- **Parco della Favorita**, Viale Diana, on the slopes of Monte Pellegrino. Lovely park laid out by the Bourbons.

ABOVE: Palermo is rich in bars and *caffès*. **LEFT:** Vucciria market.

MONEY-SAVERS

Culture week. *Settimana della Cultura* is Italy and Sicily's culture week, when all state-run museums and historical sites are free of charge. Usually late-April or May. Crowded maybe, but you can see all that is on offer.

Free churches. The churches are extraordinary in their variety and their abundance of art. Wander in, take a look. Many close between 1pm and 4.40pm. Entrance is free.

Train Travel. Fares on trains are among the lowest in Europe. On the Italian state railway, Ferrovie dello Stato, children between 4 and 12 pay half-price; younger, they travel free. To travel around the island by train, a Trenitalia Pass is great value. The pass gives you 10 days of travel within a two-month period. And, even better, the ticket can be used for up to five people – which means five people travelling together counts only as one trip. Passes are available from main line stations in Italy and Sicily and also from Rail Europe offices (www.raileurope.com or www.raileurope.co.uk) and Italian State Railway agents (www.fs-inline.com).

Bus Travel. Buses are cheap and efficient, wherever you are. Ask at bus stations for schedules and maps to help with exploring. You'll be surprised how far you can go.

A VOLCANIC HERITAGE

Sicily's complex history has produced an
island with a unique character – proud,
introspective, enigmatic and irreverent

Sicily may be Italian, but the islanders are Latin only by adoption. They may look back at *Magna Graecia* or Moorish Sicily but tend to be bored by their exotic past. Mostly, they sleep-walk their way through history, as if it were a bad play in a long-forgotten language. Floating not far beneath the surface is a kaleidoscope of swirling foreignness against a backdrop of Sicilian fatalism.

This is the legacy of a land whose heyday was over 700 years ago. It is most visible in the diversity of architectural styles, brought together under one roof in a remarkable mongrel, Siracusa Cathedral. Yet Sicilians themselves, as they often boast, are *bastardi puri* ("pure bastards"), the product of racial overdose.

The assumption that people want overt power, leadership, laws, equality, a democratically calibrated society, is laughably unSicilian. The Greeks' lessons in democracy fell on stony ground: the Sicilians responded with a race of full-blooded tyrants. The Mafia, with greater superficial sophistication, showed equal disdain for democratic niceties: their shadowy state within a state became more effective than the pale, public model. Sicilians dismiss democracy as a system only suitable for "Nordic" countries. Until recently, most landed, educated Sicilians declined public office, preferring private gain to public good. As the Prince says in Lampedusa's *The Leopard*: "I cannot lift a finger in politics. It would only get bitten."

Poor Sicilians knuckled under or emigrated, often flourishing on foreign soil. Millions have conquered the United States with a classic Sicilian combination of contacts, cuisine and cunning, symbolised by the Pizza Connection, the Mafia's imaginative drugs cartel. The heroin distribution and money-laundering ring operated in the guise of an international pizza chain. This is the deadly product served by Sicilian history. As the writer Leonardo Sciascia says: "History has been a wicked stepmother to us Sicilians." Yet it is this heritage of doom, drama and excess that draws visitors to an island marooned between Europe and Africa.

Goethe, too, found Sicily intoxicating, from the Classical temples and Etna's eruptions to the volcanic nature of the Sicilians. "To have seen Italy without seeing Sicily," he wrote, "is not to have seen Italy at all – for Sicily is the key to everything." ❏

PRECEDING PAGES: the Temple of Olympian Zeus, Valley of the Temples; the Moorish port of Sciacca. **LEFT:** a headless Roman and a news-hungry citizen in Catania.

THE SICILIANS

Brooding, conservative, suspicious and superstitious – or self-confident, sensitive, honest and hospitable? The Sicilians are a mass of apparent contradictions

Sicilians have a reputation for being brooding, suspicious and unfathomable. Closer contact reveals stoicism, conservatism and deep sensibility. This contradictory character does not match the sunny Mediterranean stereotype of *dolce far niente*, but once over the initial hurdles, outsiders may encounter overwhelming hospitality, boundless curiosity and smothering friendship on the slimmest of pretexts.

In 1814 the British Governor of Sicily was perplexed that "Sicilians expect everything to be done for them; they have always been so accustomed to obedience." His Sicilian minister argued for absolutism: "Too much liberty is for the Sicilians what would be a pistol or stiletto in the hands of a boy or a madman." Critics claim that Sicilians remain sluggish citizens, subsidy junkies with little sense of self-help. Sicilians reply that power and prestige lie elsewhere. History has taught them to have no faith in institutions.

The meaning of family

In the face of this, the traditional responses are emigration, resignation, complicity or withdrawal into a private world. Though emigration has been the choice of millions, most Sicilians choose to stay but avoid confrontation with the shadow-state of patronage and the Mafia. They prefer to live intensely, but in private. As a result, their world is circumscribed by the family, the bedrock of island life.

Palermo is emblematic of the retreat from the world and also of an ambivalence about class. It goes against the grain of Sicilian sen-

timentality to admit that the middle classes have fled the historic centre in droves to settle in safe leafy villages or in the suburbs. Yet even here, many modest homes maintain a level of security more common to a South American dictator, with watchmen, electronic gates and savage dogs. Optimists point to a gradual return of the middle classes to the *centro storico*, with one square held up as a shining example, a socially mixed island which could be the city's salvation. But elsewhere, gentrification looks a long way off. Arab and African immigrants occupy derelict buildings by the port while neighbouring quarters are home to the underclass (*sottoproletariato*). Hovels lurk in the shadow of splendid mansions or villas.

The Sicilian upper classes lead such a separate lifestyle that a social vacuum is inevitable. In rural Sicily, the divide is further consolidated by education, Mafia affiliation and isolation.

Foreign influences

The story of private virtues and public vices is linked to Sicily's hybrid past. As the writer Gesualdo Bufalino says: "The Greeks shaped our sensitivity to light and harmony. The Muslims brought us a fragrance of Oriental gardens, of legendary *Thousand and One Nights*; but they also sowed in us a fanatical exaltation

and an inclination to deceit and voluptuousness. The Spanish gave us hyperbole and haughtiness, the magnificence of words and rites, the magnanimity of our code of honour, but also a strong taste of ashes and death." Even today, the Arab west is overladen with inscrutability, Spanish manners and ceremony. By contrast, the Greek east is more democratic, with closer links to the Italian mainland.

Sicily's miscegenation lives on in the language. *Cristiani* (Christians) is a generic word for people, just as *turchi* (Turks) refers to hea-

thens. Appearances matter in Sicily: the word *azzizzare* (to beautify) comes from the Arabic; *orfanità* is Spanish-Palermitan dialect for looking good; *spagnolismo* (Hispanicism) naturally means seeming better than you are.

Within a cocoon of personal loyalty to friends and family, individuals cultivate their patch. In a traditionally oppressed culture, one's word is one's bond; lives have depended on *parole d'onore,* so promises must be kept. But in the eyes of a pessimistic or powerless individual, betrayal can happen only too easily, sparked off by a casual rebuff. Any rejection of hospitality is seen as a betrayal. As a Palermitan lawyer says: "For us, hospitality is a joy and a duty with obligations on both sides. A refusal is not just rude but fuels our *complessi di tradimento* [betrayal complex]."

Sicilian heroes tend to be dead, ideally martyred like St Agata. However, the cult of the anti-hero and the underdog gives prime place to the bandit Salvatore Giuliano, the incarnation of rebellious bravery. By contrast, state-sanctioned heroes like the murdered anti-Mafia Judge Falcone are honoured too late; and Leoluca Orlando, his successor, had to work hard to gain the respect of the Palermitans. Any genuine hero trying to change the system is scorned with the ultimate insult: *"Idu nu du è"* (he's a nobody). The *disfattista* temperament, full of destructive criticism, is also brought to bear on new initiatives. Perhaps the natives' sombre temperament is the product of insularity.

A passion for the present

Yet, despite their melancholic immutability, Sicilians have a passion for the present. Thanks to a heightened sense of history, the islanders attach supreme importance to time. They see themselves as volatile forces of nature, as violent as Etna, but imbued with a sense of the sacred. Spirituality is expressed in spontaneous church services led by lay women. In festivals, Classical polytheism merges with Christianity. But the everyday intimacy of the relationship with God implies a chatty equality and an acceptance of Him in any guise.

Lampedusa's *The Leopard* is illuminating in unravelling this state of being Sicilian: "Sicilians never wish to improve for the simple reason that they believe themselves perfect. Their vanity is stronger than their misery. Every inva-

---

LEFT: a volcanic encounter near Mount Etna.
ABOVE: a traditional wedding in Caltanissetta.

sion by outsiders… upsets their illusion of achieved perfection, and risks disturbing their self-satisfied waiting for nothing at all."

As for the role of women, anyone who knows a Sicilian family will be aware that there is a strong basis for the belief that Sicily is in fact a matriarchy; that behind the public pretence that the man is boss, the woman is really in charge. Certainly, Sicilian women are far from being quiet, retiring, obedient vessels.

Battle of the sexes

Yet the familiar postcard image of the men of the town meeting together to play cards or talk at the end of the day is still very much a real-

community and political programmes to improve their children's prospects.

Now most women who want a more progressive existence simply leave the rural areas. Their reality is a rural exodus to university in the city, and Sicily has a long tradition of girls excelling in higher education.

Catania, Palermo, Siracusa and Messina enjoy liberal lifestyles, at least for the *borghesia* (middle classes). A relatively high proportion of women have careers and independence. The 1974 divorce law gave women equal status and, when middle-class women marry, for the most part they keep their own surnames.

The vexed question of whether Sicily is a

ity in small-town Sicily. One frequently ends up wondering: "Where are the women?"

Traditionally life was indoors, the grandmother, mother and daughter cooking, cleaning and passing the hours together. But in recent years political developments have encouraged associations of women who have got together to try to push through changes. The fight against the bomb, against an oppressive male-dominated system and most recently against the Mafia have brought women together in groups of increasing volubility. Although these are largely middle-class, educated women, more working-class women, mothers of drug addicts and minor criminals are getting involved with

matriarchy can be resolved in part by dividing Sicilian life into public and private domains: in public the man runs the family's affairs. But within the home, the woman is in charge.

Most forward-looking Sicilians bring up their children with fewer distinctions between the sexes. True, children stay at home until they are married, even in the most progressive households – but why would they move out? Property is expensive and the family is a tight-knit unit that functions very strongly at all levels and ages. In true Sicilian style, what seems traditional is, for the most part, pragmatic. ❏

ABOVE: barber's shop, Vucciria market, Palermo.

Rural Life

Secrecy and melancholy seem palpable in rural Sicily, but even the most secluded villages are building bridges to the future. Travellers will notice certain technological incongruities: fancy sports cars racing past donkeys laden with bushels of firewood; apartment building towering over clay-tile roofs or ancient cottages.

Most villages are neither wholly traditional nor wholly modern. They are in the middle, adrift between the feudal past and high-tech future. Fifty years of aid have raised the standard of living but have done little to encourage lasting economic change. Once basic services like electricity, plumbing, medical care and education were a luxury. Today, they are taken for granted. The traditional peasant dream of buying land and farming for oneself is being supplanted by the desire for a satellite TV or new car.

But while consumerism is on the rise, there is little evidence that any deep-seated changes have taken root in the countryside. Villages are being subsidised both by government funds and emigrant remittances, just enough to give them a taste of the North's wealth without fostering economic self-sufficiency.

Underemployed and undercapitalised, many people still have to piece together a livelihood from a variety of jobs. It is not unusual for a family to farm one or more tiny parcels of land, sharecrop another, own a stake in an olive press or harvesting machine. Competition is stiff, and shrewdness, or *furberia*, is considered an asset, especially in business. "Better to be a devil with a pocketful of money," the old saying goes, "than a fool with a few lire."

A man is expected to take care of his family, to take advantage of opportunities – and, if necessary, other people – without worrying too much about ethics. Generosity and kindness are highly valued. A proverb says it all: "The man who makes himself a sheep will be eaten by a wolf."

The success of the family is not mea-

sured solely by wealth, but by the accumulation of influence and prestige. In a land where government is historically weak, personal power is highly valued. The man who is able to take care of his own affairs is someone who commands respect, a man of honour. And this man of honour is not only in a position to help his family, but his friends as well. *Clientelismo* (patronage) is the only sure way of getting ahead.

Family loyalty extends to the village as a whole, too, especially when villagers face outsiders. It's not unusual to hear people refer to themselves first as members of a village, Stefanesi, Sciaccatani, Caltabel-

lotesi, and only then as Sicilians or, less commonly, Italians. Such feelings are natural enough. Small villages tend to be dominated by three or four surnames and, after years of intermarriage, the entire village may seem like an extended family.

As in an extended family, everybody knows everybody else's business, and keeping up appearances is absolutely essential to family pride. This involves dressing and behaving well, performing religious duties, maintaining the appearance of modest wealth and fulfilling family obligations. In short, it means making a *bella figura*, a good impression. Gossip is a great leveller. ❏

RIGHT: a farmer in Trápani province.

THE SHAPING OF SICILY

The island's warring tribes were subdued by the Romans, whose seven centuries of dominance were followed by a succession of foreign powers, including the Greeks, Germans, French, Spanish and Habsburgs. Although it became part of Italy in 1861, it is in many ways un-Italian

Sicilian history is a cavalcade of invasion by ancient tribes. The Sicani, Siculi, Elymni were the first. Then came the Carthaginians and Greeks, the Romans, Arabs, mercenaries and slaves, Vandals, Goths, Saracens, Normans and Spaniards. Most remained for long periods, adding rich layers to Sicily's extraordinary fusion of genes and culture.

The islanders were not great shapers of their own destiny but the powers of their subversiveness and survival were substantial. In response to invasion, they proved themselves to be a ball and chain around each conqueror's necks: sullen, slothful, uncooperative, a millstone dragging its rulers into futile conflict while leaving Sicilians free to live in their own luxurious private theatre.

The key to power

In days when the known world was limited to the lands lining the Mediterranean, the boundaries were Phoenicia (today's Lebanon) and the Straits of Gibraltar. Carthage was only 160km (100 miles) away, in Tunisia. Sicily was not only in the centre, but it divided "the world" into two. Ancient superpowers could dominate one side or the other but in order to control both, they had to possess Sicily.

Although not a large island, Sicily was big enough for enemies like the Phoenicians and Greeks to occupy separate parts yet never quite big enough to be a power in its own right, even

though Siracusa (Syracuse) was once considered the greatest city in Europe. The island was always at the mercy of larger forces swirling around its shores and dragged into almost every major Mediterranean war.

However, three indigenous groups with separate cultures and languages were established: the Elymni (Elymians) in the northwest, the Sicani (Sicans) in the west and the Siculi (Sicels) in the east.

When the Phoenicians arrived, they occupied northwestern Sicily and welcomed the resident Sicani as neighbours. They fortified their settlements like Solunto and Panormus (Palermo) only when their livelihood was

---

LEFT: a 6th-century BC Phoenician head from Mozia.
RIGHT: Venus Anadiomene, a Roman copy of a Greek original, held in the Museo Archeologico, Siracusa.

threatened by Greek expansion. On the island of Motya (modern Mozia), their base for attacking the Greeks, there were sensationalist aspects of their culture, such as sacred prostitution and human sacrifice. Numerous jars of charred babies imply that Motya was a grim place. The balance of power swung from Siculi to Sicani and back again. But since Sicily is named after the Siculi race, it is clear that they ultimately triumphed, in name at least.

Enter the Greeks

When Sicily formed part of *Magna Graecia* (Greater Greece) it had a population of more than 3 million – greater than Athens

and Sparta combined. The islanders spoke Greek and practised Greek art. Agriculture flourished and the island became the granary of the Mediterranean.

But none of this was evident when the Greek migrants first arrived. Nor were they aware that there were Phoenician settlements on the western shore. The first colony on the east coast was Naxos (734 BC). Then came Zankle (Messina), Leontinoi (Lentini) and Katane (Catania). In the south, with settlers from Rhodes and Crete, were Gela, Akragas (Agrigento), Selinunte and Heraclea Minoa. Syrakusai (Siracusa), the greatest colony, was founded by Corinthian Greeks. These colonies were ruled by "tyrants", a term that originally meant men who seized power instead of inheriting it – an early form of today's dictators.

Sicily's first taste of the battles ahead occurred in 480 BC, when the Carthaginian commander Hamilcar invaded Sicily with 300,000 mercenaries aboard 200 galleys and 3,000 transport ships. He besieged Himera (Términi Imerese) by land and sea, prompting the tyrant Theron to appeal for help from Gelon, the tyrant of Siracusa. Gelon responded with 50,000 men and 5,000 cavalry and 150,000 Carthaginians were slain in the ensuing battle.

Athens intervenes

Sicilian cities were always ready to fight at the drop of a hat and, when Selinunte and Segesta quarrelled, Selinunte asked Siracusa for help, so Segesta approached Athens. In Athens they were prudently welcoming and, when Segesta offered to pay the costs of military aid, plus a handsome premium, they sent representatives to look into Segesta's creditworthiness.

The Athenians were received with a show of breathtaking splendour at the temple of Aphrodite on Mount Eryx (Erice). On show were sacred vessels made of gold and silver and dripping with precious stones. They were too sacred to be touched, they were told, or even viewed except from a reverential distance. The ambassadors enjoyed sumptuous banquets, eating off gold and silver plates; so awed were they that they had no hesitation in recommending ships be put at the disposal of Segesta. True, on the question of payment, the city had given them only enough to cover the first month, but there could be no doubt that

---

THE NAME SICILY

The Siculi who gave their name to Sicily came from Liguria in the 13th century BC. According to Thucydides, they "defeated the Sicani in battle, drove them to the south and west of the island, and renamed it Sicily instead of Sicania." These seafarers and farmers were gradually Hellenised by Greek settlers on the east coast. However, in settlements like Siracusa, the Siculi were reduced to serfdom. They were seldom granted Greek citizenship, though a few were elevated from the status of barbarians (that is, non-Greeks), to persons qualified to marry Greeks – the ultimate accolade. Sicily abounds with Siculi settlements, with the best one at Ispica.

the balance would be forthcoming. What the Athenians didn't know was that the temple treasures were fakes. The gold and silver plate was borrowed from the Siculi, as was the silver bullion. But the fraud was never exposed and the 250 ships that sailed from Piraeus with 25,000 men was the largest ever Greek armada.

The battle for control of Siracusa's great harbour took place in 413 BC, with Greeks fighting Greeks. The Athenians were humiliated. Their generals were executed and the 7,000 captured troops were lowered 30 metres (100 ft) into stone quarries, into a hell which was stifling hot by day and freezing at night. After 10 weeks, those who survived were sold as slaves.

A year later, Hannibal attacked Akragas. But, while digging trenches, the Carthaginians had exposed corpses and a plague swept through the camp, killing Hannibal. The city eventually fell after an eight-month siege.

After blaming Siracusan generals for the defeat, in 405 BC a spirited demagogue, one Dionysius, was given full powers to sort out the military mess. He ruled efficiently for 38 years, to be followed by Timoleon (345–336 BC), who restored some sort of democracy, and then Agathocles (315–289 BC), who returned to the bellicose old days, seizing any land still occupied by Carthaginians. Finally Hieron II (265–215 BC) brought a measure of stability,

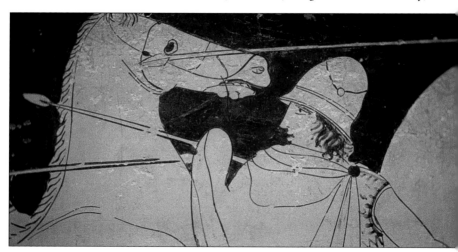

Naturally, the Sicilian Greeks went back to fighting among themselves, thus triggering a second Carthaginian invasion. Hannibal, the eldest son of Hamilcar, had a score to settle with the city where Hamilcar died. In 409 BC he arrived with a powerful force and made quick work of Selinunte. In fact, it ceased to exist.

Then he turned his attention to personal vengeance. In the massacre at Himera, 3,000 male survivors were taken to where Hamilcar had died, tortured and offered as sacrifices to the memory of the dead general.

LEFT: Perseus slays Medusa, from Temple C, Selinunte.
ABOVE: detail from vase, Museo Archeologico, Gela.

forging a treaty between Siracusa and Carthage. Then he changed the course of history; he made an alliance with the new, fast expanding Mediterranean superpower: Rome.

Rome and Byzantium

In 264 BC the Punic Wars triggered momentous changes in Sicily. Sandwiched between the rival powers of Rome and Carthage, it was a battleground. Popular images of the Punic Wars are dominated by Hannibal's crossing the Appenines with elephants to attack Rome, but the first rounds were fought in Sicily, bringing the island firmly within the Roman Empire.

Rome's takeover was methodical. First,

Akragas (Agrigento) fell in 261 BC and 25,000 of its inhabitants were sold into slavery. Then Panormus (Palermo) and Selinunte and, ultimately, after a two-year siege, Siracusa. The island became Rome's first province (as opposed to being incorporated in the Republic) because it was deemed too Hellenised, too Greek in its culture. So Greek language and traditions prevailed.

The next 50 years saw revolts by slaves which were brutally curbed. More damaging was the civil war between Octavian (future Emperor Augustus) and Sextus Popeius who seized the island in 44 BC. When Sextus lost, the retribution on the Sicilans was severe.

REBELS WITH A CAUSE

One of the richest men was Damophilus of Enna, a ruthless slave master. In 138 BC, whipped up by Eunus his court jester, 400 slaves rioted, murdered Damophilus and joined other dissident slaves. (In Sicily, a citizen probably kept about 200 slaves.) Eunus then enjoyed kingship until Rome sent an army of 20,000; the slaves were killed, Eunus imprisoned. In 104 BC, Rome was attacked by Germanic tribes, and the Senate freed slaves throughout the provinces to help fight these barbarians. The slaves promptly rebelled – in Italy, 90,000 were led by Spartacus, a gladiator. Those captured in Sicily were shipped to Rome to fight wild animals at the circus.

History is silent about the next five centuries of Roman rule, but, in common with the rest of the Empire, the Sicilians became recognised Roman citizens in AD 212 – the island was now an extension of Italy. It acquired a reputation as a Roman tourist resort; the emperor Caligula was especially fond of it. A tantalising glimpse of Sicily as the playground of rich Romans is Villa Romana at Casale *(see page 153)*. Mosaics show a phantasmagoria of bathing, dancing, fishing, hunting, wine-pressing, music and drama – a vision of paradise a wealthy, contented pagan would see while relaxing on holiday.

Vandals and Goths

Then Sicily exploded under the onslaught of the unmitigated louts of Western history – the Vandals. Having been expelled from Germany, they planned to use Sicily as a springboard back to Europe.

But Sicily, like Rome and the rest of Italy, fell to yet another Germanic race, the Goths. As Italy grew too chaotic to remain the seat of the Empire, the Emperor decamped to Constantinople, or Byzantium, as the Eastern Empire was named. In time, his Byzantine general Belisarius was ordered to invade Sicily to reclaim Greek heritage; the Sicilians sighed with relief. But joy was premature. Emperor Constans II proceeded to seize property, tax extortionately and sell debtors into slavery. It was a slave who redressed the balance in AD 668. While Constans was being soaped in his bath, the slave picked up the soap box and brought it down on the Emperor's head.

Visitors to Byzantine Sicily noted the women's love of ornament. Their jewels were a testament to the skills of Byzantine goldsmiths and a worldly counterpoint to shimmering church mosaics. Byzantine art is well served here even today, with cupolas emblazoned with austere Greek bishops and inscrutable saints. Classical naturalism ceded to Eastern stylisation and realism was replaced by decorative patterns and abstraction.

Arabs and Normans

During the Byzantine period, Sicily was the target of frequent piratical raids by Syrians, Egyptians and Moors from North Africa. As early as 652 AD, Saracens from Kairouan

(Tunisia) made incursions into the island. Then, in 827, came the fully fledged Arab invasion. This was sparked off by a failed Sicilian coup against an unpopular Byzantine governor. Euphemius, a wealthy landowner overcame the imperial garrison in Siracusa, declared himself Emperor and invited the Emir of Tunisia to help him.

A fleet of 100 ships was despatched, with 10,000 troops, mainly Arabs, Berbers and Spanish Muslims. The Arabs slowly gained a foothold and, in 878, Siracusa, Sicily's first city for 1,500 years, fell. It now took second place to Palermo, as Christianity did to Islam, and Greek to Arabic. Palermo Cathedral was converted into a mosque and resounded to Muslim prayers for nearly 250 years. There was an influx of Arab settlers known as Saracens, a term that encompassed Arabs, Berbers and Spanish Moors.

Saracen rule

As virtually an independent emirate, Sicily played a privileged role as a bridge between Africa and Europe. Trade flourished and taxation was low. The tolerant regime allowed subjects to abide by their own laws. Despite freedom of worship, Christians freely converted to Islam: there were soon hundreds of mosques in Palermo.

As well as Arabs from Spain, Syria and Egypt, there were Berbers, Black Africans, Jews, Persians, Greeks, Lombards and Slavs. Western Sicily prospered.

However, the Saracen rulers quarrelled among themselves and with their nominal superiors in North Africa and Baghdad too. But their disunity was nothing compared with the Italian dilemma. Norman knights had entered Italy and the Papacy got itself into such a pickle that in the middle of the 11th century there were simultaneously no fewer than three Popes. Against this chaotic backcloth, Western Christendom struggled to respond.

The Arab domination enhanced Byzantine art and architecture. The Emirs employed Byzantine craftsmen, so earlier decorative patterns and stylisation suffused Islamic art. A thousand years of Greek-infused values could not be so easily erased.

Sicilian conservatism made for a smooth transition from Byzantine to Islamic architecture. After the Hegira (Mohammed's flight in 622), the Arabs simply transplanted Oriental styles to Sicily. Although many churches were converted into mosques, the Arabs happily encased Byzantine art and symbolism in Islamic ornamentation. Christian and Islamic symbolism were conveniently fused.

The Arabs called the Normans "wolves" because of their ferocity, barbarism and native cunning. But, undeterred, the Emirs of Catania and Siracusa invited the Normans to invade

the western part of the island, as they were disgruntled by the concentration of power there. The Norman Hautevilles, Christian freebooters, needed no encouragement.

The Norman conquest

In 1068, Count Roger and his elder brother, Robert Guiscard, a fortune-hunting Norman knight, defeated the Arabs at Misilmeri but the crucial step was the siege of Palermo in 1072. Robert urged his men on to seize the city, which was "hateful to God and subject to devils".

The great Palermo mosque was quickly reconsecrated to Christ and a Mass of Thanks-

LEFT: Roman fresco, Palermo's archaeology museum.
RIGHT: an engraving of St John of the Hermits, Palermo, converted into a mosque by the Arabs.

giving held. Robert magnanimously shared the spoils with Count Roger (also known as Conte Ruggero and King Roger I). He was an autocratic ruler, buttressed by the Byzantine concept of divine rule but, under Arab influence, was transformed from a foolhardy crusader and rough diamond into a cultured figure.

Arab influence did not wane with the Norman conquest. The Normans recognised Saracen superiority in culture and commerce, so welcomed Muslim courtiers and merchants. Most Arabs retained their castles, palaces and lands as well as their social prestige. Arab craftsmanship was prized in the conversion of mosques to cathedrals while their administra-

ARAB ENLIGHTENMENT

On their arrival the Arabs instigated land reforms and encouraged the spread of smallholdings. Their reverence for water created the fountains, baths, reservoirs and storage towers still visible today. Mining techniques were improved. Sulphur, lead, silver, antimony and alum were refined. They cultivated citrus fruits and introduced sugar cane, cotton, mulberries, palms, melons, pistachio nuts, papyrus and flax. Ice from Mount Etna was used to make sorbets and sherbets, while sea salt was dried at Trápani. They introduced coral and tuna fishing. Nor did the Islamic faith deter these sophisticated Arabs from planting *zubbibbu* grapes for wine.

tive skills, erudition and poetry were appreciated at court. The Normans, prodigious builders, went on to plant their realm with castles, churches and palaces in Romanesque and Gothic styles, inspired by Northern architecture, but often subverted by Moorish models.

Count Roger died in 1101, leaving Sicily governed by his widow until the coronation of his son, Roger II, in 1130. Revelling in glory, this Roger spent lavishly on palaces, mosques, gardens and education. As the richest king in Christendom, he indulged his love of Arab art and culture. He also patronised astronomers and astrologers, Koranic scholars and Sicilian poets. This charismatic king was well versed in three languages. His cosmopolitan court was home to French *jongleurs* and balladeers who followed the itinerant Norman knights.

As in Arab times, this liberalism decreed that "Latins, Greeks, Jews and Saracens be judged according to their own laws". Norman French, Greek, Arabic, and Latin were all spoken. Even so, cultural and economic pressures led the Arabs gradually to retreat inland, away from the coastal cities.

Only the Normans were granted fiefdoms, and the rise of the baronial class was the most dubious Norman legacy. But these rugged kings also bequeathed an efficient administration and a relatively liberal regime. In its day, this melting pot of racial talent made for Christendom's most culturally creative society.

From Bad to Good

Roger was succeeded by William I, posthumously nicknamed "the Bad" because he aroused jealousies by being "more a Mohammedan than a Christian in belief, in character and in manners". He lived like an Arab Emir in a palace that contained a bodyguard of black slaves and a harem under eunuch management. His lifestyle was a matter of taste, not faith, because he had no qualms about raiding the Muslims in North Africa on behalf of the Pope.

His son, William the Good, was only 14 when crowned in 1166, and his reign was guided by Walter of the Mill, the English Archbishop of Palermo and architect of Palermo Cathedral. The English connection was strengthened when William's successor, the bastard Tancred, married Joanna, King Richard the Lionheart's sister. Richard raided Messina while on his way to the Crusades but presented Tancred with Excalibur, King Arthur's sword, a fitting tribute to the end of a legendary line of warrior kings.

Emperors, kings and Viceroys

The death of William the Good in 1189 without an heir sent the succession reeling back to the House of Hohenstaufen which produced the Prussian kings and Holy Roman Emperors. Apart from a few interludes, Norman and Spanish blood would reign over Sicily until 1860.

After Roger's line petered out, Henry VI, the Holy Roman Emperor, moved in. He built the palace of La Cuba in Palermo and, eventu-

between empire-building, he founded a school of Sicilian poetry, wrote a book on falconry and studied science, pondering such arcane questions as the workings of Mount Etna and the precise location of hell. He also fortified all of eastern Sicily from Messina to Siracusa and sacked Catania in 1232.

Successors such as Charles of Anjou called themselves King of Sicily, using the title as an adornment as they pursued greater ambitions abroad. Backed by the Pope, Charles plundered the island and taxed so punitively that rebellion hung in the air. Charles moved his capital from Palermo to Naples.

The Easter rebellion in 1282, the most sig-

ally dying of dysentry, was buried in a magnificent tomb in Palermo Cathedral. Next was his son, Frederick I of Sicily, who was, confusingly, crowned Emperor Frederick II. Born in Palermo of a Norman mother, he never considered himself Sicilian yet was known as a "baptised Sultan", thanks to his predilection for *seraglio* and Saracen pages. Despite the Arabian lifestyle, however, Muslims were discriminated against and rural settlements gave way to baronial estates. Nonetheless, in

LEFT: the Normans vanquishing the Saracens, sculpted on the Cathedral of Mazara del Vallo.
ABOVE: the court of Frederick II, *Stupor Mundi*.

nificant uprising in Sicily's history, was both a patriotic insurrection and a revolt against feudalism. But far from freeing Sicilians from a foreign yoke, it led to the War of the Vespers.

It all began when the Easter Monday procession in Palermo was joined by French soldiers from Charles's garrison. The festive mood turned to silence as Sicilian men were searched by the French troops for concealed weapons. As the bell called the faithful to Vespers, the French captain ordered his men to search the women too. "He himself laid hands upon the fairest, and pretending to look for a knife upon her, he thrust his hand out to her bosom." She fainted in the arms of her husband, who let out the ringing cry: "*Moranu i franchiski*" (Death to the French) and the French officer was struck down dead at the feet of the woman he had insulted.

The incident led to a riot which, with the encouragement of the local aristocracy, became an all-out revolt. The uprising spread from Palermo throughout Sicily, and in the massacre that followed no Frenchman was safe. The nobles of Palermo invited Peter II of Aragon to intervene on their behalf, and the Spaniard readily agreed, taking the title King of Sicily while promising to respect the freedom of Sicilians. Charles withdrew and French influence on the island came to an end.

THE SPANISH INQUISITION

After 1487 the Inquisition was powerful in Sicily. (Palermo still has Palazzo Chiaramonte, a severe palace that became the seat of the Inquisition with, carved on the prison walls, *pane, pazienza e tempo*, an appeal for bread, patience and time. Outside, heretics were burned.) The Spanish spy system used a grim police force to expel all Jews. Intellectual and cultural life suffocated. The system enforced the nobles' loyalty to the Spanish crown and supported baronial privileges. But, tied to feudalism, the peasants reverted to banditry. Now popularly perceived as honourable, brigandry was the breeding ground for the birth of the Mafia.

Friction between the Spaniards in Sicily and the Normans in Naples frequently erupted into open warfare until 1372 when Naples agreed to Sicilian self-rule provided that the Sicilian ruler paid an annual tax to Naples and recognised the dominance of the Pope.

This was submission under the guise of independence. Under the rule of a series of viceroys, the island was little more than a source of revenue for Spain, and was drained to fund the *Riconquista* and wars against the Turks.

A pawn in the game

After Charles II died in 1700, Sicily could do little but sit back and watch as the Wars of the Spanish Succession involved several contending European powers. The island was little more than a bargaining counter in the Treaty of Utrecht of 1713, when it was awarded to the northern Italian House of Savoy.

Victor Amadeus, Duke of Piedmont-Savoy and the new king, arrived in an English ship, Britain having decided that Sicily should be given to a weak Italian power rather than the stronger Austrian Habsburgs who still retained Naples. The Sicilian nobility hoped the new King would restore the glitter of the Spanish court and were nonplussed when he appeared in clothes made of undyed wool. The king's survey of the economy underlined how far Sicily had degenerated. Why were there so many unemployed people in Palermo when agriculture was crying out for labour? Agriculture had dwindled so seriously that cereals had to be imported. Tax collection was put out to commercial tender and the highest bidder unleashed a private army of thugs to recoup the cost.

In 1718 the Spanish invaded to recover their former land. The Sicilians, smarting under the Italian king's austerity measures, welcomed the 20,000 troops. Sicilian grandees brought their Spanish finery out of mothballs. The war climaxed at Francavilla, the biggest battle on Sicilian soil since Roman times. The victorious Habsburg Emperor became King of Sicily.

His rule was short. Another Spanish fleet arrived in 1734 and, in a bloodless coup, took Sicily back. Sicily was yet again joined to Naples, under Charles of Bourbon, the Spanish infante. Then, when he succeeded to the Spanish throne in 1759, he handed it over to his son Ferdinand, whose reign lasted 66 years.

After Nelson's defeat of the French fleet in 1798, Ferdinand felt emboldened to attack French forces in Italy but was forced to flee to Palermo under Nelson's protection. The King rewarded Nelson with the Dukedom of Bronte, an estate near Mount Etna. Britain retained an interest in Sicily, if only to prevent Napoleon from moving in. In 1806, Ferdinand IV invited Britain to take over Sicily's defence – which made Sicily richer than it had been for centuries. British subsidies encouraged mining and reduced unemployment. While Ferdinand went on hunting trips, the real governor was William Bentinck, the British commander.

Britain could never decide what to do with Sicily. In the event, an Austrian reconquest of Naples meant that Britain withdrew and in 1816, the Kingdom of the Two Sicilies was created. The kingdoms of Naples and Palermo were unified and Ferdinand became their king. Immediately he abolished the Sicilian flag and took to his court in Naples. Four years later, during the St Rosalia celebrations, Palermo rose against him, a rebellion only put down after the arrival of 10,000 Austrian troops.

Palermo again provided the flashpoint for a revolt in 1848. In the aftermath, the King offered a liberal constitution but this was rejected in favour of an independent Sicily. The Bourbon flag was replaced by the Tricolour.

Garibaldi intervenes

That was the backdrop to another revolt in Palermo in 1860, which spurred Giuseppe Garibaldi to choose Sicily as the starting point for his unification of Italy. On 11 May he arrived at Marsala with 1,000 men to liberate the island from Bourbon rule in the name of the Piedmont House of Savoy. His skill at guerrilla warfare and growing support from the Sicilian peasantry ensured victory over 15,000 Bourbon troops at Calatafimi. Within days, Garibaldi occupied Palermo and proclaimed himself dictator, ruling on behalf of Vittorio Emanuele of Piedmont.

In a plebiscite, Sicilians voted almost unanimously for unification of Italy. This meant the end of Garibaldi's brief dictatorship and the assumption of power by Count Camillo

Cavour in Turin. To many Sicilians, that sounded more like annexation than union.

Under the Italian flag

Union with Italy under king Vittorio Emanuele II did not bring prosperity. The new parliamentary system brought democracy of a sort, but as only 1 percent of the island's population was eligible to vote, most people could not see any improvement. Economically, the island's fortunes went from poor to poorer.

There were abortive uprisings – the first, in Palermo, six years after unification – which were savagely repressed. The only escape from poverty seemed to be emigration and in the last

decades of the 19th century, villages lost many of their men to the United States, Argentina, Tunisia and Brazil. In a single year, Sicily lost 20 per cent of its population.

The 20th century began ominously with the 1908 Messina earthquake which killed up to 84,000 people and destroyed thousands of homes. Then the conquest of Libya in 1912 was followed by World War I, taking a toll on the Sicilian economy. In 1934, swept along by Benito Mussolini's rhetoric in Rome, a plebiscite showed that only 116 Sicilians out of 4 million rejected Fascism.

Il Duce talked about building dams, supposedly a panacea for agricultural ills, but few

LEFT: Garibaldi's troops taking Palermo in May 1860.
RIGHT: Vittorio Emanuele II, first king of a united Italy.

materialised. Peasants still lived in one room with their animals. The railways were single-track and the extraordinary level of mule ownership was maintained by the lack of roads. Mussolini's master plan was to industrialise the influential north and use Sicily as the provider of raw materials. He also planned to bring the Mafia to heel. Initially the Mafia were all for Mussolini; not so when he despatched Cesare Mori, an expert in uprisings, to eradicate the scourge.

Mori started briskly. Various Dons were rounded up, walls were removed from roadsides where they facilitated ambushes, and the carrying of firearms was forbidden. When

THE MAFIA MEETS THE ALLIES

The Mafia played an unexpectedly important role in the Allied conquest of Sicily, and Vito Genovese, wanted for murder and other crimes by police in the United States, turned up as a liaison officer attached to a US army unit. Unwittingly, the Allies helped restore the Mafia's authority in Sicily and so erased Mussolini's only solid achievement: his bringing the country's criminal families under control. In the absence of the previous Fascist administrators, the army invited a likely-looking candidate, Don Calógero Vizzini, to take on the job without looking into his background. He had been locked up by Mussolini as one of the most undesirable *mafiosi*.

Mussolini announced that the Mafia had been eliminated, the murder rate, he said, had dropped from 10 a day to only three a week. The net result was to drive the criminal families deeper underground.

Then, as the tide turned in World War II, the Allies chose Sicily as the landing stage for the war against Hitler in Europe. The coast was defenceless, air cover minimal and, even had there been good roads, most of the artillery was still horse-drawn. The US 7th Army under General Patton landed at Gela in July 1943 while British and Canadian forces tackled the east coast. The German and Italian forces scrambled across the Straits of Messina. Once more, Sicily came under foreign control.

After the war

In 1946, Italy's new government granted Sicily autonomy in areas such as agriculture, mining and industry. In elections it would be a contest between Christian Democrats on the one hand and Socialists and Communists on the other.

The balance of power lay in the hands of prominent *mafioso* Don Calógero Vizzini. For the Mafia, the issue was merely one of choosing political partners that would facilitate the allocation of building licences, import permits and state contracts. Don Vizzini made his choice: the Christian Democrats doubled their number of seats and were comfortably installed as the majority party for the next 40 years. Subsequent demands for government action against the Mafia fell on curiously deaf ears.

In recognition that the Italian government was at last closing the economic gap between Sicily and the mainland, the United States, the World Bank and later the European Community chipped in with support.

But, just as it began to look as if the economy was faltering, Gulf Oil struck lucky near Ragusa in 1953 and later near Gela. Suddenly the island was key to Italy's oil industry and by 1966 one of several refineries was handling 8 million tons of crude a year. The petroleum industry attracted its chemical derivatives; gas was discovered and Sicily at last commanded the power to make industrialisation practicable. And then the tourism industry ground into gear. Life had begun to get sweeter. ❑

LEFT: Benito Mussolini, who won Sicily to his cause.

Sicily Today

Sicily's population is around 5 million. Relative prosperity is filtering through and *per capita* income has quadrupled since the 1950s. But while up to 20 percent of the workforce are state employees, from lecturers to museum attendants, unemployment hovers around 25 percent. On the plus side, Sicily does have the best-qualified unemployed: more than 80 percent are graduates. Despite such problems, the island received 20,000 Albanian immigrants in 1991, a figure which has to be juggled with the incalculable numbers of illegal Tunisian and Moroccan fishermen working along Trápani's African coast.

Sicilian politicians regularly proclaim the sighting of an "economic miracle". In the 1960s it was oil; in the 1970s it was greenhouses and reservoirs; in the 1980s it was a building boom; now it is fast expanding tourism.

The locals can be enterprising when it suits them. In 1992 European Community inspectors were outraged to find they had been fooled by "walking" olive trees. In order to gain extra subsidies, farmers planted their trees in tubs and moved them from field to field as the EC counting team advanced.

Young entrepreneurs struggle to change the existing business culture but are having some success in Palermo, Catania, Taormina and Siracusa. New cafés open, new shops sell upscale fashion. But corporate investors have been hesitant, complaining about the roads, railways, airports and telecommunications, even though these too are gradually improving. Perhaps investors fear the demands of the Mafia and the pervasiveness of crime. It not only runs the drug trade, extortion rings and street crime but has also infiltrated the political system. Fat state contracts, one of the mainstays of Rome's strategy for stimulating development in Sicily, are soaked up by layer upon layer of graft, kick-backs, overbilling and no-show workers. Government rolls are swollen with fraudulent pensions and do-nothing jobs that are doled out by local politicians in exchange for votes.

But, as Sicilians take care to point out, there is cause for hope, both in individual initiatives and a new political climate. A persistent political and civic effort has been made to expose Sicily's problems.

When the Christian Democrats lost their power base in Sicily in 1992, La Rete, a new reforming party committed to anti-Mafia and anti-corruption policies, moved to fill the vacuum. According to La Rete's leader, Palermo mayor Leoluca Orlando, the only requirement for party membership was honesty – but Orlando was under no illusions: the Mafia still

had a hold on some of the city's businesses and institutions.

Some people blame Sicily's problems on the so-called Southern mentality: that an ethic of voracious self-interest precludes community effort. Yet, in Sicily, where jobs are scarce and resources limited, looking out for oneself and one's family isn't just a matter of attitude, it's a matter of survival.

But as a respected Palermo publisher said: "We Sicilians have always been subjects, never citizens. The awakening of a civic consciousness is new: give us time to learn how to become citizens." Sicily may well be due for a Renaissance. ❏

RIGHT: new songs for a new generation.

Decisive Dates

20,000–10,000 BC Old Stone Age settlers live in caves on Monte Pellegrino and the Egadi Islands.
4,000–3,000 BC New Stone Age settlers from the eastern Mediterranean arrive on east coast.
3,000–2,000 BC Settlers from the Aegean bring metalwork and animals (Copper Age).
2,000–1,000 BC Bronze Age Sicilians start trading with Mycenean Greeks.
c1250 BC The Siculi (Sicels), Sicani (Sicans) and Elymni (Elymians) settle.
c860 BC Carthaginians (Phoenicians from North Africa) establish trading sites at Panormus (mod-

ern Palermo), Solus (Solunto) and Motya (Mózia).
c734 BC Naxos, the first Greek colony in Sicily, is founded by Chalcidians.
c733 BC Greeks from Corinth found Siracusa.
730–700 BC Other Greeks establish colonies at Megara Hyblaea, Gela, Selinus (modern Selinunte) and Akragas (Agrigento).
5th century BC Height of Greek civilisation in Sicily. Siracusa rivals Athens in power and prestige.
c485 BC Gelon of Gela captures Siracusa; he and Theron of Akragas control most of Greek Sicily.
480 BC Gela, Akragas and Siracusa defeat the Carthaginians at the battle of Himera.
c450 BC A revolt led by Ducetius, a Sicel, is crushed – native resistance to Greek rule ends.

415 BC Athens's naval expedition, which besieges Siracusa, is humiliatingly defeated.
409–7 BC Carthage sacks Selinus, Himera, Akragas and Gela. Dionysius takes charge in Siracusa. Plague forces Carthaginians to withdraw.
405–367 BC Dionysius I is Tyrant of Siracusa.
344 BC Corinth sends troops to defend Siracusa: they defeat Carthaginians at the River Crimisus.
310 BC Agathocles of Siracusa defeated by Carthaginians at Ecnomus.
278–275 BC Pyrrhus tries in vain to unite Sicily.
269 BC Hieron II defeats Mamertini, declares himself king of Sicily.
264–241 BC First Punic War. Sicily is the battleground as Romans wage war on Carthaginians.

ROME AND BYZANTIUM

254 BC Palermo falls to Rome.
227 BC Sicily is made a Roman province.
218 BC Siracusa backs Carthage against Rome.
212 BC Siracusa falls to the Romans in Second Punic War; all of Sicily is now ruled by Rome.
138–131 BC Syrian slave Eunus leads first slave revolt against the Romans.
104–99 BC Trifon leads second slave revolt.
44–36 BC Pompey's son, Sextus Pompeius, controls Sardinia, Corsica and Sicily with his fleets.
2nd century AD Spread of Christianity in Sicily.
395 Sicily is part of the Western Roman Empire.
410 Rome is attacked by the Visigoths.
468 Vandals from North Africa invade Sicily.
493 Sicily is overrun by the Ostrogoths.
535 The Byzantine general Belisarius conquers Sicily for Emperor Justinian of Byzantium.
651 First major Arab raid on Sicily.
726 The Byzantine emperor confiscates all Papal property in Sicily.

ARABS AND NORMANS

831 Palermo falls to the Saracens (Arabs).
842–859 Arabs capture Messina, Modica, Ragusa and Enna.
878 Siracusa is taken by storm and destroyed.
902 Taormina, the last Byzantine stronghold, falls to the Arabs.
965 All of Sicily under Arab control. Palermo is second largest city in the world (after Constantinople).
1061 The Normans land in Sicily: the beginning of 30 years of struggle against the Arabs.
1072 Norman Count Roger de Hauteville (Altavilla) takes Palermo "for Christendom".

1091 Noto, the last major Moslem stronghold, falls to the Normans, who now control all Sicily.
1130 Count Roger's son, Roger II, becomes King of Sicily. Palermo is one of Europe's finest cities.
1198–1250 Emperor Frederick II rules Sicily.
1266 Charles of Anjou is crowned King of Sicily. (Angevin rule until 1282.)
1282 The Sicilian Vespers. Popular Sicilian uprising against the French.

SPANISH RULE

1302 The Aragonese begin 200-year domination.
1442 Alfonso V, King of Aragon, reunites Naples and Sicily and takes the title King of Two Sicilies.
1502 The Spanish crown assumes control of Sicily, but the Barons retain much power.
1513 The Spanish Inquisition arrives in Sicily.
1647 Anti-Spanish uprising in Palermo quelled.
1669 Etna erupts, destroying Catania and east coast towns.
1693 Massive earthquake strikes the east.
1713 Treaty of Utrecht. Victor Amadeus II of Piedmont-Savoy becomes King of Sicily.
1720 Duke of Savoy surrenders Sicily for Sardinia. Austrian Viceroys rule.
1734–1860 The Spanish Bourbons rule Sicily through Viceroys.
1759 The Kingdom of Naples and Sicily passes to Ferdinand IV.
1798 Lord Nelson is given the Duchy of Bronte.
1806–15 The British occupation of Sicily.
1814 English-owned distilleries in Marsala begin producing a sherry-like wine.
1816 The Kingdom of the Two Sicilies is created under the Bourbons.

REVOLUTION AND UNIFICATION

1848–49 Sicilian Revolution.
1860 Garibaldi and his *Mille* (1,000) land at Marsala, and force the Bourbons off Sicily.
1861 Sicily joins Kingdom of Italy.
1908 Messina destroyed by an earthquake, which leaves around 84,000 victims.
1911 Population census finds that 58 percent of Sicilians are illiterate.
1915 Italy joins the Allies in World War I.
1922–43 Benito Mussolini rules fascist Italy.
1943 Sicily is invaded by Allies in World War II.
1946 Sicily is granted regional autonomy.

LEFT: a gleeful Greek gorgon from Gela.
RIGHT: Ferdinand I, King of the Two Sicilies, in 1816.

MODERN SICILY

1950 Land reforms: estates over 300 hectares (740 acres) redistributed as smallholdings.
1951–75 One million Sicilians emigrate to northern Italy, northern Europe and the United States.
1957 Italy is a founder member of the EEC.
1968 Disastrous earthquake in the Belice Valley.
1969 Caravaggio's *Nativity with Saints Francis and Lawrence*, now worth an estimated €30 million, is stolen from San Lorenzo Oratory, Palermo.
1973 Anti-Mafia Commission is set up.
1986 The Mafia maxi-trials *(maxiprocessi)* indict hundreds.
1992 Mafia assassinate two judges and Euro MP Salvatore Lima. Mount Etna erupts.

1995 Giulio Andreotti, seven times Prime Minister of Italy, is brought to Palermo to face charges of collaborating with the Mafia.
1996 The dome of Noto Cathedral collapses.
1999 Forest fire destroys hundreds of hectares near resort of Cefalú.
2002 State of emergency is declared as Etna erupts. Days later, Strómboli also erupts.
2006 Italy's top Mafia boss, Bernardo Provenzano, is caught after 43 years in hiding.
2008 Mayor of historic village of Salemi near Palermo sells off dilapidated houses for 1 euro each, in the hope that they they will be restored. Notorious Mafioso Totò Riina's former farmhouse is reopened as a hotel and restaurant. ❏

BUILDING FOR POSTERITY

The Ancient Greeks who held sway in Sicily left the island with an unrivalled heritage of noble public buildings and domestic architecture

Of the three great ancient civilisations that held sway in Sicily, the Greeks left the most enduring architectural legacy. The Carthaginians' buildings and artifacts were largely destroyed by Greeks – an exception being the remains at Mozia, including fine pebble mosaics. And little remains of Roman temples and public buildings – ironically because of Rome's more sophisticated building technology.

Where the Greeks built with solid stone, the Romans used cement within brick casings and faced buildings with a veneer of high-quality stone or marble. Once this was plundered by later generations, the cement and brick soon crumbled. The most enduring Roman remains include indestructable amphitheatres built into hillsides (e.g. Siracusa) and lavish additions to Greek buildings (e.g. the theatre at Taormina).

The Greeks built most of their public buildings in the Doric style, with simple, austere lines and a perfect harmony of proportion. The earliest large-scale temple (575 BC) can be found at Siracusa. Its imposing design was reproduced, with variations, over two centuries at Himera, Segesta, Akrakas (Agrigento) and elsewhere, but most splendidly at Selinunte, where at least nine majestic temples were built in the period from 580 BC to 480 BC.

ABOVE: Segesta's Greek theatre (3rd century BC). The tiers of seats face west, towards the Bay of Castellamare.

ABOVE: Temple E at Selinunte, dedicated to Hera in around 480 BC, was toppled by an earthquake but was re-erected in 1957.

LEFT: a red-figure Attic *krater* from Palermo's superb collection of Greek vases.

REMAINS TO BE SEEN

Sicily's archaeological museums are rich with artifacts from many periods and many cultures – Bronze Age, Phoenician, Greek, Roman, Etruscan, and more.

Palermo's Museo Archeologico contains Carthaginian and Egyptian remains, some Roman sarcophagi *(right)* and sculptures, notably a huge Emperor Claudius enthroned like Zeus, Greek vases and statues, and art from various temples (the friezes from Selinunte are particularly fine).

Siracusa's museum probably has Sicily's most diverse collection, featuring sensual statues, gruesome theatrical masks, huge burial urns and poignant sarcophagi.

Agrigento's museum has intriguing Bronze-Age finds, painted Attic vases, carvings and statues, and Roman tombs and mosaics. The highlight is a huge *telamon* from the Temple of Zeus.

RIGHT: the Temple of Olympian Zeus at Agrigento once had 38 of these colossal *telamones* (giants) set on its outer wall as columns. The concept of such figures was revolutionary for the time.

BELOW: the Temple of Concord (with modern Agrigento in the background) is one of the best preserved Greek temples anywhere. It was built around 430 BC.

LEFT: the theatre at Taormina was built by Greeks for drama, but later enlarged by Romans who used it for circus games.

RIGHT: a carved stone lion's head water-spout from the 5th-century BC at the Temple of Victory at Himera.

THE MAFIA

With its tradition of private justice and its code of silence, the Mafia seemed to defy authority – but then it was found that authority was implicated too

When, in October 2005, two men on a scooter opened fire on a car in the town of Partinico, the Mafia murder, with traditional sawn-off shotgun and .38 pistol, made headlines because of its rarity. The revulsion of Sicilians over the 1992 murders of Mafia-fighting judges Giovanni Falcone and Paolo Borsellino had weakened the Mafia's grip on public opinion, its greatest weapon, and dented the age-old code of loyalty *(omertà)*.

This, coupled with tougher laws and greater police determination, drove Sicily's *mafiosi* underground. Their top boss, Bernardo Provenzano – once known as "The Tractor" for his ability to mow enemies down – was renamed "The Accountant" in tribute to his concentration on low-level protection rackets, drug dealing and controlling public building contracts. But Provenzano, now in his seventies, had been evading the police for more than 40 years, and officials feared that a battle for succession might mean a return to open warfare.

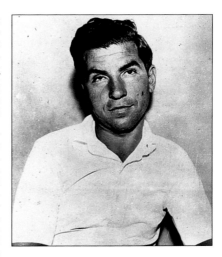

Murky beginnings

The origins of what is arguably Italy's biggest blight and its second largest company can be traced to medieval times and a mysterious religious sect, the Beati Poli, whose hooded members lurked, armed with pikes and swords, in underground passages beneath the streets of Palermo. Some say the word Mafia first appeared in the mid-1600s, meaning "a witch"; others say it derives from dialectical or Arabic words meaning "protection", "misery" or "hired assassin". What is certain is that the Mafia as we know it began to take shape in the early 19th century, in the form of brotherhoods, formed to protect Sicilians from corruption, foreign oppression and feudal malpractice. Criminal interests quickly seeped in, corruption became the preferred milieu, and before long the brotherhoods were feeding on the misery from which they pretended to defend their members.

Between 1872 and World War I, poverty and the defeat of agrarian trade unions forced 500,000 Sicilians to emigrate. Most went to the Americas. There, many joined brotherhoods based on those back home and the foundations of Cosa Nostra were laid.

In 1925, Mussolini, appalled at the Mafia's new importance as a surrogate state, sent his prefect Cesare Mori to Sicily, with almost unlimited powers. By 1927, victory was proclaimed for Mori's heavy-handed tactics. But Mori was also a threat to powerful agrarian *mafiosi*. Soon Sicily's landed interests struck a deal with the Fascists, and Mori left the island. In return, the agrarian *mafiosi* saw to it that Sicily's more criminal Mafia elements, based mainly in the cities, were almost wiped out.

But the criminals won a reprieve in 1943, when they were given the job of clearing the way for the Allied invasion. Fearing that war between the US and Italy would damage their interests, Italian-American mobsters such as Lucky Luciano had struck a deal with US

authorities in 1940. In return for their help, they were to be left alone. The operation, overseen by Don Vito Genovese, a Naples thug wanted for murder in the US, went well: the Allies hardly fired a shot. Local *mafiosi*, re-armed with weapons taken from captured Italian troops, were installed by the Allies as mayors of key Sicilian towns.

After the war, organised criminals began supporting Sicily's pro-separatist movement backed by agrarian interests. Together with the

LEFT: Lucky Luciano, who forged links between the Sicilian and American Mafias.
ABOVE: off to court in one of the 1980s maxi-trials.

authorities, the Mafia joined in the suppression of banditry, which had made inroads into its territory during the Fascist siege.

Gangland massacres

In 1957 the American and Sicilian Mafias met in Palermo's Grand Hotel et des Palmes for a summit, called to create the *Cupola* or Commission, and to establish the Sicilians' heroin franchise. The result was a criminal organisation with a clear pyramid structure.

The island's *mammasantissima* also had the satisfaction of securing the import and distribution of all heroin in the United States. It was known as the Pizza Connection since pizza parlours were a cover for the money laundering. Sicily emerged as a strategic centre for drugs, arms and international crime, confirming the shift of the Mafia's economic centre of gravity from the country to the city.

In the early 1980s a Mafia war left Palermo's streets strewn with blood and a Corleone-based clan undisputed victors. In response to strong public feeling, and to counteract accusations of government complicity, a crackdown on the Mafia was launched. Thousands of suspects were rounded up and an anti-Mafia pool of magistrates, which included Giovanni Falcone and Paolo Borsellino, was assembled. One "maxi-trial" resulted in 18 life sentences.

Murdering the magistrates

In spite of their success, the anti-Mafia pool of magistrates was mysteriously disbanded in 1988. Falcone moved to Rome as Director of Penal Affairs and lobbied for a force with powers similar to the American FBI. In May 1992, he was on the point of being nominated *superprocuratore*, its head, when the Mafia took their revenge. As he drove with his wife, Judge Francesca Morvillo, along the *autostrada* from the airport to Palermo, their car passed over a remote-controlled mine. The two judges and their three-man escort were killed instantly, their cars reduced to twisted burning metal, and a huge crater blown in the motorway.

Two months later, fellow-magistrate Paolo Borsellino, Falcone's boyhood friend and obvious successor, became another "illustrious corpse". He had just arrived at his mother's home when an 80 kg (175 lb) bomb in his car was detonated. The explosion left virtually no trace of his body, killed his five bodyguards, and broke windows several blocks away.

The terror continued in 1993 with bombs in Milan and Rome that killed bystanders and devastated churches; an explosion at Florence's Uffizi Gallery destroyed minor masterpieces. But the Mafia had miscalculated. The assassinations of the two Palermo judges and the attempt to destroy the nation's cultural treasures only served to tighten the resolve of the Italians and their government against the Mafia.

Power vacuum

In September 1995, Giulio Andreotti, 76, seven times prime minister and one of Italy's most

respected elder statesmen, was accused of being a protector and friend of the Mafia in return for votes. Although he was found not guilty, the message was clear to *mafiosi* and politicians alike: henceforth no one could be considered "untouchable". Another former prime minister and media tycoon, Silvio Berlusconi, had his business dealings investigated by an anti-Mafia police unit in 1998, though he stoutly denied charges of money-laundering for Cosa Nostra.

No one, even Palermo's successful anti-Mafia mayor Leoluca Orlando, pretended that Cosa Nostra had disappeared. It was simply changing. In 1995 it fell into debt, as income fell (fewer public works and confiscation of Mafia property) and costs rose (mainly legal fees). As the old Mafia guard languished in jail, a more sophisticated organisation, based on "old Mafia values", began to fill the power vacuum.

A new Mafia

The new-generation gangster is likely to be as ruthless on the stock exchange floor as on the streets of Palermo, be armed with a computer, and be adept at surfing the internet – the favoured new medium for laundering money.

Along with extortion and property speculation, Mafia activities now include trading arms, nuclear and conventional, between Eastern European and Middle Eastern and other embargo-covered countries. Investment features as much in Moscow as it does in Palermo. According to an Olympics official, the Mafia is prominent in providing international athletes with performance-boosting drugs.

But in Sicily, the greatest change has been in public attitudes. Where once *mafioso* activity was seen as revolt against the state, justified by centuries of foreign oppression, today the population is less tolerant. The revelations of political complicity at the highest level have destroyed any fanciful notion that the Mafia somehow represented the private citizen against the forces of authority.

While there is no doubt that Sicily still harbours some dangerous criminals, they can no longer rely on support, or even consent, from most Sicilians. The *mafiosi* haven't gone away, but they are no longer untouchable. ❏

THE BEDSHEET PROTEST

In Sicily the murder of the magistrates in 1992 sparked a popular backlash against the Mafia's excesses. On the evening of Falcone's assassination, three Palermo sisters and their daughters hung bedsheets with anti-Mafia slogans from the balconies of their neighbouring apartments. Soon other Palermitans joined in. The bedsheet protest caught on until it seemed that most of Palermo was making a personal stand against the Mafia. As anti-Mafia mayor Leoluca Orlando said later, "On certain days, you could look up at an apartment building and see where the Mafia don lived – it was the apartment without a sheet hanging from the window."

LEFT: children take part in an anti-Mafia demonstration.

Sicily in the Movies

As well as being intensely visual, Sicily is an island of extremes, a place of passion, where life and death embrace. It is a gift to film directors, from Italians such as Luchino Visconti to Italian-Americans such as Francis Ford Coppola.

Hollywood's infatuation with the glamour of gangsterland, however, has presented audiences with an image not pleasing to the Palermo tourist board. In movies, the Mafia capital, Corleone, lends its jagged rocks and sullen populace to *The Godfather* trilogy while the mountains around Montelepre, once the home of Salvatore Giuliano, Sicily's Robin Hood, echo to the sound of banditry.

The first international success in art house cinemas was Visconti's *La Terra Trema* (*The Earth Shook*, 1947) based on Giovanni Verga's *I Malavoglia*, a tale of poverty and destiny in a fishing community. Naturally, the cast were real fishermen with impenetrable Sicilian accents. Then came *Stromboli: Terra di Dio* (1950), a chronicle of torrid passion between a Lithuanian refugee and a fisherman, an affair as doomed as the brooding melodrama of the movie.

Later, while Francesco Rosi's *Salvatore Giuliano* (1961) told the tragic tale of Sicily's greatest folk hero with the grandeur of a Greek myth and with scenes of peasants grouped like a classical chorus, Visconti's glorious 1963 epic, *The Leopard*, exuded impeccable lushness, faded grandeur and decadence.

By 1984 the Italian mood was changing. The Taviani brothers' *Kaos* set in rural Sicily was a chaotic universe of legends and lost loves, of mother love and ties with the land. In one saga, a full moon rekindles sexual desire and turns a peasant into a wolf. Then *Cinema Paradiso* (1988) brought a nostalgic slice of history following the arrival of the Talkies in small-town Sicily seen through the eyes of a young projectionist, and six years later, *Il Postino* (*The Postman*) shot on the island of Salina, told a tale set in the

1950s of a fisherman's son hired to deliver mail to exiled Chilean poet Pablo Neruda. Over time, he develops an appreciation of poetry (which helps him win the heart of the local beauty) and of Communism (which finally gets him killed).

But the most recurring popular theme in the Sicilian film canon is the Mafia.

Leonardo Sciascia's anti-Mafia fiction inspired many Italian directors with strong plots and moral dilemmas, starting in 1968 with *Il Giorno della Civeta* (*Day of the Owl*). But true commercial successes, heretically, were American: Coppola's *The Godfather* trilogy, inspired by Mario Puzo's novel con-

cerning Mafia wars in the 1950s, allowed Marlon Brando to play the Godfather with relish. The three movies' atmosphere made for operatic intensity; indeed *Part III* (1990) climaxed at Palermo's Teatro Massimo during the Mascagni's foreboding opera, *Cavalleria Rusticana*.

More recently, German director Margarethe von Trotta's *Il Lungo Silenzio* (*The Long Silence*) dealt with anti-Mafia magistrates and received applause from Mafia widows, while Swedish director Mikael Håfström's *Vendetta* (1995) was a blood-and-guts yarn where two kidnapped Swedish businessmen are rescued amid a hail of bullets. ❏

RIGHT: the lavish ballroom scene in *The Leopard*.

FOOD AND WINE

Sicily's fertile volcanic soil and teeming seas
have supplied the islanders with a rich and
varied diet. The wines aren't bad either

One of Sicily's best-kept secrets is its ancient and distinguished gastronomic tradition. Only a few Sicilian dishes, like the aubergine (eggplant) side-dish known as *caponata* or the sweet ricotta-filled *cannoli*, have crossed the Straits of Messina to find fame and fortune abroad. Even Sicilians themselves are unaware of how history seasons their favourite foods.

The Greek colonists who arrived in the 8th century BC were astonished at the fertility of Sicily's volcanic soil, and with such abundance on the doorstep, Siracusa soon became the gastronomic capital of the Classical world. By the 5th century BC the city had given birth to the first cookbook written in the West, Mithaecus's *Lost Art of Cooking*, and to the first school for chefs. It was apparently a rich and elaborate cuisine. Earlier still, in the 4th century BC, a Sicilian poet, Archestratus, author of a cook book in verse, complained of an excessive use of fancy sauces.

The Arab legacy

The Arabs brought innovative agricultural and culinary techniques and introduced crops that enriched Sicilian cooking; citrus, rice and aubergines became staples. They also made Sicilian cuisine sweet and spicy. Cane sugar was introduced, as was the Middle Eastern taste for sumptuous sweets – still a Sicilian trademark. The most famous dish of Arab descent is *cassata siciliana*, the spectacular, overpoweringly sweet gateau filled with ricotta cream and decorated with almond paste and candied fruit.

By the end of the Saracen occupation, the

mould of Sicilian cooking had been set. The Normans employed Arab chefs and, until the Renaissance, Sicily exported luxury foods (pasta, sugar, confectionery and citrus) to Northern Italy. But while the Spanish brought chocolate and tomatoes from the New World and French chefs were fashionable in the 19th century, significant developments in Sicilian cuisine took place along class lines. The poor survived on bread and wild greens; the aristocracy enjoyed the costly and conspicuous dishes of the *cucina baronale*.

As for the emerging *borghesia,* they borrowed from both classes to create what is essentially contemporary Sicilian cooking. In essence it is extravagant in its festive dishes, straightforward in its daily fare but always dedicated to exalting the extraordinary flavours of the produce.

The food

To start: *Sarde a beccafico*, sardines rolled in breadcrumbs, with a pine-nut and currant filling and baked with bay leaves vie for attention with *involtini di melanzane*, stuffed aubergines in tomato sauce. These *antipasti* stars share the table with humbler but equally delicious snacks: chickpea fritters *(panelle)*; potato croquettes *(crocche di patate)* and fried rice balls filled with chopped meat and peas *(arancine)*.

proper first course. Under Arab rule, Sicily was the first place to produce dried pasta on a commercial scale. Today's best loved pasta dish is *pasta con le melanzane*, known in eastern Sicily and elsewhere as *pasta alla Norma* (after Bellini's operatic heroine). Here, tomatoes, basil, fried aubergines and a sprinkling of salted ricotta melt into a magical blend.

A host of other vegetables are served with pasta, ranging from fancy preparations like *fritella*, a spring sauté of new peas, fava beans and tiny artichokes, to simpler combinations garnished with sautéed courgettes or boiled with wild borage or mustard greens.

Western Sicily's most famous pasta dish is

In the mountain towns of the Madonie and Nebrodi, rustic products are served as *antipasti*. These include salami, cow's milk cheeses *(caciotta* and *caciocavallo)*, sheep's milk cheeses *(tuma,* or *primiticcio)* and wild mushrooms *sott'olio*. On the coast, the sea provides the inspiration. It may be a classic *insalata di mare (*seafood with oil, lemon and herbs), *pesce spada affumicato* (smoked swordfish) or a dish of tiny fried cuttlefish, each no bigger than a thumbnail.

However, most Sicilians feel pasta to be the

made with fish. Legend has it that the exotic *pasta con sarde* was invented in the 9th century by Arab army cooks who used whatever was at hand: sardines, saffron, pine nuts, dried currants and sprigs of wild fennel. In the east, a potent sauce of anchovies and breadcrumbs is still popular *(anclova e muddica)*. In another dish, grated smoked tuna roe mixed with olive oil and parsley is poured over spaghetti.

In the Trápani area, where the Arab influence is strongest, a local version of *couscous*, steamed in a fish broth, is a substitute for pasta. **Fish or meat:** Meat as a main course is often disappointing. Beef can be tough unless stuffed and braised in tomato sauce or skewered and

LEFT: a Siracusa *formaggeria* (cheese shop).
ABOVE: olives for sale at Palermo's Vucciria market.

grilled *(involtini alla siciliana)*. But lamb and pork raised in the mountain pastures and forests of the Madonie and Nebrodi is exceptional. However, to the peasants and farmers a daily *bistecca* is a sign of new prosperity.

Poor meat is compensated for by exceptionally good seafood. Sicily seems to have endless numbers of seasonal varieties.

Given the superb quality of the vegetables it is hard to forgive restaurants for relying on an undistinguished *insalata mista* (mixed salad) to accompany the main course. Maybe it is because they consider trays of grilled vegetables to be *antipasti*. But *melanzane alla parmigiana* (aubergine baked with parmesan

cheese) was a Sicilian invention after all, so you do expect better.

Perhaps artichokes fried, stuffed, roasted on coals, or braised with oil, parsley and garlic are compensation. Or bright green cauliflower boiled and served with oil and lemon, or as a special dish cooked with anchovies, cheese, olives and red wine. The interior boasts a survivor from Classical times: *maccu*, a thick purée made from dried fava or broad beans flavoured with oil and wild fennel seeds.

Sweets: Choice becomes hardest towards the end of a meal. The Arabs introduced sorbets, to the Sicilians' eternal gratitude. Etna provided snow throughout the summer and its

preservation and sale was the lucrative monopoly of the Bishop of Catania.

Sicilians, rich and poor alike, have had a passion for ice cream since the 18th century. Home-made ice cream, in a bewildering and tantalising variety of flavours and shapes, is available in bars and restaurants everywhere.

Then there are Sicilan pastries. From the chewy *mustazzoli* biscuits or the nut and fig flavoured *buccellato* to the opulent Arab tradition of *cannoli*. For centuries, the chief pastry cooks were nuns: Palermo alone had more than a score of convents, each famous for a particular sweet. A few convents still sell their pastries or, as in Erice, the tradition is carried on by women who learned their trade in convent orphanages.

On All Souls' Day, Sicilian children traditionally awake to find sugar dolls and baskets of fruit at the foot of their beds, left there by "the souls of their forefathers". The fruit is made of marzipan, known as *pasta reale* or *martorana*, one of Sicily's most delightful culinary traditions. Nowadays, *martorana* are readily available all year round in the standard forms of fruits and vegetables though visitors with more salacious tastes may be transported by other versions, the nuns' sweet triumphs: virgins' breasts *(minni di vergini)* or chancellors' buttocks *(fedde del cancelliere)*.

The wines

Grapes and wine have always formed a major part of the Sicilian economy. For a time they had little more than commodity value, being despatched north to bump up the strength and colour of other wines because traditional, bush-trained vines develop prodigious amounts of sugar under Sicily's powerful sun. More recently, though, there has been a full-scale return to producing wines for drinking, not blending, and to harnessing native grape varieties to that end.

White wines have taken the lead. Light, dry, delicately floral white wines emerge from grapes harvested before their acidity drops too low, which are then carefully fermented at cool temperatures to conserve their aromas. These rival some better known names of the wine world and are ideal for drinking with Sicilian dishes in a Sicilian climate.

The Regaleali estate, near Vallelunga in Caltanissetta province, is owned by the Conte Tasca d'Almerita, whose vineyards lie between 450 and 650 metres (1,500–2,100 ft) above sea level. This together with the strong, cooling breezes the hills attract and their distance from the sea, gives cool nights to balance hot days – almost ideal conditions for vine growing.

The estate's reputation hangs on two particular wines: *Nozze d'Oro* (Golden Wedding), a white, first made in 1985 to mark the Count's 50th wedding anniversary, that is refined, rounded, herby and long-ageing, and the Count's favourite, *Rosso del Conte*, made from the Nero d'Avola and Perricone grapes. Intense, full and powerful, it too ages slowly.

The Sicilians cannot agree as to which of the two indigenous grapes, Catarratto or Inzolia, makes superior white wine. The producer Tenuta di Donnafugata has chosen Inzolia. Try *Vigna di Gabbri* (a refined wine made from Inzolia grapes) or the standard white, *Donnafugata Bianco* (a Catarratto-Inzolia blend).

Duca di Salaparuta, with wines under the Corvo label, is also keen on Inzolia. The producer is based at Casteldaccia, just east along the coast from Palermo, and buys grapes from numbers of small growers. The basic but good drinking wine is *Corvo Bianco* but the star is the premium *Colomba Platino* (platinum dove). Even finer still is the oak-matured *Bianca di Valguarnera*.

Further west lie huge wine estates under the name of Alcamo, a controlled *Denominazione di Origine Controllata* (DOC) area. Try any wines under the Rapitalà estate label. And try *Cerasuolo di Vittoria* (*cerasuolo* means cherry-coloured) produced in the southeast, around Vittória. The wine is another DOC, made from a blend of the red variety, Nero d'Avola, and the best local variety, Frappato.

On the island of Pantelleria they favour the Moscato variety, called Zibibbo, trained as low, individual bushes against the incessant winds. Try the delicate but sweet *Moscato di Pantelleria* or the classic, rich *Passito di Pantelleria*, made from grapes that have been left to dry and concentrate rapidly in the sun after picking.

The island of Salina has a similar tradition but with Malvasia rather than Moscato vines.

Try wines from the estates of Carlo Hauner, Caravaglio or Cantine Colosi.

Wines from the slopes of Etna tend to have a heavier and fruitier flavour than those from other parts of the island. In theory, Etna should produce Sicily's best red wines but the expertise in the west of the island is often lacking in the east. An exception should be made for the white and red Murgo wines from the estate of Barone Scammacca.

Sicily's rosés deserve mention. Made predominantly from Nerello Mascalese, a light-coloured red grape ideally suited to making delicately fruity pinks, they are often the ideal accompaniment to many classic dishes.   ❑

A FORTIFIED MARVEL

Marsala, best known of all Sicilian wines, is produced in and around the town of Marsala. It is made by strengthening (fortifying) a base wine with grape brandy and ageing the result. At its best, marsala rivals top sherries, madeiras and ports.

Although marsala is often thought of as a cheap, sickly-sweet liqueur, the best (known as *Vergine* or *Riserva*) are excellent, dry, smooth sherry-like wines. Marco De Bartoli's respected range, for example, spans sweet and dry, ultra-long-aged and youthful; all are based on Inzolia and Grillo, the latter being the perfect grape for marsala.

LEFT: roasting artichokes on hot ashes for a picnic.
RIGHT: Sicily's red wines are often robust.

SICILY'S WILD PLACES

The island's lush green interior and beautiful seashore are
at last receiving some protection from development,
as regional parks and natural reserves

The wild areas of Sicily's countryside and coast have been protected and made more accessible to visitors. More than 80 reserves have been created and laws have been drawn up to protect the natural habitats and control development. This has not always been a straightforward process. Ingrained suspicion of government, plus economic hardship and lack of job opportunities, have often provoked local opposition to protecting an area.

The *Forestale* authorities responsible for the care and development of the reserves are also, in effect, building control officers, a difficult role made more complicated by regional divisions and poor communication between authorities and residents. Local agreements for grazing sheep and cattle on environmentally sensitive areas may have been traditional for generations so those affected by limits on land use often see little benefit to themselves. More positively, there is a fierce pride in the wild beauty of Sicily and a strong tradition of rural pursuits and small-scale agriculture, both of which are gradually working in harmony with the reserves' ideals.

Protected areas

Hot summers and mild winters combined with a mineral-rich soil provide an ideal environment for flora and fauna. In spring and autumn Sicily is an important staging post for thousands of migrating birds. Like the native species, these benefit from the protection of the habitat and the controls on hunting and fishing.

In addition to indigenous plants like *erba bianca* (woody absinthe), myrtle, arbutus (the strawberry tree), lentisk and tree spurge, the island is host to a number of successful "invaders", like the huge prickly pear, the riverbed-loving oleander, the carob, the eucalyptus and the umbrella pine which produces the delicious pine nuts used in *pesto* sauce.

There are three types of protected area: regional parks, natural reserves and sea reserves. All three categories are sub-divided into zones, designated A, B, C or D, to define the level of protection and, therefore, the activities permitted in the zone. General regulations are available at every park office and information point and are important for both personal safety and the protection of the environment. Most are common sense, but it is particularly important to be aware of the high risk of fire. Camping is forbidden.

There are organised walks in some parks and details of these, plus maps, books on the flora, fauna and history of the region, can be obtained at information points.

The regional parks

Parco dei Nebrodi is Sicily's largest park, covering the mountainous region from Santo Stefano di Camastra, roughly halfway along the northern coastline, to the foot of Etna. Nebrodi was designated a reserve in 1993. The area includes towns and villages, and areas of

The **Parco dell'Etna** enveloping Etna's dramatic mountain and crater became a park in 1987. It offers many long and short organised treks, including the five-day *Grande Traversata Etnea*. These provide the best options for exploring. There are good walks from bases in the foothills, some accessible by bus. Hiking in the high areas is not possible in the winter due to snow and bad visibility.

This park's variety is remarkable: lush citrus groves and bananas on the lower slopes give way to mixed woodland, to pines and, finally, to volcanic desert sustaining only small hardy plants and flowers like the Etna violet that can survive the extremes of temperature.

ancient beech and oak woodland. There are lakes that provide important habitats, particularly **Biviere di Cesarù**. This park is so large that exploring without a car is difficult.

The **Parco delle Madonie** (established 1989) lies west of the Nebrodi and also takes in beautiful wooded mountainous countryside. Smaller and higher (and known for winter skiing), Madonie is easily accessible without a car. Buses run from Cefalù, Castelbuono and Petralia, and accommodation is good. Pony treks and walks are organised in summer.

LEFT: the gecko hunts for insects at night.
ABOVE: an umbrella pine on Etna's lava slopes.

ANIMALS OF THE ISLAND

Though some creatures such as the wolf have vanished, the crested porcupine is still resident, as are the red fox, hare, wild cat, pine marten, weasel and edible dormouse. Among the island's eight species of bat are the mouse-eared bat and the rare Kuhl's pipistrelle and Savi's pipistrelle. Reptiles include the common green lizard, black snake, dark green snake, grass snake and viper, and nocturnal geckos attracted by any outside light. The shy land tortoise is around, but hard to spot with its excellent camouflage. In fresh water you may see the European pond turtle. Amphibians include the common toad, edible frog, tree frog and painted frog.

The natural reserves

Many reserves have yet to establish any clear definition or boundaries. The better established reserves are listed here – plus the two major sea reserves.

The **Riserva Naturale dello Zíngaro**, a section of coast and hills near Castellammare del Golfo between Trápani and Palermo, deserves special mention as the pioneer of Sicilian reserves. In response to plans to build a main road on this unspoilt coast in 1980, a massive campaign was launched with the help of newspapers and ranks of scientists. Public support followed with a peaceful march of 6,000 people. Their efforts were recognised

by the Regional Assembly and a year later legislation was passed, securing the future of parks and reserves in Sicily.

Zíngaro is exceptionally well planned, allowing easy access for all levels of ability, though it might be too much for all but the most intrepid of wheelchair users. Its five exquisite beaches, ancient dwellings and beautiful landscape are a delight, and facilities include a natural history museum, marine laboratory, visitor's centre and archaeological museum, all housed in carefully restored existing buildings. The reserve is easily reached on public transport and there are plenty of places to stay in nearby Scopello. The tiny beaches get busy in July and August.

North of Palermo, the rocky mass of **Monte Pellegrino** juts up from the bay. In striking contrast to Zíngaro, the reserve is shared by the revered shrine of St Rosalia, patron saint of Palermo, and a collection of souvenir shops. It is a popular picnic place for families from the city. There are excellent views and walks on the rocky peak. About 15 km (9 miles) from Palermo; buses go to the shrine.

The **Ficuzza** reserve is near Marineo, 35 km (22 miles) south of Palermo, centred on the tiny hamlet of Ficuzza, a tranquil spot below the woods on Rocca Busambre. It's easiest to reach by car, but Corleone–Palermo buses do travel past. There are a few trattorias in Ficuzza for lunch.

The salt marshes of **Vendicari** (a reserve since 1984) support a highly specialised population of plants and animals. Autumn or winter is the time to visit when thousands of

BIRDS WORTH SPOTTING

More than 150 species of birds, both migratory and nesting, have been logged on the island. The notable predators include the golden eagle and the peregrine falcon. Until recently the magnificent peregrines were threatened by levels of insecticide in the environment, but happily they are on the increase again and can be seen singly or in pairs near cliffs.

They are not the only birds of prey sustained by the island's numerous small mammals and lizards: you may see Bonelli's eagles, red kites, marsh harriers, European sparrowhawks and a variety of owls (long-eared, little, scops, tawny and barn). Besides the familiar blackbirds,

crows, robins, skylarks and thrushes, you may spot the hoopoe, red-billed chough, nuthatch, coal tit, Sicilian long-tailed tit, redstart, blackcap, greenfinch, quail and cirl bunting.

On summer evenings swifts, swallows and martins join the bats swooping round the terraces. You may be startled by the sudden flight of the large European woodcock, which bursts out of the undergrowth virtually under your feet. Near fresh water, as in Nébrodi National Reserve, look out for the Sicilian marsh tit and the wonderfully named *Tachybaptus ruficolis*. The Latin means "fast-bathing red stomach", an apt description of the little grebe.

waders and ducks arrive to share the sheltered waters with flamingos, storks and egrets. There are remains of a 15th-century tower and ancient Greek fish-processing. Vendicari is about 45 km (28 miles) south of Siracusa and accessible only by car.

Newly defined as reserves, **Necropoli di Pantálica** and **Valle dell'Anapo,** accommodate extraordinary Bronze Age cave dwellings and walks along the Anapo river valley, alongside dramatic gorges and canyons. The area is rich in wildlife. About 40 km (25 miles) west of Siracusa. Accessible only by car.

Another new reserve, **Gola dell'Alcántara,** is not for the faint-hearted. Exploring can

over 40 different kinds of fish. The striking pinks and white in the waters, and the rich vegetation on the islands, make the area a visual delight. Buses from Marsala, about 6 km (3½ miles) away and ferries to the islands.

Sea reserves

The three beautiful **Isole Egadi,** only 30 minutes by hydrofoil from Trápani, are ringed with caves and creeks and miniature beaches. The clarity of the water and variety of marine life make swimming and diving a joy. All the islands have footpaths leading to the more secluded areas, but they may be difficult to follow. If you head off exploring, take plenty

include wading through the freezing waters of the river among the rainbows of spray deep in the rocky gorge, an exhilarating hour of rock and water. Buses from Taormina, approximately 15 km (9 miles) away.

Isola di Mozia, Lo Stagnone and **Saline di Trápani** make up the protected area around Mozia. Part of the Phoenician trading route in the 8th century BC, this tiny island is one of four in a lagoon 15 km (9 miles) south of Trápani.

A reserve since 1984, the lagoon and its salty waters have a rich marine life including

of water and be prepared for rocky scrambles.

There are boat trips around the islands and organised visits to the prehistoric cave drawings at the **Grotta del Genovese** on Lévanzo.

Ustica, a well-established reserve and centre for marine studies since 1987, offers a chance to explore the fabulously rich sea world of sponges, corals and fish with expert guidance or follow a sub-aqua archaeological trail complete with Roman amphorae. Sub-aqua and marine biology courses, exhibitions and conferences are held every year. Hydrofoil and ferry services connect to Palermo. ❏

● *The tourist offices in each province can supply maps of reserves and suggested routes.*

LEFT: the peregrine falcon breeds on cliffs.
ABOVE: Mozia, a tiny island, is part of a nature reserve.

PLACES

A detailed guide to Sicily and its islands, with principal
sites clearly cross-referenced by number to the maps

Sicilian scenery is dramatic, sometimes harsh but seldom graceless. Today this granary of ancient Rome contains citrus groves, pastureland and vineyards as well as endless vistas of wheatfields. Away from the accessible coast, an intriguing volcanic hinterland unfolds with wild mountains, gorges and occasional sweeps of rich ochre-coloured earth. Between Catania and Messina, Mount Etna's smoking plumes hover above the neighbouring farms, vineyards and ski slopes, and holiday houses that climb the volcano's skirts.

After breakfasting in Taormina, Cardinal Newman found it "the nearest thing to paradise". To most tourists, Taormina is the acceptable face of Sicily, a place of undiluted pleasure where culture shock is absent. Since the 19th century international travellers have been coming to this fashionable hillside town to enjoy its splendid air, its views and its access to sandy beaches. Some of Sicily's finest hotels are here. On the northern coast is Cefalù, Taormina's resort competition just 65 km (40 miles) from the bustling capital, Palermo, with a fine history of its own.

Outside these cosmopolitan pockets, the adventure begins. The souks and inlaid street patterns of Mazara del Vallo and Sciacca would not be out of place in Morocco. The perfect medieval town of Erice is a shrine to pagan goddesses. The island of Mozia retains signs of its Phoenician port and sacrificial burial grounds. Built to "intimidate the gods or scare human beings", the Greek temples of Agrigento, Segesta and Selinunte are a divine reflection of *Magna Graecia*. The Romans may not have matched these lovely sites but they left the vivid mosaics of Piazza Armerina as an imprint of a sated but sophisticated culture.

Then, at Cefalù and Monreale there are cathedrals that are a tribute to Byzantine craftsmanship, Arab imagery and Norman scale while, elsewhere, Moorish palaces, Swabian castles and domed churches are interpretations of this inspired Sicilian hybrid. To top it all, baroque explodes in the architectural fireworks of Noto and Catania.

Sicily is to be explored and, while the island's rich historical and architectural heritage beckon and reward, there are beaches accessible on most of the extensive coastline, and, wherever you are, there seem to be leisurely *caffès*, charming shops and *trattorie* with excellent food and drink ready to be served. It is all this that makes the sun-baked island and its rock-like island archipelagos what they are: remarkable. ❑

PRECEDING PAGES: the cloud-capped Nebrodi Mountains; the hilltop town of Centúripe.
LEFT: Caltabellotta, regarded by many as the loveliest village in Agrigento province.

5 4

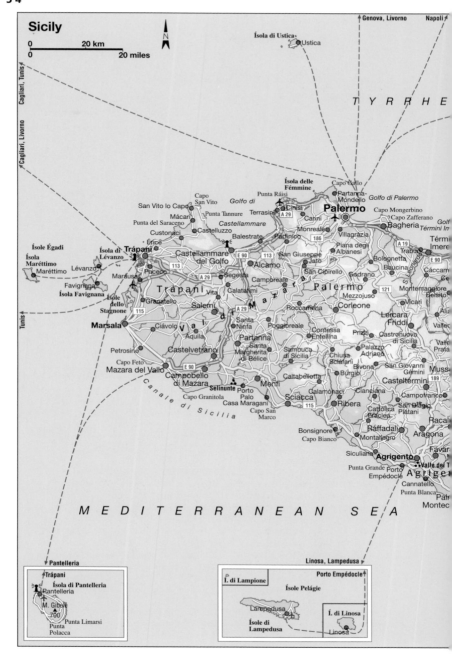

Sicily

0 ——— 20 km
0 ——— 20 miles

N

Genova, Livorno
Napoli

Ísola di Ustica
Ustica

T Y R R H E

Cagliari, Tunis
Cagliari, Livorno
Tunis

Capo Gallo
Ísola delle
Fémmine
Partanna-
Mondello
Golfo di Palermo
Punta Ráisi
Palermo
Capo Mongerbino
Capo
San Vito lo Capo
San Vito
Golfo di
Terrasini
Cinisi
Capo Zafferano
Bagheria
Golf
Términi In
Punta Tannure
A 29
Carini
Mácari
Punta del Saraceno
Castellammare
Castelluzzo
Monreale
Villagrázia
Térmi
Imere
Custonaci
Balestrate
Pachinico
Piana degli
Albanesi
186
Trábia
Érice
Ísole Égadi
Ísola di
Lévanzo
Trápani
Castellammare
del Golfo
E 90
113
San Giuseppe
Jato
Bolognetta
E 90
Ísola
Maréttimo
Álcamo
San Cipirello
Búccina
Cáccam
Ce
Maréttimo
Lévanzo
113
Paceco
Segesta
San
Marausa
Campreale
Godrano
Favignana
A 29
Calatafimi
Palermo
Mezzojuso
121
Montemaggiore
Belsito
Ísola Favignana
T r á p a n i
Vita
M
a
z
a
Vicari
ísole
dello
Granatello
Salemí
Roccamena
Corleone
Alía
Stagnone
115
Ciávolo
V
a
l
d
i
Contessa
Lercara
Friddi
Vallec
Marsala
Aquila
Santa
Ninfa
Poggioreale
Entellina
Prizzi
Castronuovo
di Sicilia
Petrosino
Partanna
Palazzo
Valle
Prata
Capo Feto
Santa
Margherita
di Bélice
Sambuca
di Sicilia
Adriano
Castelvetrano
Chiusa
Sclafani
San Giovanni
Gemini
Muss
Mazara del Vallo
E 90
Campobello
di Mazara
Bivona
Búrgio
189
C a n a l e   d i   S i c i l i a
Selinunte
Porto
Palo
Menfi
Caltabellotta
Clanciana
Casteltérmini
Capo Granitola
Casa Maragani
Galamónaci
San Blágio
Campofranco
Capo San
Marco
Sciacca
Ribera
Cattólica
Eraclea
Plátani
Racal
115
Bonsignore
Capo Bianco
Ráffadali
Montallegro
Aragona
Favar
Siculiana
Agrigento
Punta Grande
Porto
Empédocle
A g i g e
Valle del T
Cannatello
Punta Blanca
Patr
Montec

M E D I T E R R A N E A N   S E A

Pantelleria
Linosa, Lampedusa
Porto Empédocle

Trápani
Ísola di Pantelleria
Pantelleria
M. Gibéle
▲
700
Punta Limarsi
Punta
Polacca

Í. di Lampione
Ísole Pelágie
Lampedusa
Ísole di
Lampedusa
Í. di Linosa
Linosa

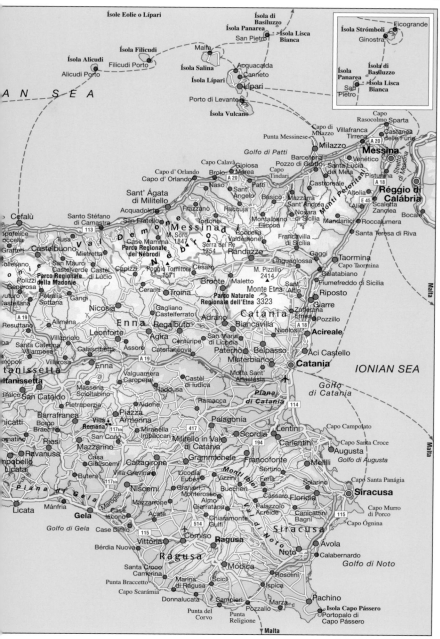

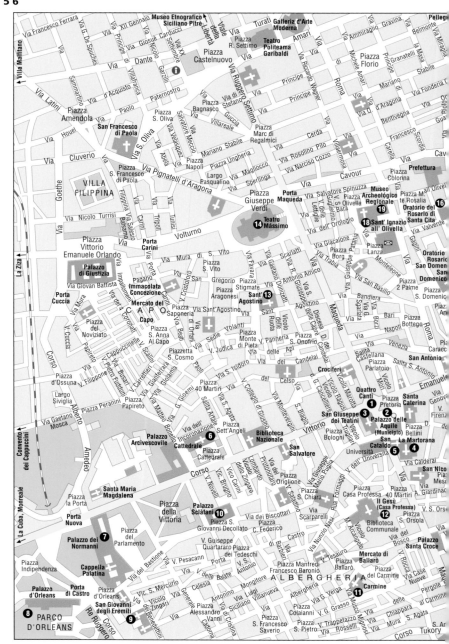

Palermo

0   200 m
0   200 yds

Molo Sud

Golfo di

Palermo

Via del Mare

za muzzo

Francesco Crispi

Via Galileo Ferrari

Via Sammuzzo

Via Galvani

Via Patuano

Via Alessandro Volta

Via Filippo Patti

Via CM. 8

orta Giorgio

Piazza XIII Vittime

Piazza Giorgio Genovesi

Via del Castello

Castellamare

iorgio Genovesi

Via Bivona

S. Alessandro Castello

Via Barilai

Via Cianciolo

Mignisi

Via Sebastiano

Piazza Castello

Mercato Ittico

Tavola

Via Tonda

Via S.

Piazza Castello

Piazza Cap. di Porto

Piazza Fonderia

V.Ces

Cala

Porta Felice

La Cala

Cala

Porta Carbone

Santa Maria della Catena
17

Vittorio Emanuele

Piazza S. Spirito

29

Materassa

Piazza F. Matera

Via Cassari

Terzana

Via Chiavettieri

UCCIRIA

Internazionale delle Maionette

Mura delle Cattive

VILLA

Piazzetta Dogana

28

V. Niscèmi

A

Via del Parlamento

Corso

Via Bottai

Piazza Marina
24

Palazzo Butera

MARE

Oratorio di San Lorenzo
27

San Francesco d'Assisi
26

Santa Maria dei Miracoli

Palazzo Chiaramonte
23

Via de Francisci

Via Butera

Salita Mura di Cattive

Cardil

Via Resuttana

Piazza S. Francesco d'Assisi

Palazzo Mirto
25

V. P. Merlo

Via di Blasi

Via IV Aprile

Via Scopari

La Pietà

zza Cassa Risparmio

Alessandro

Paternostro

Calascibetta

V. Lungarini

Cefalà

Via Scarri

Alloro

Via Alloro

Galleria Regionale
(Palazzo Abatellis)
22

Porta Dei Greci

Santa Anna

ici za ina

Via dei Corrieri

Vicolo

V. S. Carlo

Paternostro

Via Schiavuzzo

Via C. all'Alloro

Via Castro

Francesco Riso della Venerà

La Gancia

Savona

Santa Teresa

Piazza della Kalsa

V. P. Cr. Deuespiri

V. Aragona

Via Filippo

Piazza S. Eumo

Piazza Spasimo

Via S. Teresa

Piazza Spasimo Ventimiglia

Via Cecilia

Divisi

Via Garibaldi

Via del Sole

LA KALSA

Vicolo del Pallone

Cervello

etta

V.S.

Piazza Rivoluzione

Palazzo Aiutamicristo
21

La Magione
20

dello

Lo Spasimo

Porta Reale

Abramo

Foro Italico (Umberto I)

Lincoln

inese

V. Monte Santo

Via Maestro d'Acquia

Via

Via Magione

Piazza Magione

C. Pardi

VILLA GIULIA

Roma

Via

Gorizia

Via della Pace

Via G. Filangieri

Lincoln

Via

Milano

Corso

Via Manzoni

Porta Castro Filippo

ieste

Porta Garibaldi

Via Paci

Abramo

Via A. di Rudini

Antonio

Via V.M. Cipolla

Archirati

Ugo

ORTO BOTÁNICO
30

Piazza Giulio Cesare

Via dei

Via Rosario Gregorio

Mille

Balsamo

V.P. Randazzo

Via Gaspare Mignosi

a Segno

Via Trio

Stazione Centrale

San Giovanni dei Lebbrosi

Bagheria

PALERMO

At first sight Palermo is yet another crowded city with faded architectural beauty. But after decades of political instability and neglect, Sicily's under-rated capital is turning once again into a vibrant city

Palermo is both an essay in chaos and a jewel-box: hectic traffic and crowded streets are blended with a wonderful selection of palaces and churches, many neglected but others ready to delight.

A Phoenician colony existed here from the 8th century BC, perched on the water's edge of a fertile plain sheltered by a ring of mountainous hills, but it was only after Palermo fell to the Arabs in 831 AD (having been under Roman rule since 254 BC) that the settlement came into its own, growing, with Arab colonization, to the size of a city. By the 9th century it had developed into a great centre of scholarship and art, the home of Jewish and Lombard merchants, Greek craftsmen, Turkish and Syrian artisans, Persian artists and Negro slaves. It had the most multiracial population in Europe.

A golden age

Under Arab rule, it is said, there were 300 mosques, and the city was ringed by pleasure palaces like La Ziza and hunting lodges like La Cuba. Citizens acquired a love for Arab ornamentation. By 1091 when Norman rule began, it coincided with Palermo's own golden age, one of expansion, enlightenment, prosperity and cultural riches, incorporating Greek, Roman and Arab traditions.

Under Spanish rule that followed, the Moorish city was remodelled along grand baroque arteries. This attempt to impose order on the chaotic Arab maze provided a misleading semblance of control. Behind the grand new crossroads of Quattro Canti that divide the city into four *quartieri* (districts), the old Moorish city continued to swirl with crooked alleys, lively markets and impoverished housing. The revised urban design separated nobles and artisans, rich and poor.

Map:
pages
56–7

LEFT: Palermo seen from Monte Pellegrino.
BELOW: on the look-out for custom.

Part of the Fontana Pretoria, whose many naked statues once gave offence.

In a sense, little has changed since then, but it is only recently, as restoration becomes a reality, that many of the middle-class families that deserted the city centre in modern times have begun to return. The cosmopolitan city was badly damaged during the Allied invasion of Italy when, in 1943, Allied bombs destroyed the port and much of the historic centre. After the war, the problems were compounded as the Mafia, in league with corrupt politicians, stepped in, accepting funds from Rome and, later, the European Union, for the rebuilding of the devastated centre, only to siphon off the money for their own pleasures.

Nothing was achieved until 1992 when, following the Mafia murders of magistrates Giovanni Falcone and Paolo Borsellino, two high-profile public prosecutors, public attitudes changed. Palermitans experienced a wave of revulsion, and its citizens were no longer willing to be silently dominated by the Mafia.

After an extensive period of political instability and stagnation, a feeling of hope now permeates the air as the authorities combat corruption with some success. A new civic pride seems to have taken root and, as a result, hotels are updating themselves and, on the hour, tourist coaches appear to deposit their countless guided sightseers. As commerce is revived, so shopping streets again compete with the more sophisticated cities of mainland Italy. More than a million people live within Palermo and its periphery.

The historic centre

The city of Palermo is divided into four traditional sections by the **Quattro Canti ❶**, the hectic crossroads at Piazza Vigliena, where "four corners of the city" are formed by two great arteries, Via Maqueda (created in 1580s) and Corso Vittorio Emanuele. To give added importance to this constricted traffic junction, the four facades of buildings were embellished in 1620 with ornamental stonework and fountains by d'Avanzato.

Northwest of Corso Vittorio Emanuele is the **Capo** quarter and southwest, the **Albergheria**. North-

Getting Around

By Bus
The city is well serviced by the municipal bus service (AMAT). Tourist offices have up-to-date route maps. Tobacconists *(tabacchi)* and many newspaper kiosks sell €1.10 tickets. Tickets entitle you to transfer when you like to your destination within the city centre and must be franked on the bus machine at start of a trip. After franking they are valid for 2 hours. Day tickets: €3.50. Info tel: 091 690 2690.

By Metro
The Metropolitana metro service runs 6.10am–8.35pm with trains every 25 minutes. Single trip €1.05. Fairly safe (but beware of pickpock-

ets). The service is more useful for commuters travelling through Stazione Centrale than tourists because there are only 12 stations.

By Taxi
There are many cab stands in the city, usually near busy junctions. You can also hail one in the street. Drivers are licensed by the city and must use their meters. You should "remind" the driver to put it on if he seems to have "forgotten". Minimum charge is €3.81. A supplement of €0.32 is added for luggage and €1.91 after 10pm and on Sundays and holidays. Disabled passengers get a 30 percent reduction per trip.
To telephone for a cab:
Autoradio Taxi: 091 513 311
Radio Taxi Trinacria: 091 225 455

By Carriage
A horse-drawn carriage tour is a less romantic option in practice than it might seem due to the city's heavy traffic, summer heat and pollution. Prices are negotiable, but expect to pay €50 for a tour. A *carrozza* can carry five passengers.

By Car
Driving is stressful because of the frantic driving style, the many one-way streets and poor signing. Parking is a great problem; most spaces are valid for one hour or less. The solution is a hotel garage or one of the many "protected" car parks. Rates are usually €1 an hour; overnight rates are variable, usually around €15.

● Car rental firms: page 64.

east of Via Roma is **Vucciria** and southeast, the **Kalsa**.

Not to be missed a few paces (south) along Via Maqueda from the junction is **Piazza Pretoria ❷**, a piazza almost completely filled by the Fontana Pretoria. This baroque square was once disparagingly nick-named Piazza della Vergogna (the Square of Shame) because of its abundance of flagrantly nude statues that make up the fountain. More than 30 naked or near-naked nymphs, tri-tons, gods and youths of varying sizes and quality surround its vast circular basin. It was designed mid-1500s by Camillo Camilliani, a Tus-can, for a villa in Florence but was sold to Palermo instead in 1573 where Camillo's son and Michelan-gelo Naccherino established it in the square. Why it was sold, no one is sure but, allegedly, it was the local nuns who chopped off the noses of many of the naked men (but stopped short of castration). The statues were recently restored and ornamental railings surrounding the enclosure were closed to ensure that future vis-itors do little damage.

Adjoining the square is the **Pal-azzo delle Aquile** (Mon–Fri 9am–1.30pm, 3–7pm, Sat 9am–1pm), the municipal hall, with an eagle deco-rating its exterior. Built in 1463, it was later enlarged and restored. The towering presence here, however, is **San Giuseppe dei Teatini ❸** (Mon–Sat 7.30am–noon, 5.30pm–8pm; Sun & hols 8.30am–1pm, 6–8pm), built by Giacomo Besio (1612–45) with a cupola in majolica. During the 17th and 18th centuries the baroque interior was theatrically decorated with multicoloured marble and with eight massive columns in grey marble to support the dome, which is emblazoned with a fresco of the *Triumph of Sant'Andrea Avellino* (1724) by Borremans.

On neighbouring Piazza Bellini the campanile of **Chiesa della Mar-torana ❹** (Mon–Sat 8.30am–1pm, 3.30–7pm, winter closes 5.30pm, Sun 8.30am–1pm) stands tall along-side the three small red domes of **San Cataldo**. La Martorana was estab-lished in 1143 by Georgio di Anti-ochia, an admiral whose successes brought such fortune to Norman

Map: pages 56–7

San Giuseppe dei Teatini.

BELOW:
Piazza Pretoria, filled with the statues of Fontana Pretoria.

BELOW: the Cattedrale, dedicated to Our Lady of the Assumption.

Sicily that Roger II honoured him with the title Emir. (The church was originally called Santa Maria dell' Ammiraglio, or St Mary of the Admiral, to honour him. It also once had a dome on top of its tower.) To add perfect embellishment the admiral chose Greek Byzantine craftsmen to make the splendid **mosaics**. In the cupola is *Christ Pantocrator Blessing from the Throne*; elsewhere, with angels and apostles, are scenes from the *Ascension*, the *Annunciation*, the *Birth of Christ* and *Roger II crowned king by Christ*. It is one of the most beautiful Norman churches in Sicily but may have been even finer had not the nuns from the nearby convent demolished and altered much of it to suit the needs of their Order. The Order, founded by Eloisa Martorana, was given the church in 1233 but Mussolini returned it to the Greek Orthodox parishioners in 1935 to be their cathedral.

The triple-domed church of **San Cataldo ❺** (Mon–Fri 9.30am–1pm, 3.30–6pm, Sat–Sun 9.30am–1pm; entrance fee) is one of the last sacred buildings built in the Arab-Norman style. The interior was never decorated but if it appears plain, it is probably only because of comparison to its gilded neighbour, La Martorana. Subdued light reveals the three domes supported by squinches and piers; the Fatimid capitals are so delicate they appear to float. The mosaic floor and lattice windows are original; in the crypt are sections of Palermo's ancient Roman walls.

The Cattedrale

West from Quattro Canti, Corso Vittorio Emanuele leads away from the port towards the cathedral, separating the Albergheria and Capo quarters. This main thoroughfare was once known as Via Cassaro Vecchio, *vecchio* being old and *cassaro* derived from *qasr*, Arabic for castle. Beyond the **Biblioteca Nazionale** (which contains more than 500,000 volumes and 15th- and 16th-century manuscripts) are Piazza Cattedrale and the cathedral itself.

The **Cattedrale ❻** (daily Nov–Feb 9.30am–1.30pm, March–Oct 9.30am–5.30pm; hols 8am–1.30pm, 4.30–6pm. www.cattedrale.palermo.it)

was begun in 1185 on the site of a basilica that replaced a mosque in the 9th century. The original cathedral was the work of an Englishman, Walter of the Mill, who went on to become Archbishop of Palermo in 1168. The mosaic over the door is believed to have come from the original Byzantine church. An inscription from the Koran on the left-hand column is from the original mosque. Its soaring towers are late 14th-century.

However, it was in the 18th century that Ferdinando Fuga made alterations to the interior and added the cupola. The baroque interior is a cool shell with an enclosed setting for six **royal tombs** that include that of Roger II, the first king of Sicily (d. 1197) and Frederick II (d. 1250), Emperor of Germany and King of Sicily. The tombs were moved in the 18th century into their present position in the side chapels by Fuga. Borne by crouching lions, the sarcophagi are made of rare pink porphyry and sculpted by Arab masters, the only craftsmen who knew the technique in Norman times. In the nave are **statues** of saints by Antonello Gagini, moved from the high altar by the busy Fuga. In the **treasury** are items found in some of the royal tombs, including the crown of Constance of Aragon (d. 1222), a cap sewn with jewels. Constance was 24 when she married Emperor Frederick II, age 14. In the **crypt** are 23 tombs, many of them Roman.

The Albergheria Quarter

South of Corso Emanuele, the **Albergheria** quarter was once the home of Norman court officials and rich merchants from Pisa and Amalfi. Although many dilapidated houses are home to illegal immigrants, a sense of community prevails over scenes of urban decay.

Beyond the cathedral on the Corso is **Piazza della Vittoria**, with a spacious garden sheltered by countless palm trees and with a triumphal gate spanning the road. The gate is the **Porta Nuova**, the new gate erected in 1535 to celebrate Charles V's victory in Tunisia. Also here is the **Palazzo dei Normanni** ❼, the eclectic royal palace and centre of power since Roger II con-

TIP

An interesting tour led by volunteers shows visitors the underside of the Albergheria. It includes a bird's-eye view of the city from a tower normally closed to the public, a visit to a carob factory or a cart-painter's workshop, with a meal in a cosy inn or street snacks in the Ballarò market. It's run by Albergheria Viaggi, Piazza San Francesco Saverio 3. Tel: 091 651 8576.

BELOW: the courtyard of the Palazzo dei Normanni.

Gagini and Serpotta

The city has an abundance of works of art that define the periods of its history. Two names of which locals are inordinately proud are Antonello Gagini and Giacomo Serpotta. Gagini, a marble sculptor like his father Domenico, is considered the most significant Renaissance sculptor in Sicily. Between 1510 and 1536 he and his studio sculpted in marble, terracotta and stucco. Among his abundant work in Palermo is the Madonna della Scala (1503) in the cathedral.

Serpotta (1656–1732) was a master in stuccowork. His exquisite work in the Oratorio di Santa Cita (1685–88) makes the walls look as if they are draped in cloth (see page 67).

TIP

● **Car Rental**
Avis, Via Crispi 115.
Tel: 091 586 940
*Hertz, Via Messina 7.
Tel: 091 331 668
Sicily by Car, Via
Mariano Stabile 6.
Tel: 091 581 045 *
● **Motorbike Rental**
Motorent, Via Amari
91. Tel:091 602 3455
Rent a Scooter, Via
Amari 63. Tel: 091
336 804
● **Bicycle Rental**
Cannatella, Via
Papireto 14. Tel: 091
322 425

BELOW: marriage rites.
RIGHT: mosaic in the
Capella Palatina in the
Palazzo dei Normanni.

verted the original 9th-century Arab towered castle into his residence, an Arab-Norman palace. It houses the city's must-see site, the superb Cappella Palatina (Palatine Chapel). Now the seat of the Sicilian parliament, this cube-shaped palazzo has walled gardens overgrown with orchids, papyrus, banyan trees, ficus beniamine as well as dwarf palms, whose leaves are reputed to take 50 years to grow, and African kapoks, said to be a favourite with monkeys in their natural habitat because they store water in their barrel-like trunks. As the main building was turned into the home of the Regional Assembly in 1947, its visiting hours are limited (Mon, Tues, Thur, Fri, Sat 8.30am–noon, 2–5pm, Sun & hols 8.30am–12.30pm; entrance fee).

Cappella Palatina

Leading off a lovely loggia is the superb **Cappella Palatina** (Mon–Sat 8.30am–noon, 2–5pm, Sun & hols 8.30am–12.30pm; entrance fee), the royal chapel built for Roger II between 1130 and 1140. He ensured each of the religions in his kingdom was represented in some manner within the Christian chapel: Arab, Greek, Muslim and Christian. The interior is famous for its wonderful glittering **mosaics** on the dome and apse, designed to recall the life of Roger II as well as record the subjects vivid to the Christians. These include sumptuous Biblical scenes incorporating the *Annunciation*, the *Raising of Lazarus*, the *Building of the Ark*, the *Nativity* and the *Destruction of Sodom*. The inlaid floors, marble walls, columns and candle holders and a 3-metre (10-ft) tall paschal candlestick, richly decorated with animals carved in white marble, were made by Romans, while Arab craftsmen created the exquisitely carved and painted wooden ceiling; it portrays Christian paradise (as seen through Muslim eyes) with naked maidens surrounded by Normans prudishly clothed and crowned with haloes. The ceiling is remarkable. Where else can you see Persian octagonal stars meet Islamic stalactites with palm trees and peacocks while men play chess, hunt and drink among

entwined dancers and female musicians? Unique in a Christian church, it is a composition of ineffable Oriental splendour.

On the top floor of the palace are the **Royal Apartments**, mostly decorated in the 19th century, but the **Sala di Re Ruggero** has splendid mosaics of hunting scenes created in 1140. The **Sala da Ballo** has a fine view to the sea.

Through Porta Nuova is Piazza Indipendenza with, behind Palazzo d'Orleans, the **Parco d'Orleans** ❽ (Mon–Fri 9am–1pm, 3–6pm, Sat–Sun 9am–1pm), the lush gardens open to the public. The park belongs to the palazzo, the official residence of the Regional President. Mothers play here with children, men play cards and office workers eat ice creams sandwiched in buns, a Palermitan speciality.

The romantic **San Giovanni degli Eremiti** ❾ (currently closed for restoration), with its distinctive five red cupolas, lies just south of the royal palace on Via dei Benedettini. It illustrates the Arab influence favoured when its construction was begun by Roger II in 1132, a year after he had been elected king. Its elegant Norman cloisters are overgrown with jasmine, citrus, mimosa and bougainvillea. The shape of an early mosque is still visible, so is a piece of 12th-century fresco but little more. The wealthy church was stripped long ago.

Arab architectural motifs haunt **Palazzo Sclafani** ❿, a fortified medieval palazzo north of San Giovanni, built in 1330 by one of the most powerful feudal families. Further east, in Piazza del Carmine, is the fabulously-domed church of **Carmine** ⓫ (daily 9–10.30am) with fine paintings and majolica.

This area is really the heart of **il mercato di Ballarò**, the **Ballarò market**, a noisy haunt of artisans and students, housewives and bootleg-

gers. Currently Palermo's liveliest daily market, it is raucous, authentic and sprawling, with the hurly-burly of the exotic food stalls clashing with the second-hand clothes stalls. Sicily's first Jesuit church, **Il Gesù** ⓬ (daily 7.30–11.30am), is on Piazza Casa Professa. Also known as **Casa Professa** for its learned Jesuit origins, its interior is beautifully decorated with colourful marble, sculptures, tritons and cherubs. It has been restored after being damaged in World War II. The atrium of Casa Professa is part of the Biblioteca Communale, founded in 1760.

The Capo Quarter

The battered **Capo** *quartiere* lies north of the cathedral. Since its origins as the slave-traders' quarter, the Capo has been isolated, historically the poorest area of the city. It is a maze of streets but the quarter's centrepiece, on Via Sant' Agostino masked by market stalls, is the church of **Sant'Agostino** ⓭ (Mon–Sat 7am–12pm, 4pm–6pm, Sun 7am–12pm), part of the imposing monastery that ran the region in

Map: pages 56–7

The multicoloured dome of San Giovanni degli Eremiti.

BELOW:
San Giovanni's exotic gardens and cloisters.

The atmospheric alleys of Vucciria.

medieval times. Although built in 1275, the sober church was enlarged by the powerful Chiaramonte and Sclafani dynasties. Their crests and some lava mosaics decorate a delicate late-13th-century portal surmounted by a 14th-century rose window, over the Via Maestri dell' Acqua entrance. Inside are gilded stuccoes by Giacomo Serpotta (c. 1711) and important frescoes and paintings. Charming 16th-century cloisters surround a small garden.

In the narrow streets are many churches from the 15th, 16th and 17th centuries. Some, like the restored **Immacolata Concezione** on Via Porta Carini, have beautiful carved interiors while others lie abandoned and derelict. Some are put to other uses, like **San Marco**, which is now a home for the elderly. These streets are the setting for the **mercato del Capo**, an excellent source of food, clothes and household goods.

Within walking distance of the market, northwards on Via Maqueda, historic Capo gives way to 19th- and 20th-century Palermo with **Teatro Massimo** , the city's well restored,

vast opera house dominating Piazza Giuseppe Verdi (tours: Mon–Sat 10am–3pm, unless there's a rehearsal). The harmonious building, first opened in 1897, was designed by Palermo's illustrious Giovanni Battista Basile in eclectic rather than neo-classical style. The portico, graced by Corinthian columns, is of Greek inspiration, while the cylindrical shapes of the building and the cupola owe more to Roman ideal. The interior is equally eclectic: while the grandiose main staircase is baroque, the decor, rich in floral motifs, is decidedly Art Nouveau. This remarkable theatre, with an enormous stage, seats 3,400 for performances of opera and ballet. It was reopened in 1998 with a glittering production of Verdi's *Aida*, after a scandalous 25-year closure that can be blamed on lethargy, financial shortcomings and political infighting. For programme details tel: 091 605 3111; www.teatromassimo.it.

The two **kiosks** on the piazza were designed by Battista Basile's son Ernesto in the Liberty/Art Nouveau style that he used for much of his work in Palermo. To one side across the road is the thriving **Teatro al Massimo** (tel: 091 589 575; www.teatroalmassimo.it), where plays in Italian are presented.

The Vucciria Quarter

The name of this quarter is a corruption of the French *boucherie*, thanks to the quantity of meat traditionally on sale in the **Vucciria market**. The stalls straggle along alleys from Via Roma to **San Domenico** (Mon–Fri 9–11.30am, Sat–Sun 5–7pm), a baroque church with an impressive facade that has its foundations in the 1300s but was altered around 1636 by the Domenican order. In the 18th century, the Spanish viceroys tried to impose order on Palermo's most chaotic market but failed dismally. Little has changed and the names of

the surrounding streets echo the old local trades: silversmiths, ironmongers, pasta makers, shoemakers. The colourful stalls display capers and pine nuts, spices and sun-dried tomatoes, endless varieties of meat and sausages and bootleg tapes, and are particularly charming as night falls and the red awnings are illuminated. However, the success of Ballarò market means that the Vucciria market truly bustles only on Saturdays. If the Vucciria palls, leave the market and consider a drink in the faded belle-époque grandeur of **Grand Hotel et des Palmes** at 398 Via Roma. Wagner reputedly completed *Parsifal* in a gilded salon here in 1882, while the wartime Mafia boss, Lucky Luciano, later held court in the dining room.

Behind the church of **San Domenico**, on Via Bambinai, a doll makers' street that has stayed close to its roots by selling Christmas crib figures as well as votive offerings, is a baroque jewel, the **Oratorio del Rosario ⓕ** (Mon–Sat 9am–1pm). It is a theatrical chapel created by Serpotta, with *putti* playing cellos amidst seashells, eagles and allegorical exot-

ica. The altarpiece, the *Madonna of the Rosary,* is the work of **Van Dyck** (c1624) and considered one of the finest in Sicily and Italy.

Oratorio di Santa Cita

Just around the corner, on Via Valverde, lies another celebrated oratory, **Oratorio di Santa Cita ⓖ** (Mon–Sat 9am–1pm), reached through lush gardens. The oratories were places where nobles gathered, centres for charitable works as well as for displays of personal status and wealth. In Santa Cita, Serpotta's ravishing stuccowork depicts the *Intercession of the Virgin in the Battle of Lepanto* with all of the boats exquisitely differentiated.

Beyond the chapel is **La Cala**, the scruffy portside edged by Via Cala. Fishing boats bob against a backdrop of bombed palazzi whose cellars house immigrant families. However, regeneration is gradually seeping into this semi-derelict quarter with the restoration of churches, like **San Giorgio dei Genovesi** (Mon–Sat 9am–1pm), which is now an exhibition centre.

Oratorio del Rosario in San Domenico.

BELOW: traditional puppets are made in this part of Palermo.

TIP

Street Markets
The city is known for its bustling street markets where locals shop every day for fresh produce: meat, fish, fruit, vegetables, spices. The narrow winding lanes of the Ballarò, the Vucciria, the Capo and the Borgo Vecchio (east of Teatro Politeama) are reminiscent of an Arab souk. Some stalls will grill fish, squid and octopus while you wait. Keep exploring and you find everything is available, from clothes to bootleg DVDs and CDs.

BELOW:
the courtyard of the Museo Archeologico Regionale.

Sandwiched between the port and Piazza Marina is **Santa Maria della Catena** ⑰ (Mon–Fri 9am–1pm), a well-restored 15th-century church with an early-Renaissance portico at the top of a flight of stairs. *Catena* means chain, so the church may have been named after the chain that shut off the harbour in times of war. Inside a 16th-century *baldacchino* covers a charming 14th-century fresco of *Madonna and Child*.

From the port, if you retrace your steps to Via Roma and turn into Via Bara, you come to Piazza Olivella, part of a charming artisans' quarter of puppet-makers, *pasticcerie* and trattorie. The grand baroque church of **Sant' Ignazio all' Olivella** ⑱ (Mon, Tues & Sun 9–10am, Thur–Sat 9–10am, 5–6pm) begun in 1598 but with a 17th-century facade, has some fine pictures, as does the neighbouring **Oratorio di San Filippo** (known also as **Sant' Ignazio**, currently closed for restoration), with its interior created in 1769 by Filippo Pennino.

Adjoining the Olivella church is the **Museo Archeologico Regionale**

⑲ (Tues–Fri 8.30am–1.15pm, 3–6.15pm, Sat–Mon 8.30am–1.15pm; entrance fee), the essence of Classical Sicily encased in a late Renaissance monastery, with artefacts that illustrate the region's glorious historical roots, from prehistoric times to the Roman era. There are inscrutable Egyptian priestly figures found near Mózia *(see page 100)* and anthropomorphic sarcophagi stare out of Semitic faces and square bodies. In a large cloister is a tangle of lush vegetation and a lily pond.

The museum's most important treasures are in the fabulous **Sala di Selinunte**, including carved stone reliefs (the metopes) that were set above the columns about 470 BC at Selinunte *(see pages 102–4)*. They show deities, the *Sacred Marriage of Zeus and Hera on Mount Ida*, a winged sphinx, *Hercules and the Cretan Bull*, *Actaeon turning into a Stag*, the *Rape of Europa* and many more equally evocative legends.

Also here is an Etruscan collection, the **Collezione Casuccini**, accumulated by a Sicilian historian. There are sculptures and painted terracotta works from around the 6th to 5th centuries BC uncovered in Chiusi (Tuscany). Also, superb Greek vases of the same period depict the *Myth of Tripolemus* and the *Battle of Athena against the Giants*.

In the museum, too, are terracotta votive offerings from Selinunte and other ancient sites in Western Sicily, as well as the celebrated bronze *Ram* that once stood over the gate of Castello Maniace in Siracusa. There are casts of engravings from Addaura on nearby Monte Pellegrino and a Roman mosaic showing Orpheus enchanting wild beasts.

La Kalsa

In Arab times the Kalsa quarter was where the Emir lived in splendour and in the Middle Ages it became the chosen district for the homes of

wealthy merchants. The word *kalsa* comes from the Arabic *khalisa*, meaning pure or chosen.

Little of this purity shows today. La Kalsa may be picturesque, but it is impoverished having been badly damaged during World War II as it fringes the harbour. When Mother Teresa's mission settled close to bomb-struck **Piazza Magione**, wealthy Palermitans were horrified to be lectured by an Albanian nun, even one incarnating sainthood. Her message was that since Palermo was as poor as the Third World, charity should begin at home. The message, however, seems to have struck a chord since the area is being slowly regenerated with a cheerful materialism heralded by new bars and palazzo restoration, especially close to the gentrified **Piazza Marina**.

However, this seemingly abandoned corner of Palermo does house a wonderful Norman church as well as the late Mother Teresa's nuns. On Piazza Magione, Moorish filigree windows and blind arcading announce the ancestry of the church of **La Magione** (daily 9am–noon, 3–6.15pm). This imposing Cistercian church was founded in 1151 as the Chiesa della Trinità but was then given in 1197 to the Imperial Teutonic Order by Henry VI as their base. The interior is plain without being austere. It is a fine example of Arab-Norman architecture, with a gracious interior complete with 14th-century altar beneath a painted *Crucifix*. The delicate cloisters (Mon–Sat 9am–7pm, Sun 9am–1.30pm) contain a 15th-century fresco of the *Crucifixion*. Outside is a charming garden of palm trees.

On Piazza Magione is a memorial to the magistrate Giovanni Falcone, assassinated by the Mafia in 1992 and, to one side of the piazza, is **Teatro Politeama Garibaldi** (1861), a small theatre saved from ruin by the Comune but in need of restoration. Just south, in the honeycomb heart of the Kalsa, is **Lo Spasimo** (Mon–Fri 8am–8pm, Sat–Sun 9am–8pm; tel: 091 616 1486), an exhibition and entertainment complex set in a former 16th-century monastery. Concerts are held in the cloisters and the roofless church, which, given a sultry, starry night and swaying palms, creates a romantic, Moorish atmosphere.

Via Magione leads into Via Garibaldi with, among the palazzi, **Palazzo Aiutamicristo** , an enormous Catalan-Gothic mansion built in 1490 containing a loggia and porticoed courtyard. It was along Via Garibaldi, and what is now Corso dei Mille, that Giuseppe Garibaldi made his triumphant advance into Palermo on 27 May 1860.

Regional art gallery

Just east, Via Alloro, the city's patrician centre in the Middle Ages and the principal street in the Kalsa, leads to **Palazzo Abatellis** (1488), a grand Catalan-Gothic mansion restored after the war and converted in 1954 into the **Galleria Regionale** (cur-

Map: pages 56–7

TIP

Internet facilities
● Internet Cafe, Via Candelai. Open Tues–Sun from 7pm. Tel: 091 327 151
● Internet Cafe, Via Spinuzza 51. Open daily 11am–3am. Tel: 091 662 2229
● Free internet point: Villa Trabia, Via Salinas (9am–7pm). Tel: 091 740 5941

BELOW:
Palazzo Abatellis, now the regional art gallery.

BELOW: the Fontana del Garraffo in the Piazza Marina.

rently closed for restoration). This regional gallery houses Sicily's most endearing art collection. The treasures are matched in scale and quality by the charming setting.

Off a Renaissance courtyard and loggia, on two floors, there are rich rooms of 15th to 16th-century sculpture, a serene bust of *Eleanor of Aragon* by Francesco Laurana, engaging Gagini sculptures, wonderful Sicilian paintings of the 13th, 14th and 15th centuries, including a haunting *Annunciation* (1476) by Antonello da Messina, considered Sicily's greatest painter of the 1400s.

The undoubted masterpiece is a fresco that once was on the walls of Palazzo Sclafani. The mid-15th-century work of two unknown painters, it is the powerful *Triumph of Death*, with a skeleton archer as the grim reaper of Death riding on a spectral horse, cutting a swathe through wealthy bishops, nobles and fair maidens. Here, Death shoots only at those who do not want to die because they are enjoying life to the full; he ignores the poor and disabled, who pray for divine interven-

tion and a release from their earthbound troubles. The subject is macabre but strangely compelling.

Next to the Gallery is the austere **La Gancia**, originally the 15th-century church of Santa Maria degli Angeli (Mon–Sat 9.30am–noon, 3–6pm, Sun 10am–12.30pm). Paintings here include works by Antonello Gagini, Vincenzo da Pavia and Pietro Novelli as well as stuccoes by Giacomo Serpotta.

Palazzo Chiaramonte

A short walk away is **Palazzo Chiaramonte** ㉓ (Tues–Sat 9am–1pm, 2.30–6.30pm, Sun 10am–2pm; entrance fee) a massive palace built by the baronial Chiaramonte family in 1307. It became the palace of the Spanish viceroys and then the seat of the Inquisition from 1605 to 1782. Carved on the grim prison walls inside is a poignant plea for *pane, pazienza e tempo* (bread, patience and time). Heretics and dissenters were burned to death outside. Commonly known as **Lo Steri**, the building was restored for the Chancellor of Palermo University and is sometimes used for concerts. The gorgeous inner courtyard and the salon with a coffered Moorish ceiling are well worth a visit.

Alongside Palazzo Chiaramonte is **Piazza Marina** ㉔, originally a muddy inlet of the sea that silted up and was reclaimed in Saracen times. Since then the square has witnessed the shame and glory of city history. It was used by the Aragonese for weddings and jousts and, because it was close to the prisons, for public executions too. In the centre is **Giardino Garibaldi**. As it is the only gentrified square in the old quarter, the locals are self-consciously proud of its shady park and well-tended banyan trees. The square holds a bric-a-brac market on Saturday afternoons and Sunday mornings. Across the square is the charming

Renaissance church of **Santa Maria dei Miracoli** (Mon–Fri 9am–5pm, Sat 9am–1pm).

Close to the church, at 2 Via Merlo, is **Palazzo Mirto** , an unprepossessing palazzo with a delightful interior. In 1982 the palace and its contents were donated to the State by the descendants of the Princes of Lanza Filangri, whose ancestors have lived in the palazzo since the 17th century. Now a museum (daily 9am–6.30pm; entrance fee), the palazzo is a fine example of how a grand family lived and a testament to the eclectic tastes of 18th-century nobles in Palermo. Below *trompe l'oeil* ceilings are Louis XVI chairs, rustic panelling, heroic tapestries and crib figures. A Chinoiserie salon has lacquered Oriental cabinets, porcelain and pagoda-style seats.

Near the stables are two important works by Italy's great sculptor, **Antonio Canova**, the funerary stele of *Giambattista* and *Elisabetta Mellerio* (c.1830). To prevent them leaving the island, they were purchased by the region of Sicily in 1978.

A Gothic classic

Just beyond Via Roma, Via Paternostro leads into a piazza with the 13th-century church of **San Francesco d'Assisi** (daily 8am–noon, 4–6pm), one of Palermo's loveliest Gothic churches, its austerity softened by a beautiful portal and delicate rose window. It was damaged in World War II but well restored. The nave (1255–77) is edged with 14th-century chapels and eight statues by Serpotta (1723).

Nearby, on Via Immacolatella, is the **Oratorio di San Lorenzo** (Mon–Sat 9am–5pm; entrance fee), under plans for restoration. The interior is a whimsical yet overwrought extravaganza of stucco by Giacomo Serpotta, a masterpiece based on the lives of Saints Francis and Lawrence, with every surface awash with cheeky cherubs and lavish allegories. One of Caravaggio's last paintings, a *Nativity*, hung over the altar but was stolen in 1969. Locals believe the painting was taken by the Mafia for ransom but is likely to have been destroyed as they failed either to raise a ransom or sell it.

Opposite the church of San Francesco, at 58 Via Paternostro, is **Antica Focacceria di San Lorenzo**, a legendary local inn with battered bow windows matched by marble slabs and a gleaming brass stove. This period piece, open 8am–11pm, has a reputation for rustic snacks like *panini di panelle* (fried chickpea squares) and, an acquired taste, *pani cu' la meusa* (tripe served in a bun).

Much of this area was reduced to rubble by Allied bombing during the war, including **Palazzo Butera** , eulogised by Goethe. Once Sicily's grandest palace, it is now used for receptions and exhibitions. As part of the ongoing regeneration of the area, the council has restored the terraced **Mura delle Cattive** below the Butera. This terrace, decorated with statues, was named *Wall of the Nasty*

Map: pages 56–7

TIP

On the third Sunday of every month an antiques and retro market is held in the courtyard of the Palazzo Butera. What's more, the terraces of the palace provide one of the best panoramas of Palermo.

BELOW: creating a stir at Antica Focacceria.

Women in honour of the sour-faced widows and spinsters who once glowered at lovers strolling by. In the 18th century, when the people of Palermo were renowned for being sexually liberated, this was where lovers would meet in the evenings on the pretence that the terrace had fine views over the seafront to Monte Pellegrino and that the heat here was less oppressive. It is now the evening meeting place for teenagers. The marina below was once Palermo's grand seafront until the Belle Epoque and was both a public parade and chance for louche encounters. Now known as **Foro Italico ㉙**, the stark waterfront is yet another thoroughfare with heavy traffic.

Off Via Butera, in Piazzetta Niscemi, is the Puppet Museum, **Museo Internazionale delle Marionette** (Mon-Fri 9am–1pm, 3.30–6.30pm, Sat 9am–1pm; entrance fee), with an amusing international collection of around 3,000 puppets from Palermo, Catania and Naples and many from Africa and the Far East. There are performances during the week and a festival of puppet shows in the

autumn, the *Festival di Morgana*. Children are encouraged to make their own puppets.

Off Foro Italico, not far from the elegant **Porta Reale** (1786), is the **Villa Giulia** (daily summer 8am–8pm, winter 8am–5pm) with an attractive garden and the **Orto Botanico ㉚** (April & Oct daily 9am–6pm, May & Sept daily 9am–7pm, June–Aug daily 9am– 8pm, Nov–Mar Mon–Sat 9am–5pm, Sun 9am–2pm; entrance fee), botanical gardens dotted with pavilions, sphinxes and a lily pond. There are clumps of bamboo and bougainvillea, banyans and magnolias, pineapples and petticoat palms.

The southern suburbs

From the scruffy waterfront at **Foro Italico**, a short drive or stroll southwest leads to a couple of lesser-known Arab-Norman sights in a dismal area of the city. It is hard to believe in the 10th century this was described as an earthly paradise.

On Corso dei Mille, the **Ponte dell' Ammiraglio**, a stranded Norman bridge built in 1113, stands in urban sprawl (open daily). Once it straddled the now-diverted River Oreto.

On Via Cappello, just off the Corso, is **San Giovanni dei Lebbrosi** (Mon & Wed–Sat 11am, 4–6pm, Tues 9–11am), built of limestone and brick as a castle chapel for Count Roger I in 1072. The domed church is one of the city's earliest Norman monuments and was later used as a leper hospital. Hence its name: Saint John of the Lepers.

The western suburbs

Some distance out of the Capo quarter, off Via Guglielmo Buono, is Piazza Ziza and one of the most impressive examples of Arab-Norman secular architecture in Sicily. It is purely Islamic in its inspiration. In Norman times palaces encircled the city "like gold coins around the neck

of a bosomy girl," – the vivid description by the Arab poet, Ibn Jubayr. None were finer than those, here, in what was then the kings' private park reserved for hunting. The poet's words evoke the pleasure dome of **Castello della Ziza** (daily 9am–6.30pm; entrance fee).

Begun in 1160 by William I, and known as **La Ziza** (from the Arabic for magnificent), this was to be a house of joy and splendour. An Arabic inscription by its entrance conjures up earthly paradise within. With the passage of time it was converted into a fortress and, in 1635, converted yet again, this time into a residence. It was opened to visitors in 1990 after years of neglect.

An Arab arch leads to a palace built on the site of a Roman villa so that it could exploit an existing aqueduct. By installing a system of canals, water from the aqueduct fed a charming fountain at the centre of the ground floor hall and this, in turn, fed a pond outside. In fact, La Ziza's most charming spot is the vestibule, adorned by honeycomb vaults, the fountain and a glorious mosaic of peacocks and huntsmen. In this breezy chamber the Emir and his court listened to the lapping of water. On the top floor, the central hall was originally an atrium with small rooms on either side believed to have been a harem.

South of La Ziza, screened by barrack walls, is **La Cuba** (daily 9am–6.30pm; entrance fee), the final piece of the Moorish jigsaw. This quaint pavilion lies along Corso Calatafimi, opposite Via Quarto dei Mille, but in Arab times it was set in a lovely artificial lake within the luxuriant grounds of La Ziza. In *The Decameron* Boccaccio set a story of illicit love in this "sumptuous villa" which is now, although partly restored, a ruin marooned in an army barracks. Originally La Cuba had a dome.

The **Convento dei Cappuccini** (daily: Mar–Oct 9am–noon, 3–5.30pm, Nov–Feb 9am–noon; entrance fee), the Capuchin friars' convent with its grim catacombs, lies on Via Cappuccini midway between La Cuba and La Ziza. In macabre Sicilian style, corpses of the clergy,

Map: pages 56–7

Mummified priest in the Convento dei Cappuccini.

BELOW: Castello Ziza, once a house of joy and splendour.

View from a balcony.

nobles, lawyers and the bourgeoisie were mummified here from the 16th century to 1881. In these galleries embalmers have stored over 8,000 dearly departed souls. Many are hung on walls, dressed and apparently grinning at visitors.

North and Conca d'Oro

Travelling northward towards Mondello with its numerous villas and beaches, you come to the city outskirts and the legendary "golden shell", the Conca d'Oro plain, carved between coast and mountains. This should be carpeted with marigolds and citrus groves but land speculation and Mafia funding has ensured that Palermo's countryside is mostly encased in concrete, with environmental laws circumnavigated by unscrupulous builders.

Villa Igiea, Palermo's deluxe seaside hotel on Salita Belmonte on the east coast, is a survivor, a fine example of the city's Liberty days. Ernesto Basile, son of the architect of the Teatro Massimo, designed it for the Florio family, Sicily's finest entrepreneurs, who chose this terraced setting overlooking the sea. The glorious Art Nouveau dining room is a harmonious composition of elegant cabinets, functional furnishings and ethereal frescoes.

On the northern outskirts, the road leads on to Palermo's large park, the **Parco della Favorita** (open daily) at the foot of **Mount Pellegrino**; this was purchased by the exiled Bourbon king Ferdinand III in 1799 to make his exile from Naples more bearable. His domineering consort, Maria Carolina, conceived of the **Palazzina Cinese** (closed) as a Petit Trianon to rival the creation of her sister, Marie Antoinette.

Next door is **Villa Niscemi** (Sun 9am–12.30pm, Mon–Sat from 9am by arrangement; tel: 091 740 4822), whose fate seems assured as an entertainment centre. The villa was used as Giuseppe di Lampedusa's model for Tancredi's home in *The Leopard*. Owned by a noble family who came to Sicily with the Normans, the villa combines elegance with rustic charm.

Di Lampedusa's own ancestral home, **Villa Lampedusa** (daily 9am–12.30pm), built in 1770 but bought by the Principe around 1845, is also nearby and well signposted.

Also here is the **Museo Etnografico Siciliano Pitrè** (closed for restoration), which houses an extraordinary ethnographic collection that illustrates Sicilian life, customs and folklore. There are costumes, painted carts, musical instruments, carriages and much more, including a model of the towering 18th-century *Carrozza di Santa Rosalia*, which was towed by teams of mules through Palermo's streets on 15 July, the feast day of Santa Rosalia. On board were garlanded maidens, musicians with their instruments and, beneath a cupola surrounded by winged angels, a huge statue of the saint.

From the coast, a scenic road climbs **Monte Pellegrino**, the city's

holy mountain, passing citrus groves and shrubland. In the sandstone slopes, the **grotto di Adduara** caves (closed) have revealed prehistoric drawings carved into the walls. It is a beautiful location, crowded at weekends with cars and picnickers. From the terraced slopes, sweeping views span the bay of the Conca d'Oro.

On the mountainside the **Santuario Santa Rosalia** (daily 7am–7.30pm) is a shrine to Palermo's revered patron saint with a chapel and grotto. Her origins are mysterious but, according to legend, Rosalia renounced the world on the death of her father, going to live as a religious recluse in a hermitage on the mountain. She died there in 1166.

But in 1624, while Palermo was in the throes of a deadly plague, she appeared to a visitor on the mountain asking him to search for her remains in the cave and give her a Christian burial. Her grave found, she was disinterred and her relics were carried in procession into Palermo where the plague, instantly and miraculously, ceased. Such was the spread of religious devotion to her that within a year a chapel with its cavern sanctuary was established in her honour, a place of pilgrimage. Mountain views and souvenir stalls are the additional rewards for trailing up to this sanctuary.

Mondello

Set in the lee of Monte Pellegrino is the fashionable resort of **Mondello**, reached easily from Palermo by bus from Viale della Libertà. The resort, pioneered by the Bourbons, began as a tuna-fishing village but was turned into a garden suburb by a Belgian entrepreneur in the 1890s and reached its heyday in the interwar years. Nowadays Liberty/Art Nouveau villas are surrounded by modern buildings.

It is a popular meeting place for the people of Palermo who come to the lido to swim, socialise and dine on fresh fish. The centre of attraction is the striking maroon and ochre Art Nouveau pier. Other attractions are slight but seductive, from summer sea breezes to a ruined medieval watchtower, as well as busy discotheques and decorous dining. ❏

Map: pages 56–7

Watermelon custard
Crema di Anguria *is a fragrant Sicilian speciality. The sweet red pulp of watermelon is mixed with a little sugar, corn starch and jasmine water, then heated to a creamy consistency. As it cools, pieces of candied pumpkin and plain chocolate are mixed into the custard. It's served chilled. In Palermo many sweet pastries are filled with this, often called* gelu di miluni.

BELOW: the summer resort of Mondello.

Isola delle Femmine and Terrasini

Further along the coast, away from Mondello on the A29, are two more resorts. Isole delle Femmine is best avoided. It may face an island of the same name, but is surrounded by an industrial zone and the sea is often polluted. Terrasini, however, overlooks the Golfo di Castellamare and is a former fishing village with sandy beaches and clean sea. It has three museums: Antiquarium (Piazza Falcone-Borsellino) with ancient finds from the sea, Museo Etnografico (Via Carlo Alberto della Chiesa) with a folklore collection and Museo di Storia Naturale (Via Cala Rossa), a natural history museum. (Usually open all year, Mon–Sat 9am–12.30pm.)

RESTAURANTS AND CAFÉS

Palermo

Standards in the majority of eateries are high and establishments off main thoroughfares offer particularly good value. Many of Palermo's top hotels also have renowned restaurants, particularly the Villa Igiea and Principe di Villafranca. They are expensive, of course, so if you want to splash out, you might also consider somewhere like **La Scuderia** or **Regine** for excellent food outside a hotel ambience. Or venture further to the renowned **Charleston le Terrazze** at Mondello lido, 11 km (7 miles) away.

The streets around Corso Scina and Via Emerico Amari have a concentration of Tunisian restaurants with names like Medina and Aladin, some of which have belly dancing.

Not all pizzerie are of the same standard, but if the place is full of locals, it's good.

Expensive

Cucina Papoff
Via Isidoro La Lumia 32.
Tel: 091 586 460.
www.cucinapapoff.com
Refined yet imaginative Sicilian cuisine in an Art Nouveau setting. Friendly atmosphere. Try the fish and *u maccu*, broad beans with fennel.

Closed Sat lunch, Sun and Aug. €€€

Osteria dei Vespri
Piazza Croce dei Vespri 6.
Tel: 091 617 1631.
www.osteriadeivespri.it.
An upmarket restaurant in a lovely sheltered square, with outdoor tables in summer. The cooking is creative Italian, and the wine list one of the city's best. Closed Sun. €€€

Regine
Via Trapani 4.
Tel: 091 586 566.
regine@ristoranteregine.it
For Sicilian specialities, this is the place. Known for wide-ranging antipasti (look for *peperoni ripieni alla palermitana*, stuffed sweet peppers Palermo-style) and their ways with fish. Closed Sun and Aug. €€€€

Santandrea
Piazza Sant'Andrea 4.
Tel: 091 334 999.
Quietly located in a picturesque piazza in the busy Vuccirìa market. Only a few tables, so it's wise to reserve. Fine traditional cuisine, seafood, delicious antipasti and Sicilian desserts. Dinner only; closed Sun. €€€

Sapori Perduti
Via Principe di Belmonte 32.
Tel: 091 327 387.
A fashionable place with chic, modern decor and a suitably imaginative menu. Closed Sun dinner and Mon. €€€

La Scuderia
Viale del Fante 9.
Tel: 091 520 323.
www.lascuderia.snc.it
At the heart of the Parco della Favorita, a "historic" restaurant, famed for its food and location. Highly praised and popular. Extensive traditional Sicilian cuisine. Closed Sun and last 2 weeks Aug. €€€€

Trattoria Normanni
Piazza della Vittoria 25.
Tel: 091 651 6011.
This well-established restaurant near the Palazzo dei Normanni has a varied menu; the house speciality, *spaghetti ai Normanni*, comes in a prawn and aubergine sauce. Closed Sun. €€€

Moderate

Biondo
Via Carducci 15.
Tel: 091 583 662.
pascipa@pascipa.it
Warm and welcoming trattoria, but simple. Best known for its mushroom dishes when in season. Closed Wed and Aug. €€

Al Covo de' i Beati Paoli
Piazza Marina 50.
Tel: 091 616 6634.
www.alcovodeibeatipaoli.com
With tables set out on the pretty piazza, this is a pleasant spot in summer. The pizzas are good, although service can be slow. Dinner only. €€

Primavera
Piazza Bologni 4.

Tel: 091 329 408.
Located in the old centre close to the cathedral. Some tables on the piazza. Traditional cuisine, excellent *pasta con le sarde* (fresh sardines), *pasta con i broccoli* and grilled calamari. Closed Sun dinner and Mon. €€

Questione di Gusto
Via Principe di Scordia 104.
Tel: 091 328 318.
Busy neighbourhood trattoria a short walk from busy food market. Hence excellent antipasti (especially roasted vegetables), vegetarian dishes and fresh fish. *Spaghetti vongole e cozze* (with mussels and clams) is a meal in itself. Good grilled meats too. Closed Fri. €€€

Al Santa Caterina
Corso Vittorio Emanuele 256.
Tel: 338 808 2388.
A very varied menu, including excellent pizzas. It's worth booking to ensure you get one of the balcony tables overlooking the corso. Closed Wed. €€

Trattoria al Vicolo
Piazza San Francesco Saverio
Tel: 091 651 4032.
A bustling local trattoria in the Albergheria district, with tables on the piazza outside in summer. There are plenty of pasta dishes to choose from, and fish is also a speciality. Closed Mon. €€

A'Vucciria

Via dei Chiavettieri 7.
Tel: 091 982 1050.
Excellent seafood served in the heart of the market. Also try their own pasta specials, especially *spaghetti a'vucciria*. Close to Piazza Marina. Closed Thur. €€

Inexpensive

Antica Focacceria San Francesco

Via Paternostro 58.
Tel: 091 320 264.
www.afsf.it
Not to everyone's taste but it is quaint, hectic, always open, cheap, and rough and ready. The place for *trippa* (tripe), *arancine, panini* and, of course, slices of different kinds of focaccia. Closed Tues Oct–May. €

Basile

Via Bara 76.
Tel: 091 335 628.
Near the Teatro Massimo, this lunch-only place is a little chaotic but excellent value. Choose from a range of daily, mainly meaty specials, then pay at the counter and collect your meal. Closed Sun. €

Gigi Mangia

Via Principe di Belmonte 104. Tel: 091 587 651.
mangia@tin.it
Trattoria with delicatessen (that delivers food and wine worldwide). Patronised for its delicious vegetarian appetisers and *il colonnello va a Favignana*, a pasta dish with tomatoes, herbs and *bottarga* (tuna roe). Closed Sun. €€

Pizzeria Bellini

Piazza Bellini.
Tel: 091 616 5691.
A bustling pizzeria in a lovely location, suitable after a visit to La Martorana church. It is open until 2am in summer so makes an attractive spot from which to view the illuminated church at night. Most tables taken by 9pm. Closed Mon. €€

Shanghai

Vicolo dei Mezzani 34.
Tel: 091 589 702.
Not the smartest place in Palermo, nor is it Chinese. But its balcony overlooks the Vucciria food market and fresh produce is delivered continuously. You know you are in Sicily here. Closed Sun and Feb. €

See and Be Seen

Antico Caffè Spinnato

Via Principe di Belmonte 107. In the pedestrian street alongside Grand Hotel et des Palmes, this is where smart people gather for aperitifs, accompanied by in the evenings. Part of the Spinnato group known for their excellent ice creams, *cassata* and *cannoli* that are served here and at **al Pinguino**, Via Ruggiero Settimo 86 and **il Golosone**, Piazza Castelnuovo 22. €

Bristol

Via Amari 28.
Tel: 091 320 667.
www.barbristol.it
This newly restored café-bar is a popular spot for a pre-dinner *aperitivo*, but is busy throughout

the day, from breakfast till late. Hot and cold snacks, as well as ice-cream and pastries. €

Mondello

At 11 km (7 miles) from Palermo, this seaside town with its Liberty villas and well-appointed beach lidos is a fashionable summer dining place. Most trattorie have outdoor terraces with sea views.

Expensive

Charleston le Terrazze,

Via Regina Elena.
Tel: 091 450 171.
Many claim this is Sicily's finest restaurant. And it might well be. In an Art Nouveau beach establishment over the water, it offers the highest standards of cuisine and service in a gracious setting. For many Sicilians this is Sicilian food at its finest. Smart, well dressed clientele, particularly in the evenings. Admired especially for its way with fish. Book. Closed Wed Nov–Apr and early Jan– early Feb. €€€€

Moderate

Trattoria Sympaty

Via Piano di Gallo 18.
Tel: 091 454 470.
A charming trattoria decorated with a nautical theme as it is known for dishes based on fish and seafood. Regulars go for lobster. Varieties of seafood pasta are delightful. Closed Fri at dinner and end Nov–mid-Dec. €€€

Inexpensive

Billy's

Via Mondello 41.
Tel: 091 689 3793.
For anyone homesick for steaks, burgers and Mexican food, it's here. Closed Tues. €€

Bye Bye Blues

Via del Garofalo 23.
Tel: 091 684 1415.
info@byebyeblues.it
On the road into Mondello. Ignore its nightclub name – this place is known for excellent food at excellent prices. Booking, therefore, essential. Fresh produce, fresh fish. Closed Tues and Nov. €€

Terrasini

Primafila

Via Saputo 8.
Tel: 091 868 4422.
Popular, welcoming establishment close to the waterfront. Tables outside. Good traditional Sicilian fare. Closed Mon and Nov. €€€

La Ruota

Via Lungomare.
Tel: 091 868 5151.
A trattoria with grilled fish as its speciality. Open all year. €€

Caffè del Duomo

Piazza Duomo.
The place for snacks, ice-creams and cakes. €

PRICE CATEGORIES

Three-course dinner and half-bottle of house wine:
€ = under €15
€€ = €15–30
€€€ = €30–60
€€€€ = over €60

A FLOWERING OF FLAMBOYANCE

The earthquake of 1693 wiped the architectural slate clean in many Sicilian cities and gave free rein to the new, ornate tastes of the ruling class

The baroque of the 18th century was a golden age for Sicilian architecture, a tantalising game of silhouettes and perspectives, an opportunity for wild ornamentation, with sculpted cornices, fanciful balconies and flowing staircases. In Palermo, *spagnolismo*, the love of ostentation, found its natural soulmate in baroque taste. Urban planning led to grandiose squares and fancy streets. Convents, churches and oratories sprang up in the historic centre, and city *palazzi* competed for attention. Balconies and cornices were adorned with angels, nymphs, gargoyles and grimacing monsters. In Bagheria, villas acquired opulent staircases and marble-encrusted ballrooms. The distinguished baroque cities of Ragusa and Módica indulged in spatial experiment, theatrical vistas flanked by flights of steps. In Noto, baroque meant spaciousness, symmetry and loftiness. It is a stage set of a city, sculpted in golden stone, exuding a sense of joie de vivre.

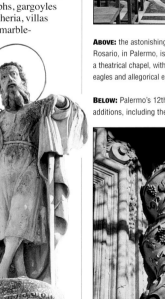

RIGHT: St Paul is one of the 12 sculpted apostles who flank the broad staircase leading to San Pietro in Módica. The cathedral was rebuilt after the 1693 earthquake.

ABOVE: the astonishing stucco work in the Oratorio del Rosario, in Palermo, is Giacomo Serpotta's finest work. It is a theatrical chapel, with *putti* playing cellos amidst seashells, eagles and allegorical exotica.

BELOW: Palermo's 12th-century cathedral has many later additions, including these ornate baroque pillars.

ABOVE: reminiscent of a wedding cake, San Giorgio in Ragusa is Rosario Gagliardi's masterpiece. The sandstone church occupies a raised terrace and its blue neoclassical dome is a landmark. It took more than 40 years to build.

BELOW: fountains abound in Sicily but this one in Palermo's Piazza Pretoria is exceptional. Its riot of nude tritons, nymphs, gods and goddesses once caused the square to be nicknamed Piazza della Vergogna – the Square of Shame.

THE PLASTER MASTER

Giacomo Serpotta, born in Palermo in 1656, was a genius in stucco, who elevated Sicilian plaster work from a craft to an art. His most breathtaking creations can be seen today in several of Palermo's oratories. His Oratorio di San Lorenzo has a fragile beauty bordering on the overblown, every surface festooned with allegorical stucco figures. The lavish Oratorio del Rosario di San Domenico combines frothy statues of the Virtues with a joyful abundance of capering cherubs.

The Oratorio del Rosario di Santa Cita is generally regarded as Serpotta's masterwork. A host of exuberant angels and cherubs clamber over walls and window frames, allegorical statues seem to float in space, while an intricate stucco panel depicting a sea battle in relief employs metal wire for the ships' rigging.

RIGHT: six balconies with extravagantly sculpted buttresses adorn the classical facade of Noto's Palazzo Villadorata, a baroque jewel restored to its former glory. Around the windows are friezes of mythical monsters, a snarling parade of griffons, sphinxes, sirens, centaurs and cherubs. Arabesques climb the walls, clashing with crested cornices and billowing wrought-iron balconies.

PALERMO PROVINCE

Leave the bustling capital to explore Monreale's
glittering Arab-Norman cathedral, the remote
Madonie mountains, the brooding
heartland that was home to the
Mafia, and the island of Ustica

O utside **Palermo ❶** is a
province of extreme light and
shade, of exuberant festivals
and shimmering cathedrals. This
was once the Mafia heartland with
gulleys and mountain lairs nurtured
by the mythology of banditry and
poverty. Now, as the small towns
begin to flourish again, the spiritual
isolation that made this a wild
province is evaporating.

Monreale

These remote rural pockets feel far
away from the Moorish voluptuousness and sophistication of **Monreale
❷**, 8 km (5 miles) from the capital.
In the words of a Sicilian proverb:
"He who goes to Palermo without
seeing Monreale leaves a donkey
and comes back an ass."

Certainly, its sumptuous cathedral
is the apogee of Arab-Norman art.
The **cathedral** (summer Mon–Sat
8am–6pm, Sun 8am–10am, 3.30–
5.30pm; winter Mon–Sat 8am–
12.30pm, Sun 8am–10am, 3.30–
5.30pm) and Benedictine monastery
were built by William II, c.1183, on
a hill overlooking the Conca d'Oro.
Flanked by square bell towers, the
cathedral dedicated to the Assumption is not instantly awe-inspiring,
yet its details are exquisite. An
arched 18th-century **Romanesque
portal** frames a greenish **bronze**

door decorated with Biblical scenes
by Bonanno da Pisa (1185). The portal displays sculpted bands of garlands, figures and beasts alternating
with multi-coloured mosaics. To the
left, a Gagini porch shelters another
bronze door, by Barisano da Trani
(1179), inspired by the delicacy of
Byzantine inlaid ivory. The **apses**
are Sicily's most opulent: interlacing
limestone and lava arches, sculpted
as delicately as wood.

Monreale drew craftsmen from
Persia, Africa, Asia, Greece, Venice,

Map
on page
82

LEFT:
Monreale Cathedral.
BELOW: ancient
Roman architecture
at Términi Imerese.

Pisa and Provence. The glistening gold interior fuses Arab purity of volume with Byzantine majesty. The shimmering (restored) **mosaics** are unequalled anywhere. Their scenes show the Norman attachment to Christianity: the *Assumption of the Virgin*, *Jacob's dream*, *Sts Peter and Paul* and more. The whole series is a *bibbia pauperum*, a poor man's Bible.

In the apse the *Christ Pantocrator*, about 6 metres (20 ft) tall, is an authoritarian God presiding over the Madonna, angels and saints. Look for Thomas a'Becket, who entered sainthood after Henry II of England had him murdered. (Henry was William's father-in-law.) Above the royal throne is a mosaic of *Christ crowning William the Good*, a tribute to the king whose world embraced concubines, eunuchs and negro slaves. Other delights include Cosmati paving, Roman capitals incorporating busts of Ceres and Proserpine, and a gilded ceiling whose rafters resemble the spines of beautifully bound books.

The garden **cloisters** (daily 9am–6.30pm; entrance fee) express William's love of Islamic art and are the most sumptuous 12th-century cloisters in the world. Every second pair of white marble columns has a vivid zigzag mosaic pattern spiralling up the shaft. Many sculptures echo the mosaics but add a personal note, including the name of a mason, or musicians playing Sicilian instruments. The *Allegory of the Seasons*, an enchanting marble composition, depicts tree-planting and pig-killing. In one corner, a loggia creates a *chiaroscuro* effect with a glorious, slightly phallic fountain. Shaped like a palm tree trunk, the shaft is crowned by lions' heads.

After raucous Palermo, Monreale exudes provincial calm, and while the town is probably an anticlimax after seeing the cathedral's mosaics, a stroll offers a chance to savour the

The striking mosaic of Christ Pantocrator in the middle apse dominates Monreale Cathedral.

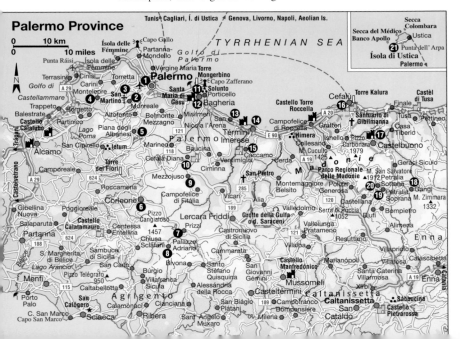

pedestrian-only streets of the centre, with its crumbling baroque churches and shops selling ceramics or fine ices. The **Chiesa del Monte** has stuccos by Serpotta while the church of **Madonna delle Croci**, set higher on the hill, offers a last lingering view from the cathedral to the coast.

Bandit country

In the lushly mountainous landscape towards **Boccadifalco** is the hill resort of **San Martino delle Scale** with the Benedictine **Abbazia di San Martino ❸** (Mon–Sat 9am–noon, 4.30–6.30pm, Sun 9–11am, 5–6.30pm). Reputed to have been founded by St Gregory the Great in the 6th century, the abbey was destroyed and rebuilt a number of times over the centuries. Now part convent, part school, it is known for its monumental staircase, monastic library and 18th-century paintings, including Marabitti's *St Martin and the Beggar*. The surrounding pine forests are a cool escape in summer.

A short distance away is **Montelepre ❹**, of which John Addington Symonds wrote in 1873: "The talk was brigands and nothing but brigands." This was especially true on the eve of World War II when the tragic outlaw Salvatore Giuliano reigned over these desolate crags. If Mafia chroniclers are correct, this is still bandit country. Certainly local graffiti defiantly revives Giuliano's name. Montelepre and its neighbour **Partinico** are examples of grim Sicilian impoverished reality and desolation. On the surface, apart from recent ugly building, little appears to have changed since Giuliano's mysterious murder in 1950.

The medieval heart of Montelepre is enclosed by scruffy alleys and courtyards coiled around the Chiesa Madre. Its castle was built in the 15th century by the Archbishop of Monreale. On the edge of town are boulders and cacti and views of deserted farms and fields that once formed parts of feudal estates.

Partinico is a byword for urban poverty. In the 1950s Danilo Dolci, an Italian poet and writer dedicated to helping Sicily's poor, chose benighted western Sicily to set up his centres in an attempt to improve local conditions. Known by many as Sicily's Gandhi because of his non-violent attitude, his *Inchiesta a Palermo* (1956 English edition: *Poverty in Sicily*) brought the region into international recognition by exposing the power of the Mafia. His work undimmed, he died unnoticed in poverty in 1997.

Piana degli Albanesi ❺, along the SS 624, appears suspended above a lake. Lush pastures are encircled by hills, once home to 15th-century Albanian settlers. The community moved here in 1488 after Turkish troops invaded their homeland. Since then, generations have kept their customs and their Orthodox faith in this cheerful town. Marriages and funerals, Epiphany and Easter are times for traditional Byzantine ceremony and folk costumes. They tempt hun-

Map on page 82

TIP

Two very different movies relate the story of the local bandit Salvatore Giuliano. Michael Cimino's 1987 *The Sicilian* embraces the romantic "Robin Hood" view. But Francesco Rosi's 1962 documentary-style *Salvatore Giuliano* offers much greater insight into the social and political forces of the late 1940s. Both are available on DVD.

BELOW: bandits traditionally hid out in these mountain regions.

TIP

Don't waste time in
Corleone trying to
follow in the footsteps
of the Corleone clan in
The Godfather movies.
The town was too
developed by the early
1970s for director
Francis Ford Coppola's
taste and the Sicilian
scenes were shot in
Sávoca *(see page 251).*

BELOW: Corleone,
with its Castello
in the foreground.

dreds of tourists to visit. The community speaks Greek at home; signs are in Greek as well as Italian. Local cuisine is a cultural stew: *stranghuie* (gnocchi), *brumie me bathé e thieré*, a filling bean casserole, or *dash*, castrated ram, Albanian-Greek style. It was the citizens of Piana degli Albanesi who gunned down Salvatore Giuliano at Portella della Ginestra, just above the artificial lake, **Lago Piana degli Albanesi**. The lake provides drinking water for Palermo and irrigates the fields of the Conca d'Oro.

Corleone

Corleone ❻, perched along the rural SS 118, is enfolded in desolate hills and high verdant plains, its old town surrounded by unattractive buildings. In the centre looms the **Castello**, a rocky outcrop topped by a Saracen tower. A prison until 1976, it is now home to Franciscan friars who take their vow of poverty seriously. Below, the rooftops are stacked in a chromatic range of greys. At first sight, Corleone fails to live up to its infamous reputation as the cradle of

the Mafia. It was from here, after all, that Mafia boss Toto Riina ruled before moving to Palermo where he went into hiding until his arrest in 1993. Bravely, the town has changed the name of its central piazza to Falcone-Borsellino, to honour the anti-Mafia magistrates gunned down by the Mafia. It also opened a **Mafia Museum** in 2000 – more of a repository for the documents and videos of anti-Mafia agencies than a Disneyland experience. The town was established in 1237 and its **Chiesa Madre** contains 16th–17th-century wooden statues and stalls.

To the southeast lies the medieval town of **Prizzi ❼** with its sloping checkerboard of rust-tiled roofs. The town is celebrated for its bizarre traditional Easter festival known as the *ballo dei diavoli* (dance of the devils). Dating back to Sicani times, the dance depicts the eternal struggle between Good and Evil, winter and spring, Christianity and paganism. The gap-toothed devil masks are primitive but menacing while the atmosphere of ritualised violence appears to echo Mafia lore.

The neighbouring village of **Palazzo Adriano** ❽, 10 km (6 miles) southwest, encapsulates the rivalries of these provincial backwaters. Two sombre churches share the main square in mutual antipathy: the Orthodox **Santa Maria dell'Assunta** scorns the Catholic **Santa Maria del Lume**. Ironically, the square starred in the warmly evocative movie *Cinema Paradiso*. From here, the route back to the coast passes the hilltop village of **Mezzojuso** ❾, snug in the Ficuzza woods. Like many others, the village has mixed Albanian and Arab ancestry and religious frictions. **Annunziata**, the Catholic church, is overshadowed by the Orthodox **San Nicola**, home to lovely Byzantine icons.

Nearby, **Santa Maria delle Grazie** houses frescoes and the finest iconostasis in Sicily, while the adjoining monastery displays precious Greek manuscripts and miniatures. **Cefalà Diana** ❿, just north, is firmly in the Arab camp, with a tumbledown castle and the island's best-preserved Moorish bathhouse.

East of Palermo

From the capital to Cefalù, the coast curves past fishing villages and coves to Capo Zafferano and the ruins at **Solunto** ⓫ (Mon–Sat 9am–6.30pm; Sun 9am–1pm; entrance fee). Set on majestic cliffs, the ruins are less impressive than the wild location. The solitary ruins were originally Solus, one of the earliest Phoenician trading posts on the island, until destroyed by Dionysius of Siracusa in 398 BC as he tried to clear Sicily of all non-Greeks. Later, it was taken by invading Carthaginians who invited Greeks to return, so Hellenising the settlement. Then in the First Punic War, in 254 BC, it fell to Rome, only to be abandoned during the 3rd century AD as it failed to become wealthy. As a result of these changes, there are traces of the three

civilisations remaining. The highlights among the extensive ruins are the floor **mosaics** (including *Leda and the Swan*) and a luxurious villa dwelling with a colonnaded peristyle. From the agora there are stunning views of the Casteldaccia vineyards, an ancient castle and the coastal resort of Cefalù. Beyond the wizened olive trees and battered boulders are charming swimming spots near the lighthouse on the cape. **Porticello**, on the shore just below Solunto, is a straggling fishing village popular with Palermitans for a seafood Sunday lunch.

Bagheria

Just inland is **Bagheria** ⓬, 15 km (9 miles) from Palermo, which developed during the **Ottocento** (19th-century) vogue for ostentatious summer villas surrounded by orange trees but declined during the 20th century due to unbridled land speculation. These patrician villas are mostly in late Renaissance style, with grand staircases and a central body flanked by sweeping concave wings. The U-shaped lower wings

Map on page 82

The Saracen castle at Cefalà Diana was an important stronghold on the Palermo–Agrigento road.

BELOW: Solunto.

were reserved for servants, with underground chambers (*stanze del scirocco*) used by the patricians as retreats from the humid summer heat. The villas were encircled by French formal gardens.

While views of cement works often mar the pastoral idyll, some villas are pitiful wrecks, others retain their grandeur. A fine example is **Villa Cattolica** (Tues–Sun, summer 9.30am–2pm, 3–7.30pm; winter 9am–1pm, 2.30–7pm). Built around 1737, it houses the **Museo Guttoso**, a bizarre collection of contemporary paintings and the tomb of Renato Guttuso (1912–87), one of Sicily's best known modern painters. A sculptor friend made him a surreal blue tomb to match the sky, a capsule of kitsch among the cactus and lemons.

The **Villa Palagonia** (daily, summer 9am–1pm, 4–7pm; winter 9am–1pm, 3.30–5.30pm; www.villa palagonia.it) is the strangest of the villas (*see box below*).

Términi Imerese

Further east, 8 km (5 miles) outside Términi Imerese, is **San Nicola**

Stirring statue of Giuseppe la Masa in Términi Imerese.

BELOW:
the surreal statues of Villa Palagonia.

l'**Arena** N, a picturesque fishing village with a 15th-century crenellated castle overlooking the harbour. Now a nightclub, the castle belongs to aristocrats from Palermo. Beside it is a solid brick **tonnara** (tuna cannery), a reminder that the coast was devoted to tuna fishing until recently.

Términi Imerese N itself is an unfortunate jumble of industry, resort and Classical ruins. However, the upper town remains fairly unspoilt, with a 17th-century **cathedral** (the statue of Jesus in one of the chapels has real hair) and the **Museo Civico** (Tues–Sat 9am–1pm, 4–6.30pm, Sun 8am–12.30pm), which has an art collection and archaeological finds.

Known to the Romans as Thermae Himerenses, the city was famed for its hot mineral springs and baths, used in the treatment of urological problems. They can be tested in the lower town at the **Grand Hotel delle Terme** built on the site of the Roman baths. Just east of town is an impressive Roman aqueduct set in a wild olive grove.

Inland is **Cáccamo** N, a dramatic, 12th-century castle (daily, summer

Villa Palagonia

This villa, built in 1715 by Tommaso Maria Napoli, is famous for its crumbling interior with cracked mirrors and its garden full of grotesque statues of monsters, dwarves, tormented souls and fantastic animals. Most, it is said, were created by the surreal imagination of the wealthy Prince Palagonia and are said to represent his faithless wife's lovers. Beside the main entrance, two gargoyles with gaping mouths were used to extinguish the footmen's torches. A flamboyant double staircase ascends to the piano nobile, with the salon's mirrored ceiling representing the sky. Engraved over the door is the message: "Mirror yourself in these crystals and contemplate the image of human frailty."

Map on page 82

9.30am–1pm, 4–8.30pm; winter 9.30am–1pm, 3–7.30pm; entrance fee), one of the most important Norman strongholds in western Sicily and possibly the island's best preserved castle. It was the base of the local dukes of Caccamo until sold to the Region in 1963. The towers, battlements and ramparts look convincingly medieval, even if parts were redesigned during the baroque period.

There are collections of art and arms in its restored rooms, one of which, the **Sala della Congiura**, is where the duke and fellow nobles plotted to overthrow William the Bad in 1160. The coup failed; the duke died in the king's dungeon. The **Duomo** (remodelled in 1614) contains a 14th-century painted crucifix and many statues and sculptures.

Himera

The site of ancient **Himera** (Mon–Sat 9am–6.30pm, Sun 9am–1pm; entrance fee), founded as a colony of Zancle (Messina) in 648 BC, is nearby, east of Términi Imerese, in an industrial zone near Buonfornello. Himera was the scene of the 480 BC defeat of the Carthaginians by Theron of Agrigento and his brother Gelon of Siracusa, when the advance of the Carthaginian leader Hamilcar, determined to rid Sicily of all Greeks, was thwarted. Hamilcar perished in the defeat but in 409 BC his son Hannibal returned with a stronger force and devastated the city. There are ruins of a Doric temple and traces of houses as well as an extensive museum containing findings from the site.

Cefalù

A return to the coast at **Cefalù** 🔟 is a chance to visit the province's great counterpoint to Monreale Cathedral. Sitting snugly below the massive hill of **La Rocca**, Cefalù is the west coast's rival to Taormina as a tourist centre. The consensus is that, although Taormina has better hotels, nightlife, sophistication and atmosphere, Cefalù is as lovely, as picturesque, has more beaches and is more family-friendly.

The cathedral, or **Duomo** (daily 8am–noon, 3.30–6.30pm), was built in 1131 by Roger II with a bold twin-towered facade and a triple apse with

The Grand Hotel delle Terme, Términi Imerese.

BELOW:
Términi Imerese.

Detail from the Duomo in Cefalù.

blind arcading. (The King confidently had a porphyry sarcophagus made for himself but he and the sarcophagus are now in Palermo Cathedral as he died before this cathedral was completed.) Inside, a severe nave is flanked by 16 ancient columns with Roman capitals surmounted by Gothic arches. A sense of space and majesty is created by the concentration of other-worldly **mosaics** in the presbytery and over the altar. A superbly compassionate *Christ Pantocrator* in the apse holds an open book with Greek and Latin biblical text (John 8:12): "I am the light of the world, he who follows me will not walk in darkness." The open-timber roof has traces of the original Arab-Norman paintings. Below is a Norman font guarded by leopards, the symbol of King Roger's Hauteville dynasty.

Out of season, **Piazza del Duomo** is a delightful sun trap with a view of the cathedral at the foot of steep cliffs running up to the fortifications. The square is also framed by the Corso, a Renaissance seminary and a porticoed **palazzo**. Here, the Caffè Duomo is the place for an *aperitivo*. Cefalù's **old port**, tangibly Moorish and home to Tunisian fishermen, has been a backdrop in countless films, including *Cinema Paradiso*.

A warren of alleys leads west from **Corso Ruggero** and reveals Renaissance facades, Gothic parapets and mullioned windows overlooking tiny courtyards. An underground spring bubbles up in the arcaded Arab baths, sited at the bottom of curved steps. **Via Porto Salvo** passes battered churches and flourishing craft shops. In summer, the town is a delightful tourist trap with quaint craft boutiques selling ceramics and gold jewellery, matched by sophisticated restaurants catering to the fastidious. **Porta Pescare**, one of the surviving medieval gates, opens onto a creek, beach and boatyard. In the evening, the seafront, bastion and Corso become a parade devoted to the pleasures of the *passeggiata* and *gelati*.

From Piazza Duomo, a steepish hill leads down to **Museo Mandralisca** (daily 9.30am–12.30pm, 3.30–7pm; entrance fee). Apart from several Madonnas, this is a dusty collection, except for Antonello da Messina's *Portrait of an Unknown Man* (*c*.1460). The painting once served as a door to a pharmacy cabinet on the island of Lipari where an assistant, unnerved by the sneering expression, scratched the unknown man's face.

Above the medieval town is **Rocca**, where the original Arab town was sited, with a panorama overlooking Cefalù and the sea. After the Norman conquest in 1063, the populace left the looming crags for the port below. **Salita Saraceno** leads up three tiers of city walls to the restored fortifications of the crumbling stone castle. There are traces of a pool, fountain, cistern and prison. Nearby is the so-called **Tempio di Diana**, circa 4th century BC, built over an earlier cistern.

The Madonie mountains

Compared to the neighbouring Nebrodi mountains, the Monti Madonie range are higher (Pizzo Carbonara 1,979 metres/6,495 ft), more accessible and more open to tourism. Unlike a lot of Sicily, the Madonie range has not been scarred by deforestation or urban blight. **Piano Cervi** and **Monte San Salvatore** are riddled with aqueducts and streams. Majestic firs have grown on these rugged ridges since the Ice Age and were used to create the roof of Monreale Cathedral. In the remoter regions, wild cats and eagles still thrive. A consortium, Parco Regionale delle Madonie, was established in 1989 to ensure the region survives as a natural habitat that welcomes visitors (www.parcodellemadonie.it).

Thanks to low-key tourism based on outdoor pursuits such as trekking and horse-riding, the Madonie region has largely escaped grinding poverty and rural emigration. In summer, agriturismo (farm stays) make an appealing way of exploring the area. There are signs on the snaking roads that lead you to them. The tiny **Piano Battaglia** ski resort is the only winter sports option.

Gibilmanna

After Cefalù, coastal olive groves give way to pine woods and rugged valleys before reaching the impressive religious site of **Gibilmanna**, with its monastery that has a venerated sanctuary and an underrated museum devoted to rural life and sacred art (daily, summer 9.30am–12.30pm, 3.30–7pm; winter 9am–1pm, 3–5pm). The Capuchin friars rebuilt this monastery in 1535 on the site of a 6th-century one.

Isnello, 7 km (4 miles) south, a winter ski resort, has a ruined Byzantine castle overlooking majolica-encrusted spires and limestone cliffs.

A vastly superior feudal castle towers over **Castelbuono** ⓱, 12 km (7 miles) east, a civilised, prosperous, well-kept place that could be mistaken for Tuscany. Castelbuono lobbied successfully to be an exit point from the Palermo–Messina motorway. As such, it is reaping the benefits in the weekend influx of visitors drawn to the lively atmosphere, well-restored churches and welcoming restaurants. The castle, c.1438, (Tues–Sun 9am–1pm, 4–8pm; entrance fee) is austere but with a pleasant chapel.

The rural route follows the SS 286 south to **Geraci Siculo** (22 km/14 miles) and then winds up to **Gangi** ⓲, a tortoise-shaped town with a crumbling watchtower that is now a hard-working rural centre. On the second Sunday in August, in a custom said to have originated in the days of Demeter, sheaves of wheat tied with red ribbons decorate the streets for *Sagra della Spiga*, a celebration of the year's harvest.

Petralia Soprana

Follow the SS 120 west and the jagged skyline of **Petralia Soprana** ⓳ comes into view. This seemingly

Map on page 82

TIP

A day trip offered by travel agents from Palermo and Cefalù visits mountain enclaves and fortified villages linked to the feudal Ventimiglia dynasty. There are also buses from Cefalù to the towns and villages. To truly explore, however, a car is best. For tours contact the Ente Parco delle Madonie, Corso Ruggero 116 (tel: 0921 923 327; www.parco dellemadonie.it).

BELOW: the medieval Lavatoio in Cefalù was used until recently for washing clothes.

Map
on page
82

*Petralia Sottana rises
out of the misty
Madonie mountains.*

BELOW: Ustica's port.

prosperous town, set on a spur, has covered passageways leading to a belvedere with bracing views, marred only by a vast car park on stilts. The **Chiesa Madre** was built in the 1300s by the Ventimiglia family. Half-hidden in alleys are striking mansions with balconies and watchtowers.

Petralia Sottana ②⓪ (the lower town), nestling in the wooded hillside, also exudes a quiet ease. Now a mountain resort, this former Norman citadel has Romanesque, Gothic and baroque churches. The **Chiesa Matrice** is perched on a belvedere and swathed in mist; inside is a precious Arabian candelabra.

The road west to **Polizzi Generoso** passes *masserie*, feudal farmsteads that were as self-sufficient as most villages. The **Chiesa Madre** has a 16th-century Flemish triptych and Venetian organ. Polizzi is a trekking centre which, in season, sustains walkers with pasta and asparagus *(pasta cu l'asparaci)*.

From here, the fast A19 returns to the coast, as does the winding route via the ski resort of Piano Battaglia.

Ustica

The lovely island of **Ustica ②①**, 60 km (37 miles) from Palermo, is connected daily to the city by hydrofoil and ferry services (1 hour and 2½ hours respectively) and can be visited on a day trip. It is extremely popular with swimmers and nature lovers, but serious divers or underwater photographers will choose to make the island their base.

Ustica is Sicily's best-established and best-preserved marine reserve. The rugged coastline is riddled with caverns and coves, partly accessible along coastal paths, and below its clear waters is an explosion of colour and life that includes corals, sea sponges and anemones as well as barracuda, bream, scorpion fish and groupers. Useful offices are: Centro Accoglienza per la Riserva Marina, tel: 091 844 9456, for information about the nature reserve sites and boat trips; Mare Nostrum Diving, tel: 330 792 589; booking@marenostrumdiving.it, for scuba information, lessons and dives.

The volcanic, black, turtle-shaped island turns itself into a riot of colour in spring when wild flowers are abundant; true landlubbers can enjoy visits to the ruins of a Saracen castle (a long climb), the church of **San Bartolomeo** with its colourful ceramic saints, and call in at the small **museum**, open in summer only, which contains items found in the surrounding sea. A walk around the island will take about four hours, covering 10 km (6 miles).

Boat trip

One of the pleasures is an excursion by boat from **Cala Santa Maria**, the island's port. There is even a glass-bottomed boat for viewing the marine reserve. There are 10 grottoes, too, mostly on the eastern side of the island. **Grotta Azzurra** with its azure water is the most famous, 100 metres (330 ft) long. ❏

RESTAURANTS

Monreale
La Botte
Contrada Lenzitti 20, Circon-
vallazione Monreale.
Tel: 091 414 051.
On ring road around the
centre. Closed Aug.
Open Sat at dinner and
Sun at lunch only. €€

Dietro l'Angolo
Via Piave 5.
Tel: 091 640 4067.
A brief stroll from the
Duomo, this restaurant
has a lovely terrace with
great views. The pasta
dishes are reasonably
priced, and there are set
menus. Closed Tues. €€

Riccardo III
Contrada da Grotte-
Monreale. Tel: 091 414 237.
Characterful place inside
an old stable with a var-
ied menu. Fri–Sun only.
Closed Aug. €€

Taverna del Pavone
Vicolo Pensato 18.
Tel: 091 640 6209.
www.tavernadelpavone.eu
Pleasant surroundings in
an old building. Interest-
ing local dishes. Closed
Mon and 2 weeks Jan.
€€€

Cefalù
La Botte
Via Veterani 6.
Tel: 0921 424 315

Small, charming, with
tables outside in warm
weather. Varied menu,
meat and fresh fish.
Closed Mon, 2 weeks Feb
and 2 weeks Nov. €€

La Brace
Via XXV Novembre 10.
Tel: 0921 423 570.
www.ristorantelabrace.com
Highly respected cooking
served in a simple trattoria in an alley. Booking
essential. Closed Mon &
Tues lunch and 15 Dec–
15 Jan. €€€

Kentia
Via Nicola Botta 15.
Tel: 0921 423 801.
Known for its charm, cui-
sine and garden. Expen-
sive but good. Sample the
scaloppine ai funghi and
panzerotti di magro. Inexpensive set menu. Closed
Tues and Jan. €€€

Magno
Via Belvedere 4.
Tel: 0921 923 348.
Traditional trattoria right
by the Duomo. €€

Ostaria del Duomo
Via Seminario 5.
Tel: 0921 421 838.
Lovely open-air location
overlooking the cathedral.
Seafood specialities.
Authentic caponata,
penne and carpaccio di
tonno, thin slices of raw
tuna in a gentle mari-
nade. Open Mar–Nov.
€€€

Lo Scoglio Ubriaco
Via Corso Ortolani di Bor-
donaro 2. Tel: 0921 423 370.

A terrace overlooks the
harbour, so you can
watch the fishing boats
while enjoying spaghetti
al cartoccio (baked
spaghetti in a paper
envelope). Closed Tues
(except in summer) and
two weeks in Nov. €€

Vecchia Marina
Via Vittorio Emanuele 73.
Tel: 0921 420 388.
Terrace overlooks the
fishermen's beach. Try
the casareccie con gam-
beri e carciofi (home-
made pasta with prawns
and artichokes). Closed
Tues and Jan. €€€

Gangi
Tenuta Gangivecchio
Gangivecchio.
Tel: 0921 689 191.
www.tenutagangivecchio.com
A former monastery out-
side Gangi that is a
charming family hotel
with the best Sicilian cuisine. €€

Gibilmanna
Fattoria Pianetti
Contrada Gratteri.
Tel: 0921 421 890
www.fattoriapianetti.com
An agriturismo on the
hillside. Excellent cook-
ing with homegrown
organic produce. €€

Isnello
Piano Torre
Park Hotel, Piano Torre.
Tel: 0921 662 671
www.pianotoreparkhotel.com

This charming hotel at
the heart of the reserve
has an excellent restau-
rant with a varied Sicilian
menu. Closed Mon. €€€

Ustica
Around the port there
are a number of trattorie,
all about the same in
standard and price.
Those crowded with Sicil-
ians and Italians are
invariably the best. Two
to consider in the centre
of the village:

Mamma Lia
Via S. Giacomo 1.
Tel: 091 844 9594.
Very good fish. Open
Easter–Oct. €€

Da Mario
Piazza Umberto I 21.
Tel: 091 844 9505.
More fish. Open Easter–
end Sept. €

RIGHT: fresh octopus features on many menus.

TRÁPANI PROVINCE

Western Sicily is the most seafaring part of the island, famous for its North African atmosphere, nature reserves, endless beaches and, above all, its remarkable ancient sites and treasures

Palermo

Map on page 94

As the least definable yet most varied province, the Provincia di Trápani is a collection of contradictions. This seafaring region represents a swathe of ancient Sicily, from Phoenician Mózia to Greek Selinunte, medieval Erice and Arab Mazara del Vallo. The landscape spans salt-pans, vineyards, woods and coastal nature reserves.

Trápani city

In ancient times Drepanon (hence **Trápani ❶**) was the port of Eryx *(see Erice, page 95),* famous in the Mediterranean for its wealth and magnificent temple of Venus, goddess of fertility. As a seafaring power, its history lay at the heart of the Mediterranean world.

As the capital of the province, Trápani remains an important town, and its **Stazione Marittima** off Piazza Garibaldi is an embarkation point for the Egadi Islands *(see page 107)* and the remoter island of Pantelleria *(see page 111),* as well as Sardinia, Naples and Tunis. Trápani's traditional industries of coral, tuna fishing and salt production linger on and it is said the town may also be a Mafia money-laundering centre – a rumour borne out by the city's countless small banks.

Visually, Trápani is appealing from a distance: a patchwork of shallow lagoons bounded by thin causeways. In summer, drying in the sun, there are also heaps of salt roofed with red tiles. Close up, the promontory with the old town has a superficial charm with its 11th-century Spanish fortifications but it is marred by the bland urban surroundings. The sights are not monumental but can occupy an enjoyable morning before taking a ferry trip to the outlying islands. Apart from the **Pescheria**, the fish market, on the Lungomare, the town offers a grace-

LEFT: Trápani fishermen
BELOW: Trápani harbour, with Erice in the background.

ful Gothic church, a fine arts and crafts collection and a cluster of dilapidated baroque palazzi.

Off Via Torrearsa there is the austere church of **Sant'Agostino**, *circa* 1340, that was the Knights Templars' church, and on Corso Vittorio Emmanuele is the cathedral of **San Lorenzo**, 1635. On Via Generale Giglio there is the church of **Purgatorio**, 1683, with a fine dome and 20 wooden statues (17th–18th century) of the **Misteri** that are carried through the streets in a Good Friday procession, while the church of **Santa Maria del Gesù**, founded by Emperor Charles V, contains a charming terracotta *Madonna of the Angels* by Andrea della Robbia sheltering under a marble baldecchino by Antonello Gagini. Currently there is talk of restoring the churches, so they may, or may not, be open. Centred on Via Giudecca, the small Jewish quarter has a decayed charm epitomised by the

Trápani harbour.

Palazzo della Giudecca while, on the tip of its promontory, is the **Torre di Ligny**, a fortress built in 1671. The salty port offers *cuscusu* (fish soup) and lobster in boisterous fishermen's haunts.

About 3 km (2 miles) north of the old town is **Santuario dell'Annunziata** (daily 7am–noon, 4–7pm), a Carmelite church founded in 1315 but rebuilt in 1760. This sanctuary of the Madonna is considered Trápani's main monument. Its charms are a baroque belltower, a Gothic rose window and a doorway decorated in a zigzag pattern. Inside is a rococo nave and a cluster of exotic domed chapels. Dedicated to fishermen, the frescoed **Cappella dei Pescatori** (1481) embraces Byzantine and Moorish elements, as well as a Spanish diamond-point design. Behind the high altar is the lavish **Cappella della Madonna**, with sculptures by Antonino Gagini and the revered statue of the *Madonna di Trápani* by

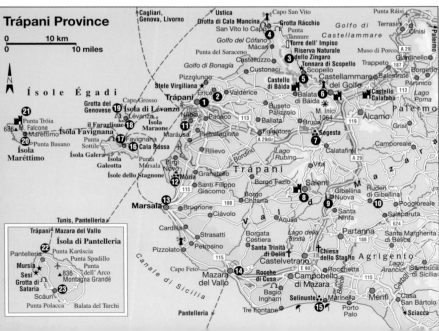

Nino Pisano, crowned in jewels. This venerated Madonna is credited with miraculous powers.

The **Museo Regionale Pepoli** (Mon–Sat 9am–1.30pm, Sun 9am–12.30pm; entrance fee) is the city's eclectic museum, housed in the former convent adjoining the cathedral. Off the cloisters lie Gagini sculptures, important Sicilian paintings and sections devoted to the decorative arts made locally between the 17th and 19th centuries. Exquisite craftsmanship is visible in the coral cribs and gilded figurines, the enamelled Moorish lamps and majolica tiles. Gaudiest of all is a coral crucifix by Fra Matteo Bavera, with a salmon-coloured Christ against an ebony and mother-of-pearl cross.

The mystic mountain

Just north is a more enticing base than Trápani for exploring – and staying. In spring, the winding road climbs past views of acacia, wild gladioli and waxy lemon blossom to the legendary Mount Eryx (today's **Monte San Giuliano**). Swathed in seasonal mists or in a carpet of flowers, **Erice ❷**, perched at 750 metres (2,460 ft), is an exquisite, tiny medieval walled town. The Carthaginian walls survive, rough-hewn slabs inscribed with Punic symbols, while nearby is the charming Quartiere Spagnolo, the 17th-century Spanish bastion.

As ancient Eryx, this mystical city was founded by the Elymni (Elymians), the mysterious settlers of Segesta who worshipped the Mediterranean fertility goddess known as Astarte to the Elymni and the Phoenicians, as Aphrodite to the Greeks, and as Venus to the Romans.

The entrance to the town is **Porta Trápani**, a medieval gate leading directly to the **Chiesa Madre**, dedicated to The Assumption (9.30am–12.30pm, 3–6pm). Its porch dates from around 1426 while its **campanile**, originally a watchtower, is dated around 1315. The neo-Gothic interior was created in 1852.

There are a number of churches within the walls, but it is the views from the gardens of the **Villa Balio** on the summit of the hill that justify a pilgrimage. Below stretch ragged

In Erice, the Romans followed earlier customs of worship including the cult of sacred prostitution at the temple. Sicilian historian Diodorus wrote: "The Romans put aside the gravity of office and entered into play and intercourse with women amidst great gaiety."

BELOW: ropemakers at work, Trápani.

Where Ecology Counts

Trápani province is the most Arab and Phoenician in its ancestry and, as such, it has garnered a reputation for being somewhat lethargic and morally compromised. Yet environmentally it is often at the forefront. Trápani takes a stand against pollution, building speculation and the destruction of coastal salt-pans. Here, both windmills and marshes are protected, and there's a nature reserve along the road between the port and Marsala. It was Trapáni that launched *pescaturismo* (fishing tourism), offering visitors excursions with fishermen in order to discover aspects of the coast and its marine parks, as well as learning about the fishing industry itself.

*Castello di Venere,
built on a rocky
outcrop in Erice.*

turrets, wooded groves and vineyards; a tapestry of salt-pans and sea slip all the way to the turtle-shaped Egadi Islands and to Cap Bon in Tunisia. As the English poet Fiona Pitt-Kethley concluded: "If you want a good view, go up Eryx, not Etna." Wintry weather is another story: many older citizens wear a *burdigliuno*, a blue hooded cape, as a wind shield.

On a rocky outcrop is the **Castello di Venere** (daily 8am–1.30pm, 3.30–6pm). Inside the crenellated Norman walls is the site of the fabled **Tempio di Venere**, now the battered marble remains of a temple, beside a well. **Castello Pepoli**, with its mediaeval tower, the **Torretta Pepoli**, a neo-Gothic fantasy created by Count Pepoli, adds to the scene. Castello Pepoli is still owned by the Pepoli family and is not open to visitors.

Virgil compared Eryx to Greece's Mount Athos for its altitude and spiritual pre-eminence. Not that Erice remains a sanctuary today. Its orphanages and convents have become ceramics and carpet shops or nightclubs and chic restaurants. Still, behind this public face lies a private Erice, one of wall-hugging cobbled alleys, grotesque baroque balconies, votive niches and secret courtyards. In keeping with Arab traditions, such courtyards were where women and children could sit in private, working or chatting by the well. Erice is a paradox. In winter, it resembles a windy Umbrian hill town yet in summer bursts with tourists and bijou boutiques recalling the Côte d'Azur. Look for the local brightly coloured, geometric patterned carpets (*frazzate*). They are still handwoven.

The town is packed in season yet suffers from depopulation. However, the September Festival of Medieval and Renaissance Music is making a name for itself. This sleepy-looking citadel is also home to scientific conferences, centred on the internationally renowned **Centro Ettore Majorana**, a scientific and cultural institute set in a lovely old convent. Curiously, none of this bustle affects the town's sense of harmony.

Sweet Indulgence

Like many Sicilian towns, Erice has a name for exceedingly sweet pastries based on almonds and dried fruits. As in Palermo with its *martorano* marzipan confections, *dolci ericini* were originally made by novice nuns in a closed convent. But in 1975 this convent closed and locals lament that the sweets are not as home-made as they were. However, Maria Grammatico, who learnt the trade when a novice nun, vies for the title of having Sicily's best bakery in her Pasticceria Maria in Corso Vittorio Emanuele. Apart from *pasta reale* (marzipan coated with fine icing), her sweets have such poetic names as *sospiri* (sighs) and *belli e brutti* (beauties and beasts).

Along the coast

This coast was once noted for its rich tuna-fishing grounds but most *tonnare* (tuna fisheries) have fallen into ruin. However, the sea road passes the renowned **Tonnara di Bonagia** on the way to Sicily's finest nature reserve. The **Riserva Naturale dello Zíngaro ③** is set on a rocky headland pierced with coves and bays but containing no official roads. The reserve was created with the support of the council, citizens and ecologists but, cynics say, it could not have been achieved without Mafia approval too. Locals claim that these sheltered coves continue to be the destination for tiny fishing boats bringing ashore heroin from the Middle East. Whatever the truth, the reserve is also a glorious home to buzzards and falcons as well as palms, carobs and euphorbia.

Cynical Sicilians dismiss Lo Zíngaro as a fabricated Disneyworld, but most visitors are only too happy to find a semblance of order and efficiency in any Sicilian site.

On the headland lies **San Vito lo Capo ④**, a burgeoning resort noted for its fine coast, sandy beaches and lively fish restaurants rather than its sophistication. The northern entrance to Lo Zíngaro lies 11km (7 miles) southeast, just before the ruins of a tower, the **Torre dell'Impiso**. The coastal road south skirts the reserve, passing primeval mountains, shepherds' huts, abandoned tuna fisheries, ruined towers and ragged rock formations at sea. The changing coastline continues to Castellammare, with the rugged journey made by boat, on horseback or on foot.

Scopello

Scopello ⑤, 10 km (6 miles) before Castellammare, marks the southern entrance to the reserve and has an information desk and car park. This fishing village is based around a *baglio*, an imposing medieval farm-stead. On the road are paths leading to attractive bays: Cala Bianca, Cala Rossa and Baia Guidaloca. Apart from a rustic trattoria and a chance to buy farm-fresh cheese, the only site of note is the **Tonnara di Scopello**, once the finest tuna fishery on the coast, which overlooks the bay and a shingle beach popular with swimmers (privately owned but open 9am–12.30pm). The atmospheric complex contains a pink villa, chapel, storerooms and the barracks where the tuna crew stay in the fishing season. Above are a couple of rugged Saracen towers, designed to combat piratical invasions.

A leisurely four-hour marked trail begins in the south, beyond **Galleria di Scopello**, and hugs the coast, passing coves and beaches, until it meets the road at **Uzzo**, in the northern end of the nature reserve.

Castellammare del Golfo

Castellammare del Golfo ⑥, an overgrown fishing village, enjoys panoramic views across the gulf and, from the port, a boat ferries visitors to Lo Zíngaro nature reserve (tel:

Map on page 94

TIP

In spring, the Riserva Naturale dello Zíngaro is a magnet for bird-watchers. Bird types include Bonelli's eagle, the Sicilian Rock partridge, the Peregrine falcon, the buzzard, the kestrel and the red kite. Many trails crisscross the reserve, including the *sentiero della costa*, a coastal footpath that runs for 11 km (7 miles) from Scopello to San Vito lo Capo, roughly a five-hour walk.

BELOW:
Scopello's beach.

BELOW:
Segesta's dramatic
5th-century BC temple.

0924 35108). The sweet, pastel-coloured cottages and idyllic harbour with its trattorie belie the town's bloody past as a Mafia haunt. In the 1950s, around 80 percent of the male population had been to jail and the internecine Mafia warfare led the port to become the chief embarkation point to the US.

Gavin Maxwell lived among the tuna fishermen in the 1950s, recording their destitution and illiteracy in his book *Ten Pains of Death* (1958). Even then, there was a clash between old and new lifestyles: "From my eyrie in the castle I watched Castellammaresi women come down to the sea to bathe and swim fully dressed in their everyday clothes, and to meet, while so floundering, bronzed visiting nymphs in bikinis and snorkels."

Segesta

In rolling countryside south of Castellammare lies **Segesta** ❼ (daily 9am–1 hour before sunset; entrance fee), one of the most romantic Classical locations. The site can also reached along the A29 from Trápani.

The vast, largely unexcavated city of **Egesta** (today's Segesta) is believed to have been founded by the Elymni in the 12th century BC. The settlers claimed to be refugees who escaped the Fall of Troy but some scholars believe them to be an iconoclastic tribe of Iberian-Ligurian descent. Elymnian writings found at Segesta are in an unfathomable language although written in the Greek alphabet. However, the Trojan link could explain their hatred of the Greeks, an enmity that led to their role in the razing of their rival nation at Selinunte in 409 BC. (Segesta itself was sacked by Siracusa in 307 BC when nearly 10,000 residents were killed and the rest sold as slaves.)

Crowning a low hill on the edge of a ravine is a great Hellenic monument, the roofless **Doric temple** that lacks a *cella* (inner chamber) and fluting on its 36 columns, but is no less lovely for that. No one knows to which god the temple was dedicated, or if it was ever completed. It appears to have been abandoned, unfinished, around 420 BC.

A regular shuttle bus takes visitors to the next level on **Monte Barbaro**

3 km (2 miles) away with its **theatre** built in the 3rd century BC. (Only the fittest should attempt the 30-minute climb on foot.) Well preserved, the theatre measures 63 metres (207 ft) in diameter and has 20 rows of seats facing the fabulous view of the Golfo di Castellammare. Greek plays are staged here in summer.

Further away, but hard to get to, is the partly excavated **Sanctuary of the Elymians**, 6th century BC. An easier option is to visit the **Terme Segestane**, the sulphur baths at Ponte Bagni, 4 km (2½ miles) away. The Greeks used to go there too.

The earthquake zone

In 1968 a major earthquake struck western Sicily, including Calatafimi, Salemi, Partanna and Gibellina. Over 50,000 people were left homeless and many still live in makeshift accommodation. The reasons for this are unclear but would appear to involve bureaucratic inefficiency and yet another curious disappearance of funds earmarked for the project. **Salemi** ❽, a benighted hill-top town 30 km (19 miles) north of Castelvetrano, is the most intriguing of the earthquake spots. Since the 13th-century castle has been ineffectually propped up, the main interest lies in the narrow, blackened medieval alleys and crumbling churches. Just east lies **Gibellina Nuova** ❾, a strangely ugly new town built after the earthquake flattened the original city, 18 km (11 miles) to the west.

The town is dominated by a 1970s conception of futuristic architecture that bears little relation to its history: open-air exhibits such as a petal, plough and tomato overlook lifeless streets. Although Gibellina is trying to position itself as a centre of technology, **Ruderi di Gibellina** ❿, the rubble of a devastated city, has been left as it fell in 1968. A primitive stage has been erected on the ruins and is used for performances of macabre "memorial" concerts, Greek tragedy and contemporary theatre.

The North African coast

South of Trápani is the so-called North African coast, closer to Tunisia than to mainland Italy. It is

Map on page 94

TIP

The water in the Terme Segestane thermal baths, which reaches 47°C (117°F), is claimed to relieve everything from acne and dandruff to arthritis and diabetes. Details: Ponte Bagni 1, Castellammare del Golfo, Trápani Province. Tel: 09 2453 0057.

BELOW: imagining a performance on Monte Barbaro.

BELOW: cheese for sale in Marsala.

known for its **salt-pans**, a reminder of an industry that has flourished since Phoenician and Roman times thanks to ideal conditions: low rainfall, regular tides, and the absence of estuaries that would dilute the salinity. The industry represented the mainstay of the local economy between the 14th and 17th centuries. Today's *Via del sale* (the salt road) stretches from Trápani to the Stagnone Lagoon with the island of Mózia and on further to Marsala, taking in another stretch of salt-pans and newly renovated windmills, with the brackish lagoons home to wild ducks, grey herons, common puffins and African cranes. As a result, this coastal area has been declared a nature reserve focused on the workings of the salt-pans and the passage of migratory birds.

At **Núbia** , only 5 km (3 miles) out of Trápani, is the **Museo delle Saline** (Tues–Sat 9am–noon, 3pm–6pm), a working museum, opened in 1988, to illustrate the ancient salt industry and the way it is extracted here from the marshes. (In February and March seawater is drawn into

the salt-pans where it evaporates in the sun. By July the salt is dry enough to be harvested into pyramids, covered with tiles, and allowed to dry out before being taken away for cleansing and packaging.)

Further south, a stretch of salt-pans and shallow lagoons embraces the marshy **Saline dello Stagnone**, the largest lagoon on Sicily's coastline. Poetic views across the shallow salt-pans are intensified at sunset. On the coast is a newer, well-organised salt museum, **Mulina Salina Infersa** (daily 9am–8pm), housed in a converted windmill.

Mózia

From a small jetty here it is possible to take the ferry across the lagoon to **the island of Mózia** , Sicily's chief Punic site (tel: 0923 712 598 for the custodian if there is no ferry waiting). A submerged Phoenician causeway just below the surface links the island to the shore, but this is now impassable.

Mózia, first known as Motya, looms on the far side of the Stagnone lagoon, its largest island. As Motya, it was established as a Phoenician colony in the mid-8th century BC, set within a ring of ramparts and towers, and protected by a landward bastion. When the Phoenicians founded a colony Lilybaeum (Marsala) as their new home, Motya fell into total neglect. It was bought, centuries later, by the Marsala wine merchant Joseph Whitaker (1850–1936), who made the excavations his life's work. As Mózia was never again colonised, Whitaker discovered a secret city more complete than Carthage.

The ruins of Motya are still only partially excavated but the remains of the city walls, cemetery and small manmade harbour, the **cothon**, are visible. There is also a **tophet**, dedicated to the goddess Tanit, where it is believed the Phoenicians sacrificed their first-born children. There are ruins of many houses, some with mosaics. The **Casa dei Mosaici** has a black and white pebble floor that depicts lions attacking a bull.

The genteel **Whitaker Museum** contains pre-Punic pottery and nearly 1,000 burial urns, many still with the remains of their occupants. One particular treasure is a remarkably fine Greek statue from early-5th century BC of a sinuous youth, possibly a charioteer, known as *The Man in a Tunic*. The quality of this piece is superb.

Marsala

Marsala ⓭ occupies the next cape, 10 km (6 miles) south, and takes its name from the Arabic *Marsa-al-Allah*, harbour of God. The view of Capo Boeo, the most western point of Sicily, was enjoyed by refugees from Mózia in 396 BC when it became Carthaginian **Lilybaeum,** the best-defended Punic naval base in Sicily, and the only city to resist Greek expansion westwards. (Marsala, in turn, has given its name to a famous dessert wine produced in the local vineyards.)

At the centre of the old town is the **cathedral** dedicated to **St Thomas di Canterbury**, built on the site of a church dedicated to St Thomas Becket. Begun in 1607 but ruined in 1893 when the dome collapsed, the church was rebuilt in the 20th century, with the Baroque front completed in 1958. There is much work by Domenico and Antonello Gagini, including two statues, *St Thomas the Apostle* and *St Vincent*.

Close to the cathedral on Via Giuseppe Garraffa is the small **Museo degli Arazzi** (Tues–Sat 9am–1pm, 4.30–6pm, Sun 9.30am–1pm; entrance fee), containing 18 richly coloured Flemish **tapestries** given to the church in 1589 by the Archbishop of Messina. The fine tapestries, made in Brussels between 1530 and 1550, depict the *Capture*

of Jerusalem. On Via Scipione l'Africano is the domed church of the **Addolorata**, whose 18th-century interior contains the venerated statue of the *Madonna* wearing a very untraditional black cloak. Paces away is an original entrance to Marsala, **Porta Garibaldi** (previously Porta di Mare) erected in 1685.

The original site of Lilybaeum is on the city's promontory awaiting further excavation. In the Baglio Anselmi (a former distillery) is the **Museo Archeologico** (daily 9am–6pm; entrance fee), its old warehouses used as halls for prehistoric collections as well as finds from Mózia, exquisite Hellenistic gold jewellery and countless funerary monuments and figures. One room contains a superb **Punic ship** reconstructed after being recovered from the Stagnone Lagoon in 1971. At 35 metres (115 ft) long, it was manned by 68 oarsmen. For some unexplained reason its original iron nails have not rusted.

On the seafront is the **Stabilimento Florio** (Mon–Fri 9am– noon, 3–5.30pm), one of the most typical of

Map on page 94

Porta Nova, Marsala.

BELOW: windmills and salt-pans, Marsala.

*Spreading the word
in Mazara del Vallo.*

BELOW: taking the
tour of Selinunte.

the Marsala distilleries, most of which are set in *bagli*, that is, traditional walled estates with elegant courtyards. The Florio founders are probably Sicily's greatest entrepreneurs but the amber-coloured dessert wine was pioneered by British wine merchants *(see box below)*. The Florio museum has a fine collection of vintages, including illicit bottles sent to the USA during Prohibition, when Florio cunningly labelled the alcohol as seasoning or medicinal tonic.

From Marsala, the lovely coastal road passes salt-pans and marshes south to **Mazara del Vallo** , a place of moods rather than specific sights. The fishing port feels like a North African town and indeed flourished under Arab rule. A ragged **Norman castle** overlooks the seafront and palm-filled park, while the **Norman cathedral** has been given a baroque veneer and contains two dramatic Roman sarcophagi.

The best church is at **Porta Palermo,** located in the heart of the fishing quarter. This is the crenellated Norman-Byzantine church of **San Nicolò Regale** overlooking the port,

and has abstract Roman mosaics. Since the town is now home to one of Italy's largest fishing fleets, the Mazaro river is packed with trawlers all the way to the fish market. **Via Pescatori** is full of Tunisian fishermen but the women are hidden away. Behind lies the Casbah, the Tunisian quarter, an intriguing den of arcaded, tapering alleys and backstreet charm. **Piazza Bagno** has a *hammam* with baths and massage. Nearby are a ritual butcher's and several Tunisian cafés with North Africans smoking *chicha* bubble pipes.

Selinunte

As the most westerly Hellenic colony, 30 km (19 miles) east of Mazara, **Selinunte** was a pocket of Greece in the part of Sicily under North African control. Set in a richly arable plain on the edge of the sea, the ancient city was founded in 650 BC by colonists from Megara Hyblaea *(see page 195)*. It took its name from *selinon*, Greek for the wild celery that grew here in abundance. By the 5th century BC it had become a prosperous city with great

Marsala wine

A British merchant, John Woodhouse, discovered that when Marsala wine was fortified with alcohol it survived the lengthy sea voyage back to England, and in 1773 he began shipping the new fortified product in greater quantities. Soon other merchants opened their own wineries, among them Benjamin Ingham in 1806 and Vincenzo Florio in 1883 (names still going strong although they are now owned by the Cinzano group). The wine comes in different "flavours", most sweet, though Marsala all'Uovo (with egg yolks) is sweetest of all. The dry Marsala Secco, served chilled, is a pleasant *aperitivo*, while Marsala Vergine, matured for at least five years, is considered best of all.

temples and two harbours, where the rivers Modione and Cottone that then framed the site reach the sea. At that time Selinunte and the city of Siracusa were allied in their hatred of powerful Carthage (in today's Tunisia) but, in 409 BC, when the Carthaginians attacked the city with the help of the people of Segesta, it was ransacked and destroyed. The city never fully recovered and when in 250 BC it was again attacked, the population decamped and resettled at Lilybaeum (Marsala). However, an aerial view of Selinunte's collapsed columns reveals that they fell like dominoes, evidently the result of an earthquake not man's destruction.

Surprisingly for Sicily, the huge **archaeological site** (daily 9am– 5pm, until 4pm in winter; entrance fee) is not overshadowed by building but is left in splendid isolation, flanked by two rivers and the ancient ports, both silted up. The oldest temples, named alphabetically **Ⓐ**, **Ⓑ**,

Ⓒ and **Ⓓ**, lie in the acropolis, while the main temples **Ⓔ**, **Ⓕ** and **Ⓖ**, were built on the eastern hill.

A curious entrance directs visitors from the ticket office and car park through tunnels in sandbanks to the reconstructed **Temple E** that was possibly dedicated to Hera (Juno) wife of Zeus, queen of heaven. Its lovely sculptures are in the Museo Archeologico in Palermo, much to the chagrin of locals who would like the *metopes* and friezes to return, especially the statue of the *ephebe*, a noble youth, which was unearthed by a local farmer.

Temple F, the oldest on the hill, is the most damaged of the trio, dedicated, perhaps, to Athena, goddess of war, while **Temple G**, probably dedicated to Zeus (Apollo), is now a vast heap of rubble with one restored raised column. Each column in this temple was built using stone drums weighing 100 tons and remained incomplete. Fragments of their

Maps:
Area 94
Site: 103

The Marinella seafront near Selinunte.

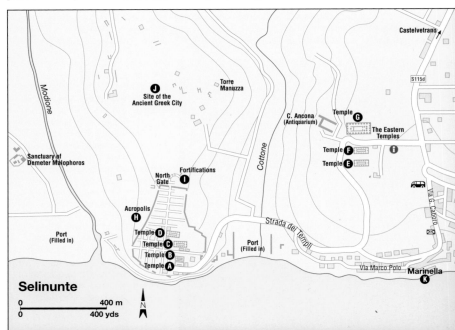

Selinunte

0 ____ 400 m
0 ____ 400 yds
N

Modione

Castelvetrano

S115d

Torre Manuzza

Ⓙ Site of the Ancient Greek City

C. Ancona (Antiquarium)

Temple Ⓖ
The Eastern Temples

Sanctuary of Demeter Malophoros

Cottone

Temple Ⓕ   Ⓘ

Temple Ⓔ

Fortifications

North Gate Ⓘ

Acropolis Ⓗ

Strada dei Templi

Via G. Caboto

Port (Filled in)

Temple Ⓓ
Temple Ⓒ
Temple Ⓑ
Temple Ⓐ

Port (Filled in)

Via Marco Polo   Marinella Ⓚ

Maps:
Area 94
Site: 103

Temple A – what's left of it – stands on the acropolis at Selinunte.

painted stucco have been unearthed.

Sited within a walled enclosure, the **acropolis** retains some original **fortifications** . Five towers and four gates have been identified. **Temple O** is barely visible with only the stylobate (platform) remaining; no building or superstructure survives. **Temple A** is equally elusive even though its stylobate is there along with pieces of its original 36 columns. Both temples date from around 480BC.

On the knoll of the hill is the conspicuous **Temple C**, dated at around mid-6BC. The largest temple of all, it appears to have been dedicated to Apollo, the great Olympian god. Some of the columns are monoliths and when they all collapsed in an earthquake in the 8th century they flattened a Byzantine village that had grown around them. (There are crosses carved into some of the fragments found here.) The giant columns are nearly 2 metres (6½ ft) in diameter except for those on the temple corners which are even thicker. The columns were rebuilt into a towering colonnade in 1927. Only the platform

remains of **Temple B** while **Temple D** has its platform and some blocks from the columns.

North of the acropolis is the **Ancient City** , and on either side of it lies a **necropolis** that has to be excavated. The **Sanctuary of Demeter Malophoros**, across the river Modione, was built c.575BC with a huge sacrificial altar at its centre. The Sanctuary was a sacred area enclosed by walls. More than 10,000 votive figures of Demeter were found here.

Selinunte is a tragic yet hauntingly lovely spot. The sight and sound of the waves merge with squabbling magpies and fast yellowback lizards. In cracks of the ruins grow aromatic wild fennel, parsley, mandrake, acanthus and beds of yellow flowers. It is deeply therapeutic.

A lengthy visit to the sprawling site can be followed by a swim along the sandy coast. Framed by temples, the seafront at **Marinella** is lined with lively restaurants.

Vanquished city

Between Selinunte and Castelvetrano a road leads to **Campobella di Mazara**, a wine-producing town. Further on are the **Cave di Cusa**, the ancient quarries that provided the stone to build Selinunte. Set 4 km (2½ miles) south of Campobella di Mazara, this charming rural site is always open (daily times vary, however) and is now overrun with wild flowers. Huge column drums lie chiselled, as if ready to be transported to Temple G at Selinunte, 18 km (11 miles) away, before being abandoned.

The fascination lies in the complex mechanics of construction. Old sketches show how half-carved capitals were levered and pillars were hauled to Selinunte in carts. The poignancy lies in the fact that all work stopped the moment Selinunte was destroyed. The vanquished city just disappeared under the sands. It is yet to be excavated. ❑

RESTAURANTS

Trápani

Ai Lumi
Corso Vittorio Emanuele 75.
Tel: 0923 872 418.
www.ailumi.it
An elegant, fashionable old establishment serving good traditional local dishes. Closed Nov. €€

Cantina Siciliana
Via Giudecca 36.
Tel: 0923 28673.
www.cantinasiciliana.it
Simple *osteria* with 1950s decor serving only local dishes. €€

P & G
Via Spalti 1 (by Villa Margerita park).
Tel: 0923 547 701.
Casual seafood place serving Trapani classics like *neonata* (baby sardines), pizzas and couscous. Closed Mon. €€

Paradiso
Lungomare Dante Alighieri 22. Tel: 0923 22303.
www.tavernaparadiso.com
A highly regarded taverna. Specialities: *neonata* (baby sardines), *spaghetti ai ricci* (spaghetti with sea-urchin) and tuna. Book. Closed Sun. €€€

Safina
Piazza Umberto I 35 (opposite the railway station).
Tel: 0923 22708.

PRICE CATEGORIES
Prices for three-course dinner per person with a half-bottle of house wine:
€ = under €15
€€ = €15–30
€€€ = €30–60

Huge portions at low prices. Closed Wed in winter. €€

Trattoria del Porto
Via A. Staiti 45.
Tel: 0923 547822.
A family-run trattoria in the port area with fish and seafood specialities and outdoor tables. Try the fish couscous. €€

Erice

Al Ciclope
Viale Nasi 45.
Tel: 0923 869 183.
Can be expensive. Closed Tues except in summer. €€€

Moderno
Via Vittorio Emanuele 67.
Tel: 0923 869 300.
www.hotelmodernoerice.it
Classic Sicilian cooking. Charming terrace that has panoramic views. Closed Mon in quiet season. €€€

Monte San Giuliano
Vicolo San Rocco 7.
Tel: 0923 869 595.
www.montesangiuliano.it
Very good traditional Trapanese cuisine. Try the *involtini di melanzana* (stuffed aubergine rolls). Closed Mon. €€€

La Pentolaccia
Via Guarnotti 17.
Tel: 0923 869 099.
www.ristorantelapentolaccia.it
Former monastery. Fish and couscous specials. Good choice of local wines. Closed Tues. €€

Ulisse
Via Chiaramonte 45.
Tel: 0923 869333.

Just off the main square, this restaurant serves up excellent pizzas as well as pricier meat and fish dishes. Garden. Closed Thur in winter. €€€

San Vito lo Capo

Alfredo
Contrada Valanga 3.
Tel: 0923 972 366.
Good seafood. Known for pasta dishes with *bottarga* (cod roe). Garden. Closed Mon and mid-Oct–Nov. €€€

Riviera
Via Litoranea 57.
Tel: 0923 972 480.
Unpretentious trattoria with lively crowd. Closed Nov–Dec. €€€

Tha'am
Via Abruzzi 32.
Tel: 0923 972 836.
Arab influences show in the decor and North African dishes. Closed Wed Oct–May. €€€

Marsala

Delfino
Lungomare Mediterraneo 672. Tel: 0923 751 076.
www.delfinobeach.com
On waterfront 4 km (2½ miles) from centre. Great seafood. Closed Tues except Apr–Oct. €€€

Divino Rosso
Via XI Maggio.
Tel: 0923 969 565.
divinorosso@libero.it
Fabulous selection of wines sold by the glass. Excellent meat and fish dishes. Book for dinner. Closed Feb and Mon. €€

Nashville
Piazza Pizzo 24.
Tel: 0923 95186.
Crispy pizzas are served outside on the piazza in fine weather, and there's a menu of traditional Sicilian fare too. €€

Mazara del Vallo

Al Pesciolino d'Oro
Lungomare San Vito 109.
Tel: 0923 909 286.
www.alpesciolinodoro.it
Seafood of all kinds. Closed Thur. €€

Baby Luna
Lungomare Mazzini.
Tel: 0923 948 622.
www.ristorantebabyluna.com
Near the cathedral. Busy, popular. Closed Mon and Nov. €€

Del Pescatore
Via Castelvetrano 191.
Tel: 0923 947 580.
www.ristorantedelpescatore.com
Try the swordfish and spicy pasta dishes. Closed Mon. €€€

Alla Kasbah
Via Itria 10.
Tel: 0923 906 126.
Regulars go to enjoy the fish couscous. Closed Mon. €€€

Selinunte
Hotel restaurants in this area are good value.

Pierrot
Via Marco Polo 108 at Marinella. Tel: 0924 46205.
www.ristorantepierrotselinunte.it
Emphasis on seasonal fish. Closed Tues in winter and two weeks in Jan–Feb. €€€

THE EGADI ISLANDS AND PANTELLERIA

As the easiest offshore islands to visit, the Egadi attract summer crowds, but out of season they offer peace and traditional charm. Much further south lies Pantelleria, Sicily's island close to the shores of North Africa

The archipelago of the small Egadi Islands (**Isole Egadi**) lying off the western coast, 50 minutes to two hours by ferry from Trápani, is totally involved with the sea. And it is a particularly rich and beautiful sea that surrounds Favignana, Lévanzo, and Maréttimo. Crystalline and multi-coloured, it teems with marine life.

Today the islands are a paradise for sailors and scuba divers (and for anyone who enjoys fish served on a plate), although crowds of invaders brought by ferries and hydrofoils from Trápani threaten to overwhelm the peaceful rhythm of island life, especially on Favignana. Coincidentally, although the summer weather lasts from May to October, these are also the months of the *mattanza (see page 110),* when tuna is brought to the shore for slaughter. It has become an unlikely tourist event.

Cave drawings

The Egadi have 15,000 years of history and the caves of Favignana and Lévanzo contain traces of the islands' prehistoric settlers. In Lévanzo cave drawings in the **Grotta del Genovese** etched 12,000 years ago show bulls and deer as well as hunting man. It is thought the archipelago was once part of a land bridge linking Africa to Italy.

The islands were the springboard for the Arab conquest of Sicily and the great traders, the Phoenicians, then settled here and remained until despatched by the Romans. Over the centuries the Saracens and the Normans followed, then the Aragonese and, finally, the Genoese. The Normans and Aragonese fortified the Egadi while the Spaniards encouraged the growth of a coral industry.

When Spain sold them in 1637 to bankers Pallavicino in Genoa, the new owners began to develop the

Map on page 94

LEFT:
tuna fishermen, with
Forte Santa Caterina
in the background.
BELOW:
Pantelleria seascape.

islands economically. By the early-19th century when they were purchased by the Florio family, both tuna and tufa (volcanic rock) were being exported. Today fishing and tourism keep the economy alive.

Favignana

At 20 sq. km (7.7 sq. miles), Favignana, home to around 4,400 people, is the largest and most populous island of the group. Ancient tufa-quarrying remodelled the landscape until it was brought to a standstill in the 1950s by the high cost of extracting and transporting the rock.

The island is a homage to stone, its slopes dotted with tufa houses. Even cliffs and caves represent a pleasing spectrum of ochre, russet and cream-coloured rocks. However, if cyclists heading for one of the coves stop to peer over the roadside stone walls, they will discover an abundance of sunken gardens. These sheer stone walls, overgrown with wild fennel and capers, give shelter from the sweeping sea winds to the orange and lemon trees, as well as the figs and tomatoes planted below on the floor

of the abandoned quarries. Other quarries were carved at the very edge of the sea too so that the tufa could be loaded directly onto the boats transporting it to the mainland. Stone from the maze-like **Cala Rossa** helped build many cities in Sicily and North Africa. The chiselled walls and eroded geometry of the seaside quarries make Cala Rossa a popular spot for picnics and swimming.

In the bustling medieval town of Favignana, to one side of the ferry quay in the **port** , near where the ferry docks, stand beautiful vaulted warehouses in which the big black-bottomed tuna boats, the long nets and huge anchors are stored during the winter. The still waters of the harbour reflect the tiled roofs and stone smokestacks of the **Tonnare Florio**, a former tuna cannery, which closed in the 1990s (all processing is now carried out in Trápani).

In Florio's time, a day's catch could be as high as 10,000 fish. Today, it has shrunk to under 2,000 a month because of overfishing and pollution. Even so, the tuna industry survives, with traditional techniques

A fisherman from Favignana.

BELOW:
Favignana's port.

allied to hi-tech sonar detection, used to spot the shoals.

Palazzo Florio, built in 1876, and the statue of Ignazio Florio in **Piazza Europa** are a reminder of better days. Also in town is **Forte San Giacomo**, a fortress built by Roger II in 1120 which was converted into a Bourbon prison in 1837 and performs a similar function today as a maximum-security prison for some of Sicily's finer *mafiosi*. The prison offers the town's men employment as guards and general staff.

The tourist office is at Largo Marina 14 (tel: 0923 545 511).

Paleolithic caves

Eastwards along the shore is **Punta San' Nicola**, awaiting excavation of its caves that were inhabited in Paleolithic times, **Bagno delle Donne** (once the women's baths), and **Cala Rossa** where the sea was said to have turned red in 241 BC during a bloody battle between the Carthaginians and Romans. A little further on is **Parco del Cavernicolo**, a modern swimming pool complex.

At the island's centre is **Monte Santa Caterina** with a prohibited military zone containing **Forte Santa Caterina**. This fort, founded by Roger II, was once a prison.

Lévanzo

The smallest island, and the one closest to the mainland, bears witness to the islanders' bond with the sea. Much of the coast is still inaccessible, except by boat. The port of **Lévanzo** 🔞 (or **Cala Dogana**, because the Customs offices are here) consists of a handful of houses with rooms to let, a couple of small hotels, several cafés and trattorie.

Its one tarred road turns into a dirt track as it leaves town and winds along a gentle valley between the peaks of the Pizzo del Mónaco and the Pizzo del Corvo. The stony slopes are covered with *macchia*

mediterranea, arid-looking grey-green scrub that turns lush with the winter rains and blooms in spring.

At the head of the valley the track forks: the left-hand path zigzags down the steep coast towards the sea, leading to the **Grotta del Genovese** 🔞, a deep cavern overhanging the rocky shoreline. It is Lévanzo's greatest treasure. If the sea is calm and the wind right, you can reach the grotto by boat, combining a visit to see the ancient carvings with sailing and swimming from a craft hired at Cala Dogana (or book with the custodian of the grotta: Signor Giuseppe Castiglione at Via Calvario 11, near hydrofoil quay, tel 0923 924 032).

The **rock carvings** are prehistoric and not found until 1949. Etched into the soft stone about 10,000 years ago, they include impressions of human dancers and wild animals in naturalistic poses. More recent ones of men, women and fish were created about 5,000 years ago.

Most of the rest of the island is inaccessible except for the fit and determined and there are only a few inlets for swimming.

Map on page 94

The Palazzo Florio, built in 1876, was once the home of the tuna tycoon Ignazio Florio. Today it contains a gallery and cultural centre.

BELOW: Favignana's rocky shore.

The Great Tuna Massacre

Tuna fishing is rooted in the Sicilian psyche. Nowhere is this more so than in Favignana where it is considered the sea's ultimate challenge to man, as well as the island's traditional livelihood. The tuna's only predators are the killer whale, the Mako shark and man, and their ritual death here at the hands of fishermen is both gruelling work and a disturbing spectacle. But, as the proverb says: "Tuna fishing shortens your arms and silences your tongue."

The season lasts from May to mid-June, with the ritual *mattanza*, the traditional method of tuna slaughter, as the inexorable fate of the passing shoals.

The fast-swimming tuna hunt off the coast of Norway but spawn in the Mediterranean's warm waters. Shoals circle Favignana where they are captured in a system of huge chambered nets *(tonnare)* introduced by the Arabs in the 9th century.

Buoys mark out a 100-metre (330-ft) rectangle; up to 10 km (6 miles) of nets are suspended between the floats. Halfway along lie five antechambers. The innermost section is the *camera della morte*, the death chamber 30 metres (100 ft) deep.

At dawn, or when the winds are right, eight black boats set off to check the nets. The helmsman leads the fleet in prayers, aided by an image of the Madonna. The 60-strong crew sings and chants the *cialoma* in guttural tones. Entreaties are uttered by the *rais*, a Moorish title given to the chief fisherman, who travels in a separate boat and constantly checks the entrance to the *camera della morte*.

The black boats encircle the nets. When the *rais* decides that the currents are right, the shoal is steered into the death chamber and the gate closed. As it fills with fish, the floating death trap sags, like a heavy sack. To the command of "*Tira, tira!*" (pull, pull!) the net is pulled tight. The *rais* chants the fateful battle cry. Each verse of this bloodthirsty sea shanty has a chorus of "*Aiamola, aiamola*", perhaps derived from *Allah! Che muoia!* (Allah, may it die!).

As the net is drawn in to the length of a football pitch, the fish circle frantically in the *sarabanda della morte*, the dance of death. The chanting stops and the slaughter begins. The frantic fish are harpooned and caught behind the gills with long pole-gaff hooks to be dragged onto the boats. Some of the tuna are man-sized and their razor-sharp tail fins can kill.

As the silvery fish are pierced, the frothing water is stained red. It takes a frenzied 15 minutes and a sea of vivid red to slaughter about 200 tuna, although some die of heart attacks or over-oxygenation. With true Sicilian logic, the tuna's breeding grounds also become their tragic end.

In the past, one day's *mattanza* could determine the island's fortune for the rest of the year, but no longer as tuna numbers are fast declining and Japanese fleets now compete for catches in the Mediterranean. (To meet this decline, fish farms off the coasts of many Mediterranean islands are now breeding tuna in their pens as well other fish such as bream.) The cruel ritual is both a gory tradition and a gruesome tourist spectacle that survives despite conservationists' concerns and the contravention of conventions on driftnet fishing. ❑

LEFT: blood on the quay as tuna are weighed.

Maréttimo

The most mysterious, mountainous and greenest of the Egadi Islands, Marétimmo lies to the west, separated from its sister islands by a stretch of sea rich in sunken treasure. Here lie the remains of the Carthaginian fleet destroyed by the Romans in 241 BC.

The little port of **Maréttimo** ⓴ has no hotel but a few serviced apartments, and the locals (a total of 800) happily accept guests in their homes. Tourism does not seem to feature prominently in this tiny place. Peace and natural beauty are what draw visitors here. Scuba divers come to explore the 400 caves and grottos scattered along the coast; plant-lovers study the Mediterranean vegetation at its purest. The rest simply want to relax, swim in the aquamarine waters, or take 3-hour trips in the brightly coloured traditional boats around the coast.

Ambitious visitors will climb up to survey the island from **Monte Falcone** (686 metres/2,250 ft). An easier walk is an excursion to **Case Romane**, not houses but ruined Roman fortifications not far from the village. (From the port follow directions to Pizzeria Filli Pipitone.) Beside the ruins is a crumbling Arab-Norman chapel.

An alternative hike leads north along the cliffs and cuts across an isthmus to **Punta Tróia** ㉑, a rocky promontory dominated by a Saracen castle. Originally a watchtower, the castle was enlarged by Roger II and converted by the Spanish into its present form, with an underground cistern that later did service as a dreaded prison. But such sombre thoughts quickly float away on this restful, thyme-scented island.

Pantelleria

Pantelleria is closer to Tunisia's Cap Bon, 70 km (44 miles) away, than to Sicily, which is 110 km (68 miles) distant, and is reached on a six-hour ferry crossing from Trápani, or by air. At 83 sq. km (247 acres), it is the largest island off Sicily with a population estimated at 7,600. The island's evocative name probably derives from the Arabic "daughter of the winds", after the winds that can buffet this rocky outpost, even in August. The island is dotted with cube-like, low-domed houses (*dammusi*) and surrounded by terraces used for growing capers or grapes; even the vines are trained low to protect them from the winds. The landscape is dramatic and relatively bleak but enlivened with hot springs, jagged rocks and coves instead of beaches. Many mainland Italians, especially from Milan (like fashion designer Giorgio Armani) have getaway summer homes here.

Pantelleria town

Pantelleria town ㉒ was bombed heavily during the Allied forces invasion of Sicily in World War II, so many of its original buildings have been lost. It is now modern with only a little visual charm. But

Map on page 94

TIP

You can bring a car on the *traghetto* (ferry) from Trápani. However, on Pantelleria it's easier to rent a moped or use the bus service between the town and Scauri and Tracino. Bicycles and motor-scooters can also be rented in town.

● The tourist office is on Via San Nicola (tel: 0923 911 838).

BELOW: the stony slopes of Lévanzo.

Map
on page
94

TIP

In summer, hikers should always carry bottled water with them, especially on Maréttimo. On these parched islands, water is more precious than wine.

BELOW: out of season, the harbour at Pantelleria is tranquil.

the island itself has a lively air as well as an exoticism encapsulated by the white-cubed houses and restaurants that serve fish couscous.

Pantelleria was founded originally as a trading post by the Phoenicians. Its small harbours provided excellent protection for the small ships of the day. The island was captured by Rome but eventually – after the Vandals and Byzantines – it was the Arabs who claimed the island and introduced farming.

A rewarding hike or a bus ride from the Pantelleria town to the port of **Scáuri** on the southern coast passes the traditional white-washed *dammusi* houses, with their domed roofs as well as the terraced vineyards, small settlements and expanses of blackened, lava stone landscape. The dry stone walls enclose citrus groves and often appear to have hardy, locally bred, donkeys peering over them.

The route also passes strange Neolithic dome-shaped funerary monuments, known as *Sesi*, conceivably built by early settlers who arrived here around the 18th century

BC. Little is known of the Sesi people; it is assumed they came from Tunisia on foot before the Mediterranean Sea developed. They built circular domed structures using the island's volcanic rock, similar in shape to the *dammusi*. At **Mursia** their village with *Sesi* structures was protected by walls. Its name, Alta Mura, means High Wall.

The island's volcanic origins are visible in the presence of lava stone, basalt rock, hot springs, *stufe* (volcanic steam vents) and a landscape pitted with small *cuddie* (baby spouts), which are extinct volcanic craters. On **Monte Grande** (836 metres/2,743 ft), near the hamlet of Bugebera, lies a lake in an old crater full of warm, bubbling, sulphurously brown waters, known as **Specchio di Venere** (Venus's mirror) and used by local bathers to cure myriad ills. The water here can reach 50°C (122°F) because of a hot spring. **Bagno d'Acqua** is another small lake inside a former crater, and visitors are drawn to it too in order to cover themselves with beautifying volcanic mud.

As for coastal scenery, the craggy shore is studded with coves, with rocks shaded from red through green and black. For swimmers and divers, the absence of beaches is compensated for by the privacy occasioned by secluded coves and hot springs, and by the quality of the underwater landscape, with sightings of ancient wrecks as well as sea sponges and coral. In fact, the great **excursions** on the island are a tour in a car or by boat. By boat is better.

Famous wines

Pantelleria is famous for its sweet raisins and for its wines, especially **Moscato di Pantelleria** produced from its sweet moscato grape, *Zibibbo*. The wine made from raisins is **Passito**, usually highly scented with almonds. ❏

RESTAURANTS

Favignana

La Bettola
Via Nicotera 47.
Tel: 0923 921 988.
Simple, inexpensive trattoria. No frills, but with a wide selection each day of tuna and swordfish dishes. Closed Thur. €€

La Tavernetta
Piazza Madrice 62.
Tel: 0923 921 939.
Local specialities given star treatment. Excellent fish. Book. €€€

Egadi
Via Cristoforo Colombo 17.
Tel: 0923 921 232.
www.albergoegadi.it
Popular hotel restaurant renowned for its fish, especially tuna. Closed Oct–Mar. €€€

El Pescador
Piazza Europa 38, Porto.
Tel: 0923 921 035.
Run by a fishing family. Simple cooking, the speciality is spaghetti with fresh tuna and capers. The restaurant can be relied on to take the pick of the fresh catch. Closed Wed (except summer) and Feb. €€€

Il Nautilus
Via Amendola 6, Porto.
Tel: 0923 921 671.
Excellent tuna carpaccio and *spaghetti con tonno e gamberi* (with tuna and prawns). Inexpensive set menu includes spaghetti with shrimps, capers and tomatoes. €€

Sorelle Guccione
Via Colombo 17.
Tel: 0923 921 232.
mgguccione@virgilio.it
Alongside the Duomo, simple setting for traditional cooking. Fish. Dinner only. Open Easter–end Oct. €€

Lévanzo

Paradiso
Via Lungomare 8.
Tel: 0923 924 080.
Simple hotel restaurant overlooking the sea. Closed Oct–Mar. €€

Pensione dei Fenici
Via Calvario 18.
Tel: 0923 924 083.
Pensione with a terrace restaurant. Closed Oct–Jan. €

Maréttimo

Le Rose dei Venti
Punta S. Simone 4
Tel: 0923 923 249
www.isoladimarettimo.it
Family hotel with modest restaurant serving excellent fresh fish as well as lobster. Closed Nov–Mar. €

Onda Blu
Piazza Umberto.
Tel: 0923 923 103.
Pasta with wonderful sauces, grilled vegetables, fish, all served at tables on the square. Open summer only. €

Pantelleria

Il Cappero
Via Roma 33.

Tel: 0923 912 601.
By the port. Simple dishes; fish too, of course. And pizza. Popular. Closed Mon. €€

I Mulini
Via Kania 12, Contrada Tracino. Tel: 0923 915 398.
imulini@galactica.it
A charming old windmill typical of the countryside adapted with enthusiasm. Good local cooking; garden in summer months. Popular. Must book. Dinner only. Closed Tues. Open Easter–end Oct. €€€

La Nicchia
at Scauri Bassa.
Tel: 0923 916 342.
Pizzeria and ristorante where specialities are fish and couscous. Some tables outside. Dinner only. Closed Wed. Open Easter–end Oct. €€

Papuscia
Contrada Sopra Portella 28, Tracino. Tel: 0923 915 463
www.papuscia.it
Hotel restaurant. Dinner only, with simple but delicious dishes. €€

Gabbiano Azzurro
Riva al Mare
Tel: 0923 911 909.
Cheap and cheerful establishment. Closed Fri. €

Zabib
Porto di Scauri.
Tel: 0923 916 617.
Good restaurant, open only for dinner. €€€

PRICE CATEGORIES

Prices for three-course dinner per person with a half-bottle of house wine:
€ = under €15
€€ = €15–30
€€€ = €30–60

RIGHT: seafood is an obvious choice on the islands.

AGRIGENTO AND THE VALLEY OF THE TEMPLES

The town may be a curious mixture of modern ugliness and antiquity, but the Classical splendour of the Valley of the Temples is a major attraction

Map on page 116

Siracusa may have been the most powerful city in Greek Sicily but **Agrigento** (known as Akragas to the Greeks, Agrigentum to the Romans) was the most wealthy and luxurious, a city that reached from the acropolis high on the ridge down to the blue sea below. It was first settled by people from Gela in 580 BC, attracted there by the abundance of springs and the prospect of a dreamy, well-fortified site. It was Benito Mussolini who, in his campaign to unify Sicily and all Italy under one flag, changed its name to Agrigento.

Maverick city

At first sight, little remains of the ancient splendour. Not that the "modern" city, with a population of around 55,000, is wholly poor, or even modern. Agrigento is a living contradiction, an unaesthetic muddle concealing a fascinating urban mix. The town's medieval core is a maze of Moorish streets and substandard housing while, in contrast, the new quarter overlooks the temples in an attempt at bourgeois chic, but one that went horribly wrong when landslides, aggravated by overcrowding and shoddy building, killed many in 1966.

This particular scandal was compounded by the discovery that feckless Mafia surveyors had cut corners

by not checking for land subsidence, and that their contractors had used poor quality cement. Nowadays, charmless middle-class apartments gaze across at the temples, often from within the confines of the park. Beyond the richness of the Valle dei Templi that is the city's glittering inheritance, lies a somewhat soulless town centre, complete with neglected public buildings and a rapacious attitude to the bounties of tourism. Even so, don't be dismayed. The image of a parasitical city living

LEFT: The Tempio della Concordia seen from the Tempio di Hera.
BELOW: the town of Agrigento, seen from the temples.

Agrigento's crest.

off its past glories can be dispelled by a starlit night, a heady southern Sicilian wine and a dinner of grilled swordfish as an alternative to tuna.

City sights

If you are in the Agrigento area only for a day, head straight for the **Valle dei Templi** (Valley of the Temples) and restrict your visit to the town of Agrigento itself for dinner and an evening stroll. Parking problems and an unreliable public transport system, added to the disparate nature of the archaeological sites and their rel-

ative distance from the city, make it inconvenient to combine both places, even for meals. (If you are not staying in a hotel close to the Valle dei Templi, consider taking a picnic lunch and mineral water to the archaeological sites.)

The tourist office is at Piazzale Aldo Moro 9 (tel: 0922 20454).

Above Via Atenea, Agrigento's pedestrianised main shopping street as well as the entrance to the historic quarter, stands the **Chiesa di Santo Spirito ❶**, the church of a fine Cistercian abbey founded in 1290.

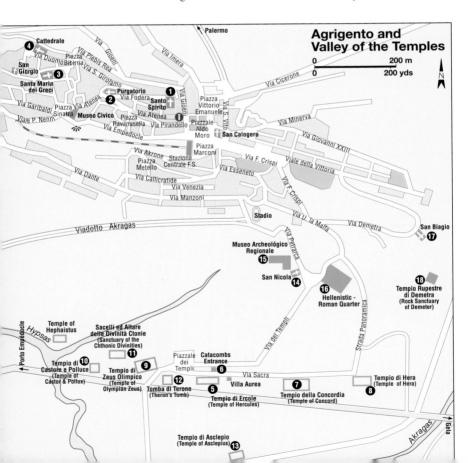

Map on page 116

Often known as the **Badia Grande**, it is the finest church in the city. It is a complex of cloisters, chapter house and refectory in Chiaramonte style *(see margin note)*. The church has a Gothic portal and rose window, plus a panelled ceiling and baroque interior with stuccos attributed to Serpotta. The vaulted Gothic dormitory leads to a chapter house with mullioned windows and a bold portal, all emboldened with Arab-Norman geometrical motifs. The abbey is undergoing restoration but the commercial spirit triumphs in Agrigento.

The sacristan in the house opposite will gladly open the church for a tip, while the Cistercian nuns sell sweet almond and pistachio pastries shaped like snakes, shells and flowers. Faced with such delights, the French writer Dominique Fernandez was torn between the "baroque opulence" of the architecture and the "Arab unctuousness" of the cakes. The cakes won.

Dominating Piazza Purgatorio, just off Via Atenea, is the 17th-century church known simply as the **Purgatorio ❷**, built on an ancient sacred site, but better known for its riot of baroque allegorical stuccowork by Serpotta, and for its elegant facade. To the left of the church, a stone lion guards an entrance to the ancient underground drinking water and drainage system. Created in the 5th century BC, these were known as one of the wonders of the world. Linked to the underground chamber beneath San Nicola church, the system used conduits and cisterns to channel water to the city. There are plans to open the chambers to the public and create a copy of a Roman food store complete with a lava-stone grinding mill.

Further west is **Santa Maria dei Greci ❸**, a Norman church set among Agrigento's alleyways, in the heart of the medieval quarter. A Chiaramonte Gothic portal leads to a Norman nave, a coffered ceiling and some Byzantine fragments. Below ground is the greatest surprise: the church is constructed around a 5th-century Greek temple dedicated to Athena. A narrow gallery contains the bases of six fluted Doric columns, the remains of

The Chiaramonte, the dominant feudal dynasty of the 14th century, gave its name to the Catalan-Gothic architectural style, in which fortresses doubled as palaces, with decorated facades, vaulted rooms and lavish, painted ceilings. The best of these tower houses had an austere beauty.

BELOW:
the alleys of Agrigento.

Agrigento's lurid past

The city abounds in Classical anecdote regarding its fabled wealth. For example, the Tyrant of Akragas kept wine in reservoirs hacked out of solid rock; each giant cellar contained 4,000 litres (900 gallons). And returning Olympic heroes were welcomed by cavalcades of chariots drawn by white horses, which were legendary in the Greek world. One ruler of this sybaritic city supposedly burned his enemies alive in a large bull made of bronze.

The people, it was said, "built for eternity but feasted as if there were no tomorrow". The city rivalled Athens in the splendour of its temples, but in its hedonistic lifestyle Akragas was the Los Angeles of the ancient world.

Exploring the Tempio della Concordia.

the temple peristyle and stereobate. The sanctuary spans Greek and Christian cults: tradition has it that St Paul preached here.

On Via del Duomo is the 14th-century cathedral, the **cattedrale ❹**, which surmounts a ridge and is designed in eclectic style, with Arab-Norman, Catalan-Gothic and baroque elements, from Catalan blind arcading to a Norman bell-tower. The Norman-Gothic nave boasts an inlaid, coffered ceiling and a section frescoed to simulate a dome. Graceful baroque stuccowork in the choir contrasts with a severe Gothic chapel. The cathedral was restored after being damaged in the 1966 landslide and is currently being restored due to subsidence.

In summer, the Classical city stages open-air performances of drama in tribute to Persephone. The modern city responds with *passeggiate* along tree-lined **Viale della Vittoria**. From this road there are some excellent views of the Valley of the Temples. At the far end is the mediaeval church of San Biaggio and the Sanctuary of Demeter.

Valle dei Templi

It is here, for a fleeting moment, that the Classical world comes alive. The Valley of the Temples is not really a valley but a string of Doric temples that stand imposingly on a ridge south of the city facing the sea. An ideal first glimpse of the temples is by night, during a drive along the **Strada Panoramica** and **Via della Valle dei Templi**. The temples glow in the dark countryside, radiating a sense of cohesion, security and serenity. This crest of temples was designed to be visible from the sea, both as a beacon for sailors and to show that the Gods guarded the sacred city from mortal danger.

An early start guarantees enough solitude to slip back into the Classical world. But unless you plan to view the **Tempio della Concordia** (the Temple of Concord) from the elegant restaurant in Villa Athena, come armed with a picnic. Otherwise, the on-site snack bar could bring you back to the present times with a bump.

Piazzale dei Templi, the entrance to the main temples, was once the

agora (market place) and is still alive to the ancient trading spirit. The local guides operate a monopoly, refusing to allow unauthorised rivals to present the archaeological park, and small boys often demand money to protect tourists' cars from unknown dangers, a feature of many Sicilian sites. The archaeological park falls into two sections: the enclosed Western Zone (daily 8.30am–7pm) and the unenclosed Eastern Zone (open access) which is best viewed in the early morning or late afternoon – or perhaps from afar when it is floodlit at night.

The first treasure visible in the Eastern Zone is the **Tempio di Ercole** (Temple of Hercules) ❺. Built in 520 BC in Archaic Doric style, this is the oldest temple, second in size here to the Temple of Zeus and of roughly the same proportions as the Parthenon in Athens. It once had a gorgeous entablature emblazoned with lions, leaves and palms but now it presents an almost abstract puzzle. Although much is in ruins, Alexander Hardcastle performed a truly Herculean task by re-erecting eight columns in 1924.

Villa Aurea, set in olive and almond groves beside the former Golden Gate, once belonged to Hardcastle, the Englishman who devotedly excavated the site. The grounds are riddled with catacombs and water cisterns, which run under rocks and orchards the length of the Classical site. A path on the left leads to the **catacombs** ❻, which emerge in a necropolis on the far side of the villa. Now excavated and well-lit, the passages cut through the rock and reveal a cross-section of tombs and fossilised bones.

Arches link circular rooms *(tholoi)* containing circular honeycomb cells stacked high with shelftombs. Though the oldest tombs here date from the 4th century BC, the main Roman necropoli lie just to the south while Greek burial grounds are scattered around the city.

At the end of the Via Sacra lies the **Tempio della Concordia** (Temple of Concord) ❼, abutting ancient city walls. After the Theseion in Athens, it is the best preserved Greek temple in the world. The pastoral surround-

Map on page 116

The Tempio della Concordia was used as a church for 12 centuries. Mass was celebrated there until 1748, when a local prince obtained permission to return the building to its Classical simplicity.

BELOW: the Tempio della Concordia.

BELOW:
the Temple of
Juno Lacinia.

ings are at odds with the temple's bloody history: on this bulwark thousands were slain in battle against Carthage. Dating from 430 BC, the temple was saved from ruin in the 6th century by being converted into a church. The peristyle was sealed by dry stone walls, and the *cella* opened to form twin naves, although sadly the *metopes* and pediment were destroyed.

The tapering columns tilt inwards imperceptibly, creating an ethereal grace and airiness that belie the weighty entablature. A further refinement is that the fluted columns have different spacing, narrowing towards the corners. They were originally coated with glazed marble dust to protect the flaky sandstone, then painted with vivid polychrome scenes, predominantly bright blue or blood-red. Now lichen-coated, the temple still represents sheer perfection in line. The only jarring image is the distant cityscape with its high-rise apartment buildings and cemetery but, seen though a heat haze, even that shimmers obligingly. The temple is transformed by light: locals

say that one has not lived until seeing Concord changing with the seasons, at dawn and sunset, dusk and moonlight.

Unfortunately, the temple is fenced off and partly propped up by scaffolding, with entry forbidden because of "work in progress", a familiar Sicilian refrain. Moreover, in the year 2000 there was a controversial decision made to remove damaged sections of the temple and replace them with replica columns. The architectural establishment reacted to the decision with dismay but, if the temple is to survive it might yet be the best solution. Certainly space to display the originals could be made in the city's well-designed archaeological museum.

The **Tempio di Hera** (Temple of Hera) ❽ surmounts a rocky ridge which formed part of the city ramparts. Known as Juno to the Romans, Hera was protector of engaged and married couples. Fittingly, hers is held to be the most romantic of temples, set "high on the hill like an offering to the goddess". Yet Zeus's sister and wife was perceived as a bloodthirsty goddess, to be appeased by sacrifice at an altar beside the walls. Part of the *cella* and 25 columns remain intact along with the drums of columns; the rest fell over the hill during a landslide. The stones bear reddish traces of fire damage where they were singed by flames.

The Western zone

After retracing your steps to the entrance, cross the road to the **Tempio di Zeus Olimpico** (the Temple of Olympian Zeus) ❾. Even at the peak of its golden age, the temple was unfinished. With the area of a football pitch, it was the largest Doric temple ever known. The U-shaped grooves on the stone blocks represent primitive pulley marks formed during construction. Today's

fallen masonry is a challenge to the imagination: the best stone was plundered to build the port of Empédocle 9 km (5½ miles) away. A frieze on the east side depicted the battle between Zeus (known also to the Romans as Jupiter or Jove, that is, Giove), and the Giants, matched by the War of Troy on the western side.

The facade was supported by 38 *telamons* (columns carved as male figures) – a revolutionary concept for the time. In this way, the weight of the pediment was shared by the giants and by the columns of the peristyle. The *telamons* also had allegorical and aesthetic functions. They both broke up the uniformity of the peristyle and illustrated the war against Zeus; like Atlas, the defeated giants were compelled to carry the world on their shoulders.

A sandstone copy of a *telamon* lies on the ground, dreamily resting his head on his arms, and one of the originals is on display in the archaeological museum. On the temple, these male *giganti* (also known as *atlantes*, or Atlas figures) alternated with female caryatids and represented the three known racial types of the time: African, Asian and European.

Confusing quarter

West of the Temple of Zeus is the most confusing quarter, dotted with shrines dating from pre-Greek times. The Via Sacra leads to the **Tempio di Castore e Polluce** (Temple of Castor and Pollux, or the Dioscuri) ❿, spuriously named after the twin sons of Zeus. Although it has become the city symbol, the building is theatrical pastiche, erected in 1836 from the remains of several temples. Even so, it is a graceful and evocative reconstruction. Locally, the temple is known as **tre colonne**, since only three of the four columns are visible from the city. Despite its name, the temple was first dedicated to Persephone and Demeter, Chthonic (Underworld) deities, along with Dionysus.

This theory is supported by the temples in the surrounding area. Known as the **Sacelli ed Altare delle Divinità** (Sanctuary of the Chthonic Divinities) ⓫, the quarter

Map on page 116

TIP

The temples provide a striking backdrop each February for the annual almond blossom festival (Sagra del Mandorio) and international folk festival. There are parades, shows, crafts exhibits, and a chance to listen to anything from Filipino groups to Scottish pipe bands.

BELOW:
a sleeping giant among the temples.

San Nicola's facade.

conceals sacrificial altars and ditches, a veritable shrine to fertility, immortality and eternal youth. Pale-coloured beasts were offered to the heavens but black animals were sacrificed to the gods of the Underworld. The altars took the form of flat, concentric circles or deep, well-shaped affairs. Now bounded by a gorge and an orange grove, this sanctuary of death was also the fount of life, with lush gardens and a lake full of exotic birds and fish.

Close to Piazzale dei Templi lies **Tomba di Terone** (Theron's Tomb) **⓬**, a tribute to Agrigento's benevolent tyrant. This truncated tower in Doric-Ionic style is essentially a Roman funerary pyramid, more a celebration of conquest than glory to a local hero. Outside the ancient walls is the isolated **Tempio di Asclepio** (Temple of Asclepius) **⓭**, half-hidden in an almond grove. Dedicated to the god of healing, it lies between the river Akragas and a sacred spring. It is of a curious design, with solid walls and no peristyle, possibly because the interior housed chambers for dream inter-pretations as well as wards for recuperation or for taking the waters.

From Piazzale dei Templi, a short drive along Via dei Templi leads to the **Villa Athena** with its restaurant (tel: 0922 596 288), the **museo archeologico** (*see below*) the Hellenistic-Roman quarter and a clutch of pagan shrines. En route are fortifications, a reminder that Agrigento was once enclosed by walls, towers and massive gates, of which the perimeter and craggy foundations remain. The sandy landscape is dotted with olives and pines. Subsidence has created strange slopes and whirling patterns on the soil.

San Nicola **⓮** (daily 9am–6pm) on Via Petrarca, is a Romanesque church with 15th-century cloisters whose severe but grand facade is reminiscent of monuments in ancient Rome. This is not so far-fetched given that the church is built from Greek stone raided from the ruins and also purports to be a Roman temple dedicated to the sun god. A chapel contains the **Sarcophagus of Phaedra**, an exquisitely carved scene of Phaedra's grief at the loss of her lover and stepson Hippolytus.

Regional museum

Next door is the well-presented **Museo Archeologico Regionale** **⓯** (daily 9am–1pm; Wed–Sat 2–5.30pm) incorporating a church, courtyard and temple foundations. The Graeco-Roman section is the centrepiece, along with a Bronze Age urn from a Sican tomb and a three-legged Trinacria, the ancient symbol of Sicily. Exhibits include a wealth of painted Attic vases dating from 5th century BC, Greek lion's-head water spouts, an *ephebe* (Classical youth) and a vibrant Roman mosaic of a gazelle. A poignant marble sarcophagus depicts the death of a child amidst weeping. The highlight is a *telamon* in all its massive glory accompanied by other power-

ful giant heads. Elsewhere are votive offerings and statues associated with orgiastic rites: phallic donkeys compete with a libidinous pigmy and a hermaphrodite.

The **Hellenistic-Roman Quarter** ⑯ (daily 9am–1hr before sunset) lies opposite, an ancient commercial and residential area laid out on a grid system. Whereas the Greeks created the grid system, the Romans overlaid it with a rational arrangement of public and private space. The well-preserved remains of aqueducts, terracotta and stone water channels are visible, as well as vestiges of shops, taverns and patrician villas. The frescoed villas are paved with patterned mosaics protected by glass enclosures.

On the far side of Strada Panoramica is a stretch of Greek walls and **San Biagio** ⑰, a Norman church perched on a rocky platform (currently closed for restoration). It is carved into an ancient temple to Demeter and Persephone. Two circular altars lie between the church and another tribute to the goddess of fertility. At the foot of the cliff is the **Tempio Rupestre di Demetra** (the Rock Sanctuary of Demeter) ⑱, the oldest sanctuary in the valley, dating from the 7th century BC.

When visiting Sicily in 1885, Guy de Maupassant was lucky enough to see the temples without tourists or modern desecration. The writer was struck by their air of "magnificent desolation; dead, arid and yellowing on all sides". Yet with falcons hovering above, lizards scurrying at one's feet, the air heavy with the scent of blossoms, today's landscape throbs with life. ❏

Map on page 116

Popular local dishes are salsiccia al finocchio *(pasta and fennel),* coniglio in agrodolce *(sweet and sour rabbit), and* involtini di pesce spada *(stuffed swordfish). Combinations of shellfish, artichokes, pasta and pilchards are common, as are sweet Arab staples such as* cassata *and* cannoli.

Restaurants

Agrigento

Le Caprice
Via Cavalieri Magazzeni.
Tel: 0922 411 364.
Sicilian specialities in a garden setting. One of Sicily's best restaurants. Delicious array of antipasti and shellfish; tasty swordfish, shrimps and mussels. Pizza at dinner only. Closed Mon in winter. €€€

Concordia
Via Porcello 8.
Tel: 0922 22668.
Good for grilled fish and seafood-based pasta dishes – try the spaghetti with prawns. Reasonably priced fixed menus too. Outdoor seating in summer. Closed Sun in winter. €€

La Corte degli Sfizzi
Via Atenea Cortile Contarini 4. Tel: 0922 602 529.
A trendy and fairly inexpensive restaurant/pizzeria. Several set menus at differing prices. Pizza available at lunchtime. Closed Tues. €€

Da Giovanni
Piazzetta Vadalà 2.
Tel: 0922 21110.
A small restaurant, but if you want to try truly Sicilian dishes, this is the place. Ask to be guided through the menu. Booking essential. Closed Sun and first 2 weeks Jan. €€

Kalos
Piazza San Calogero.
Tel: 0922 26389.
Worth a visit for *involtini di pesce spada* (rolled and stuffed swordfish). Closed Sun. €€€

Per Bacco
Vicolo lo Presti.
Tel: 0922 553369.
A small trattoria that's a favourite with locals, specialising in fish dishes. Dinner only. Closed Mon. €€

Trattoria dei Templi
Via Panoramica dei Templi 15. Tel: 0922 403 110.
Comparatively new establishment with high reputation. Excellent seafood but also good traditional Sicilian meat dishes. Closed Sun in July and Aug; Fri from 1 Jun–end Jun and 2 weeks in Jan. €€€

Villa Athena
Via dei Templi 33.
Tel: 0922 596 288.
www.athenahotels.com
This lovely hotel-restaurant scores highly on atmosphere and fine views across the Valley of the Temples. Wide selection of Sicilian wines and liqueurs. Reservation advisable. Dress code: no jeans or T-shirts. €€€

Bar la Promenade
Via Panoramica dei Templi 8.
Tel: 0922 23715.
A *caffè* and *pasticceria* of note, especially if you like Sicilian specialities made with almonds: cakes, marzipan, granita, ice cream and *latte di mandorla* (a milky almond drink). Closed Tues.

PRICE CATEGORIES

Prices for three-course dinner per person with a half-bottle of house wine:
€ = under €15
€€ = €15–30
€€€ = €30–60

AGRIGENTO PROVINCE

This enigmatic province embraces everything from earthquake-struck towns to spectacular hilltop villages, from mineral spas and coastal forts to the distant Pelagie Islands

People from Agrigento are a mysterious breed, often referred to as *né carne né pesce*, neither fish nor fowl. Yet this elusive province has produced exceptional Sicilians: Empedocles, the pre-Socratic philosopher; Pirandello, the playwright; and Sciascia, the political novelist. All were gifted mavericks who shared a bitter-sweet relationship with their homeland. Empedocles committed suicide on Etna. Pirandello was the master of split personalities. Sciascia called his land a "wicked stepmother" yet rarely left, except to visit Paris.

Outside the capital, Agrigento is barely touched by tourism. There are no obvious sights in this low-key province. Instead, there are myriad chance discoveries of a lesser order: distinctive hill-top towns; deserted Classical sites; coastal fortresses; remnants of former feudal estates; Arab-Norman ports; prosperous vineyards.

The *provincia* also has more than its fair share of unpleasant surprises: shabby towns; suburban sprawl; neglected fields; and the scars left by disused sulphur mines. The province is an inward-looking place whose insularity and lassitude make only a few concessions to visitors' demands for charming hotels, reasonable service and well-maintained roads. Agrigento's additional drawbacks are exceptional poverty, the lingering grip of the Mafia, and a torpor conditioned by centuries of failure.

An eastern foray

The route into the hinterland east of Agrigento passes rugged hill-top towns of Arab origin which were fortified during the Moslem conquest and later. Many of these were sulphur-mining centres until the early 20th century and, despite a

Map on page 126

LEFT: repairing the nets at Sciacca.
BELOW: one of the giant heads made of lava near Castello Bentivegna.

slight agricultural revival or diversification into wine, have yet to recover from the collapse of the traditional industry.

Leaving **Agrigento** ❶ in the direction of Caltanissetta, follow the SS 122 through the rolling countryside to **Favara**, a former sulphur centre, with a dilapidated Chiaramonte castle (rebuilt in 1488 from an original 1275 castle), two 16th-century churches, the **Purgatorio** and the **Rosario**, and an elegantly baroque main square.

From here, choose the hilly road east to the nearby medieval hilltop town of **Naro** ❷, an important agricultural centre. Some of Italy's finest produce passes through Naro. It is an appealing place, with battlement walls (c.1265) enclosing a late-13th-century Chiaramonte castle and some impressive baroque mansions.

Follow the SS 410 south to the sea: the rewarding 17-km (11-mile)

drive lined with olive trees and vineyards leads to **Palma di Montechiaro** ❸ with panoramic views over the coast. The town, with a population of 25,000, may strike a romantic chord with readers of Lampedusa's *The Leopard*. It was established in 1637 by the Prince of Lampedusa, an ancestor of Giuseppe Tommasi di Lampedusa who used much of the life in this town as his inspiration for the novel.

Today, however, the town conjures up a catalogue of Sicilian ills: Mafia intervention, disturbing images of poverty, unemployment, public indifference, despair and dogs. The once splendid late-17th-century **Palazzo Ducale** is crumbling and the town's only dusty glory is the **Chiesa Madre**, built above imposing steps between 1666 and 1703, decaying under the weight of civic inertia. To qualify for funding, the church steps must be restored in the same stone as

Sicily's Carnivale at the beginning of Lent involves entire communities in parades and contests.

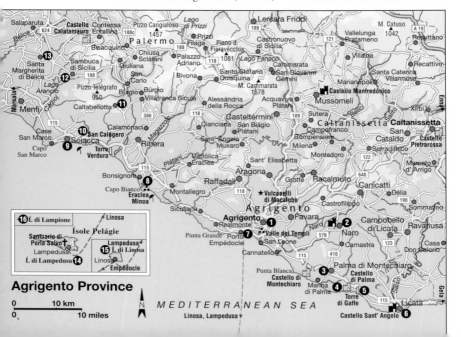

Agrigento Province

0   10 km
0   10 miles

MEDITERRANEAN SEA

Linosa, Lampedusa

Map on page 126

before. However, the original quarry is closed, so Sicilian bureaucracy decrees that renovation is impossible.

About 4 km (2 miles) south, the coastal road ends in the fishing port of **Marina di Palma**. From here, the SS 115 leads back to Agrigento. However, castle aficionados can follow the same road east to see the remains of a string of fortifications along the coast, notably the striking castles of **Castello di Palma** ❹ and, just east, **Torre di Gaffe** ❺.

Licata

Further east still lies sad, unattractive, downtrodden **Licata** ❻, marking the eastern confines of the province. Although a working port (the invading Allied forces landed here in 1943), Licata also has a 16th-century castello, layers of palazzi, the 17th-century convent of **San Francesco** that is now a school and a 17th-century church dedicated to **San Domenico** with two paintings by Filippo Palladini.

The dull **Museo Archeologico** (Mon–Sat 9am–6.30pm, Sun 9am–12.30pm; entrance fee) has prehistoric and Greek period relics. The beach is uninviting.

The southwestern coast

Just outside Agrigento city, the hamlet of **Caos** on the Porto Empédocle road is where Luigi Pirandello, one of Italy's greatest and most wideranging writers, was born in 1867. The irony of the village name was not wasted on Pirandello who called himself a "son of chaos".

The traditional farmhouse in which the "master of the absurd" was born is now a small but pleasing **museum** (daily 9am–1pm, 2–7pm; entrance fee). In 1936, in accordance with his wishes, the playwright's ashes were buried in the countryside. Although this once idyllic spot now overlooks industrial sprawl, Pirandello, whose life was a lesson in defeat snatched from the jaws of victory, would have appreciated his posthumous fall from grace.

Just 7 km (4½ miles) south of Agrigento is **San Leone**, the city's pleasant but unexceptional seaside resort, which a humble fishing village until the 1960s, and **Porto**

Giuseppe di Lampedusa, a Sicilian aristocrat born in 1896, wrote his only novel, Il Gattopardo (The Leopard) a short time before he died in 1957. The action takes place in Sicily in 1860 as the Kingdom of Naples and Sicily is brought to an end by Garibaldi and his army invading Sicily in order to forge a united Italy.

BELOW: the farmland is rich in this province.

Luigi Pirandello

The playwright and novelist, born in Caos in 1867, won the Nobel Prize for Literature in 1934, two years before his death. His pervasive influence on European drama challenged the conventions of the day in their naturalism, personal relationships, disillusionment and reality, and his play *Sei personaggi in cerca di Autore* (Six Characters in Search of an Author), written in 1921, is still in constant repertory around the world. His writings anticipated the works of Brecht, Beckett and O'Neill. His novel *L'Esclusa* (The Outcast) broke all society's rules when published in 1901 as it concerned a woman's desire for independence in Sicily's patriarchal society.

Sciacca has engaging weather-beaten buildings.

BELOW: Eraclea Minoa.

Empédocle ❼, just west of San Leone, an unmitigated blackspot, despite its illustrious past. The port authorities quarried the Classical site for stone to build its harbour walls and, it would seem, in revenge the temple gods cursed it with ugliness. The benighted city with cement works and high-rise buildings should be avoided unless you are taking a ferry trip to the remote **Isole Pelágie** *(see page 131)* and a visit is inevitable.

Fortunately, the SS 115 soon passes through sparsely populated countryside leading to the province's most delightful, but isolated, Classical site. En route are views of the coast, which borders a fertile valley and overlooks neat orange plantations and smoothly contoured fields.

The Classical site of **Eraclea Minoa ❽** (daily 9am–one hour before sunset; entrance fee) squats on bleached soil alongside olive-covered slopes at the mouth of the river Platani. As one looks down from this idyllic headland, there is a view over the white cliffs of **Capo Bianco** emcompassing a crescent of golden sands and pine groves. Eraclea was a satellite of Selinunte but suffered a grim fate at the hands of the Carthaginians when it was depopulated and became a no-man's-land in Greek and Punic territorial disputes. The name Minoa suggests a Minoan settlement and evokes the legend of King Minos of Crete who pursued Daedalus from Crete to Sicily, but the connection is tenuous.

While the site is delightful and the atmosphere therapeutic, the excavations have been laborious and the results far from spectacular. So far, Eraclea has revealed substantial city walls, a Hellenistic theatre (4 BC), a necropolis, and ruined villas dating from Greek and Punic times. Concerts and productions of classical drama are put on in July and August (tel: 0922 846005).

Sciacca

Further along the coast is Sciacca ❾, a working fishing port with a population of 42,000, many of Arab descent. The town was evangelised by San Calógero and prospered in Arab times thanks to its location,

Leonardo Sciascia

Sciascia (1921–89), born at Racalmuto, remained emotionally tied to Sicily all his life and said he had never left the island for more than three months (then generally to Paris). He was an intellectual and one of the greatest Italian writers of the 20th century, and his novels were infused with Sicilian life that revolved around the sulphur mines and the farms. His most famous novels include *Il Giorno della Civetta* (The Day of the Owl, 1961) and *A ciascuno il suo* (To each his own, 1966). In *The Moro Affair* he tackled the murky world of Italian politics in the 1970s. A Communist Party member of Palermo City Council, he later became a member of the European Parliament.

midway between Mazara and Agrigento. Its name derives from the Arabic *As-saqah*, meaning "cleft" – a reference to the caves of Mount Kronion whose thermal springs were to make the area an important spa.

In the 16th century Sciacca was torn apart by two warring families, the Norman Perollo and the Catalan Luna, and it suffered a gradual decline until the revival of the port and mineral spa, aided by an injection of Mafia funds and its close links with North Africa.

Sciacca lacks great architecture, but some exhilarating sea views and an engaging ensemble of tawny, weather-beaten buildings justify a visit to the town.

Corso Vittorio Emanuele, the main street, has sumptuous palazzi from all periods, including a Moorish mansion converted into a jeweller's, one of many which used to belong to the landed gentry. The loveliest civic building there is the **Palazzo Steripinto** (1501), with a crenellated facade of diamond-shaped design, a rusticated style borrowed from Neapolitan architecture.

The terrace of **Piazza Scandaliato** is the bustling baroque centre of both the town and the Corso. Its scenic balcony is perfect for drinking in the views of the sea over an *aperitivo*. On summer evenings, the square belongs to Tunisian hawkers (unless moved on by the police) selling exotic clothes, leather goods and local ceramics.

The **Duomo** (daily 8.30am–6pm) presents a confused image, with Arab-Norman apses buried in a baroque facade. It was built in 1656, replacing a church erected in 1108. It has considerable charm as well as statues by Antonino and Gian Domenico Gagini.

The neighbouring **Museo Scaglione** (Wed & Fri 9am–1.30pm, 3–7pm) was established in 1988 in the **Palazzo Scaglione** with works of art collected in the 19th century by Francesco Scaglione. Exhibits include paintings, ceramics, sculpture and a much admired 18th-century crucifix.

From Piazza Scandaliato, steps lead down to the port and numerous fish restaurants. After the slightly oppressive hinterland, visitors tend

Map on page 126

TIP

Two of Sciacca's best beaches, combining fine sand with clear water, are the San Marco and the Contrada Sobareto. The tourist resort of Torre Macauda, 9 km (5½ miles) to the east of town, is not overpriced and has unspoiled beaches. The open-air pool in its thermal spa is available to visitors in summer.

BELOW: the Moorish port of Sciacca.

After the Saracens invaded Sicily in the 9th century, Sciacca became the main port for the export of grain to North Africa, and the town's fishing industry thrived as well. In 1101 Count Roger bequeathed the town to his daughter, Juliet. She replaced the mosques with Christian churches and monasteries.

to appreciate this forthright, living town, noted in the province for its sandy beaches, spa waters and for seafood platters.

Sciacca's churches embrace all periods and styles. **San Calógero** and **San Domenico** are sober baroque works while the **Convento di San Francesco** combines clean lines with Moorish cloisters. The **Chiesa del Carmine** is a Norman abbey with a Gothic rose window and half-hearted baroque restoration. Facing is a sculpted medieval gate and the Gothic portal of **Santa Margherita**.

To the east is the ruined Romanesque **San Nicolò** church which contrasts with **Santa Maria della Giummare**, a Catalan Gothic church with crenellated Norman towers and a baroque interior. Just within the walls is the **Badia Grande**, an impressive 14th-century abbey.

Set among almond and olive groves just 2 km (1¼ miles) outside Sciacca, **Castello Bentivegna** (May–Sept 10am–noon, 4–8pm; Oct–Apr 9am–1pm, 3–5pm; closed Mon) is also called the "enchanted castle". It is a folly in stone created

by a peasant sculptor, a forest of statues that is the work of one man. In 1946, after great personal tragedy, Filippo Bentivegna returned from the United States and bought a patch of land in his native town. Using the rocks at the foot of Monte Kronio as his material, he sculpted 3,000 primitive heads of devils, politicians and knights. Not content with his work above ground, the sculptor set about carving heads from olive wood and creating frescoed caverns in the mountain. Bentivegna died in 1967.

The Sciacca spa, known to the Romans as Thermae Selinuntinae, is open from April to November. Used since prehistoric times and praised by Pliny, the spa's mud baths and volcanic vapours are available in a grand Art Nouveau establishment that attracts well-heeled Italians with promises of cures for rheumatic and respiratory conditions.

Just north is the **San Calógero** ❿ spa on Monte Kronio that harnesses the powers of a "mini" volcano, with bubbling hot springs and vapour-drenched grottoes used as saunas. The galleries, seats and water channels were hollowed out in ancient times by the Sicani or, according to the myth-makers, by Daedalus. The place takes its name from a saint particularly venerated in these parts as he was patron of the harvest.

The rugged west

From Sciacca, a circular route and winding road leads 20 km (12 miles) inland, up to the mysterious mountain village of **Caltabellotta** ⓫, the highlight of this rural route, with its cluster of towers, churches, grey roofs and a population of 4,500. The commanding village is spectacular, whether seen through spring blossom or swathed in mist. On the highest level, below the hulk of the ruined castle, is the Norman **Chiesa Madre** with its original portal and pointed arches fully restored for the

BELOW: Filippo Bentivegna's heads carved from lava.

year 2000. On the level underneath is the lopsided **Piazza Umberto** and the handsome **Chiesa del Carmine**, which has also been restored recently. Below stretch shadowy mountain views from the spacious **Belvedere** and the white **Chiesa San Agostino**. The peace that brought the Sicilian Vespers to an end in 1302 was signed here. On the edge of the village lies the **Eremo di San Pellegrino**, an abandoned hermitage with stupendous views of a mountainside studded with necropoli. Legend has it that a dragon lived here and feasted on young maidens until killed by the saint.

Sambuca di Sicilia

Northwest of Caltabellotta, but linked by circuitous country roads, is **Sambuca di Sicilia** ⑫, an Arab-Norman town with its old centre near Piazza Navarro showing its Islamic antecedents. There is also a popular lake and facilities for watersports and barbecues. Amateur archaeologists are drawn to the neighbouring Zona Archeologica di **Monte Adranone**, where the remains of a Greek colony have recently come to light, as well as huts and burial chambers from an Iron Age village.

Further west still is **Santa Margherita di Bélice** ⑬, bordering Palermo and Trápani provinces. In recent times it has become better known as the epicentre of the earthquake zone. Between here and the coast lies **Menfi**, another earthquake-damaged town, and a centre for the province's winemaking.

Isole Pelágie

This remote, sun-baked archipelago of three islands lies amid strong currents off the North African coast, closer to Tunisia's Cap Bon than the Sicilian mainland. Although there are pockets of agriculture, the islands are unnaturally barren, an ecological

disaster, due to wanton deforestation, neglect, water shortages and strong winds that have caused a virtual disappearance of the native olive groves and juniper and carob plantations. Fifty years ago, much of this lunar landscape was farmland bounded by drystone walls but today the local economy rests on fishing, from sponge fishing to canning, supplemented by Lampedusa's developing tourist industry. However, the islanders have belatedly realised the error of their unecological ways and have started small-scale forestation programmes.

In terms of cultural heritage, there are no outstanding sites but the waters are translucent and rich with marine life, while the rugged native character and cuisine are distinctly Tunisian. Highlights of a stay on this Sicilian outpost include Moorish *dammusi* houses in local stone, excellent couscous and, of course, fish, as well as quiet coastal walks. Except for the summer months in Lampedusa, peace and quiet reigns. Although in the winter the islanders turn in on themselves, in summer

Map on page 126

TIP

Getting to the Isole Pelágie:
There is a direct air link to Lampedusa's airport from Palermo, as well as Catania and Trápani in summer. Regular Siremar ferries sail from Porto Empédocle, outside Agrigento. Siremar tel: 0922 636 777. www.siremar.it An extra seasonal hydrofoil service links Lampedusa to Linosa. Ustica Lines: tel: 0923 873813. www.usticalines.it

BELOW: Caltabellotta.

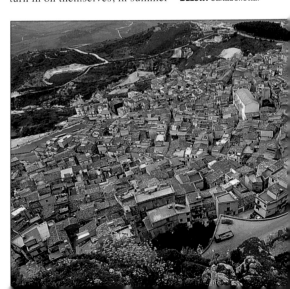

they are extremely welcoming. A curious feature of the islands in summer is the virtually continuous breeze and the chilly nights.

Lampedusa

Due to its location, **Lampedusa**  is known as "a gift from Africa to Europe" or, thanks to its recent popularity with illegal immigrants, "the backdoor into Italy". Today there is a population of around 6,000.

The island was first settled by the Phoenicians and Greeks but was later owned by the Princes of Lampedusa. The family turned down a bid for ownership by Queen Victoria in favour of one by Ferdinand II of Bourbon in 1843 and the Bourbons soon populated it with Sicilians. These, however, have mostly been assimilated or usurped by weather-beaten Tunisian fishermen, who live on the south coast. Sponge fishing is the mainstay of the island's economy, with a local cannery used to process a wide range of Mediterranean fish.

The Allies bombed Lampedusa in 1943 as a prelude to invading Sicily and the rest of Italy. Since then, the island's greatest claim to fame has been its use as a US radar base for a bombing raid on Libya. In 1986 a Libyan launch fired rockets at the island base in retaliation for the American bombing of Tripoli. In fact, Gaddafi's missiles landed harmlessly in the sea, but the Italian government was concerned enough to order the closure of the US base. In recent years Lampedusa has been in the Italian newspaper and television headlines again with regularity as boatloads of illegal immigrants (known generally as *clandestini*) are caught landing on the island's more remote beaches, intending to make their way to the Italian mainland.

Lampedusa port, with its ferry service to Porto Empédocle and nearby Linosa, contains a rabbit-warren of a casbah that reeks of spices, sardines and anchovies. Indeed, the port is the best place for sampling such distinctive dishes as pasta with sardines, sweet and sour rabbit or typical Sicilian candied fruit and spicy desserts. Buses from the port are infrequent so, despite the rocky roads, bicycles and mopeds are a popular way of exploring the interior.

At the centre of the island is **Santuario di Porto Salvo**, a church in a lush garden draped in bougainvillaea and surrounded by grottos that was once home to Saracen pirates. The white-steepled sanctuary contains a venerated statue of the **Madonna**, paraded on the saint's feast day every September. Other corners of the island that have escaped deforestation include the cove of **Cala Galera**, which has pockets of pine and Phoenician juniper. While the interior can be explored by bicycle, a boat trip is the best way of appreciating Lampedusa's secluded grottos, craggy inlets and sheer limestone cliffs. The island of **Conigli**, just off shore, is a nature reserve with the **Baia dell' Isola degli Conigli** (Bay

The "sponge king" of Lampedusa.

BELOW:
Lampedusa port.

of the Island of Rabbits), the island's greatest attraction.

Linosa

Linosa ⓯ (pop. 500) is the island closest to Sicily and can be reached on a day trip from Lampedusa, 42 km (26 miles) to the north. The island is formed by the tips of three vast submerged volcanos (**Monte Vulcano**, **Monte Nero** and **Monte Rosso**), the last link in a volcanic chain that stretches to Mount Vesuvius outside Naples. Although the three visible volcanic cones are now extinct, the beaches still strewn with black boulders show their origins and can coat every visitor with black volcanic ash and grit. Even so, despite the summer heat, most visitors congregate on the lava grit beaches or quickly develop an interest in scuba-diving.

There is little to do here except rest, roast, swim, trek along dusty paths through vineyards or spot *dammusi*, the pastel-coloured cubelike houses with white window frames. These traditional Arab houses date back to designs created by the first Tunisian settlers. The domed roofs are designed to keep the interior cool. Massimo Errera (tel: 0922 972 082) organises trips around the island as well as days trekking and excursions to the craters.

About two hours by boat from Lampedusa, **Lampione** ⓰ is an uninhabited island, with a modest area of just 1.5 sq km (370 acres), scorched dry thanks to man's negligence. Its drama lies underwater: the translucent sea is unpolluted and rich in marine life, from sponge beds to basking sharks. Sicilian pleasures are notoriously double-edged. ❑

Volcanic Linosa is far more fertile than Lampedusa, and produces carobs, whose leathery pods are made into animal fodder, fertiliser or a chocolate substitute.

Restaurants

Caltabellotta

Trattoria La Ferla
Via Colonnello Vita.
Tel: 0925 951 444.
A lovely restaurant with authentic rural cuisine in a scenic village in the mountains. Closed Mon and two weeks which vary every year. €€

Sciacca

The best fish restaurants are in the lower town, near the port, and are mostly inexpensive. While in Sciacca try the *tabisca*, a traditional local pizza with onion and cheese.

Le Gourmet Verso
Via Monte Kronio 7, at San Calogero. Tel 0925 26460
legourmet@tin.it

Classic Sicilian cooking. Locals come here for fish. Garden. Closed Tues and Nov. €€€

Hostaria del Vicolo
10 Vicolo Sammaritano.
Tel: 0925 23071.
Unpretentious establishment, but known for its gastronomic approach to food and wine. Good pasta and seafood. Extensive selection of wine. Closed Mon and Nov. €€€

Miramare
Piazza Scandagliato 6.
Tel: 0925 26050.
Wide variety of special fish dishes and also excellent pizza. With fine sea views from the terrace. €€

Lampedusa

Al Gallo d'Oro
Via Vittorio Emanuele 45.

Tel: 0922 971297.
A friendly trattoria with excellent fish dishes, as well as some Arab-inspired options. Closed Nov–Easter. €€€

Gemelli
Via Cala Pisana 2.
Tel: 0922 970 699.
milano@ristorantegemelli.it
Close to the airport. Excellent dishes typical of the island, including dishes of Arab origin, are served under a delightful pergola. Dinner only. Open June–end Oct. €€€

Lipadusa
Via Bonfiglio 12.
Tel: 0922 971 691.
At the heart of the island, serving ambitious local cuisine. Dinner only. Open Easter–end Oct. €€€

Grand Caffè Royal
Via Roma 83.
Tel: 0922 971 032.
Join the locals for home-made ice cream and granita. €

Linosa

Anna
Via Vittorio Veneto 1.
Tel: 0922 972 048.
www.linosavacanze.it
Simple, inexpensive trattoria that also has rooms to rent. Good home cooking. Closed winter. €€

PRICE CATEGORIES

Prices for three-course dinner per person with a half-bottle of house wine:
€ = under €15
€€ = €15–30
€€€ = €30–60

FESTIVALS SACRED AND PROFANE

Christianity and paganism, historical memory and folk tradition all combine without inhibition in Sicily's frequent and fervent celebrations

Many Sicilian festivals mark a historical event with an overlay of religious worship.

Palermo's feast of Santa Rosalia, for instance, celebrates the saint reputedly saving the city from plague in 1624 with a mixture of prayer and wild festivities. Other *feste*, although tied to the Christian calendar, have pagan elements lurking just beneath the surface. Thus *Carnevale* (literally "farewell to meat") marks the beginning of Lent and a period of abstinence, but is celebrated in many towns and cities with a licentious abandon that echoes the ancient Saturnalia.

Easter is the dominant Christian festival, but is celebrated in a variety of forms: processions of *tableaux vivants* or holy relics, re-enactments of the Passion by chosen citizens, respects paid to the *Addolorata* (Our Lady of the Sorrows), and often more obscure rites besides. On Easter Sunday in Prizzi, for instance, the *Abballu de li diavoli* has devils in grotesque masks, led by Death himself, trying to prevent the Madonna meeting the resurrected Christ. It's a dramatic reworking of the Christian story, but also an unconscious echo of Lupercalia, a distinctly demonic pre-Christian festival.

LEFT: the Greek tradition is easily detected in festivals celebrated in the style of the Eastern Byzantine Church in Piana degli Albanesi, an enclave of Greek Orthodoxy.

ABOVE: the Easter procession in Trápani tours the town for 20 hours non-stop, from early afternoon on Good Friday, through the night until Saturday morning.

ABOVE: in Enna on Good Friday, 2,000 white-hooded members of the medieval fraternities hold a procession in total silence.

SECULAR CELEBRATIONS

Not all of Sicily's *feste* have a religious basis. Historical events, real or imagined, are commemorated with equal gusto throughout the island. In Adrano, Piazza Armerina and elsewhere, the exploits of Roger II are recalled with medieval pageants involving a great deal of flag-waving, jousting and other pseudo-Norman jollity.

The *Festa della Castellana* in Cáccamo sees a procession of 500 costumed characters representing notables in the town's history.

The stars of Messina's annual procession *(above)* are two giants, Grifone and Mata, the mythical founders of the city, represented by ancient 8-metre (26-ft) mounted wooden figures.

The first signs of spring are excuse enough for a festival in many places, including Agrigento, where, in February, the *Sagra del Mandorlo in fiore* celebrates the blossoming of the almond trees.

LEFT: Palermo's foremost festival is *U Fistinu*, six long days of fireworks, processions and general mayhem. It's all carried out in the name of Santa Rosalia.

BELOW: in Agrigento, on the feast of San Calógero, bread rolls are baked to be thrown to the crowds – literally a bun fight.

RIGHT: these sugar statues promote sweet memories. They are made to be eaten beside the graves of ancestors at *I Morti*, the bizarre Festival of the Dead celebrated on All Saints' Day in Palermo.

CALTANISSETTA PROVINCE

At the heart of Sicily's west, this dramatic, often wild, landscape is a beguiling place with its craggy scenery, traditional customs and Mafia lore

The **provincia di Caltanissetta** is a place of subtle moods rather than specific sights. Although from the hilltop villages there are spectacular views of mountain ridges and purple canyons, abandoned farms and ruined Norman castles, the province is sparsely populated and a visitor is often alone with this beguiling scenery.

"This is ancient Sicily, the land of *latifundia* (feudal estates), sulphur mines, hunger and insecurity", wrote the French writer Dominique Fernandez, relishing the feeling of its desolation and lawlessness.

A province betrayed

Caltanissetta occupies a central position on a sulphur-bearing plain, its yellowish soil scarred with disused mines. Yet the province is far from uniform. There is a difference in character between the siege mentality of the bleak hilltop towns and the more accessible Greek flavour of Gela's coastal plains. This is a province that feels betrayed by recent history: just as the sulphur mines brought hardship and a high mortality rate to the hinterland, so coastal industrialisation brought pollution but not prosperity, and mass emigration brought depopulation and despair. Although not the most poverty-stricken province, Caltanis-

setta is arguably the most aggrieved.

Caltanissetta ❶, the provincial capital with a population of around 63,000, is a harsh summation of the region's struggle for survival. Its name reflects its cosmopolitan past: Arab conquerors added the prefix *kalat* (Arab for castle) to the name *an-nisa*, meaning ladies. The first documented reference to the city is dated 1086 when Conte Ruggero (Roger the Norman) took the region under the jurisdiction of the Catholic church, conquered the fort of

Map
on page
138

LEFT: Umberto I gazes at Caltanissetta.
BELOW: the Fountain of the Tritons, Caltanissetta.

Pietrarossa and established the abbey of Santo Spirito. As befits an ancient bastion on hilly ground, it is a closed city, its defences raised against outsiders. Modern war damage means that medieval monuments are restricted to the outskirts, along with the original Greek settlements. Architecturally, the city is mostly 19th-century, with only the occasional baroque monument to relieve the blandness.

Nonetheless, Caltanissetta is no mere market town but the agricultural heart of Sicily's interior, with grain and cotton long grown in the countryside. As the historical hub of Sicilian mining operations, the city fell into decline in the 1960s with the collapse of the sulphur industry. Potassium and magnesium mining have now supplanted sulphur and the city has achieved modest prosperity. Still, life here has always been tough, even by Sicilian standards. Although the grinding poverty is no

This province is well known for its terracotta pottery.

more, the city today appears characterised by a wilful torpor verging on deadly passivity that even colours Caltanissetta's approach to crime.

Mafia lore

As the headquarters of the Criminal Justice magistrates courts, Caltanissetta is entrusted with trying the most controversial Mafia cases. Ironically, the province is itself tainted by Mafia association, while local citizens have been, arguably, the most reluctant to express the resurgence in civic values that characterises optimistic new Sicily.

In 1992, despite public dismay, the town was entrusted with the investigation into the murder of Judge Falcone, his wife and bodyguards *(see page 37)*. Much to the astonishment of American FBI agents cooperating on the case, Caltanissetta magistrates hoped to compete with the Mafia without access to a computer. Despite its presumed

Caltanissetta Province

0   10 km
0   10 miles

MEDITERRANEAN SEA

probity, the city's magistrates court remains Sicily's most understaffed and overworked. Cynics may say that this is intentional, giving *mafiosi* suspects a head start.

City sights

Caltanissetta's heart, in so far as it has one, lies in Piazza Garibaldi. Here, the baroque **Duomo** (1570–1622) flanked by bell towers, overlooks the ugly neo-Romanesque church of **San Sebastiano**, the baroque Town Hall and a bronze statue of Neptune. The cathedral interior is an engaging explosion of kitsch, highlighted by sugary ceiling paintings by Wilhelm Borremans (1720) the Flemish painter. In chapels to the right of the nave, saints in glittering glass cases compete for attention. A triumphal angel and cherubs adorn a gaudy glass and gold coffin, a Sicilian disguise for a rotting corpse.

Behind the Town Hall, Via Palazzo Paterno leads to the crumbling **Palazzo Moncada**. This was the home of the Moncada dynasty, the feudal rulers of the region from 1406 onwards. The baroque mansion is emblazoned with snarling lions posing as gargoyles. Emblematic of Sicily, the building was never finished and its leisurely "restoration programme" implies that it never will be.

Corso Umberto, the main street, is lined with dark, dilapidated buildings and scruffy bars. Oblivious to the rain, wizened men congregate outside to discuss politics or building permits. Inside, dry-tasting pastries are washed down with *Amaro*, a reminder that Caltanissetta is the main producer of this famous *digestivo*. The unwelcoming atmosphere is pervasive since the **Nisseni**, the locals, are suspicious of outsiders. The remaining sights are quickly dispensed with, unless you wish to stay and sample the local speciality: *stigliole*, stuffed kid's entrails.

The **Museo Archeologico** (daily 9am–1pm, 3.30–7pm; closed last Sun of month; entrance fee), on Via Napoleone Colajanni, has prehistoric and Greek remains from local settlements, including rock tombs. Finest are the Attic vases, painted

Map on page 138

The highlight of Easter Week in Caltanissetta is the Maundy Thursday procession of the Mysteries of the Passion, with sculptures borne by representatives of the ancient guilds. The mournful dirges of the cortege are a throwback to Arab and Greek cultures.

BELOW: fountain in Caltanissetta's Piazza Garibaldi.

The Sulphur Mines

At the height of demand for sulphur in the 19th century, mainly from Britain and France, more than two-thirds of all of Sicily's production came from sulphur mines in the Caltanissetta region. But aggressively marketed production from the United States destroyed its competitiveness and, by 1945 the industry had collapsed, causing widespread emigration. Today it is possible to visit a number of mines and see the long corridors where the dangerous extraction and processing were carried out. Many of the workers sent to the narrowest and deepest shafts were boys under 15. There are sites at Delia, Montedoro, Sommatino, Riesi and San Cataldo.

BELOW:
candles are held in Caltanissetta's Procession of the Royal Craftsmen, a tradition that dates to the Middle Ages.

urns, a terracotta model of a temple and the earliest Bronze Age figures found in Sicily.

Around the capital

Fortunately, the disappointing provincial capital is a stone's throw from several significant medieval or prehistoric sites which, although neglected, are worthy of more than cursory interest. **Santa Maria degli Angeli**, on the city's eastern outskirts, is a ruined Norman church with a richly carved Gothic porch. Almost next door is the stump of **Castello di Pietrarossa**, perched on a jagged spur, the city's most dramatic monument. Frederick II sought refuge in this baronial fiefdom during his battle for supremacy with the Chiaramonte and Ventimiglia dynasties. However, the 1567 earthquake tossed the Norman-Arab castle into its present pitiful heap. Further east, the **Abbazia di Santo Spirito**, established by King Roger in 1153, has some pleasing 15th-century frescoes.

Five km (3 miles) south of Caltanissetta on the San Cataldo to Pietraperzia road, lies the **necropolis** of **Monte Gibil Gabel**, (the Mountain of the Dead, in Arabic). This prehistoric site was also home to a Hellenised settlement, the original site of Nissa. Tumbledown fortifications remain, together with prehistoric and Greek tombs carved into the rock. The necropolis is open on request at the gate, 9am–1pm.

On the flanks of **Monte Sabbucina** lies a more impressive prehistoric necropolis, even if the best finds are now in Caltanissetta's Museo Archeologico. Take the SS 122 road from Caltanissetta to Enna, leaving town through the barren Terra Pilata. The road crosses the Salso river at **Ponte Capodarso**, a delicate 16th-century Venetian bridge: 6 km (4 miles) along the Enna road, a scenic route is marked to the archaeological park of **Sabbucina** ❷ (9am–sunset). This Bronze Age settlement was later occupied by Hellenised Siculi (Sicel) tribes, who flourished here from the 6th to the 4th centuries BC. The Sicels lived within a square-towered fortress, parts of which sur-

vive. The remains include boundary walls, defensive towers, a sanctuary, two wells, the tracery of grid patterns and house foundations.

The wild west

A sweeping circular route west of Caltanissetta passes a series of shabby but atmospheric hill towns. Settlements were traditionally restricted to hill tops, whether castles or fortified towns, both for defensive purposes and as refuge from the malaria-infested plains. It was common practice for farm-workers to commute to the country from their home villages.

As for the fortresses, although feuding barons once inhabited these lofty strongholds, depopulation and desolation have turned many into virtual ghost towns. From such windswept eyries stretch views of ravines and deserted plains, sulphurous hills and abandoned mines.

Santa Caterina Villarmosa ❸, 20 km (12 miles) north of Caltanissetta along the SS 122 *bis*, is worth a cursory glance if you are interested in looking at lace and delicate embroidery, the town's main claim to fame.

Villalba ❹, about 35 km (22 miles) west, just off the SS 121, is a notoriously down-at-heel Mafia haunt, once held by Don Calógero Vizzini. Vizzini was the main Mafia boss from 1942 until his death in 1954 and as mayor he ran this scruffy town like a private fiefdom. His tombstone in Villalba cemetery laments the death of a gentleman and praises his Robin Hood status as a defender of the weak.

Even before the rise of the Mafia, Villalba was doomed to be forever milked by absentee landlords whose revenues from the production of wine and grain here provided them with a noble lifestyle in Palermo. Once a ducal hunting estate, Villalba is just one of the seemingly inaccessible settlements that characterise Caltanissetta province. Along with

other local Norman towns, it was a source of cheap labour for the feudal estate of Micciche, now known as **Regaleali**. The Regaleali wines, produced these days by Count Tasca d'Almerita, have overtaken many of the Corvo and Donnafugata wines in terms of popularity.

More than most surrounding market towns, **Mussomeli ❺**, 20 km (12 miles) south of Villalba, has suffered from Mafia mythology and emigration. New York received some of Mussomeli's finest Mafia members in the 1960s.

Just east of town, on the Villalba road, stands **Castello Manfredónico**, named after Manfredi Chiaramonte, Frederick II's son, killed defending his kingdom against Charles of Anjou. Set on an impregnable crag, the lopsided castle blends into the rock. From the fortress are vertiginous views over the desolate valley below.

Mussomeli has always lived dangerously. This was the home town and political base of Don Genco Russo, the Mafia overlord from 1954, after Vizzini's death, until the

Map on page 138

TIP

Regaleali, the noted wine producers near Vallelunga, run traditional cookery courses on their estate. Guests stay on the estate, living with members of Conte Tasca d'Almerita's family. Most courses are taught in English or Italian. Details: Regaleali Cookery School, Viale Principessa Giovanna 9, Mondello, Palermo. Tel: 091 450727. www.tascadalmerita.it

BELOW: Castello Manfredónico.

Don Genco Russo, based in Mussomeli, was one of the Mafia's capo di tutti capi *after the death of Calógero Vizzini.*

late 1960s. Mafia expert Clare Sterling described him as a masterly political fixer despite being "a coarse, sly, half-illiterate ruffian loved by none". Known as Zi Peppi Jencu (Uncle Joe the Little Bull), he helped organise the Sicilian takeover of the American heroin cartel.

During his trial in the 1960s, the Don presented a petition with 7,000 signatures from Mussomeli alone. The petition claimed the Don had "dedicated his life to our welfare, setting an example in probity and rectitude". According to Sterling, the trial's turning point came with the threatened publication of telegrams from 37 Christian Democrat deputies, one of them a Cabinet Minister, politely thanking the Mafia's *capo di tutti capi* for helping them get elected. Don Genco Russo was acquitted and died a natural death in Mussomeli in 1976.

The country road zigzags south for 13 km (8 miles) to **Sutera** ❻, the first of several ragged towns set on rocky outcrops in old mining country around Caltanissetta. Beyond a series of acrobatic bends lies Sutera's shadow, **Bompensiere** ❼. (From Sutera, follow the SS 189 south for 4 km/2½ miles before taking the rural road east towards Caltanissetta.) **Serradifalco** ❽, 15 km (9 miles) east, is another neglected hill-top town, linked across a ridge to Villalba. **San Cataldo** ❾, nestling in wooded hills to the east, was once the administrative heart of a great agricultural estate, but is today noted for its crafts, especially terracotta pots and wrought ironwork. Nearby is the archeological site of **Vassallaggi** (9am–1pm) where there are traces of a Greek settlement.

South to the coast

Sinuous upland roads link the craggy countryside on the Gela plains to the south. The higher peaks are covered in mountainous vegetation but the wooded slopes soon give way to olives and almonds. The journey passes sleepy towns with populations reduced by emigration. They share a battered rural economy and dignified poverty. **Sommatino**, **Riesi** and **Niscemi** are typical of such spots, though the ruined castle

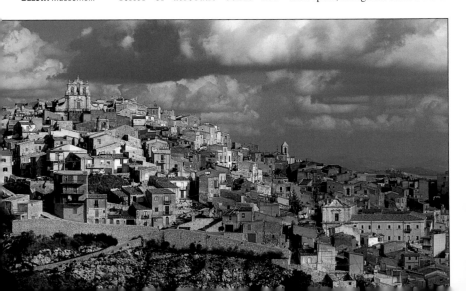

at **Délia** ❿ helps distinguish it from its neighbours.

From Caltanissetta, the SS 626 bridges the rugged hinterland and the coastal plains towards Gela. **Mazzarino** ⓫ lies 10 km (6 miles) east of the main thoroughfare, reached along the SS 190. The town's modest reputation rests on Mafia lore and a ruined **castle**. Founded by the princes of Butera, the castle retains its original keep and some defensive walls.

Ragged palazzi and a couple of undervalued churches add to the atmosphere of gentle nostalgia. **Chiesa San Domenico** contains a touching *Madonna* by Paladino while **Chiesa dei Carmelitani** houses an 18th-century marble tabernacle encrusted with ivory, ebony, coral and tortoiseshell.

In the 1960s this bedraggled country town hit the headlines as a Mafia stronghold run by a licentious abbot. Tales of the friars' orgiastic lifestyles were rife, gleefully embroidered by the press. Sensationalism aside, the good friars were far from blameless and admitted their Mafia ties. The Mazzarino friars acted as messengers between the Mafia and their victims. At their trial in 1962, the friars were accused of extortion, intimidation and murder, as well as the creation and distribution of pornography. Under cross-examination, they admitted to writing some of the blackmail and ransom notes "but only because the *mafiosi* were illiterate and did not own a typewriter". Allegedly, verbal threats were delivered via the confessional.

Butera

Butera ⓬, a crumbling hill village perched on a chalky crest 18 km (11 miles) south, is the most attractive in the province. The fief prospered under Spanish rule, held by the Branciforte family, the Princes of

Butera. Although currently closed, the battlemented 11th-century castle is fairly well preserved, with a powerful keep and mullioned windows. The **Chiesa Madre** has a Paladino *Madonna* and a Renaissance tryptich. Nearby, the **Palazzo Comunale** (Town Hall) has an intricate 14th-century portal and panoramic views over the Gela plains to the coast.

Butera was a former Sicani colony, heavily marked by the Hellenistic influence at Gela. Sanctuaries, funerary rites and fortifications in the region owe much to Greek influence. North of town, **step tombs** dating from the 8th century BC attest to this, their doors decorated with Greek spiral shapes.

Just east of Butera as the crow flies is **Lago di Disueri** ⓭, a dam with a late Bronze Age necropolis on its rocky shores.

Southeast of Butera, on the SS 117 *bis*, the curious mound of **Il Castelluccio** ⓮ presents a dramatic break in the fertile Gela plains. This tumbledown castle keep, jutting out of fields of artichokes and wheat, was built by the warlike Frederick II.

At the Chiesa Madre, Mazzarino.

BELOW:
on the battlements of Butera Castle.

The lure of quick commissions attracted the finest Greek literary and artistic talents to affluent Sicily. Among them was the founder of Greek tragic drama, the Athenian playwright Aeschylus, who died an extraordinary death at Gela in 456 BC. An eagle seized a tortoise and, looking down from a great height for a rock on which to drop and break it, mistook Aeschylus's bald pate for a polished stone. That was the end of the tragedian.

BELOW:
Castello di Falconara.

Nearby is a modern **war memorial**, a reminder that these fields witnessed the Allied landing in Sicily in 1943. Il Castelluccio overlooks the fertile **Gela plain**, rich in grain, wine and olives as well as artichokes and oranges, lemons and cotton.

This land of plenty was once an open invitation to the Greeks, the first and most welcome wave of settlers. **Gela** ⓯ is often called the only truly creative Greek colony. It was renowned for its entrepreneurial spirit, inspired military architecture and artistic excellence. It became a Doric colony in 688 BC, settled by Greeks from Rhodes and Crete. However, the indigenous Sicani tribe transmuted the superior Greek culture into a unique shape. Exquisite coins, terracotta figurines, sculpted walls, and flourishing agriculture remain a testament to these times.

From here, Hellenistic influence spread to the rest of Sicily. Yet Gela was sacked by the Carthaginians in 405 BC, a year after Agrigento's fall, and was eventually razed by the Tyrant of Agrigento in 282 BC, who deported the entire population. The

most recent devastation was in 1943 when the Allies liberated Sicily and, in the process, bombed Gela to smithereens. Arguably, even more recent industrialisation has been its ultimate desecration, its environment ruined, sacrificed to the northern Italian economy. The city is hideous and only those with a passion for Greek archaeology will brave the polluted outskirts. But, that said, it is prosperous again due to its industry and massive oil refinery and, with this regeneration of wealth, local youth are no longer moving to cities or mainland Italy for work and few bemoan their new-found wealth.

Unlike the hill towns of the interior, Gela has no tradition of aristocratic rule. As a result, it has no castles or noble *palazzi*, nothing between its glorious Greek heritage and today's grim sprawl. Still it is worth sifting through the industrial debris to reach the ancient city. Occupying the western slopes of Gela, the main archaeological site presents a strange contrasting scene. The walls built by Timoleon, the good Tyrant of Siracusa, are set amongst mimosa, eucalyptus and pines; just beyond the sand dunes are futuristic domes and glittering pipes of modern power generation.

The **Museo Archaeologico** (daily 9am–1.30pm, 2–7pm; entrance fee), on Corso Vittorio Emanuele, is built alongside the ancient **Molino a Vento** acropolis, with its recently excavated remains of Hellenistic houses open to inspection. The museum itself displays painted Attic vases, coins, Ionic capitals and terracotta sarcophagi. Gela terracotta was renowned throughout *Magna Graecia*, prized for its painted designs and the delicacy of the figurative work. The star piece is a noble terracotta horse's head from the 6th century BC, part of a temple pediment. **Parco della Rimembranza**, close by, is a park with a single Doric

column, the remains of a temple to Athena. From here, there are views over the Gela plain, embracing the long horizon of the Golfo di Gela (Gulf of Gela) and the Mediterranean, marred by the industrial mass on the beach below.

Outside the city, the 5th-century BC walls and the site of **Capo Soprano** (9am–1 hour before sunset; entrance fee) are Gela's chief glory. Situated at the western end of town, on Viale Indipendenza, these romantic walls were covered by sand dunes, preserved in their full height and glory, until 1948 when excavation was begun. Running parallel with the sea, the battlemented ramparts were rebuilt by Timoleon after the Carthaginians razed the city. The thick walls are topped with angle towers and sentry posts, with the remains of barracks inside the northern sections. The **Greek baths**, the only ones to have survived in Sicily, date from the 4th century BC.

Golfo di Gela

From here, you can visit the moonscape of the Gela coast, travelling northwest to Agrigento or turn east to Ragusa and Siracusa. West of Gela, the sandy shore is littered with military pillboxes, relics of Gela's most recent defences and invasion. They are often polluted by the neighbouring oil refinery.

Falconara ⑯, to the west, is a small resort with two appealing beaches, **Manfria** and **Roccazzelle**. The stretches of golden sands beckon invitingly. **Castello di Falconara**, the local castle, is set in lush grounds overlooking the sea. Built in sandy-coloured stone, the feudal castle has crenellations and a 14th-century keep. This atmospheric spot is used by Palermitan aristocrats for their summer residences.

If the oil-laden winds are blowing the wrong way, take the SS 117 bus north across the plains, passing eucalyptus and cork plantations en route to Piazza Armerina and Roman Sicily. These are Virgil's celebrated **Campi Geloi**, the plains in which the poet Aeschylus supposedly met his death *(see margin note opposite)*. Archaeologists are still searching for the great tragedian's tomb. ❑

TIP

Sicily's most depressing towns often have excellent cuisine. If you're marooned on the Gela riviera, at least sample macaroni with aubergines or *stigghuilata 'mpanata*, focaccia-style bread stuffed with vegetables, meat or fish – a meal naturally accompanied by aristocratic Regaleali wines.

Restaurants

Caltanissetta

L'Archetto
Via Palmieri 10.
Tel: 0934 210 31.
A friendly trattoria with fish specialities including a couscous paella, and pizza. Closed Tues. €€

Cortese
Viale Sicilia 166.
Tel: 0934 591 686.
The pretty, flower-strewn restaurant offers traditional Sicilian specialities at moderate prices. Closed Mon and two weeks in Aug. €€

Delfino Bianco
Via Scovazzo Gaetano 19.
Tel: 0934 254 35.
Fresh, modern decor and a varied and inexpensive menu of meat and fish dishes. Closed Sun. €€

Il Gattopardo
Via Pacini 20.
Tel: 0934 598 384.
Both restaurant and pizzeria. Dinner only. Closed Mon and one week in August. €

La Lanterna
Piazza Dante Alighieri 26.
Tel: 0934 346 565.
A simple trattoria-pizzeria; with outdoor tables, it also makes a good spot for an aperitif and a bit of people-watching. €€

Gela

Casanova
Via Venezia 89.
Tel: 0933 918 580.
Near the port, with cooking that is both traditional and adventurous. Small, so booking essential. Closed Sun evening and Aug. €€€

Centrale Totò
Via Generale Cascino 39.
Tel: 0933 913 104.
Simple regional cuisine. Useful if stuck in Gela. Closed Sun. €€

Mazzarino

Alessi
Via Caltanissetta 20.
Tel: 0934 381 549.
Restaurant and pizzeria. Pizza only for dinner. €€

Mussomeli

La Baracca
Via Dogliotti.
Tel: 0934 952 190.
Friendly *caffè*. Shut Fri. €

PRICE CATEGORIES

Prices for three-course dinner per person with a half-bottle of house wine:
€ = under €15
€€ = €15–30
€€€ = €30–60

ENNA PROVINCE

This elevated inland province possesses the island's greatest Roman villa and a succession of hill towns and strategic castles in its fertile landscape

The desolate, sun-parched centre of Sicily is the only province without an outlet to the sea. Yet there is much to proclaim, from the Roman Villa at Piazza Armerina, one of the wonders of the ancient world, to a hinterland studded with hilltop towns and Norman castles. Around its historical sites is an agricultural province producing corn, olives, cheese, nuts and wine.

Enna ❶, known as Sicily's navel for its central position 942 metres (3,090 ft) above the countryside, is sacred thanks to the cult of Demeter (the Olympian goddess of corn and sustainer of life) and the myth of Persephone (Demeter's daughter by Zeus, carried off by Hades to be queen of the Underworld).

Despite Persephone's gift of spring, Enna often feels cloaked in winter, shrouded above the plains in mist or blown by wintry gusts. However in summer, while Sicily swelters, this elevated position offers locals a refuge from the heat.

City in the clouds

Enna's sights are fairly compact, but if the mist falls, expect to cling to the city walls between churches. Tradition has it that the restored **cathedral** (daily 9am–noon, 4–7pm), was begun by Eleanor of Aragon in 1307, but a fire in 1446 swept away most of the treasures. Nonetheless, the cathedral on **Via Roma** is a fascinating romp through Enna's mystical past. The elaborately carved white pulpit is encrusted with cherubs and rests on a Graeco-Roman base removed from a temple to Demeter, as does the marble stoup nearby. The quaint portico is matched by Gothic transepts and apses, while the wrought-iron sacristy gate once graced a Moorish harem in the **Castello di Lombardia**. There are works attributed to

Map on page 148

LEFT:
outside the walls of the Castello di Lombardia, a bronze monument commemorates a slaves' rising in 137 BC.
BELOW:
Enna's cathedral.

The gates of Enna's cathedral.

Paladino and the beloved 15th-century statue of the *Madonna della Visitazione* (the city's patron saint), which is carried through the streets in procession on 2 July.

Enna's esoteric past would appear to make it susceptible to pagan magic. The black basalt base of the capitals incorporate sculptures of Hades and demonic symbols in an attempt to crush evil forces by fair means or foul. The adjoining **Museo Alessi** (currently closed) displays the contents of the cathedral's **treasury**, including the prized **Coronna della Madonna** (Madonna's Crown), a sacred 17th-century enamelled diadem studded with precious stones.

Along bustling Via Roma lies a string of dignified mansions and churches, such as the Catalan-Gothic **Palazzo Pollicarini** and the baroque **Chiesa San Benedetto**. Via Roma is pedestrianised for the evening *passeggiata* and contains a good *pasticceria* as well as cosy restaurants. At the bottom are sweeping views from the *belvedere* and **Torre di Federico II**, a tumbledown octagonal tower built by Frederick II. The tower is linked by secret passageways to **Castello di Lombardia**

(daily summer 8am–8pm, winter 9am–5pm) at the top of the hill, at the other end of Via Roma in Piazzale Lombardia. As one of Sicily's largest medieval castles, this imposing fortress began as a draughty Byzantine keep but acquired towers with each wave of invaders, from the Normans to the Swabians. A series of three courtyards leads to the majestic eyrie of **Torre Pisano**, the tallest of the castle's six surviving towers, which has views over the entire island.

Just beyond the castle looms a massive boulder on the tip of the plateau, the **Rocca di Cerere**, also known as the Temple of Demeter, though no temple exists. Legend has it that Demeter's daughter Persephone was abducted by Hades and swept off into **Lago Pergusa**, gateway to the Underworld *(see margin note)*.

The interior

This circuitous route explores the castle-studded landscape north of Enna. Facing the city is **Calascibetta ❷**, a decrepit but atmospheric-looking hill village built by the Arabs while besieging Enna in 951. Rust-coloured buildings cling to the slopes and the **Chiesa Madre** is perched on top of a blustery cliff.

From here, the SS 121 winds north to **Leonforte ❸**, a 17th-century Branciforte fiefdom best known for its colourful Good Friday procession and its **Granfonte**, a delightful fountain that is a testament to feudal largesse. Set on the edge of town, the graceful arched fountain fills troughs from 24 spouts.

Picturesque **Sperlinga ❹**, north of Leonforte on the SS 117, may well be Sicily's most intriguing castle (daily summer 9.30am–1pm, 3–7pm; winter 9.30am–1pm, 2.30–6.30pm; entrance fee), with battlemented towers and bastions that reach to the bottom of the cliff. Above ground, the village is a string of modest cottages; below the castle, the rock is riddled with chambers, a secret underground city. Dating from 1082, the Norman castle *(see box below)* was donated to the town by Baron Nicosia, its feudal owner, in 1973. The castle and tunnels can be visited.

Map on page 148

The cavern of Hades is still on the south bank of Lago Pergusa but his chariot and black horses are now replaced by hi-tech Formula One cars. The lake, 9 km (5 miles) south of Enna, is the focus of summer sailing competitions and is encircled by a deafening motor racing track and fast food restaurants.

BELOW: the imposing Granfonte at Leonforte.

Sperlinga's castle

After the bloody Sicilian Vespers in 1282, Sperlinga became the Angevins' last stand. The castle was besieged but the French forces within held out for more than a year, protected by a system of trap doors that deposited invaders in underground pits. The only access is still a staircase hewn out of the rock. Steep, switchback paths climb to the summit, festooned with warning notices. From the crenellations stretch sweeping views over oak woods, olive groves and pasture. The rocky slopes of the village are also pitted with caves, some of which have been inhabited since Sicani times. The caves were occupied by Sperlinga's poorest peasants and their livestock until the 1980s.

Nicosia , 8 km (5 miles) southeast of Sperlinga, is a charming mediaeval town set on four hills and ringed by rocky spurs. It has been a Greek city, Byzantine bishopric, Arab fort and Norman citadel. In the Middle Ages it was riven by religious rivalry between Roman Catholic newcomers from the north and the indigenous population who, in Byzantine tradition, followed the Greek Orthodox rite. After pitched battles, the matter was settled in favour of the natives.

The 14th-century **San Nicolò** triumphed as the city cathedral, with its 14th-century facade and lacey campanile. From the cathedral, which dominates the town, Salita Salamone climbs to **San Salvatore**, a Romanesque church that would look at home in Burgundy.

Piazza Garibaldi, the main square, is dotted with dingy bars and **circoli**, working men's clubs. Old men sit and chat in *gallo-italico*, a Lombard dialect stemming from northern settlers and shared with Aidone, Piazza Armerina and Sperlinga. Half the adult population emigrated between 1950 and 1970 and Nicosia has been further isolated by the route of the new motorway. Leading off Piazza Garibaldi are myriad *vicoli*, crooked alleys climbing Nicosia's hills. From here, the steep **Via Salamone** winds above the cathedral, passing dilapidated palazzi and convents encrusted with garlands or gargoyles.

At the top is **Santa Maria Maggiore**, built in 1767. After an 18th-century earthquake, the Norman church was rebuilt in baroque style. This elegant shadow faces a montage of bells that fell when the campanile came down in the last earthquake, in 1978. From the terrace, the tumbledown castle is visible, overgrown with cacti and thistles on a rocky spur. *Cardi* (fried thistles) are a rustic delicacy but the Trattoria La Pace in Via della Pace believes in heartier fare.

The SS 120, a meandering mountain road, leads 20 km (12 miles) northeast to **Cerami **, a jagged village dominated by a ruined castle. The wooded countryside is interspersed with orchards and lolling cattle.

Just north of the SS 120 is the scenic **Lago di Ancipa**, a lake set in a lush wilderness. East of Nicosia are windswept views across the bleak Nebrodi mountains.

The highest stronghold

Further along the SS 120 lies **Troìna **, at 1,120 metres (3,674 ft), the loftiest town in Sicily, which occupies an Arab-Norman stronghold on a solitary ridge. This citadel has declined into an austere hill town with a nest of churches crammed into winding medieval alleys. Tall, draughty convents look out over scruffy terraces and the makeshift houses of returning emigrants. The churches are grand, as befits the first Norman diocese in Sicily. The Norman **Chiesa Matrice** has a fortified

The crooked alleys climb Nicosia's hills.

BELOW: line-up of locals in Nicosia.

16th-century bell tower, nave, crypt, tower and solid external walls.

In this citadel Count Roger and wife were besieged by Saracens in 1064. The couple escaped by classic Norman cunning: while their enemies were lulled into a drunken stupor, the Normans scurried along secret vaulted passages that burrow deep under the ruined castle.

Inside, the fusty church has been revamped in baroque style, complete with flaking gold leaf and late Byzantine art. Outside, an arched walk slopes under the bell tower and returns to the atmospheric Norman stronghold. The terraces are scarred with jagged bits of castle and chapel. On the *belvedere*, Troìna's youth gather to enjoy rugged windswept views over the distant blue-grey hills. On the last Sunday in May devotees gather in Troìna to celebrate the **festa di San Silvestro**, wreathed in laurel leaves with processions and banquets.

Agira , a tortuous 30 km (19 miles) south of Troìna, is set on a hill surmounted by a Saracen castle. The slopes once housed a Siculi settlement but are now given over to olives, grapes and almonds. These hills saw heavy fighting during the Sicilian campaign in 1943, hence the Canadian war cemetery on the town outskirts. Though not striking, the churches contain precious works of art. **Santa Maria Maggiore**, in the shadow of the castle, has a 15th-century triptych and sculpted Norman capitals, while **Santa Maria di Gesù** contains a painted crucifix by Fra Umile da Petralia. Laden down by a 16th-century facade, the Gothic **San Salvatore** has a treasury containing a bejewelled medieval mitre.

Further east, past **Lago di Pozzillo**, an artificial lake, a minor road leads off the SS 121 through orange and olive groves to **Centùripe**. The name supposedly comes from the Latin for steep

slopes, justifying the town's tag used by Garibaldi in 1862, *il balcone della Sicilia* (the balcony over Sicily), with its magnificent valley views to Catania and Etna.

At the town centre is a pink and white 17th-century **Duomo**, contrasting with the town's modern, ugly buildings. Classical statues, terracotta and vases are visible in the **Museo Archeologico** (Tues–Fri 8.30am–1pm, Sat–Sun also 3–7pm; closed Mon). On the outskirts, further finds have been made at **Castello di Corradino**, the site of a cliff-top Roman mausoleum. At the foot of Monte Calvario are the ruins of a Greek villa and, in the Bagni valley, the remains of Roman baths. From here, the A19 motorway leads back to Enna.

Echoes of Ancient Rome

The territory south of Enna has its fair share of crumbling hill towns but the countryside is also home to several Greek settlements and Roman outposts, notably the magnificent Roman villa at Piazza Armerina. Southwest of Enna are a couple of

Map on page 148

Agira's war memorial.

BELOW: drinks in this area are not for the weight-conscious.

Section of a mosaic in the Villa Romana, Piazza Armerina.

isolated hill towns on the Caltanissetta border. **Pietraperzia** , a market town stacked up on the slopes south of Caltanissetta, lives off the land but once provided a living for the land-owning Barresi dynasty.

Barrafranca lies 10 km (6 miles) to the southeast of Enna, set on a spur in the **Monti Erei** (Erei Mountains). Established by the Arabs who gave it the name Convicino, it was conquered by the Normans before being swallowed up by the Barresi feudal estates in 1330. In the 16th century they changed its name to Barrafranca. The baroque **Chiesa Madre**, with campanile and arabesque dome, has fine paintings. The pleasures here lie in the sampling of local produce, including olives, almonds and grapes.

Piazza Armerina

Further east is **Piazza Armerina** and the **Villa Romana** at Casale, Sicily's greatest wonder of the Roman world.

As a town, Piazza Armerina is upstaged by the Roman villa but it has a faded elegance all of its own.

The closure of the sulphur mines cast a pall over the local economy; the town today, population 22,500, sees its salvation in tourism. In the *centro storico* where there is little room for hotels (they are on the outskirts) there are countless licensed bed-and-breakfast establishments. However, if time is short, skip the town and head straight for the Villa.

Surrounded by rich greenery of farmland and trees, until the 8th century the settlement was known simply as Piazza, but as it grew it took on the name Armerina after one of the three hills it spread over. From the 8th century BC the site was favoured by the Romans, the Byzantines and the Arabs until the arrival of the Normans when it grew into a city. This event is celebrated on 13 and 14 August each year with the **Palio dei Normanni**, races with riders and horses in period costume.

In town, a series of flights of steps and alleys leads to the baroque **Duomo**, crowning the terraced hill. Erected in 1604 on the site of another church, theatrical staircases accentuate the spacious *belvedere* and the cathedral's baroque facade. A Catalan-Gothic *campanile* (c.1490) with blind arcading remains from the original church and sets the tone for the lavish, spacious interior. Bordering the cathedral is **Palazzo Trigona**, a sober 18th-century counterpoint to the baroque flights of fancy.

The hilltop quarter radiates from Piazza Duomo and Piazza Garibaldi. In keeping with 13th-century urban design, this is in fishbone formation, with tiny alleys fanning out delicately along the contours of the slopes. Beside Palazzo Trigona, Via Floresta leads to the picturesque Aragonese **castle**.

Further south, the steep Via Castellina nudges the city walls and an old watchtower. A stroll down the steep Via Monte, the medieval main street, reveals an evocative slice of

history, passing palazzi dating from Norman and Aragonese times.

Turnings right lead past turreted mansions to **San Martino**, a 15th-century church. A kilometre stroll north from the compact hillside quarter reaches **Sant' Andrea**, an unadorned but delightful Norman priory with a frescoed interior designed in a Coptic cross plan.

Villa Romana del Casale

Nestling among oak and hazel woods, the **Villa Romana del Casale** (Roman Villa at Casale) **⑬** (daily 8am–one hour before sunset; entrance fee; www.villaromanadel casale.it) lies 5 km (3 miles) south-west of the town at **Casale**. A route signposted for Villa Romana cuts through the side of the town and hugs the foot of the hill emerging, with flashes of olives and forsythia, into open countryside. The excellent hunting in these forests was the bait that drew the villa's original Roman

owners. It was occupied throughout the Arab period but destroyed by the Norman King William the Bad in 1160 and then again, later, by a landslide. While the remains suggest its size, it is the extraordinary mosaics covering the floors that make Villa Romana unique. The Villa has been declared a UNESCO heritage site.

The villa's fluid, impressionistic mosaics may have inspired the Normans in their designs for Palermo's Palazzo dei Normanni. In splendour, the only rivals are Hadrian's Villa at Tivoli or Diocletian's palace at Split. But Sicily's mosaics better reflect the flux of Roman politics, with the emergence of separate Eastern and Western Empires. One theory is that, after Diocletian realised that the Roman world was too vast to be ruled by one mind and retired to his villa in Split, so Maximian withdrew to contemplation here.

Whether hunting lodge or country mansion, the villa disappeared under

Maps:
Area 148
Villa 153

Visitors inspect the mosaics of hunting scenes at the Villa Romana del Casale.

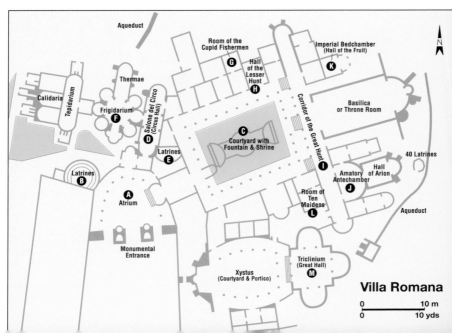

Villa Romana

0   10 m
0   10 yds

To the Romans, hunting meant food, sport, sensuality, adventure and pleasure.

BELOW: two of the Ten Maidens in the Villa Romana.

the landslide for 700 years but, after a hoard of treasure was found in 1950, serious excavations were begun. Much remains to be unearthed in the hazelnut orchards, from the slave quarters to the water system. A typical Sicilian muddle caused excavations to be abandoned in 1985 and has delayed the restoration of mosaics that suffered flood damage in 1991 as well as later vandalism. Many were discoloured and some superficially damaged, including those in the Great Hall.

If this were Venice, there would be a public outcry; since this is Sicily, manpower and funding focus on security, discouraging looters and custodians from indulging in night raids. On top of everything, plastic roofing used as a protective shelter turns the site into a sauna in summer. However, the authorities have finally been galvanised into action, with a decision to place the site under Regional protection and a coherent plan to restore the villa in line with international curating standards.

To avoid the visiting crowds, coaches and the heat, it is worth arriving early in the morning or late in the day. The vaulting may be lost and the frescoes faded but the villa's magic lies in the 40 rooms covered in Roman-African mosaics. Their vitality, expressive power and free-ranging content set them apart from models in Tunisia or Antioch. The stylisation of these mosaics is under-cut by humour, realism, sensuality and subtlety. Above all, the mosaics' visual energy shines through.

From the ticket office the path leads to a massive triumphal arch leading into an **atrium Ⓐ**, surrounded by a portico of marble columns, then crashes down, left, to earth in the male **latrines Ⓑ** that were once well appointed with marble seats. Mosaics here are in a composition of a Persian ass, ram and pouncing leopard. Despite the savagery of the scene, the latrines look more civilised than many modern ones. The villa's centrepiece is the **courtyard Ⓒ**, with peristyle, pond and statue. The mosaics depict whimsical animals' heads framed in wreaths, from a fierce bear and tiger to a horse with a stunted nose. The design has a symmetry, pairing domestic and wild or male and female animals; a fierce ram thus sits beside a gracious deer.

The **Salone del Circo** (Circus Hall) **Ⓓ** illustrates chaotic races at the Circus Maximus. These are the most extensive of their kind so far uncovered anywhere. Nearby, outside the **Thermae**, the thermal baths complex, is the small **latrine Ⓔ**, with bidets for women.

In the octagonal **frigidarium Ⓕ** (leading to the warm and hot rooms) are vestibules and plunge baths adorned with tritons, centaurs and marine monsters, while in the anointment room next door, a man is depicted being massaged and perfumed by his naked servant.

Off the Courtyard the **Room of the Cupid Fishermen Ⓖ** depicts a

naked mermaid clasping a dolphin in the presence of fishermen with bare buttocks or chests. Nearby is the **Hall of the Lesser Hunt** , with a frenetic deer hunt, the snaring of a wild boar, and a toast to a successful day's sport. To the Romans, hunting meant food, sport, sensuality, adventure and pleasure, preferably all at once.

Edging the courtyard is the **Corridor of the Great Hunt** , the finest mosaics ever known, a gloriously animated work meant to be appreciated while walking. In this swirling mass of movement, chariots, lions, cheetahs, rhinos and huge swans merge in lovely autumnal colours. A mosaic sea separates Africa and Europe, echoing the division of the Roman Empire. Africa is personified by a tiger, elephant and a phoenix fleeing a burning house. The exotic, bare-breasted Queen of Sheba is being ogled by a tiger as well as by Romans.

Sport and erotica are often neatly entwined in the mosaics. The **amatory antechamber** , part of the Empress's suite, features Cupid fishermen netting a fine catch. The

Imperial bedchamber is decorated with figs, grapes and pomegranates, snatching at Greek fertility symbols. The **Room of Ten Maidens** presents prancing girl gymnasts in costumes that prove conclusively that the bikini was not invented by Coco Chanel in the 1950s.

Nearby, steps lead up to the **Triclinium** (Great Hall), the villa's masterpiece, 12 metres (39 ft) square and with deep apses, where the mosaic of the central pavement is a flowing mythological pageant based on the **10 Labours of Hercules**. It is a symphony of pathos and poetic vision worthy of Michelangelo: the gods are threatened by chaos and decay; tortured giants writhe in agony; and a mighty nude Hercules is glorified. Passion is present in Cerberus, the three-headed dog; and in the fierce Hydra, which has a woman's face but snake-encrusted hair.

All the scenes normally excluded from Christian art lie here. Villa Romana depicts a kaleidoscope of everyday life, highlighting intimate pleasures such as child's play and youthful dancing, massage and love-

> Maps:
> Area 148
> Villa 153

Aphrodite is dead: the ideal goddess of beauty has been superseded by this plurality of particular girls, portrayed on a pavement where the feet of huntsmen can trample them.

– VINCENT CRONIN
ON THE "BIKINI GIRLS"

BELOW:
the Queen of Sheba appears in the Corridor of the Great Hunt.

Map
on page
148

Worth visiting outside Morgantina on Contrada Vanelle is Centro Formaggi, famed for its excellent cheeses made from ewe's milk. There is a hard cheese called pecorino, including a black pepper version (pecorino pepato) and a softer version known as caciotta that also comes blended with olives.

BELOW:
Enna is primarily an agricultural province.

making. A timeless quality also infuses the mosaics' undisguised eroticism: the female nudes may have odd-shaped breasts but they dance in pagan abandon. The more accomplished male nudes are studies in virility, heightened by the use of chiaroscuro and tonal shading. The Romans worshipped heroism and masculine valour, a vitality crushed by cool Christian art. In essence, this villa remains a temple of paganism.

Greek influence

When you are sated with Roman sights, consider picnicking in the surrounding pine and eucalyptus woods. Alternatively, **Aidone** ⑭, 10 km (6 miles) northeast of Piazza Armerina and built of redstone, represents a window on the Greek world. The centre has a ruined castle and a clutch of austere churches enlivened by elaborate arches and warm brickwork. San Domenico is noted for its diamond-point design on the facade. The **Museo Archeologico** (daily 9am–1pm, 3– 7pm; entrance fee), set in a restored 17th-century Capuchin monastery in the upper part of the village, is an introduction to the rural site of Morgantina, perhaps the most legible site in antiquity.

Morgantina ⑮ (daily 9am–1 hour before sunset; entrance fee, includes Museo Archeologico at Aidone), just 5 km (3 miles) east, occupies a rural paradise worthy of Persephone, its slopes covered in calendula, pines or olives and framed by grey-blue hills. In two parts, Serra Orlando is on the ridge to the west, Cittadella on a hill to the east. Between is a deep valley. This huge ancient Siculi settlement was Hellenised by a Chalcidian colony in the 6th century BC and survived for 500 years.

The remains are not aesthetically beautiful like Piazza Armerina, but they are supremely clear, an exposition of a Classical city in stone. The site reveals a civic and sacred centre bounded by a commercial district and a residential quarter.

Cittadella, the hill site of a Bronze Age settlement, is pitted with chamber tombs. Visible Hellenistic sections include: the *macellum* (covered market), designed like a shopping mall; a schoolroom complete with benches; a gymnasium with an athletic track; the *bouleuterion* (town hall); and boutiques, a granary and a theatre with good acoustics. Several of the noble villas contain the earliest known mosaics in the Western Mediterranean, including a floor inscription saying welcome (*euexei*).

Theatrical steps lead to the *agora*, complete with aqueducts and fountain. Nearby stands a temple with a *bothros*, a round well-altar once used for sacrifices.

This is a reminder that Enna marked the crossroads of *Trinacria*, ancient Sicily's three provinces. According to one historian, Enna is the hub of a giant geomantic chart, lying on ley lines spanning the island. This network of sacred spots supposedly provides the key to the region's occult power. ❏

RESTAURANTS AND CAFÉS

Enna, the provincial capital, has a reasonable selection of places to eat. The smaller towns all have trattorie, but the choice and quality are limited.

Enna

Ariston
Via Roma 353.
Tel: 0935 26038.
A long-established restaurant serving regional dishes. Closed Sun and two weeks in Aug. €€

Centrale
Piazza VI Dicembre 9.
Tel: 0935 500 963.
www.ristorantecentrale.net
Another long-established restaurant, this one at the heart of the town. Good family fare, reasonably priced. Try the pasta and lamb when on menu. Benito Mussolini's signature is in the guestbook. Closed Sat lunch. €€

La Fontana
Via Volturno 6.
Tel: 0935 25465.
A simple family-run trattoria. €

La Griglia
Via Falantano 19.
A characteristic trattoria with tasty *bruschetta* and *maccheroni alla norma* (with aubergine). €

Grotta Azzurra
Via Colaianni 1.
Tel: 0935 24328.
This lively restaurant has been serving up good-value, hearty meals for almost half a century. Closed Sat in winter. No credit cards. €

Pasticceria Caprice
Via Firenze 17.
Tel: 0935 25281.
The best ice cream and Sicily's famous *cassatella*. €

Pasticceria Il Dolce
Piazza Sant' Agostino 40.
Tel: 0935 24018.
Considered to have the finest *cannoli*, almond biscuits, ricotta-filled cakes and more. If you have a sweet tooth, this is an essential place to visit, especially at weekends. €

San Gennaro
Via Belvedere Marconi 6.
Tel: 0935 24067.
Family-run restaurant serving hearty soups, stuffed lamb, grilled vegetables. Outside tables with view. Closed Wed. €€

Tiffany
Via Roma 487.
Tel: 0935 501 368.
Near the Duomo, this restaurant specialises in fish – try the *pennette* pasta with artichoke hearts and prawns – but offers pizza and some meaty options too. Closed Thur. €€

Centùripe

Pasticceria Centrale
Piazza Sciacca 11.
Tel: 0935 573 576.
A pleasant *caffè* with excellent snacks and pastries. €

Nicosia

Baglio San Pietro
Contrada San Pietro.
Tel: 0935 640 529.
www.bagliosanpietro.com
A small farmhouse conversion with 10 guest rooms and pool. Simple, good quality dishes. Closed Nov–Mar. €

Vigneta
Contrada San Basile.
Tel: 0935 646 074.
vigneta@hotmail.com
There is not a wide choice in this town, but Vigneta offers good Sicilian family cooking. Known for their vegetarian dishes and pizza too. Garden. Closed Tues. €

Pasticceria al Bocconcino
Via Roma 8.
Tel: 0935 638 894.
If you like almonds and hazelnuts, this is the place. €

Sperlinga

Bar Li Calzi
Piazza Marconi 1.
Tel: 0935 643 130.
The most popular place in town. €

Piazza Amerina

Centrale da Totò
Via Mazzini 29.
Tel: 0935 680 153.
Very popular with locals. Serves moderately priced Italian dishes, as well as crispy pizzas. Closed Mon in winter. €

Al Fogher
Contrada Bellia 1.
Tel: 0935 684 123.
Worth an excursion on the SS 117, 3 km (2 miles) north, for the regional cooking. Try the specials of the day. Garden. Book. Closed Mon. €€€

La Ruota
Contrada Casale Ovest (near Villa Romana).
Tel: 0935 680 542.
www.trattorialaruota.it
A good trattoria specialising in homemade pasta. Try the delicious *maccheroni*, fresh tomato pasta and *melanzane in agrodolce* (aubergines in sweet-sour vinaigrette). Book. Lunch only. €€

La Tavernetta
Via Cavour 14 (near the Duomo). Tel: 0935 685 883.
This town trattoria in a steep lane serves very tasty pasta dishes. Fish specialities are also recommended. Closed Sun in winter. €€

Al Teatro
Via del Teatro 6.
Tel: 0935 85662.
Delicious, crisp pizza. Closed Wed in winter. €€

Pasticceria Zingale
Via Generale Muscarà 8.
Tel: 0935 686 111.
A welcome stop, a *pasticceria* with wide variety of local specialities. €

PRICE CATEGORIES

Prices for three-course dinner per person with a half-bottle of house wine:
€ = under €15
€€ = €15–30
€€€ = €30–60

RAGUSA PROVINCE

The province favours subtlety over drama. Rolling countryside framed by dry-stone walls gives way to Classical sites alongside sandy beaches or cave settlements close to the heart of baroque towns

iscreet wellbeing is the keynote to the region. Novelist Gesualdo Bufalino proudly described his province as *"un ísola nell'ísola"*, an island within an island. Historically, this was home to a cave-dwelling population who for millennia felt more secure clustering in grottoes or ravines, a tradition that survived until recently, with caves around Ragusa, Mòdica and Scicli inhabited until the 1980s. It is perhaps not accidental that this earthy, community-minded *provincia* is almost a crime-free haven, surviving beyond the Mafia's reptilian gaze. Here the typical conditions for Sicilian crime are absent.

Low-key tourism

Industry and tourism reached the province relatively late, with the result that Ragusa has not concreted its coast with factories or tourist villages, even if greenhouses often blight the vistas. Instead, the province has cultivated low-key tourism, selling itself as an "off the beaten track" destination. Many wealthy Italians have holiday homes here.

The city of **Ragusa** was a Norman stronghold that became a fief of the Cabrera dynasty. However, the 1693 earthquake devastated the province and reduced most of Ragusa to rubble. The merchant class responded by building **Ragusa Alta** (sometimes **Superiore**) ❶, the new city on the hill. But the aristocracy refused to desert their charred homes so recreated **Ragusa Ibla** ❷ (Lower Ragusa) on the original valley site. The towns merged only in 1926 so now Ragusa is a hill-top town divided into two parts. While Ragusa Ibla is an enchanting, timeless pocket of Sicily, Ragusa Alta is the business centre, saved only by some baroque mansions, churches and bustling restaurants. Here the

Map on page 160

LEFT: Ragusa Ibla's medieval rooftops.
BELOW: hanging it out to dry in the narrow streets of Ragusa Ibla.

Ragusa province is noted for its scented honey and robust cheeses, among the best in Sicily. Ricotta, mozzarella, provola and cacciocavallo are the main cheeses to sample, either in savoury or sweet dishes.

urban design is a mess: baroque opulence interlaid with fascistic monumentality and a modern sector riven by gorges that are crossed by three bridges.

In the upper town, **San Giovanni Battista** (daily 7am–12.30pm, 3pm–7pm) is the city's theatrical baroque cathedral with an ornate facade and soaring, pretty **campanile**. Its sense of sweeping movement is echoed by the bustle of the surrounding bars and veterans' clubs in what is an exceptionally clubby city.

Nearby, baroque mansions have wrought-iron balconies featuring sculpted cornices. One such is the 18th-century **Palazzo Bertini** on Corso Italia, with its sculpted but grotesque masks representing "the three powers": a peasant, nobleman and merchant – a fair introduction to Ragusa's class concerns.

On Corso Vittorio Veneto is the crumbling but fine baroque **Palazzo Zacco**: a gap-toothed monster sticks out his tongue, mocking the church of San Vito opposite. Just south is the gorge crisscrossed by three bridges, one of which was built by a friar who tired of the daily uphill slog to his parish. The **Museo Archeologico Ibleo** (daily 9am–1.30pm, 4.30–7.30pm; entrance fee) on Via Natelelli at Ponte Nuovo, one of the bridges, is rich in finds from Camarina and Siculi necropoli elsewhere in the province. Well displayed, the exhibits include finds from prehistoric to Roman times, Greek vases, Byzantine mosaics and a reconstruction of a potter's workshop. On the far side of the chasm is densely packed Ragusa Ibla, now easily reached by shuttle bus along the scenic ring road, faced in subtle local stone.

Santa Maria delle Scale, framed by parched hills, represents the gateway to Ibla, joining the old to the new. This Gothic church was remodelled after the 1693 earthquake. A medieval portal remains, as does the

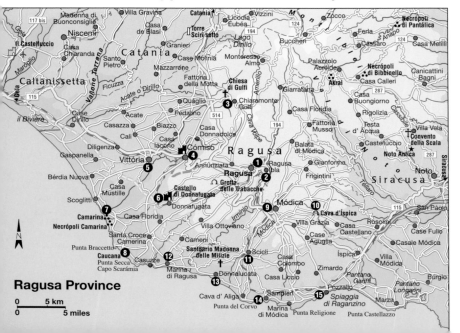

Ragusa Province

0   5 km

0   5 miles

Catalan-Gothic nave, complete with Renaissance ornamentation and arches adorned with beasts and flowers. The church is *delle scale* because from this balcony over old Ragusa, 250 steps lead down into Ibla, offering a commanding view – a panorama over isolated farms and over the blue-tinged cupola of the cathedral below.

Ragusa Ibla

In Ragusa Ibla, the baroque city recreated on a medieval street plan, an old-world charm and intimacy prevails. Snapshot vistas of Ibla capture secret shrines, family crests and baroque fountains. Shrines lurk in narrow alleys and on facades, representing a need for reassurance as well as an expression of faith and a superstitious belief in future miracles. Ibla is also oriel windows, tiny squares and showy staircases, tawny-coloured stone mansions and filigree balconies hung with washing, dark courtyards popular with ambling dogs, secret arches and yellowing palm trees.

Gentrification has reversed the neglect of Ibla in recent years. The crumbling mansions are being restored and cherished by young, middle-class couples who have tired of the bland modern city. Easier access too has helped open Ibla up to citizens from the upper town without losing Ibla's sense of separateness or leisurely pace of life. Where once Ibla was deserted in the evening, its pedestrianised quarter is now the focus for Ragusa's admittedly low-key nightlife. A number of lively bars have taken over historic palaces, with tasteful bohemian conversions coexisting with the clubby, patrician side of town.

Palazzo Nicastro, the baroque chancery erected in 1760, sits astride the winding staircase linking old and new Ragusa. To the left is **Santa Maria dell'Idria**, erected in the 18th century, a church owned by the Cosentini, one of Ibla's leading families. Given the narrowness of the alley, it takes time to gain a perspective on the robust bell tower and majolica-encrusted dome. Crushed between the church steps and Corso Mazzini is **Palazzo Cosentini**, a per-

The interior of Ragusa's Duomo, San Giorgio.

BELOW: retailing opportunity in Ragusa Ibla.

A hospitable people

Unlike much of Sicily, there is a civilised balance between ancient *cultura contadina* (peasant culture) and the creativity of the *borghesia*. Class distinctions aside, the Ragusani are a hospitable people, more open than those in the mountainous interior. The provincial economy thrives on wine-growing, cattle-breeding and cheese-making as well as market gardening, hot-house flowers and genetically modified tomatoes. Although Ragusa hoped to grow rich on asphalt and oil, the latter discovered in the 1960s, agriculture has brought more lasting prosperity. Still, given the underground nature of the people, it is fitting that the earth should become a source of wealth.

fect example of Ragusan baroque, an ancestral home adjoining the family church of Santa Maria. The sculpted balconies are a melange of fantastic bare-breasted sirens and monsters with flaring nostrils. Leering faces proffer scorpions or serpents instead of tongues, a warning not to gossip.

On Piazza della Repubblica, the next square down, stands the **Chiesa del Purgatorio**, a dramatic baroque church surmounting an elegant staircase. The bell tower is built on Byzantine city walls, visible from the steps of Salita dell'Orologio.

After the cosy claustrophobia so far, the spacious **Piazza del Duomo** below comes as a shock. The square is lined with palm trees, baroque mansions and aristocratic clubs. The far end of the piazza is dominated by Rosario Gagliardi's cathedral dedicated to **San Giorgio**, a masterpiece of Sicilian baroque. As the city centrepiece, completed in 1775, this wedding cake cathedral was patronised by the nobility (St George was considered the unofficial patron saint of the Sicilian aristocracy). The sandstone church occupies a raised terrace and tricks one's eyes up from its convex centre, seemingly writhing with statues, in a crescendo to the balconied campanile, topped by a blue neoclassical dome that is a city landmark. Its smaller imitator on the Corso is the church of **San Giuseppe** which gains in subtlety what it lacks in theatricality. The original church, erected in 1590, was damaged in the 1693 earthquake. Its facade is attributed to the school of Gagliardi but not the master himself. The fresco in the cupola showing the glory of San Benedetto is by Sebastiano lo Monaco (1793).

Adjoining Piazza Duomo is the arched **Palazzo Arezzo**, belonging to Baron Vincenzo Arezzo, whose family has had a stake in Ragusa for centuries. The facade is adorned with sculpted hedgehogs, the family crest. The Arezzo family still own much of the province, from farmland to villas and a castle. Given their credo of enlightened paternalism, the family has endowed local hospitals, parks and churches. Ibla's nobles have always immortalised themselves in stone, linking grand baroque man-

Detail from the cathedral of San Giorgio.

BELOW: viewing Ragusa Ibla from Largo Santa Maria.

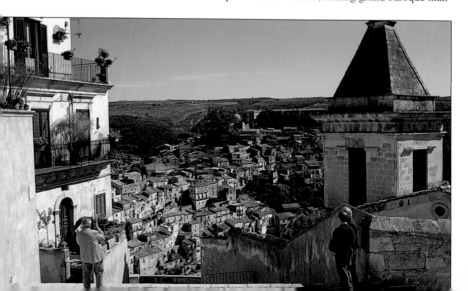

Map on page 160

sions to a graceful family chapel or even a gentlemen's club. Nearby is the **Circolo di Conversazione** (ring for admission), a literary salon founded by local noblemen and the indefatigable Vincenzo Arezzo. The belle-époque interior contains an allegorical *trompe l'oeil* ceiling but no conversation. Inspirational busts of Michelangelo, Galileo, Dante and Bellini represent art, science, poetry and music. But the art of aristocratic conversation is dead in sleepy Ibla: taciturn old fogeys gaze on frescoed nymphs or ponder news reviews over a cold coffee.

The adjoining **Palazzo Donnafugata** was the nobles' private theatre, gallery and reading club until opened to a slightly wider membership. Sadly, the sculpted marble staircase, sumptuous salons and gallery adorned with old masters are only visible during private banquets. Most symbolic is the heavily shuttered loggia on the *piano nobile*, a secret spot from which to view visitors.

Ancient Jewish ghetto

Behind the cathedral on Via Capitano Bocchieri is **Palazzo La Rocca**, an austere baroque mansion transformed into the welcoming provincial tourist office (tel: 0932 244 473), the sole city palace to which entry can be guaranteed. The facade is enlivened by bizarre balconies depicting 18th-century aristocratic entertainment: a lute player and cherub blowing a hunting horn vie with gawky, naked lovers clinging to each other in gauche poses.

The alleys in the shadow of the cathedral are what Italians readily term *suggestivo* (atmospheric). This, the heart of the ancient Jewish ghetto and artisan quarter, is slowly being restored and repopulated with younger residents and craft shops. In the square of Largo Camerina, however, a traditional cabinet-maker survives, creating tables from olive,

carob, cherry, cyprus and orange wood. More typical of the reinvigorated quarter is Al Portale, a fashionable bar carved out of former stables, close to Portale San Giorgio, or L'Antica Drogheria, on Corso XXV Aprile, a superior delicatessen selling Iblean honey and herbs, cheeses, salami and biscuits.

The **Giardino Ibleo** (8am–8pm), created in the 19th century around the (locked) church of **San Giacomo**, is a charming landscaped park set on a spur at the eastern end of Ibla. In spring, the statues, palm trees and pool are complemented by daffodils, broom and irises.

Around the grounds are three ruined churches, victims of the 1693 earthquake. The multicoloured majolica dome of **San Domenico** overlooks Gothic **San Giacomo**, built on the site of a pagan temple, and the church of the **Cappuccini**, a baroque monastic church with three works by Pietro Novelli, the *Assumption* complete with angels and apostles, *Santa Agatha in Prison* and *The Martyrdom of Santa Agnes*. On the far side of the gardens on Via Normanni is

Giardino Ibleo, the park of three churches.

BELOW: Ragusa Ibla's venerable architecture.

the dilapidated 15th-century Gothic doorway to the church of **San Giorgio Vecchio**, with a relief depicting St George and the Dragon. Carved in soft local stone, this is all that remains of the original church destroyed in the earthquake that devastated Ragusa. From this uncharacteristically lush corner of old Ibla, both ancient locals and young lovers take time to look out over terraces and dry stone walls to a valley embedded with ancient Siculi tombs.

Yet, despite its noble veneer, parts of Ibla are still poor. Within view of the heart of town are outlying quarters riddled with blind alleys, abandoned hovels and rock dwellings, side by side with remains of medieval, Byzantine and even pre-Christian Ragusa. Set below the jagged landscape of modern Ragusa, the ancient Siculi tombs now tend to be used as storerooms, wine cellars or even garages. The valley floor is cut by a river that fed several mills until the 1980s; the scene is one of whitewashed cottages, steep steps, pots of geraniums, and peppers dried on walls Arab-style.

Giardino Ibleo is the focal point of the Ibla Buskers' Festival each October, when performers from all around the world are offered free hospitality in return for entertainment.

BELOW: Fonte Diana, the Roman fountain in Cómiso.

North of Ragusa

Chiaramonte Gulfi ❸ (population 8,300) was founded in the late 7th century as Gulfi but destroyed by the Angevins in 1299. It was then revived by Manfredi I, the Count of Mòdica, one of the Chiaramonte dynasty. The town flourished until overtaken by neighbouring Vittoria which, as it grew in size, gained in prosperity and power. The infamous 1693 earthquake destroyed much of its splendour, but its *centro storica* has been preserved. The **Arco dell'Annunziata** is the one remaining medieval gateway entrance to the town. There were three.

The citizens of Gulfi added Chiaramonte to their town's name in 1881 to honour its original benefactor. Today Chiaramonte Gulfi is famous among Sicilians for the quality of its food.

At about 2 km (1¼ miles) away in the countryside is the **Santuario dell Madonna delle Grazie**, restored in 1710, but more a place for picnics than religious devotion.

West of Ragusa

From Ragusa, the rural hinterland unfolds. On higher ground, olives, almonds and carobs abound but, in well-irrigated areas, greenhouse cultivation is gaining ground. Where there is enough water, on the coast or in river canyons, dwarf palms, holm oaks, plane trees and Aleppo pines flourish. But on the plains, the view is of dust-coloured farmhouses, low dry-stone walls, endless fields, rugged limestone plains beaten to the colour of sandstone.

A dramatic descent from the Iblean hills leads across a vast plain to **Cómiso** ❹ (population 28,000), an attractive medieval and baroque town that had the misfortune to become a NATO military base in the 1980s. Peace protests were the price residents paid for housing the last cruise missiles located on European soil. As a bonus,

7,000 American soldiers subsidised the local economy until the final removal of the missiles in 1991. Since then, most of those employed by the former base have been taken on by the capacious Sicilian civil service, leaving part of the base as temporary housing for refugees. There are long-term plans to transform the base into a new airport to boost tourism to the region.

Ruled by the Aragonese Naselli dynasty from the 15th to the 18th centuries, Cómiso still has a feudal castle. The restored 14th-century **Castello dei Naselli** retains its original Gothic portal and octagonal tower, converted from a Byzantine baptistry, but the rest was remodelled in the 16th century. Although shattered by the 1693 earthquake, fragments of Classical Cómiso survive: Piazza di Município contains **Fonte Diana**, a Roman fountain whose waters once gushed into the Roman baths now under the municipal offices.

In Piazza delle Erbe there is **San Francesco** (sometimes called the **Immacolata**), with the fine marble **mausoleum** of Baldasssarre II Naselli by Antonello Gagini and, just off the piazza, is the **covered market** (1871). Adding to the baroque scenery is the vast domed **Basilica dell'Annunciata** and the slim-domed **Santa Maria delle Grazie**, a monastic chapel which offers the town's most gruesome sight: mummified bodies of monks and benefactors stacked in frightening poses.

Vittoria , further west, is a wealthy, wine-producing centre on the slopes of the Iblean hills. The city was founded in 1607 by Vittoria Colonna, the daughter of a Spanish viceroy and wife of the Count of Mòdica. Since aristocratic power in parliament was closely linked to the size of the feudal estates, Vittoria tried to make the town as populous as possible.

Today, with a population of 60,000, this neat city remains wealthy rather than healthy – although, maybe, under the surface the Mafia maintains a toehold, a theory given credence by a big Mafia massacre here in 1999. Giuseppe Fava, a Sicilian journalist murdered by the Mafia, once dismissed Vittoria as "a

Map on page 160

TIP

Around Vittória there are several wine trails, to put you on the right track for Cerasuolo di Vittória and Nero d'Avola wines and producers. Although the trails aren't yet signposted, a wine route map can be picked up from the local tourist office.

BELOW: the church of Santissima Annunziata, Cómiso.

The Castello di Donnafugata, a 19th-century palace built on the site of an Arab village, combines Venetian Gothic with Moorish whimsy.

city built by those without the time, money, imagination or background to make anywhere better".

Even so, the elegant **Piazza del Pòpolo** contains the baroque church of **Santa Maria delle Grazie**, founded in 1612 but remodelled in 1754, and the comparatively recent, but monumental, **Teatro Communale**, erected in 1877, a fine example of neoclassical architecture.

On Piazza Libertà is the **Palazzo dei Principe** (Sat 6–8pm; Sun 10am–noon, 5.30–8.30pm). Amid the bland modernity are bourgeois mansions with grand courtyards. From the city gardens are views across the fertile valley to the sea. Deforestation has made way for market gardening, with flowers and peaches added to the traditional crops of olive oil and wine. The illustrious wine producer Florio has an important base here.

South of Ragusa

Castello di Donnafugata ❻ (Tues–Sun 9.15am–2pm, 2.45–7.30pm; entrance fee) lies 20 km (12 miles) southwest of the provincial capital. Set in a carob and palm plantation,

this modern Moorish pastiche feels authentically Sicilian. The castle dates from 1648 but was redesigned as a full-blown *Ottocento* fantasy by Corrado Arezzo, the Baron of Donnafugata, in the 19th century, and remained in the family until the 1970s. Arezzo, a prominent politician and campaigner for Sicilian independence, created Donnafugata as his whimsical refuge from revolutionary politics.

The exterior is a Venetian palace transplanted by magic carpet to *The Arabian Night*s. The crenellated facade, inspired by an austere Arab desert fort, is softened by an arcaded Moorish balcony. Below the arched windows opens an amazing loggia in Venetian-Gothic style.

The finest rooms are naturally on the *piano nobile* and include a picture gallery, billiards room, winter garden and a salon for conversation. The frescoed music room illustrates the noble pastimes of painting, *bel canto* and piano recitals as well as tombola and chess. The *salotto dei fumatori* was the smokers' room.

Although once sumptuous, this palace with 122 rooms is coated in the evidence of charming Sicilian neglect and now undergoing considerable restoration. Both the *salone degli stemmi,* the room where coats-of-arms were flourished, and the faded *salone degli specchi* (the room of mirrors) with its floating drapes, tarnished gilt, inlaid tables and dusty chandeliers, conspire to create an atmosphere straight out of *The Leopard*. During World War II, the Luftwaffe commandeered the pavilion, along with the rest of the castle. However, they respected Donnafugata, so all the baron's quirky touches remain, from the cute well and the children's maze in the garden to the artificial grotto and the silly seat that squirts out water.

The vast parkland is also open to the public.

Map on page 160

The ancient Greek site of **Camarina**, the **Parco archeologico di Camarina ❼** (daily 9am–sunset), lies on the coast just 12 km (7 miles) west of Donnafugata, a short distance from the small town of Santa Croce Camarina. Founded in 598 BC, two centuries after Siracusa (the ferocity of the local Siculi tribes was a deterrent to earlier settlement), Camarina is a sophisticated example of urban planning covering three hills at the mouth of the River Ippari. But it was attacked, sacked and rebuilt many times until finally the city of perfect parallel lines was destroyed by the Romans in AD 258. The first excavations of the site were begun in 1896; then, after a hiatus, excavations continued again in 1958 and are still in progress.

In the park are traces of the 6th-century BC walls that stretched 7 km (4 miles) to protectively encircle a city that was divided into distinct public, civil and religious areas as well as marked residential zones.

Close to the **museum** (daily 9am–2pm, 3–7pm; entrance fee) there are the foundations of a **tempio di Athena** (temple of Athena). The museum contains objects retrieved from shipwrecks on this shoreline, including sarcophagi and amphora as well as a Greek bronze helmet (4th-century BC) and 1,000 coins found in a treasure chest. Nearby, the **House of the Altar** has rooms radiating from the central courtyard with a battered mosaic floor. Other Hellenistic dwellings include a merchant's house, confirmed by the presence of scales and measuring devices.

On the headland just south of Camarina, at **Punta Secca**, is the Roman port of **Caucana ❽**. Now slowly being excavated, the port was partly preserved by sand, as at Gela *(see page 144)* further down the coast. The lush site is lovely but inscrutable, a puzzle compounded by the discovery of Hellenistic amphora, Roman coins and Jewish candelabra. Amid the rubble, the clearest find is a Byzantine church with a colourful mosaic of a goat. It was in this port that the navy of Count Roger the Norman gathered in 1091 before the conquest of

The only damage done to Castello di Donnafugata during World War II was to "the friar's joke", in which an unsuspecting visitor was embraced by a mechanical friar as he entered the house. Not surprisingly, a Nazi officer disliked the joke and shot the friar to smithereens.

BELOW: a small car makes sense in traffic-clogged towns here.

In Módica call in at the Antica Dolceria Bonajuto at 159 Corso Umberto 1 (tel: 0932 941 225. www.bonajuto.it) where they will offer you I'mpanatigghi, a sweet biscuit made with meat and chocolate, or meat and carob. Signor Franco Ruta is famous for his unusual chocolate combinations. The favourite is testa di Moro, fried pastry filled with chocolate custard.

BELOW: saintly line-up at Módica's cathedral.
RIGHT: Church of San Giorgio, Módica.

Malta. To visit this **Parco Archeologico** an appointment is necessary (tel: 0932 916 142).

Southeast to Módica

Beyond farmsteads and stone walls are two high road bridges that provide a sudden, terrifying glimpse of a grey-brown town in the deep valley below. **Módica ❾**, the former regional capital, is perched on a ridge spilling down into the valley. Like Ragusa, it is two towns in one, high and low. At first sight, the setting is more prepossessing than the town, but Módica repays exploration, from its mysterious alleys and mouthwatering food to its illustrious history as the most powerful fiefdom in Sicily.

The prosperous Arab citadel of Mudiqah became a fief of the Chiaramonte family in 1296 and merged into the county of Módica. After succumbing to Spanish influence, it passed from the Caprera viceroys to the Henriquez, Spanish absentee landlords. Around town are the family crests of the three dynasties: respectively mountains, a goat,

and two castles. Módica's charm lies in the complexity of the multi-layered town, with its tiers of sumptuous churches and shabby palaces stacked up on the hill.

At the entrance to the town is the **Convento dei Padri Mercedari**, built in the 18th century and now known also as **Palazzo Mercedari**. It houses the dull **Museo Civico** (9am–1pm) and the more interesting **Museo Ibleo delle Arti e Tradizioni popolari** (daily, summer 10am–1pm, 4.30–7.30pm, winter 10am–1pm, 3.30–6.30pm; entrance fee), with exhibits of all local trades: shoemaking, construction of working carts, as well as farming and wine making. Above, visible from almost everywhere and perched precariously on the slope of the hill, the 18th-century church of **San Giorgio** (daily 9am–noon, 4–8pm) in Módica Alta (upper Módica) makes a bold statement against a backdrop of rocky terraces. This noble church surmounts a daunting baroque flight of 250 steps, but climb the stairs only if you are feeling fit: there is little to see in the church behind its

ornate facade. The writer Vincent Cronin summed it up by saying: "After such a meandering introduction, which arouses our hopes to the highest pitch, all but the greatest building would appear to fail".

But architect Gagliardi's masterpiece does not really disappoint: its imagination, movement and magic encapsulate Sicilian baroque. This frothy concoction of flowing lines and curvy ornament seems barely rooted to the spot. The vision is one of rococo splendour, shadowy recesses and a soaring belfry silhouetted against the sky.

After such spectacle, other churches play walk-on parts. However, on Corso Umberto I is the **Chiesa del Carmine**, with a marble group representing *The Annunciation,* attributed to Antonello Gagini. At the centre of town, where the Corso meets Via Marchesa Tedeschi, is the **Municipio** (the town hall), next to the church of **San Domenico**. San Domenico was damaged in the earthquake of 1613, rebuilt, then hit again by the big earthquake of 1693.

Just around the corner is the crypt, the **Cripta del Convento di San Domenico** (key and guide from the tourist office on Via Grimaldi), a mysterious retreat in the poorly restored convent, now the town hall. The medieval crypt was unearthed during renovations in 1972: in different periods of its history it was used as a burial chamber for the Dominicans and as a torture chamber linked to the Inquisition.

San Pietro

Still on the Corso, reached by a theatrical staircase along which tiers of the 12 apostles welcome visitors much like today's party greeters, is the great San Giorgio's nearest rival, the opulent church of **San Pietro** (built after 1693). Gagliardi may have designed this church, too. Close to San Pietro is the ancient

church of **San Niccolò Inferiore**, really a grotto, where three layers of frescoes dating from the 11th century were discovered in 1989.

Also on the Corso are the 16th-century church of **Santa Maria del Soccorso**, the 18th-century **Teatro Garibaldi** and 18th-century **Palazzo Manenti** with its balcony and baroque embellishments.

Museo Campailla (Mon–Fri 9am–noon) is one of the most bizarre minor museums in the province: an early syphilis clinic founded by Tommaso Campailla, a 17th-century local doctor and philosopher, and used until the early 20th century. The cure, a refinement on an 8th-century Arab practice, involved placing patients in the hot mercury chambers, heated by hot coals to produce a sauna-like effect, and subjecting sufferers to vaporous infusions. The eerie original chambers are still visible, surreally interconnected with rooms where city council workers go about their normal business.

A short distance away, back on Via Marchese Tedeschi, is the 15th-century church of **Santa Maria di**

Map on page 160

Although once known as "the Venice of the South", Módica suffered a disastrous flood in 1902 and as a result all its rivers were diverted and canals covered over.

BELOW: in Módica, love and marriage means a horse and carriage.

BELOW:
Cava d'Ispica has been inhabited since prehistoric times.

Betlem, considered by some to be the most important church in Módica. Of course it was damaged in the 1693 earthquake that shook Sicily, and then restored, but it appears to be four tiny churches linked to make one and, in the right nave, a magnificent portal opens into the late-Gothic Renaissance **Capella del Sacramento**; here the *Madonna in trono col Bambino* (Madonna and Child on a throne) is painted on stone above the altar. The facing side chapel contains a **crib** (1882) with 60 decorated terracotta figures.

Caves and tombs

From Módica, it's a short drive south to baroque Scicli and the coast, or southeast to the Ispica canyon and to Siracusa province. The **Cava d'Ispica** ❿ (daily, summer 8am–8pm, winter 8am–5pm; entrance fee) is an 11-km (7-mile) limestone gorge, typical of the gorges of the region but on a giant scale, where ghostly galleries and caves have been inhabited almost continuously since prehistoric times. There are prehistoric tombs and medieval cave dwellings.

The southern end of the narrow valley is overlooked by the **castello**, a rock shaped like a castle where dwellings were on four floors.

The better tombs are in the northern end of the gorge, close to the entrance to the site. The honeycomb of galleries conceal native Siculi oven-shaped tombs, Greek necropoli and early Christian tombs. Highlights include the **Larderia**, the most complete set of early Christian catacombs in southeastern Sicily, and the **Grotta di Santa Maria**, a rock chapel with wall paintings that was inhabited until the 1950s. A lack of funds for maintenance means that sections of the site are closed to visitors.

In the countryside at the far end of the Cava d'Ispica gorge is the **Parco archeologico della Forza** (daily 9am–1.45pm, 3–7pm), outside the small town of **Ispica**, population 15,000. The Parco too has its catacombs and traces of settlements beginning in prehistoric times. Ispica was rebuilt after the great earthquake in a safer position. On Via XX Settembre is the church of **Santa Maria Maggiore**, early-18th century with

attractive stucco work and frescoes by Olivio Sozzi. On the Corso is **Palazzo Bruno di Belmonte**, created in 1906 by Ernesto Basile as an Art Nouveau castle complete with decorative details, panels of majolica and angular towers. It is the Municipio, the municipal offices.

Scicli

Southwest of the canyons is **Scicli** ⓫, a neglected baroque gem, a forgotten town first settled in the 14th century awaiting a return to popularity. The road from Ispica reveals vistas of a grotto-encrusted hillside opening onto the restored remains of the church of **San Matteo**, part of a medieval settlement once on the slopes, now overlooking the baroque heart of Scicli on the valley floor below. Scicli's fusty city churches and fantastic baroque mansions seem out of place in this sleepy world. The ochre-coloured facades are decorated with sirens, monsters and fauns, part of the cavalcade of Christian and mythological creatures inspired by designs on Greek temples or Romanesque cathedrals.

The baroque centre has been partly renovated in recent years and the predominantly elderly population has been leavened with new arrivals, young craftspeople, from carpenters to workers in forged iron. Still, much of the battered, inward-looking atmosphere remains, but smart shops indicate that a revival is at hand.

Piazza Italia, the main square, opens with the baroque 18th-century **Duomo**, the **Chiesa Sant'Ignazio**. Its gilded interior holds a painting of an historic battle for Scicli between the Turks and Christians in 1091, where the successful intercession of a bellicose Madonna supposedly brought victory, an event celebrated in Scicli's own festival in May.

Just north, on Via Mormino Penna, the best-preserved baroque street, stands the elegant church of **San Giovanni**, with its well-restored concave-convex facade. Unlike much Sicilian baroque architecture, a dazzling exterior is matched by an equally impressive interior: the exuberantly stuccoed surface has a gaudy emerald and turquoise Moor-

Map on page 160

TIP

Anyone addicted to tomatoes should time their visit for early May, when a one-day Sagra del Pomodoro is dedicated to the fruit. Chefs in the main square of the Sampieri district of Scicli create pizzas and other tomato-based dishes, accompanied by street entertainment. Details from Ragusa Tourist Office, Via Cap Bocchieri 33, Ragusa. Tel: 0932 244 473.

BELOW:
Ragusa landscape.

Map
on page
160

*Grotesque cherubs
adorn Palazzo
Beneventano.*

BELOW: the remains
of the ancient port of
Camarina overlook
today's windsurfers.

ish design. The church was previously the preserve of cloistered nuns, who had permission to sit in balconied splendour to watch processions on feast days.

Just south, **Palazzo Beneventano** has beautiful balconies, with fantastic corbels representing mythical beasts, Moors and ghoulish human masks. Almost as splendid is nearby **Palazzo Fava**, a riot of galloping griffons and horses ridden by cherubs. Just east, at the foot of the rock, loom the majestic cupola and domed apses of **Santa Maria la Nuova**, signalling the start of Scicli's intriguing medieval quarter, dotted with modest houses, alleys and steps overflowing with pot plants.

An attractive new path that winds up to the top, where the ruined castle and Chiesa San Matteo overlook the town, has won favour as the locals' chosen summer stroll. From here, secret passageways dating from the Saracen sieges are said to lead out of town. The hill is pitted with some that were inhabited until the 1980s. They still serve a purpose

as wine cellars, garages and storerooms for farm produce.

Beside the seaside

Ragusa province has some of Sicily's best beaches. Less than 10 km (6 miles) from Scicli, the coastal landscape spans sand dunes, marshes, rocky beaches, and shingle strands dotted with heather. Sandy beaches await around the archaeological site of **Camarina**, with a secluded rocky beach on **Punta Braccetto**, the headland beyond.

Heading eastwards, **Marina di Ragusa** ⓬, lined with fish restaurants, contains the only managed beaches, equipped for windsurfing and other watersports. In summer, this winter ghost town turns into a bustling resort, with 10,000 villas let to outsiders.

Just east is the wooded coastal nature reserve of **Fiume Irmínio**, with the broad sandy beaches of **Donnalucata** ⓭ beyond, a stretch of coast rapidly being swamped by greenhouses.

A 7-km (4-mile) coastal drive leads east to the rocky headland of **Punta del Corvo**, and on to coastline that lies further south than Tunisia's northern coastline.

Sampieri ⓮ stands out for its self-consciously quaint atmosphere, a prettified fishing village popular with Ragusani out for a family romp in the sand dunes. Further along the coast, at the port of **Pozzallo** ⓯, the industrial complex is too close to the beach for comfort, although the beaches are perfectly acceptable further east, towards Siracusa province. Still, Pozzallo is a pleasant enough place to stay for a lunch of salted tuna or sardines, both caught and processed in the port.

From here, you can escape on a day trip to Malta by catamaran (Virtu Ferries, tel: 0932 954 062; www.virtuferries.com) or visit the baroque masterpiece of Noto. ❏

RESTAURANTS

Ragusa

Baglio la Pergola
Piazza Luigi Sturzo,
Contrada Selvaggio.
Tel: 0932 686 430.
info@lapergolarg.it
A popular, elegant meeting place known for its updated versions of local dishes. Fish too. Closed Tues and Aug. €€€

Duomo
Via Capitano Boccheri 31,
Ibla. Tel: 0932 651 265.
www.ristoranteduomo.it
Elegant, smart, facing the cathedral, with classical, richly flavoured Sicilian cooking. Chef wins awards for his inventive cooking. Closed Mon lunch and Sun. Also 10 days Jan & July. €€€

Il Barocco
Via Orfanotrofio 29, Ibla.
Tel: 0932 652 397.
www.ilbarocco.it
Pizzeria and restaurant. Closed Wed and 2 weeks in Aug. €€

Locanda Don Serafino
Via Orfanatrofio 39, Ibla.
Tel: 0932 248 778.
www.locandadonserafino.it
An amusing place, complete with American bar. But good Sicilian cooking and good choice of wines. Closed Tues. €€€

PRICE CATEGORIES

Prices for three-course dinner per person with a half-bottle of house wine:
€ = under €15
€€ = €15–30
€€€ = €30–60

Monna Lisa

Via Ettore Fieramosca.
Tel: 0932 642 250.
Large trattoria with a garden. Modern surroundings, Sicilian kitchen. Rich flavours. Pizza in evenings too. Closed Mon. €€

U' Sarucinu
Via Convento 9, Ibla.
Tel: 0932 246 976.
Facing San Giorgio, serving rustic dishes in a vaulted cellar. Popular. Set menu available. Closed Sun. €€

Marina di Ragusa

Eremo della Giubiliana
Contrada Gibiliana.
Tel: 0932 669 119.
www.eremodellagiubiliana.it
En route to the sea, a delightful hotel with 24 guestrooms and a pool, a winery with an excellent restaurant serving unusual Sicilian dishes. Closed Jan–Feb. €€€

Villa Fortugno
4 km (2½ miles) along road to Marina di Ragusa.
Tel: 0932 667 134.
www.villafortugno.it
Country cuisine with Sicilian sausages, pork stews and fine desserts. Closed Mon and 1 week in Aug. €€€

Da Serafino
Longomare Doria.
Tel: 0932 239 522.
www.locandadonserafino.it
A typical trattoria by the sea. Good fish and pizza too. Closed Oct–Mar. €€

Vittoria

Maria Tindara
Via Provinciale 38.
Tel: 0909 853 004.
A simple kitchen with an emphasis on meat using traditional Aeolian recipes. Garden. Open summer only. €€

Sakalleo
Piazza Cavour 12, at Scoglitti. Tel: 0932 871 688.
Simple and charming trattoria with excellent fish. Closed mid-Nov–mid-Dec. €€

Chiaramonte Gulfi

Majore
Via Martiri Ungherese 12.
Tel: 0932 928 019.
www.majore.it
Their motto here is *Qui si magnifica il porco* (here we glorify the pig). The kitchen is devoted to cooking pork and little else. But highly popular. Closed Mon and July. €€

Módica

Fattoria delle Torri
Vico Napolitano 14, Módica Alta. Tel: 0932 751 286.
Tucked away in an alley, this charming trattoria serves wonderful traditional fare in a baroque palatial setting. Dinner served under lemon trees in warm weather. Reservations essential. €€€

La Gazza Ladra
Via Blandini 5, Módica Alta.
Tel: 0932 755 655.
www.ristorantelagazzaladra.it

A pricey but excellent restaurant inside the exclusive Palazzo Failla hotel. The ambience is all refined elegance, while the cuisine has strongly Sicilian roots, with a nouvelle twist. €€€

La Rusticana
Viale Medaglie d'Oro 34,
Módica Bassa.
Tel: 0932 942 950.
Closed Sun July–Aug; Sun evening Sept–June. €€

Antica Dolceria Bonajuto
Corso Umberto I 159.
Tel: 0932 941 225.
www.bonajuto.it
A famous establishment. You can try *l'mpanatigghi*, made with meat and chocolate, or *testa di Moro*, fried pastry filled with chocolate custard, or *cannoli*, filled with sweet ricotta cheese. €

RIGHT: fresh bread from a small local bakery.

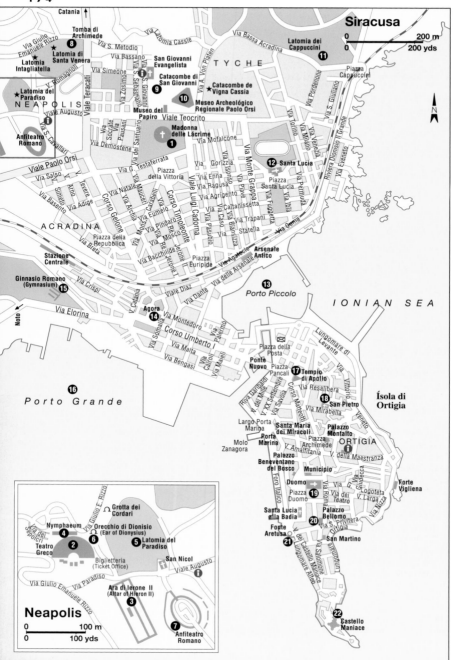

Siracusa

0 — 200 m
0 — 200 yds

Catania ↑

Tomba di Archimede

Via S. Metodio

Via Latomia Cassie

Via Bassano

Via Giulio Emanuele Rizzo

Latomia di Santa Venera **8**

Latomia Intagliatella

Via Simeone

Via Teracati

Via Zosimo

Via S. Giovanni

San Giovanni Evangelista

Catacombe di San Giovanni **9**

Via S. Sebastiano

Via A. Von Platen

T Y C H E

Latomia dei Cappuccini **11**

Piazza Cappuccini

Via Bassa Acradina

Via Pordenone

Via S. Giuliano

V. Romagnoli

Latomia del Paradiso ★

N E A P O L I S

ⓘ

Viale Augusto

Catacombe de Vigna Cassia

Museo Archeológico Regionale Paolo Orsi **10**

Via Veneta

Via Venezia

Via Mirano

Via Torino

Via S. Cavallari

Anfiteatro Romano ★

Museo del Papiro

Viale Teocrito

Via S. Santuario

Madonna delle Lácrime **1**

Via Mofalcone

Viale Paolo Orsi

Via Socrate

Via Pausani

Via Demostene

Via G. Testaferrata

Piazza della Vittoria

Viale Luigi Cadorna

Via Gorizia

Via Isonzo

Via Enna

Via Piave

Via Agrigento

Via Monte Grappa

Santa Lucia **12**

Piazza Santa Lucia

Riviera Dionisio II Grande

Via Eurialo

Via Salso

Corso Gelone

Via Natale

Via Archia

Via Muscati

Via Monte Cabanni

Via Eumelo

Via Pindaro

Via Re Mosco

Corso Timoleonte

Via Ragusa

Via Caltanissetta

Via Trapani

Via Blandizza

Via Pasubio

Via Caltanissetta

Via Fugatta

Via Perinola

Via Vela Vela

A C R A D I N A

Simeto

Tevere

Arno

Adige

Basento

Via Breta

Piazza della Repubblica

Via Bacchelide

Via Jerone

Via Re Pelliade

Piazza Euripide

Via Agatocle

Arsenale Antico

Via delle Arsenale

Via Statella

Via Gema

Stazione Centrale

Ginnasio Romano (Gymnasium) **15**

Via Crispi

Viale Diaz

Via Dante

Porto Piccolo 13

I O N I A N   S E A

← Neto

Via Elorina

Via C. Catania

Agora **14**

Via Montedoro

Via Somalia

Via Palermo

Corso Umberto I

Via Malta

Via Bengasi

Via Cairoli

Via Malaj

Piazza della Posta

Lungomare di Levante

Ponte Nuovo

Piazza Pancali

Tempio di Apollo **17**

Via Resalibera **18**

San Pietro

Via Mirabella

Ísola di Ortigia

Porto Grande 16

Riva Garibaldi

Via XX Settembre

Corso Matteotti

Via Savoia

Largo Porta Marina

Santa Maria dei Miracoli

Palazzo Montalto

Porta Marina

Piazza Archimede

V. Amalfitana

ORTIGIA

ⓘ V. della Maestranza

Molo Zanagora

Palazzo Beneventano del Bosco

Municipio

Foro Italico

Duomo **19**

Piazza Duomo

Via Roma

Via del Teatro

Via G.

Giudecca

V. Logoteta

V. Larga

Via Nizza

Forte Vigliena

Santa Lucia alla Badia

Palazzo Bellomo **20**

Via S. Privitera

del Castello Maniace

Fonte Aretusa **21**

San Martino

Lungomare Alfeo

Via Salomone

Castello Maniace **22**

Neapolis

0 — 100 m
0 — 100 yds

Via dei Sepolcri

Via Giulio E. Rizzo

Grotta dei Cordari

Nymphaeum **4**

Orecchio di Dionisio (Ear of Dionysius) **6**

Teatro Greco **2**

Latomia del Paradiso **5**

Biglietteria (Ticket Office)

San Nicol

Viale Augusto

ⓘ

Via Giulio Emanuele Rizzo

Via Paradiso

Ara di Ierone II (Altar of Hieron II) **3**

Anfiteatro Romano **7**

SIRACUSA CITY

Alluring, civilised and sleepy Siracusa is less dynamic than Catania, less sultry than Palermo, yet somehow charmingly steals most visitors' hearts as the capital of sheer indulgence

Cicero called the island of Ortigia, part of the city of Siracusa today but separated from the mainland by a narrow channel, the loveliest city in the world, and, like Siracusa itself (Syracuse in English-speaking countries), Ortigia's name resounds in academic circles abroad. Siracusa is the summation of Sicilian splendour, with an emphasis on Greek heritage. It was this cultivated city that supposedly witnessed the birth of comedy in its Greek theatre and now boasts the only school of Classical drama outside Athens.

Apart from tales of Artemis and Apollo, Siracusa gave the world architectural beauty with a baroque heart: Ortigia has facades framed by wrought-iron balconies that are as free as billowing sails. In fact, as Sicily's greatest seafaring power, Siracusa indulged an affinity with the sea that still pervades city myths and art. The city's sensual sculpture of Venus emerging from the breeze-swept sea embodies this cult of water.

Perhaps daunted by such a glorious past, today's citizens (the population is 126,000) have a reputation for being rather easy-going, possibly dreamers and underachievers, and the lack of Arab influence over the centuries in this province is often cited as an explanation for the city's low profile in terms of Mafia links.

Local lore has it that even the leaders of the criminal classes have to be drawn from the neighbouring province of Catania. It seems oddly fitting, therefore, that sleepy Siracusa should be home to the International Institute of Criminal Science.

Classical glory

The city was founded in 733 BC, a year after Naxos, by Corinthian settlers who maintained links with Sparta. Although it was ruled by a succession of cruel but occasionally

Map on page 174

BELOW: fishing boats in the channel between Ortigia and the mainland.

benevolent tyrants, Siracusa rose to become the supreme Mediterranean power of its age under Dionysius the Elder. The decisive battle was Siracusa's defeat of Athens in 415 BC at sea. During a despotic 38-year rule, however, Dionysius personified Sicilian tyranny *(see panel below)*.

City sectors

Siracusa is a diffuse, segmented city whose ancient Greek divisions still resonate deeply with residents. **Ortigia**, the cultural island at the heart of the Greek city, remains true to its vocation: despite a grand baroque and Catalan carapace, this beguiling backwater feels intimate, informal and quietly cultured. This is where the locals choose to while away the long summer evenings. By contrast, **Tyche**, the northern quarter on the mainland, can feel like the city of the dead: studded with ancient catacombs. Tyche lay beyond the bounds of Roman Syracuse and thus remains a testament to the impact of early Christianity. **Acradina**, bordering Ortigia, remains the commercial quarter, complete with railway

A bar on Via Roma.

BELOW: Santuario della Madonna delle Lacrime.

station, while **Neapolis**, to the northwest, though no longer "new", still embodies the ancient Greeks' notion of public and sacred space, ranging from theatres to sanctuaries.

While Tyche and Acradina suffered bomb damage in 1943, much of Siracusa is unscathed, and continues to slumber through natural and man-made disasters, from an earthquake in 1991 to a sluggish economy and slothful public administration in more recent years.

Both as a useful landmark and as an antidote to Classical beauty, the ugly modern **Santuario della Madonna delle Lacrime**  signals the way to the archaeological zones of Neapolis and Tyche. Visible from most of the city with its statue of the Madonna on top, this popular pilgrimage centre (daily 7am–8pm; www.madonnadellelacrime.it) commemorates a modern miracle: in 1953 a statue of Mary reputedly cried for five days and the spot became a shrine in the shape of a giant teardrop.

To the west, **Neàpolis**, the ancient quarter, is synonymous with its sprawling archaeological park,

The Legacy of Dionysius

Dionysius was a megalomaniac, a military strategist, a monumental builder, an inspired engineer and an execrable tragedian. He presided over Siracusa's golden age, with the grandest public works in the Western world. After the sun set on ancient Greece, Siracusa became a Roman province and was supposedly evangelised by St Peter and St Paul on their way to Rome. It became the capital of Byzantium, albeit briefly, in the 7th century and produced several popes and patriarchs of Constantinople. After being sacked by the Arabs in AD 878 and the Normans in 1085, the city sank into oblivion but quietly prospered under Spanish rule.

Parco Archeologico della Neàpolis (Tues–Sun 9am–7pm; entrance fee), containing rough-hewn quarries, grandiose theatres and tombs. Although set among shady fir trees and olive groves, the site is still sweltering in summer. Still, avoiding the boisterous coach parties and tawdry stalls selling painted papyrus scrolls, independent visitors can quickly melt into the spacious Greek ruins.

Teatro Greco

In the park, a stroll to the **Teatro Greco** ❷ passes the rubble of **Ara di Ierone** II (altar of Hieron II) ❸, a sacrificial altar once decorated by imposing *telamones* (giants). Surrounded by trees, the vast open theatre seats 15,000 and is often called the masterpiece of ancient Greece. This astonishing accomplishment dates from 474 BC, although much was altered in the 3rd century BC. Carved into the rock, the *cavea* (horseshoe of tiered seats) is divided into two by a *diazoma* (corridor), and vertically cut into nine blocks of seats bearing inscriptions to deities and dignitaries. A satisfying climb to

the top provides striking views over modern Siracusa and the sea. On the terrace is a **nymphaeum** ❹, a complex of waterfall, springs and grotto that once contained statues and niches for votive offerings.

In the Roman era, the theatre became an amphitheatre, with water dammed and diverted to flood the arena for mock naval battles or gladiatorial combat. But, among the Greeks, it was a stage that witnessed the first performances of all Aeschylus's tragedies. The theatrical tradition is maintained today, in alternate (even-numbered) years, with the dramas of Sophocles and Euripides played on a stage once viewed by such notables as Plato and Archimedes.

Although partially closed, above the theatre, **Via dei Sepolcri** is a path of tombs, offering glimpses of tombs and carved niches at the upper level, while the lower level leads down to the *latomie*, giant quarries that were also used as prisons in Classical times. A wooded path slopes behind the back of the Greek theatre to a secret rocky arch and the

Map on page 174

The British pop group Simply Red, whose singer Mick Hucknall owns a vineyard on the slopes of Mount Etna, released a DVD of one of their performances in the Teatro Greco. Banco di Sicilia once promoted 24,000 bottles of Hucknall's Nero d'Avola wine through its bank branches – and sold every one of them.

BELOW:
Teatro Greco, with seats for 15,000.

The Ear of Dionysius.

lush **Latomia del Paradiso** ❺. These ancient quarries were once vaulted but are now open to the sun, bursting with olive and citrus groves or overgrown with cacti and ferns.

Here, too, is the cavernous **Orecchio di Dionisio (Ear of Dionysius)** ❻, man-made and at times 47 metres (154 ft) high, with excellent acoustics. It was given its name by Caravaggio after its resemblance to an ear. The poetic painter fancied that this echoing, dank, weirdly shaped cave was used by Dionysius to eavesdrop on his prisoners.

The adjoining **Grotta dei Cordari** is scored with chisel marks, because it was here that rope makers *(cordari)* stretched out their damp strands and tested their ropes for stress. A tunnel links Latomia del Paradiso with **Latomia Intagliatella**, and a rocky arch leads on to **Latomia di Santa Venera**, lemon-scented quarries which are pitted with votive niches.

It is hard to imagine that these lush gardens were once torture chambers. After Siracusa's decisive victory over Athens, the prisoners of war were lowered by rope into these pits. There was no need to mount guard: keeping captives alive involved no more than lowering a slave's half-rations and a drop of water. After 10 gruelling weeks, the non-Athenians who had survived were hauled out and sold as slaves. Athenians were branded with the mark of the Siracusan horse and also sold as slaves.

A separate entrance (but the same ticket) leads to the **Anfiteatro Romano** ❼, the Roman amphitheatre ringed by trees but drowned by traffic noise. While this tumbledown affair is not comparable with the amphitheatre in France, at Nîmes, the site has charm. A path lined with stone sarcophagi leads to the imposing theatre dug into the countryside, its masonry the work of master craftsmen. Below a parapet circling the arena is a corridor where both animals and gladiators made their entrances for the spectacles.

Between the Greek Theatre and Roman amphitheatre is **San Niccolò**, a Romanesque church concealing a Roman cistern. A circuit along **Via Giulio Emanuele Rizzo** reveals a

cross-section of the Classical city, including an aqueduct, the tomb-studded Via dei Sepolcri and rear views of Neàpolis.

Ancient tombs

Further uphill lie the **Necropoli delle Grotticelli**, a warren of Hellenistic and Byzantine tombs, including the supposed **Tomba di Archimede** (Tomb of Archimedes) ❽, framed by a dignified Roman portico. The Romans insisted that Archimedes' death was accidental, despite his creation of diabolical death traps used against them during the city's siege. This quarter forms part of ancient Tyche, characterised by labyrinthine catacombs that often follow the course of Greek aqueducts.

The **Catacombe di San Giovanni** (San Giovanni Catacombs) ❾ (daily, summer 9am–6pm, winter 9am–1pm, 3–6pm; entrance fee) provide entry to the persecuted world of the early Christians. Escorted by a friar, visitors view early Christian sarcophagi, a 4th-century drawing of *St Peter* and a mosaic depicting *Original Sin*. The network of galleries open into space-creating rotundas. On the walls are primitive frescoes and arcane symbols, with a mysterious fish-headed boat or dead dove bound by an *alpha* and *omega*. Could this be a secret Christian code? Or a pagan transmigration of souls? Academics disagree.

In the wild garden outside is the shell of **San Giovanni Evangelista**, with its rose window and sculpted door often masked by monastic underwear drying in the sun. This modest church was Siracusa's first cathedral and is dedicated to St Marcian, the city's earliest bishop.

Crooked steps lead down to **Cripta di San Marziano** and more catacombs. Light filters in on faded frescoes of Santa Lucia, sculpted cornices and an altar supposedly used by St Paul. Amid Greek lettering and crosses are primitive

depictions of a phoenix and a bull.

Probably the finest archaeological collection in Sicily lies in Villa Landolina, fittingly built over a quarry and pagan necropolis, in the **Museo Archeologico Regionale Paolo Orsi** ❿ (Tues–Sat 9am–7pm, Sun 9am–2pm; entrance fee; tel: 0931 464 022) on the neighbouring Viale Teocrito. Beautifully arranged in sequence, the well-organised museum reveals an overwhelming succession of superb collections, prehistoric and Greek, coming from Siracusa and its colonies, ending with finds at Gela and Agrigento. In the prehistory section, the stars are reconstructed necropoli, earthenware pots from Pantalica, and depictions of Cyclops and dwarf elephants.

In the Classical sections, the tone is set by two strikingly different works: the "immodest modesty" of the headless **Venere Anadiomene** (known also as **Venus Landolina** because it was unearthed here where the villa stands) and an Archaic sculpture of a seated fertility goddess suckling her twins, found in Megara

A Greek vase in the Museo Archeologico.

BELOW: the Temple of Apollo.

The Eureka Man

The image of Archimedes leaping from his bath with a cry of *Eureka!* (Greek for *I have found it*) is, despite the efforts of generations of physics teachers, not based in fact. While testing a gold crown suspected of being a mere alloy, Archimedes realised that the mass of water displaced by an object reveals its volume, and the mass of the object divided by its volume gives its density. The crown was found to be a fake as its density was less than that of solid gold. This discovery became known as the Archimedes' Principle: the principle of specific gravity and the basis of hydrostatics.

Born in 287 BC, Archimedes worked for Hieron, the Tyrant of Siracusa. While watching the Tyrant's builders and marine engineers at work, he devised theories worth a *Eureka!* each. His greatest discoveries were the formulae for the areas and volumes of spheres, cylinders and other shapes, anticipating the theories of integration by 1,800 years.

Archimedes was not a mere theoretician. He was intensely practical in an age when Siracusa was the most inventive place on earth. Dionysius's think-tank devised the long-range catapult which

saved Siracusa from the Carthaginian fleet. Archimedes built on this tradition with the Archimedean screw, still used for raising water, and with siege engines that did sterling service against the Romans. Polybius says the Romans "failed to reckon with the ability of Archimedes, nor did they foresee that, in some cases, the genius of one man is more effective than any number of hands."

Archimedes is often quoted as saying "Give me a place to stand and I will move the world", implying that he understood the principles of leverage. It is unlikely that he anticipated the laser beam by arranging magnifying glasses to set fire to the Roman fleet at long range, but he did produce a hydraulic serpent contraption that enabled just one man to operate a ship's pumps.

He also played a part in the construction of Hieron's remarkable 4,000-ton ship. Enough timber to build 60 conventional ships was brought from Mount Etna for the hull, which was then covered with sheet lead. The ship had three decks, one of which had a mosaic floor depicting *The Iliad*. The upper deck had a gymnasium, a garden with shady walks and a temple to Venus paved with Sicilian agate. The state cabin had a timepiece, a marble bath, and 10 horses in stalls on either side.

Yet this was no pleasure craft. It carried a long-range catapult, a device fitted to the masts that swung out over an attacking vessel and disgorged a huge rock, and also had a "cannon" that fired 5.5-metre (18-ft) arrows. Archimedes designed a system of screws for launching the vessel. It was then loaded with corn, 10,000 jars of Sicilian salt fish and 500 tons of wool and despatched to Ptolemy in Egypt as a gift.

Keen to exploit Archimedes' genius, the Roman commander Marcellus wanted him taken alive when the Romans occupied Siracusa. But, as legend has it, a Roman soldier came across an old codger apparently doodling in sand. Archimedes was working on his latest brainwave, so protested sharply when the soldier unwittingly stepped on his drawing. The soldier drew his sword and casually killed one of the greatest men in the world. ❑

LEFT: a bronze statue of Archimedes.

Map on page 174

Hyblaea. Elsewhere, the collection bursts with beauty and horror: lion's head gargoyles, Aztec-like masks, a Winged Victory, a terracotta frieze of grinning gorgons; a Medusa with her tongue lolling out. Away from the horrors, smoothly virile marble torsos of *kouroi* (heroic youths) await. Beauty, both pure and sensual, lingers in the Roman sarcophagus of a couple called Valerius and Adelphia or in fragments of friezes from Selinunte and Siracusa. (The museum takes the name Paolo Orsi to honour the island's most eminent archaeologist.)

Ancient parchment

Around the corner, the **Museo del Papiro** (9am–1.30pm, closed Mon) displays collections of ancient papyrus and parchment and presents Egyptian paper-making techniques. Studios throughout the city offer to reproduce anything in papyrus, from old masters to holiday snapshots.

Off the adjoining Via Augusto Von Platen are the **Catacombe di Vigna Cassia,** catacombs with 3rd-century tombs and frescoed chambers which lead on to **Latomia dei Cappuccini** ⓫, the most picturesque quarries alongside a former Capuchin monastery. Set on the coast, these huge honeycombed pits are matched by sculptural vegetation, but currently they can only be viewed from Via Acradina above. From the adjoining Piazza Cappuccini are stirring views of the rocky shore.

Further south again, near the sports stadium, are a series of (closed) catacombs surrounding the church of **Santa Lucia** ⓬ (daily 9.30am– 12.30pm, 3–6pm; entrance fee), a Byzantine church founded by San Zozimo, the first Greek Bishop of Siracusa, and dedicated to St Lucy, the city's beloved virginal patron saint who was martyred here. The *Burial of St Lucy* (1608) by Caravaggio once hung in the church but is now in the Galleria Regionale in Palazzo Bellomo, Ortigia *(see page 184)*.

Next to the church, connected by an underground passage, is the octagonal **Cappella del Sepolcro**, which was constructed by Giovanni Vermexio in 1630 as the sepulchre for the saint whose remains were

For many visitors Siracusa is the place for market shopping. Best bets are the markets (daily except Sunday) on Ortigia, on the Lungomare close to the Tempio di Apollo, and the larger, rambling general market, La Fiera, on the outskirts, on Via Algeri. Coaches bring in the crowds from the surrounding towns and villages, so you will not be alone.

BELOW: exploring the ruins.

*Ortigia balconies
put to practical use.*

BELOW: mending nets
in the Porto Piccolo.

held in Venice. Sadly the relics are still there, interred in the Church of San Geremia.

On the bank of the **Porto Piccolo** ⓭, the small harbour, are the scant remains of the city's ancient **arsenal**. Nearby stands the Byzantine **bath-house** where legend has it that Emperor Constans was assassinated with a soap dish in AD 668. On **Piazzale del Foro Siracusano**, just behind the port, is the original Greek **agora** ⓮ of Acradina. This was the commercial centre of the Greek city but sadly suffered bombing by both the Allies and the Luftwaffe in 1943. At its centre is a war memorial.

Further west lies the ruins of the **Ginnasio Romano** ⓯, the Roman gymnasium (daily 9am–1pm; closed public holidays), a 1st-century theatre and shrine occupying a picturesquely flooded spot. Although its origins are obscure, the shrine was conceivably dedicated to Oriental deities. The raised portico is well-preserved and shimmers obligingly.

Nearby, the **Porto Grande** ⓰, where Dionysius defeated the Athenian navy in 415 BC, has become a busy industrial and mercantile port with a yacht marina.

Ortigia

A stroll across the main bridge, **Ponte Nuovo**, leads past pretty moored boats and pastel-coloured palazzi to the **Darsena**, the inner docks. This is the tiny but atmospheric island of Ortigia, jutting into **Mare Ionio**, the Ionian Sea. Rivalled only by Ragusa as a centre of aimless wandering, this partly pedestrianised island is the place for leisurely lunches, summer promenades and dreamy ruminations amid crumbling history.

Despite European Union funds earmarked for Ortigia's restoration, the city's bureaucratic lethargy and lobbying by vested interest groups mean that most projects remain stalled: the citizens grumble while the dilapidated palaces grow more dilapidated. Nonetheless, after the flight of so many families to the faceless suburbs in the 1960s, creeping gentrification is taking place, attracting a more enlightened

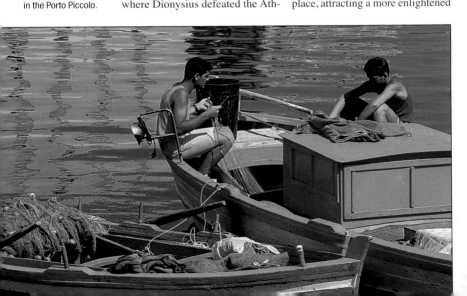

generation, particularly young professionals in search of urban charm.

Graced with two natural harbours, fresh springs and the blessing of the Delphic oracle, this seductive island was dedicated to the huntress Artemis, with the chief temple known as "the couch of Artemis". In Christian times, the goddess fused with Santa Lucia, the city's patron saint, and her cult is still venerated in city festivals.

Heralding the entrance to Ortigia is the **Tempio di Apollo** (Temple of Apollo) **⓱** in the middle of an unprepossessing square. Now sunken and dishevelled, it is the oldest city temple in Sicily, built in 565 BC and discovered by chance in 1862. This Doric temple was dedicated to Apollo, whose name is legible on the steps of the base. The squat temple has accrued Byzantine and Norman remains, and it would appear to have been at one time or another both a church and a mosque.

In the maze of streets behind the temple is the church of **San Pietro** **⓲**, supposedly founded by St Peter before being converted into a Byzantine basilica. The 8th-century apses and blind arcading are incorporated into a 15th-century shell. Just west, Via XX Settembre contains tracts of the massive Greek walls. Dionysius was an indefatigable builder and the immense wall, 5 km (3 miles) in length, was built in 20 days by 60,000 men on double time, and is still visible in other parts of the town.

Ortigia's centre

From the temple, it is a short stroll along Via Roma to **Piazza Archimede**, the grandiose centre of Ortigia. This baroque stage set, adorned by a well-restored 19th-century fountain, is framed by dignified mansions. Take refreshment at one of the *caffès* if you wish, but follow the signs to the **Duomo** **⓳** (daily 8am–noon, 4–7pm), a 5th-century temple to Athena converted into a

Christian cathedral in 640AD under the direction of Bishop Zosimus. Classical columns bulge through the external walls in Via Minerva, a sign that the temple has only been encased in a church since the 7th century. Before then, the temple was a beacon to sailors, with its ivory doors and a gold facade surmounted by the goddess Athena bearing a glinting bronze shield.

The exterior conjures up a unique spell: a rich baroque facade (1754) with dramatic *chiaroscuro* effects, including an inside porch boasting twisted barley-stick columns. Yet the cool, striking interior betrays its Greek origins; the worn but lovely fluted Doric columns set into the outer walls belong to the Temple to Athena. Notwithstanding a Greek soul, the temple also glorifies later conquerors. A Greek baptismal font rests on Norman bronze lions; above is a medieval wood-panelled ceiling; a baroque choir and Byzantine apses strike newer notes; only the Arab presence is missing. The apses were slightly damaged in the 1991 earthquake but the Greek sandstone fluted

Map on page 174

The interior of Siracusa's baroque Duomo.

BELOW: the Duomo, a 5th-century temple later converted into a cathedral.

columns survived. In the side chapel, **Capella del Crocifisso**, is a painting of *St Zosimus* by Antonello da Messina, and one of *St Marcian* attributed to the school of Antonello, also believed to have painted the 13 panels in the **Sagrestia** (Sacristy).

Also in Piazza del Duomo is the Palazzo Vermexio (1633), the **Municipio** (municipal offices), built by Giovanni Vermexio for the Senate on the ruins of a small Ionic temple possibly dedicated to Artemis.

Just a short distance away, on Via Cappodieci, stands **Palazzo Bellomo** ⑳, the loveliest Catalan-Gothic mansion in Ortigia, and the city's compact art gallery, **Galleria Regionale** (Tues–Sun 9am–1.30pm; entrance fee).

Inside, an elegant courtyard leads to the intimate gallery housing Caravaggio's masterpiece, the *Burial of St Lucy* (1608), Antonello da Messina's remarkable *Annunciation* (1474) and the grandiose **funerary monument** for Eleonora Branciforte d'Aragona by Giovan Battista Mazzolo. Other highlights include 14th- to 18th-century works, from

Byzantine icons to Catalan and Spanish paintings, Sicilian jewellery, Renaissance tombs and important pieces in gold, silver, coral, majolica, ceramics and terracotta.

Fonte Aretusa

At the southern end of Via Capodieci is **Fonte Aretusa** ㉑, a freshwater spring that is the symbol of Siracusa. Legend has it that the nymph Arethusa, a follower of great Olympian deity Artemis (Diana), was loved and pursued by the river god Alpheius after she bathed in his waters in the Peloponnese.

As she fled from his embrace to Sicily, she prayed to Artemis for help and, on reaching Ortigia, was changed by Artemis into a spring called Arethusa (Aretusa). Alpheius, however, did not give up. He flowed below the sea and mingled his waters with hers. Whether this was rape or the uniting of lovers, Siracusani continue to disagree.

After a 17th-century earthquake, however, the spring is supposed to have been mingled with sea water but, in reality, Ortigia has an abun-

dance of sweet water coming from the Iblei mountains through a peculiar geological land fault. Many houses have freshwater wells.

In any case, ducks make the clumps of reedy papyrus plants in spring water a romantic love nest. At night, the fountain sees a parade of Siracusa's youth, accompanied by flirtation and the revving of mopeds. Admiral Nelson's fleet drew water here before proceeding to Malta in 1798 and then on to the Battle of the Nile. For lovers of ancient manuscripts, the papyrus museum, **Museo del Papiro** (9am–1.30pm; closed Mon), is here, at Via Teocrito 66.

From Fonte Aretusa, the panoramic terraces of **Passeggio Adorno** lead back, parallel to the Porto Grande quays with its yacht marina and collection of private yachts, to the **Porta Marina** archway that was one of the city gates created in the 15th-century Spanish fortifications. It is a tree-lined, charming stretch, a popular place to stroll. This triumphant arch leads to the heart of the Catalan-Gothic quarter, centred on **Santa Maria dei Miracoli**, off Via Savoia, a finely sculpted 15th-century church. Excellent restaurants dot the streets around here.

The other, eastern, side of the island is skirted by **Lungomare di Levante**; you can approach this waterfront along Via Trento alongside the Temple of Apollo, through the heart of the Arab quarter, with its tortuous, narrow streets that were designed to create breezes and keep the homes cool even in summer.

You can also get to the Lungomare from central Piazza Archimede, along **Via Maestranza** and the heart of the old guilds' quarter, graced with Spanish palaces. Amid the sombre courtyards and swirling sculpture, local *pasticcerie* literally represent the icing on the cake. There is a vegetable and fish market on the Lungomare on weekday mornings.

On the southernmost tip of Ortigia, the fortified hulk of **Castello Maniace**  dominates the promontory and once served as protector of Syracusa's two shores. Constructed in 1239 by Frederick II, it takes its name from the Byzantine general, Giorgio Maniace, who was in charge of the city's defences. Until recently it was an army barracks, but is now closed for lengthy restoration and re-designation. Troops stationed here played an important role in anti-Mafia campaigns in the 1990s, with soldiers drawn from outside the province to try to prevent any collusion with local criminals. The fortress retained its military purpose until 2001, when plans were drawn up to convert it into an exhibition centre. Until then visitors who peered too long at the Gothic doorway were discouraged by nonchalant soldiers (doing their National service) waving automatic weapons.

Great escapes

Close to the city are sandy beaches and two unique spots, a Greek castle

Map on page 174

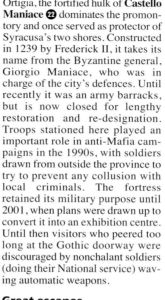

A stall at the fish market.

BELOW: Piazza Archimede by night.

Map on page 174

TIP

Siracusa has its fair share of eateries offering "tourist menus" but the small pizzerias and seafood restaurants offer better value. Pasta dishes with mussels and urchins are delicious but are not always available in summer.

BELOW: exploring caves in the region.

and a dreamy riverscape of papyrus plantations.

South of Siracusa, off the SS 115 (the route to Noto and Módica), lie popular beaches at the small resorts of **Arenella**, **Ognina** and **Fontane Bianche**. Although Siracusa's beaches tend to be full of golden bodies rather than golden sands, a more atmospheric swimming spot is 20 km (12 miles) north of Siracusa, passed Augusta, at **Brùcoli**. It is a rocky beach set around a Spanish castle that enjoys views of Etna on clear days.

In ancient **Epipolae**, 8 km (5 miles) northwest of Siracusa, is **Castello Eurialo** (daily, 9am–one hour before sunset; follow signs to Belvedere, or take the regular bus service). The fort represented the fifth component of the Greek *pentapolis* and was the most magnificent of Greek military outposts. Designed by Dionysius, the castle protected Siracusa's most exposed flank, the conjunction of the northern and southern city walls.

Apart from amazingly solid masonry and moats hewn out of the rock, the castle had labyrinthine passageways and a keep surrounded by five towers. As a final security measure, the sole entrance was concealed by a patchwork of walls. When Dionysius was in residence, he would not allow his wives into his bed unless they were first searched. According to legend, his bed was surrounded by a moat, and his wives reached it across a little wooden drawbridge, which he then drew up.

Fonte Ciane

South of the city, 5 km (3 miles) along the road for Canicattini Bagni, is **Fonte Ciane** (Spring of Ciane), a picturesque spot close to the ruined Temple of Olympian Zeus, declared a Nature Reserve in 1984. Ciane is the mythical spring and pool dedicated to a water-nymph Ciane (Cyane) who dissolved into her own pool with grief as she wept, having failed to prevent the rape of Persephone by Hades who had risen from the Underworld through the pool.

Canoes, easily rented from the tiny riverside marina from March onwards, are a way to explore the relaxing rivers, framed by canopies of lush foliage. (Unless you are lucky enough to encounter the only boatman with the right keys, expect to have to haul the canoe over a weir.)

Or you can call Signor Vella (tel: 368 7296040 or 368 3168199) to arrange a more comfortable visit on a boat. The *Ciane* weaves through groves of papyrus with tendrils as delicate as cobwebs. The origins of this wild plant are obscure: it was either imported from Egypt or native to Siracusa. Either way, its habitat is endangered but it flourishes in this idyllic backwater.

Another excursion to consider is a boat trip aboard the **Selene** from Porto Grande around Ortigia following the coastline. Call Signor Castagnino (tel: 340 0558769 or 347 1275680). ❏

RESTAURANTS AND CAFÉS

Siracusa

Antico Caffè Minerva
Via Minerva 15.
Tel: 0931 22606.
One of the oldest *caffès* in the city. Enjoy their specialities in the Tea Room or at tables outside. €

Archimede
Via Gemellaro 8. Ortigia.
Tel: 0931 69701.
www.trattoriaarchimede.it
Arguably the best or, at least, most authentic restaurant in Siracusa. Service is friendly; the menu is interesting but seafood predominates. There is always an array of subtle (and fishy) antipasti. Pizza too. Closed Sun, except Mar–Nov. €€€

Cantinaccia
Via XX Settembre 13.
Tel: 0931 65945.
Rustic cooking, good pasta and meat dishes served on a pretty veranda facing sea and garden. Closed Tues, except in summer. €€€

Castello Fiorentino
Via del Crocefisso 6.
Tel: 0931 21097.
The town's most popular pizzeria can be chaotic and you may have to queue, but it's very good value and the pizzas are superb. Closed Mon. €

Darsena da Iannuzzo
Riva Garibaldi 6, Ortigia.
Tel: 0931 61522.
www.ristorantedarsena.it
Just across the bridge, this bold, bright, popular trattoria serves the freshest fish and local dishes. Closed Wed. €€€

Don Camillo
Via Maestranza 92.
Tel: 0931 67133.
www.ristorantedoncamillo siracusa.it
Highly regarded. Extensive wine cellars. Closed two weeks July. €€€

Enoteca Salaria
Via Roma 86, Ortigia.
Tel: 0931 463 0047.
www.enotecasalaria.com
Wine bar and shop where food is served. A fine place to try local wines. €

Gran Caffè del Duomo
Piazza del Duomo
Tel: 0931 21544.
A typical *caffè*. Try their ricotta filled *cannoli* or *tiramisù* if you crave something sweet. €

La Foglia
Via Capodieci 29, Ortigia (close to the Fonte Aretusa).
Tel: 0931 66233.
www.lafoglia.it
Vegetarians welcomed. Sicilian and fish dishes also served. Features antique glasses and plates, and hand-embroidered tablecloths. Closed Tues, except in Dec and summer. €€€

La Gazza Ladra
Via Cavour 8.
Tel: 340 0602428
www.gazzaladrasiracusa.com.
This small, family-run trattoria uses the freshest of local ingredients in their daily fish specials and generous plates of antipasti. Closed Mon. €€

Medusa
Via Santa Teresa 21.
Tel: 0931 61403.
A delicious blend of Sicilian and Tunisian dishes. Lots of fish. Closed Mon and 2 weeks in Aug. €€

Minerva
Piazza Duomo 20.
Tel: 0931 69404.
Conveniently placed for lunch after a cathedral visit. Closed Mon. €€

Porticciolo
Via Trento. Tel: 0931 61914.
Near the market. Offers delicious mixed-fish grills or fresh lobster. Closed Mon and 10 days in Nov. €€

Spiaggetta
Viale dei Lidi 473, Fontane Bianche. Tel: 0931 790 334.
Modern and welcoming with windows overlooking picturesque creek. Sicilian dishes, pizzeria. Closed Tues in winter.€€

Zsa
Via Roma 73, Ortigia.
Tel: 0931 22204.
Siracusan specialities: grilled swordfish, seafood risotto, pasta *c'angiovi* (with pine nuts, sultanas and anchovies) and local *bruschetta*. Closed Mon. €€

PRICE CATEGORIES

Prices for three-course dinner per person with a half-bottle of house wine:
€ = under €15
€€ = €15–30
€€€ = €30–60

RIGHT: ice coffee is popular in hot weather.

SIRACUSA PROVINCE

Outside the city, this southeastern province offers a
cross-section of Sicily: baroque, Classical and
prehistoric blended with a leisurely way of life

The Greeks colonised this area
two centuries after settling the
rest of eastern Sicily. Since then
Siracusa has rested on its laurels,
parading its Greek heart and Levan-
tine soul with the effortless superiority of a born aristocrat.

The *provincia* has been shaped by
the cataclysm of the 1693 earthquake. Although all Norman castles
and important churches were razed
to the ground, the region responded
by building some of the greatest
baroque architecture in Sicily,
notably in the town of Noto.

Farming country

The journey southwards from **Siracusa ❶** provides a fair introduction
to the provincial landscape, with
low-slung farms, citrus orchards,
sandy beaches and a rugged hinterland. The terrain spans limestone
escarpments and rocky gorges, a flat
coastal strip and, just inland, gentle
farming country dotted with olive
and almond groves.

South of Siracusa the road leads
to **Cassibile**, an unremarkable small
town surrounded by sweeps of citrus, almonds and cereals. But it does
proudly claim its own significance,
an event marked on a stone plaque
on the route SS115. This is where, on
3 September 1943, US general
Bedell Smith signed the Allied terms

of surrender with the Italian general,
Castellano. From that day Italy's
army was no longer in World War II.

Further south is the prosperous
market town of **Avola,** a prelude to
the great baroque setting of Noto
stacked up on a hill. For many years
Avola was the centre of Italy's flourishing almond production, a role it
still plays, although more modestly,
as the demand for Italian almonds
has lessened since the United States
has entered the business commercially. On Piazza Umberto I, at the

Map
on page
190

LEFT: section of
the doorway of San
Sebastiano in Feria.
BELOW:
Noto's cathedral.

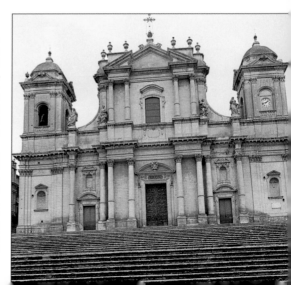

An eyewitness recorded Noto Antica's 1693 quake as "so horrible that the soil undulated like the waves of a stormy sea, and the mountains danced as if drunk." More than 1,000 people died as the city collapsed in one terrible moment.

BELOW: the Fontana d'Ercole, Noto.

centre of this hexagonally shaped town (built after 1693), is the church of San Niccolò, the **Chiesa Madre**. Dotted around are other churches, as well as a number of art nouveau buildings. On the coast, a short distance away, is **Lido d'Avola**, a simple resort that becomes a local meeting place in summer when the seasonal fish restaurants open.

Noto

Then there is **Noto ❷**, the finest baroque town in Sicily, one that is both blatantly theatrical and deeply rational. With justification, visitors praise its proportion, symmetry, spaciousness and innate sense of spectacle. Sicilians simply call it a garden of stone. For many recent years much of it lay crumbling and neglected, but with restoration in hand, the town is rapidly returning to its former glory. Noto was declared a UNESCO Heritage Site in 1996.

After the original Noto, known

now as **Noto Antica ❸**, was destroyed in the 1693 earthquake, it lay buried under rubble, abandoned ruins nestling in the foothills of the Iblei mountains, the phoenix that never rose from the ashes. It was a complex city full of Classical foundations, Romanesque and baroque churches, convents and mansions, a home over the centuries to Romans, Arabs and Normans as it grew into a flourishing medieval city. All this was obliterated in 1693.

Ten years later a new site on safer ground 10 km (6 miles) away was selected by the inhabitants and, headed by Giuseppe Lanza (Duke of Camastra) and Prince Giovanni Landolina, new Noto was planted on the flanks of a distant hill. The city was composed around three parallel axes running horizontally across the hillside, with straight streets and three squares to create interest, each enlivened by a scenic church as a backdrop. The whole design was to be

clothed in warm, golden limestone, with monumental flights of steps to enchant with tricks of perspective. The realization of this ambitious plan was the work of Gagliardi and Sinatra, gifted local architects who also worked in Ragusa province.

Despite the beauteous architecture, the glowing limestone buildings are inherently fragile and susceptible to erosion and pollution. The city faced its greatest crisis in 1996 when the cupola and roof of the Cathedral of San Niccolò collapsed after a heavy thunderstorm.

Urban theatre

The monumental gateway **Porta Reale** (1838) at the end of the tree-lined public gardens leads to **Corso Vittorio Emanuele**, the stately main thoroughfare, with a small selection of *caffès* and many souvenir shops broken by three equally monumental squares. To the left, the town slopes downwards; to the right, it rises graciously to meet **Noto Alta** (Upper Noto), with its modern buildings.

The first building on the right, on **Piazza dell'Immacolata**, gives a fine idea of what is to follow. At the top of a theatrical, grand flight of stairs (for only the fittest), the church of **San Francesco** (daily 9.30am– 12.30pm, 4–7pm) looks like the backdrop for a film set. Built between 1704 and 1745 by Rosario Gagliardi and Vincenzo Sinatra, it has a pleasant facade and simple, stucco interior. The **Seminario**, once the convent, of Benedictine monastery of **San Salvatore** (1706), sits alongside the church, facing it across the steep incline of Via Zanardelli. It has a fine 18th-century facade attributed to Rosario Gagliardi. Also on this piazza is the **Museo Civico** (opening hours vary; ask at the tourist office for the latest information; entrance fee), with a collection of contemporary art – the archeological section is awaiting restoration – and the church of **Santa Chiara** (daily 9am–12.30pm, 4pm–7pm), richly decorated with stucco and containing the 16th-century marble statue of *Madonna and Child*, attributed to Antonello Gagini.

The Corso sweeps onwards to **Piazza Municipio**, the second square, Noto's stage set at the centre

Map on page 190

Much of Noto has theoretically been under restoration, but Noto council's notion of restoration was to convert the finer mansions, such as Palazzo Trigona, into conference centres. More imaginatively, the vast monastery of San Tommaso was transformed into a sinister prison.

BELOW: on the steps of the church of San Francesco.

The gamble that failed

Economically, the province has fallen behind its more entrepreneurial neighbours, Catania and Ragusa. In the 1950s Siracusa short-sightedly allowed a sizeable stretch of the coastline to be taken over in the rush for petrochemical riches. It is now paying the price for this gain in the form of polluted beaches, poor additional industrial development and a lack of tourist facilities – just when the whole island is waking up to the fact that tourism is big business and, used properly, can enhance both local lifestyles and the environment. Most visitors, however, turn a blind eye to the faults and simply relish Siracusa's traditional sense of *discreto benessere*, discreet wellbeing.

BELOW:
the drawing room of the Palazzo Ducezio.

of the town. The golden grace of the buildings matches the majestic proportions of the design; the set is framed by man-made scenery. On the square is **Palazzo Ducezio**, (9am–1.30pm, 3–7pm; later hours in summer; entrance fee), the elegantly grand town hall designed by Vincenzo Sinatra in 1746.

Opposite is **San Niccolò**, the once splendid, towering **cattedrale**. Above the grandiose, theatrical staircase, its wide 18th-century facade and cool pastel interior were clad in scaffolding until a long-awaited restoration in 2007. The story of the restoration is told in a museum behind the cathedral (entrance on Via Cavour; daily 9.30am–1pm, 3.30–8pm; entrance fee), which also contains some of the cathedral's precious artefacts.

Next to the cathedral is **Palazzo Landolina**, the Bishop's Palace that was once the home of one of Noto's benefactors.

The Corso progresses to **Piazza XVI Maggio**, graced by gardens of palms, monkey puzzle trees and a fountain of Hercules taken from Noto Antica. (The helpful tourist office is

in this garden; tel: 0931 573 779.) Dominating the shady garden lies the recently restored church of **San Domenico**, a curvilinear Gagliardi church with a beautiful facade influenced by Roman and Spanish baroque. It is a Gagliardi masterpiece.

Facing it is the restored, ornately gilded 1850 **Teatro Vittorio Emanuele** (theatre season Oct–May; entrance fee). Also surveying the spacious square is **Collegio dei Gesuiti**, now a school, and, on the slope downwards where Via Ruggero VII meets Via Ducezio, stands **Santa Maria del Carmine** (9.30am–12.30pm, 4–7pm), created by Gagliardi's assistant, Vincenzo Sinatra, its concave doorway guarded by two *putti* (cherubs), the symbol of the Carmelite order.

Palazzo Villadorata

Palazzo Villadorata on Via Nicolaci, which leads uphill from Piazza Municipio, is Noto's pride and joy, though currently closed to the public. Also known as **Palazzo Nicolaci** after its noble owners, this baroque jewel with wonderful balconies has

been restored to its former glory. Don Giacomo Nicolaci, a patron of the arts, donated part of his huge library to the Biblioteca Communale and a wing of the palace to the city library. Around the windows are friezes of mythical monsters, a snarling parade of griffons, sphinxes, sirens and cherubs. Arabesques climb the walls, clashing with crested cornices and billowing wrought-iron balconies. The sloped courtyard was designed for carriages and includes an access ramp so that the prince could ride directly into the *piano nobile*.

Palazzo Villadorata plays a starring role in the city drama away from the Corso, but secondary characters should not be overlooked, especially convents and churches. On Via Cavour, parallel to the Corso, is the church of **Montevergine** (1748–50) with its concave frontage, while Via Giovanni XXIII, behind San Niccolò, reveals subtle details as niches for statues, sculpted cornices and bulging "goose-breast" balconies.

The spacious lower town was originally only for the clergy and aristocracy. On the hill above the grandiose public face of Noto rises the *popolare* district, clustered around the hilly Piazza Mazzini, dominated by the **Crocifisso**, a domed church attributed to Gagliardi that has a portal flanked by Romanesque lions rescued from Noto Antica. Its interior holds a Francesco Laurana masterpiece, *Madonna della Neve* (1471), a serene sculpture amid the frenzy of baroque.

The massive building with an attractive facade stretching from Via Trigona to Piazza Mazzini is the former monastery, **Monastero di San Tommaso** (1720), now a prison.

The **Giardino Pubblico** at the eastern end of the Corso is a peaceful end to any visit to Noto.

The southern coast

Southeast of Noto, there are well-signposted sandy beaches that become busy only in the height of the summer season – that is, end of July to end-September. Both the **Lido di Noto** and **Lido d'Avola** have modest facilities: *caffès*, restaurants, hotels and bed-and-breakfast arrangements. Although "foreigners" enjoy them, they are essentially holiday destinations geared to Sicilian and Italian families.

Eloro ❹ is a Classical site on the unpolluted stretch that leads south to Capo Pàssero. Now in ruins, the Siracusan city of Elorus (open 9am–1pm) was founded at the end of the 6th century BC. Well-preserved turreted walls survive, as do porticos, a pair of gateways, the agora and a Sanctuary of Demeter. Just outside the site stands the **Colonna della Pizzuta**, a curious Hellenistic funeral column that looks like a chimney stack. In the neighbouring hamlet of **Caddeddi**, a villa from the same period has been unearthed, along with mosaics depicting hunting scenes.

The 6-km (4-mile) journey south to the deserted **Vendìcari wetlands** passes citrus and almond groves. The Vendìcari salt marshes, declared a

The ceiling of the baroque Crocifisso in Piazza Mazzini.

Map on page 190

BELOW: detail from Palazzo Ducezio's hall of mirrors.

Sunrise at Marzamemi.

nature reserve in 1984 because of their biological importance, are popular with nesting and migrating birds. Most Siracusani are sun-worshippers rather than ornithologists, but for anyone simply in search of an invigorating walk, Vendìcari has much to offer: the reserve embraces a sweeping crescent of sand and four distinct marshes, with medieval water channels cut to reach the salt pans. The site also includes battered remains of medieval fortifications, a tower built by Pietro d'Aragona in the 5th century and some abandoned tuna-processing sheds. A marked trail leads through the salt marshes.

Marzamemi

Further down the coast lies **Marzamemi ❺**, the most appealing fishing village in the province. As a former feudal domain, the village retains a crumbling noble palace, adorned with the Villadorata family crest. Despite its recent elevation to small-time summer resort and its growing yacht marina (suitable only in summer months), at heart Marzamemi remains a working fishing village, complete with lobster pots and the obligatory fishing nets drying in the sun. *Cernia* (grouper), like *pesce spada* (swordfish), is a prized Mediterranean fish but mullet, mussels and tuna are also on local menus.

In summer, Sicilians from Catania and Siracusa also flock to **Pachino ❻** and the sandy beaches around Capo Pàssero. The pillboxes littering this stretch of coast are a testament to troubled times. In July 1943 the Allied invasion of Sicily took place on these shores. While General Patton and the American forces landed near Gela, General Montgomery and the British 8th Army landed between Pachino and Pozzallo. Giuseppe Tornatore's film *Malena* includes a dramatic re-enactment of the landing on Pachino's beaches. Nowadays, Pachino is a quiet wine-producing centre with a faded baroque heart. The hinterland is devoted to market gardening but the coast is rapidly developing resort amenities.

Beyond is **Capo Pàssero ❼**, the southernmost tip of the province, and home to several low-key seaside resorts that were, until recently, villages dependent on tuna fishing and processing. Today, only one tuna fishery remains, run by Don Bruno di Belmonte. Energetic visitors can rent a boat to row to Isola di Capo Pàssero and the other island rocks here.

North of Siracusa

Swimming is not advisable on the northern stretch of coast, in the **Golfo di Augusta** between Siracusa and Augusta, except at Brucoli, just north of Augusta, where the Golfo di Catania begins. As the coastline reputed to have Europe's highest concentration of chemical effluents, this area is an ecological disaster. Petrochemical plants based around Augusta have destroyed 48 km (30 miles) of beach. At night, however, this stretch has a savage futuristic beauty of its own, with its glittering

towers, gargantuan oil tanks and livid smokestacks.

The Classical sites of Thapsos on Penisola Magnisi and neighbouring Megara Hyblaea are too close for comfort to the belching fumes. Acrid fumes threaten to engulf the important site of **Megara Hyblaea** ❽, one of the earliest Greek cities in Sicily, founded in 728 BC. Cypresses shield it in poetic desolation, but industrial blight is tangible. A wall and a group of sarcophagi front the ramparts of a Hellenistic fortress. Beyond are the foundations of an Archaic city, as yet unexplored.

As a smaller mirror image of Siracusa, **Augusta** ❾ once had charm and prestige. However, while its islet setting, double harbour and faded baroque centre remain, so does rampant industrialisation. Cement works and petrochemical plants blight views of the park, *castello* and causeway. Augusta's good restaurant, Donna Ina, provides scant compensation.

The ancient interior

The rocky, wild, sparsely populated hinterland is one of Siracusa's charms. The summer-parched slopes and odd mounds conceal several significant Classical sites. The desolate countryside generates an austere appeal that is matched by the dusty baroque country towns along the route. This is Sicily with its roots laid bare, a prehistoric and Siculi land that predates Siracusa city by centuries. The rocky tableland is home to **Pantálica**, the region's foremost prehistoric site. The drive to Pantálica skirts the bleached white or pale green Iblean hills before reaching the lush **Anapo Valley**.

Dedicated hikers with a full day to spend in Pantálica will choose the northern entrance, reached through Palazzolo and Ferla. However, for more convenient access and less walking, choose the southern route through **Sortino**, following signs for Pantálica Sud. This rural drive passes country villas, citrus groves and dry stone walls.

Despite their importance, the **Necrópoli di Pantálica** ❿ (daily 9am–sunset) are off the beaten track. However, Siracusani have long been drawn to the lush gorges, a verdant paradise remote from the barren image of the Iblean hills. Apart from the loveliness of this sprawling site, Pantálica offers a slice of Sicily's earliest history: this Siculi necropolis contains rock tombs dating from the 13th to the 8th centuries BC. As the largest Bronze and Iron Age cemetery in Sicily, it contains over 5,000 tombs carved into the sheer cliffs of a limestone plateau, not to mention cave dwellings. Although Pantálica's history is shrouded in mystery, tradition claims it as Hybla, the capital of the Siculi king who allowed Greek colonists to occupy Megara Hyblaea. Certainly, some of these gaping holes are 3,000 years old.

The tombs lie at the end of a gorge carved by the River Anapo and studded with citrus trees and wild flowers, acanthus and prickly pears. In

Time for a chat in Pachino.

BELOW: the prehistoric Necrópoli di Pantálica.

Map on page 190

Map on page 190

Among the Greek ruins at Akrai are reliefs cut directly into the rock face. This one shows heroes banqueting.

BELOW: the beach at Capo Pàssero.

this secret garden lie tiered rows of tombs, a honeycomb-pitted surface of jagged rectangular openings cut into the pale rock. Mule tracks and marked paths follow the river towards a disued railway line, with easier paths marked "A", and more challenging ones marked "B". Walkers are rewarded with discreet picnic spots, as well as views of sheer rock-faces and deep ravines. Apart from the tombs and dwellings, there remains a Byzantine rock chapel, and early Christian frescoes. In spring this sacred chasm is a beauty spot bursting with snapdragons, asphodel and daisies.

A country drive leads southwest to **Palazzolo Acrèide** ⓫, a sleepy town with Norman origins, a population of 9,204, and what seems an air of surprise when they discover that outsiders should stray so far. The baroque centre displays several theatrical set pieces, whose charms are only slightly diminished by the air of abandon. The town's rough-hewn charms are apparent in **Palazzo Zocco** on Via Umberto, with its chaotic baroque ornamentation, and

the 17th-century **Chiesa Annunziata**, an early baroque church that has a portal guarded by Spanish barley-shape columns. However, many of the town's rewards are low-key: the occasional gargoyle, carved door-post or billowing balcony.

Palazzolo Acrèide is also known for its traditional carnival before Lent and its marvellous feast day that celebrates San Sebastiano. The local pork sausages are much favoured too, from Casa della Salsiccia, Via Roma 183 (tel: 0931 882 410; closed Wed pm).

Akrai

A signposted road for **Teatro Greco** leads to the Classical city of **Akrai** ⓬, a Greek site set on high windy moorland. The attractive walled park (daily, summer 9am–one hour before sunset, winter 9am–2pm; entrance fee) encloses quarries and temples founded in 644 BC by Siracusa, and a Greek theatre (3rd century BC but then also used by the Romans. It is built on a grand scale, far larger than required by the 600 spectators who watched the performances).

The confusing site contains stone carvings, votive niches, commemorative plaques, a necropolis, catacombs and the remains of a Temple to Aphrodite. The most impressive views are of the deep quarries framed by dry stone walls, firs, bay trees and wild olives. The lovely site suffers from poor management, with temples and sculptures arbitrarily locked. Across the hillside are the **Santoni** (Holy Ones), a series of 12 crudely carved sculptures, made in honour of the goddess Cybele, the Magna Mater whose esoteric cult originated in Asia. These precious finds lie a few fields away and a visit to the site requires a custodian's presence.

Leading out of town, the **Strada Panoramica** circling Akrai lives up to its name, offering views across the Greek settlements towards Ragusa province. ❑

RESTAURANTS AND CAFÉS

Augusta

Donna Ina
Località Faro Santa Croce
Est. 4 km (2½ miles) out of
town. Tel: 0931 983 422.
Seasonal seafood specialities prepared with
care. Closed Mon unless
it is a public holiday. €€

Avola

Finocchiaro
Piazza Umberto I 81.
Tel: 0931 831 062.
Renowned *caffè* with
cannoli, fruit flans and
nougat made with local
almonds. €

Rustico
Via Santa Lucia 52.
Tel: 0931 831 084.
Ignore the setting, this
simple *ristorante* serves
excellent dishes inexpensively. Delicious *spaghetti
al vongole*, grilled swordfish and Nero d'Avola
wine. Pizza too. €€

Noto

Il Barocco
Via Cavour 8.
Tel: 0931 835 999.
An atmospheric courtyard setting and tasty
dishes – pasta, pizza and
grilled meat and fish. €€

Carmine
Via Ducezio 9.
Tel: 0931 838 705.
www.trattoriadelcarmine.it
Home cooking and local
dishes, including rabbit.
Closed Mon, except
summer. €

RIGHT: marzipan treats
for a final course.

Neas
Via Rocco Pirri 30.
Tel: 0931 573 538.
The speciality here is
seafood. Mixed grilled
fish is a must. Closed
Mon. €€€

Giglio
Piazza Municipio.
Tel: 0931 838 640.
www.ristoranteilgiglio.it
Typical trattoria with
excellent pasta dishes.
Choose the ravioli. €€

Al Terrazzo
Via Baccarini 4.
Tel: 0931 839 710.
In the centre, off the
Corso. Worth visiting to
try the delightful table of
antipasti. Pizza too. €

Caffè Sicilia
Corso Vittorio Emanuele
125. Tel: 0931 835 013.
caffe.sicilia@tin.it
Traditional Sicilian *pasticceria* with homemade

pastries, *granita* and ice
creams. Good selection
of wines and jams to
take away. €

Costanzo
Via Spaventa 7.
Tel: 0931 835 243.
Try the ice creams;
locals do. Enjoy them
with a brioche. €

Marzamemi

Adelfio
Via Marzamemi 7.
Tel: 0931 841 307.
www.adelfionline.com
Traditional seafood: tuna
roes, smoked swordfish,
fresh fish baked in salt.
Very popular. €€€

Portopalo di Capo Passero

Da Maurizio
Via Taglimento 22.
Tel: 0931 842 644.
The best of Sicilian cook-

ing served on terraces,
weather permitting. Fish
arrive direct from the fishermen. Evening pizzeria.
Closed Tues and Nov. €€

Vendicari

Il Roveto
Contrada da Roveto.
Tel: 0931 66024
www.roveto.it
This restored farmhouse
is a charming place to
stay. It also has a small
welcoming restaurant
with good family cooking
that uses fresh produce
from the farm. €€

PUGNACIOUS PUPPETS AND COLOURFUL CARTS

Flamboyant manifestations of the nation's folklore, boisterous puppets and garish carts portray Sicily's history in brash primary colours

The travelling puppet show has provided entertainment in Sicily for centuries, telling tales of saints, bandits or heroes, but most commonly the Paladins, the knights of Charlemagne's court, and their battles against the Saracens. The Christians traditionally strut on the left of the stage, the turbaned, baggy-trousered Saracens on the right. The audience knows all the characters – the knights Orlando and Rinaldo, the beautiful Angelica and the wicked traitor Gano di Magonza – and identifies with them as characters in a familiar soap opera. Feelings run high, especially in the noisy battle scenes.

The puppets are up to 1.5 metres (5 ft) tall and exquisitely attired. Metal wires move their hands and a thicker bar turns their heads. A puppeteer is judged by his skill in directing the battle and by his sophisticated sound effects.

The artists who paint the sculpted carts raid motifs from their multiracial heritage: Arab adornment and arabesques; chivalric legends and Biblical epics; the Crusades and the Napoleonic wars. The few carts that survive today are found in tourist areas, but come into their own on feast days and at funerals.

LEFT: wars between Crusaders and Saracens are still a popular theme for cart-painting: here artist incorporates a self-portrait into the battlefield action. The brilliant yellows, reds and blues of the carts echo the vibrancy of the puppet theatre itself.

LEFT: puppets from Acireale are usually taller and heavier than their Palermo counterparts. Here, a gallant Acireale Orlando does battle with a giant.

RIGHT: knight dress: four Paladin knights in immaculate bronze armour on display in the Museo Internazionale delle Marionette, Palermo.

EXHILARATING POTTERY

Traditional Sicilian ceramics display the same vivacity and vibrant use of colour as the island's puppets and carts.

Thanks to the inexhaustible deposits of clay surrounding the town, Caltagirone had a reputation for pottery even before the Arabs introduced local craftsmen to the glazed polychromatic colours – particularly blues, greens and yellows – that have become typical of Sicilian ceramics. As well as functional items such as vases, bowls and jugs, Caltagirone craftsmen also produce decorative tiles, medallions and figurines in the same lively colours.

Santo Stéfano di Camastra is the second great ceramics centre on the island. On the Messina–Palermo road, the small town seems overwhelmed with its pottery: tiers of dishes, tureens and bowls line both sides of the road. The traditional style here has a rustic look and feel, often featuring fish designs. The other local speciality is tiles decorated with smiling suns and saints.

ABOVE: the side panels on a cart in Palermo depict scenes from *Orlando Furioso*, a bloodthirsty drama by Ludovico Ariosto (1474–1533) that is traditionally enacted by puppets. The drama centres on the battles of two knights to win the hand of a beautiful Indian princess.

ABOVE: puppet battles are not just between Christians and infidels: the knights also slay dragons, crocodiles and any other monsters the storytellers can devise.

RIGHT: a painted cart in Monreale, now a tourist attraction, displays a finely carved backboard as well as the traditional vivid panels.

CATANIA CITY

As Sicily's second city, Catania is a bold baroque affair bustling with commerce, the region's great shopping destination and the natural springboard to Mount Etna

atania is a city of contradictions: brash, belligerent and beleaguered yet also vibrant, cultured and resilient. It is a commercial success as well as a showcase of Sicilian baroque. But the city has an edginess, not least because its 340,000 people live permanently in the southern shadow of Mount Etna, a volcano that can seem menacing, glowing red in the night sky. The approach to Catania along the *circonvallazione* (ring road) reveals the extent of nature's wrath. Etna's recent volcano flows are visible between the grim tenements or piled like black slag heaps by the roadside.

A brief history

This ancient Siculi settlement was colonised by settlers from Naxos in 729 BC and, as it increased in wealth and power, so became known as *Catana*. By 415 BC it had become an Athenian base, and, as an ally of Athens, it incurred the wrath of Siracusa. When Dionysius attacked and conquered in 403 BC, its citizens were sold into slavery. By contrast, after the Roman conquest in 263 BC, the new regime brought with it a considerable degree of prosperity.

A sharp citizenry

The people of Catania, the Catanesi, have long had a reputation for being

sharp operators with a flair for commerce and industry. The city has produced many of the island's best engineers and entrepreneurs – as well as many of the Mafia's most active leaders. In the 1960s, Catania won plaudits for being commercially vibrant, the Milan of the South. But several decades later the chaotic politics and corruption in both Milan and Catania gave the praise a hollow echo. Catania's crime rate climbed to such heights that the city earned itself a new label as Little Chicago,

LEFT: eel seller in Catania market.
BELOW: the Elephant Fountain in Piazza Duomo.

Catania's best beaches are to the south of the city, on the Golfo di Catania.

despite the fact that most citizens had no knowing contact with the Mafia. Nonetheless, various city administrations were compromised by their presumed criminal links and according to reports from *pentiti* (people who repent, a polite way for saying Mafia turncoats), by the 1980s Cosa Nostra had switched key operations from Palermo to Catania.

Today, however, there is no outward sign of their presence. What crime there is seems limited to bag snatching or breaking into cars.

Culturally there has been an explosion of artistic activities, including large-scale open-air events, and the best nightlife in Sicily, with the creation of new bars, restaurants and clubs in the historic centre. This is also an energetic university city with an active arts scene, including good drama, classical music, a September jazz festival and myriad pop-rock spectaculars.

City sights

Visually, Catania seems the most homogeneous Sicilian city. From 1730 it was stamped with the vision of one man, Giovan Battista Vaccarini, an architect from Palermo influenced by grand Roman baroque. His work has a sculptural quality allied to a native vigour. Billowing balconies, sweeping S-curves and a taste for *chiaroscuro* are intermixed. Until your eyes adjust, the dark colour of the volcanic stone can seem oppressive, but the clever chromatic effects are skilful.

Piazza del Duomo ❶ is the baroque centrepiece, a dignified composition on a grand scale. The buildings in the square make use of flat facades, restrained decoration, elegant windows and huge pilasters. The ensemble seems harmonious, despite being designed by several architects. At the centre is the city's famous (and much copied) symbol, the delightful **Fontana dell'Ele-**

Catania

0   200 m
0   200 yds

IONIAN SEA

fante. This is Vaccarini's idea of a fountain that would enhance a city and an important piazza: a black elephant made from lava supporting a towering Egyptian obelisk taken from the Roman circus.

The **Duomo** ❷ (daily 8am–noon, 4–7pm), the cathedral dedicated to Sant'Agata, was begun by Count Roger in 1092 and rebuilt by Vaccarini after the 1693 earthquake. It is a magnificently confused summation of Catanese history: Roman theatres were raided for granite columns to adorn the lugubrious baroque facade, and the interior conceals vaulted subterranean Roman baths and a Romanesque basilica under the nave.

Roman and Byzantine columns line the transepts. St Agata's chapel, a gaudy shrine of multicoloured marble, has been restored, as have the tombs of the 14th-century Spanish rulers of Sicily. More controversially, these were moved to the nave, including the graceful tomb of Costanza d'Aragona, wife of King Federico III, and the Roman sarcophagus containing the ashes of other Aragonese royals. The tomb of Catania's famous

composer, Vincenzo Bellini (1801–35), is here, too. St Agata's relics are displayed on feast days and are believed to have miraculous powers.

Across Via Vittorio Emanuelle II is the church of **Sant'Agata** with its grand dome, and on the piazza itself are the **Municipio** (1741) with its decorated windows, and **Porta Uzeda**, an archway (1696). This leads into a small, popular park where pensioners while away time and also to **Porto Vecchio**, Catania's port. In Via Museo Biscari is **Palazzo Biscari** ❸, the most accomplished baroque mansion in Catania. It is still partly owned by the Moncada family, the Biscari descendants, but the public can attend concerts in the *salone della musica*, a rococo wonder, with a grand staircase, minstrel's gallery and allegorical ceiling. Via Dusmet offers the best view of the facade, with its frolicking cherubs, caryatids and grinning monsters. On weekdays a colourful fish market fills the neighbourhood streets.

The city's ancient remains are unlike the spacious marble theatres

Catania's Duomo.

BELOW:
the rich interior of
Catania's Duomo.

Catania's regeneration

While Catania's architecture is less ebullient than that of Noto or Siracusa, this is still trail-blazing baroque, a city with spacious streets and sinuous churches. However, as Sicily's commercial powerhouse, modern Catania stands accused of selling its soul to property speculation and neglecting its baroque heritage. Until recently, the city centre was undervalued and dilapidated, the province of students and the poor, at least after nightfall. But after years of lethargic city administration, the city has acquired European Union funding for inner-city regeneration schemes. The cathedral has been restored and the reorganisation of the main classical sites is under way.

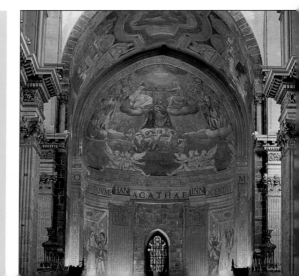

The house where Vincenzo Bellini was born in 1801 is now the Museo Belliniano, housing the composer's death mask, original scores, photographs and other memorabilia.

BELOW:
Catania's most popular beach, Lido di Plaia, south of the city.

or golden sandstone temples found elsewhere. Instead Catania offers cramped, low-lying monuments in sombre black lava stone. If you traipse down unpromising alleys, the rewards are worthwhile. While most Classical remains enjoy splendid isolation, Catania's are fully integrated in the urban fabric, generally in dilapidated parts of town, where every second turning reveals the odd Roman column, tomb or hypocaust (a space under a floor where heat from a furnace accumulated).

A good example is the **Teatro Romano ❹** (daily 9am–1.30pm, 3–5pm; entrance fee), with its entrance at 266 Via Vittorio Emanuele. The theatre was built on the site of a Greek theatre but has Roman underground passages and *cavea* as well as some of the *scena* and *orchestra*. The original marble facing was plundered by the Normans to embellish the cathedral. Next door is the semicircular **Odeon**, used for oratory and rehearsals. The building materials were chosen for their contrasts: volcanic stone, red brickwork and marble facing. It was first excavated in the 18th century when demolition of encroaching buildings began.

Tributes to Bellini

On Piazza San Francesco is the newly restored church of **San Francesco** and the **Museo Belliniano ❺** (daily 9am–1pm, Tues & Thur also 3–6pm), with a shabby baroque facade concealing a museum of musical memorabilia and original scores of the composer's work.

The father of *bel canto*, Bellini is buried in the cathedral but he is also commemorated in the richly decorated **Teatro Massimo Bellini ❻** (tel: 0957 150 921), which opened in 1890 as Teatro Massimo with his opera *Norma*. The season runs from October to May, with tickets for all operas, concerts or ballets difficult to obtain, especially at the beginning of October when the most important, prestigious event is the *Premio Bellini d'Oro*, a competition to find a great interpreter of Bellini's works.

Beyond the arch of **San Benedetto** (1777) leading off Piazza San Francesco is **Via Crociferi**, arguably

Catania's most charming street with its succession of monumental 18th-century baroque churches, convents and noble palazzi. Excavations have brought to light signs of a Roman city beneath the street. North along the street stands Vaccarini's church of **San Giuliano ❼** (1739–51), distinguished by a graceful loggia. Its elliptical interior contains a 15th-century painted *Crucifix*.

From here, Via Clementi leads to Piazza Dante with the monumental church and monastery of **San Niccolò l'Arena ❽** (daily 9am–1pm). It resembles a grim religious factory rather than a church complex. As the largest church in Sicily, this 16th-century work was conceived on a colossal scale but never completed because its sheer size would be unable to withstand an earthquake. It has an eerie, amputated look, with truncated stumps of columns framing the door like elephant tusks. Inside is a Hollywoodesque folly, Sicily's first classical staircase. After a long period of closure, the church is being restored, including the vast cupola, 62 metres (203 ft) high.

The adjoining **Monastero di San Niccolò ❾** was the Benedictine monastery and now houses Catania University's Faculties of Arts and Philosophy. The original monastery was almost totally destroyed in the 1693 earthquake, then rebuilt on an even grander scale after 1703. Long-term archaeological excavations are under way in the entrance courtyard, but beyond lie the charming former cloisters, complete with a battered garden and a curiously decorated folly.

North along Via Crociferi is the church of **Sant'Agata al Carcere ❿** (St Agatha in Chains; closed at time of writing for restoration). According to legend, and supported by graffiti on these Roman walls, it was here that Sant Agata was imprisoned before her martyrdom. Although the

site was converted into a fortified church in the 12th century, the 3rd-century crypt remains. More impressive is the Romanesque portal, moved from the cathedral after the 1693 earthquake. Sculpted with griffons and glowering beasts, the door conjures up suitable horrors of the church's original function as a prison.

Anfiteatro Romano

Further on, adjoining Via Etnea lies the **Anfiteatro Romano ⓫** (daily 9am–1.30pm, 3–7pm), the battered remains of the largest amphitheatre in Sicily, dating back to 2nd or 3rd century AD and able to seat 16,000 spectators. This is where Santa Agata supposedly met her fate and where earthquake ruins were dumped in 1693. Ancient *necropoli* stretch north and east of this site and are visible in many spots, including below the Rinascente store in Via Etnea.

The grandiose **Via Etnea**, the main city thoroughfare, runs parallel to Via Crociferi and climaxes in a stunning view of Mount Etna. Busy throughout the day, the street is particularly popular at night when the Catanesi

Map on page 202

TIP

Find refreshment in summer at *chioschi* (kiosks), which serve fruit syrups drunk with *seltz* (soda water) and sometimes salt. The usual one is *seltz e limone con/senza sale*, a soda water and crushed lemon concoction with or without salt.

BELOW: people-watching in the piazza.

Map on page 202

In 1169 the city had its first recorded major earthquake, and many followed. A devastating eruption in 1669 struck the city centre while 12,000 people were attending Mass, covering the city in molten lava. In 1693, another quake killed two-thirds of the population. The next serious damage was inflicted by the Allied forces during the 1943 invasion.

BELOW:
bargaining at
the fish market.

indulge in the evening *passeggiata*, to parade past chic shops selling fashion, jewellery, shoes, fruit sorbets and nougat ice cream.

The most elegant, richer, section of the street lies between Piazza Duomo and **Villa Bellini** ⑫, not a palazzo but public gardens. This delightful and well-kept public park represents a retreat from Catania's constant bustle. One part is named *labirinto* after the maze of paths, all leading to aviaries and an Oriental bandstand. Between the fig trees, palms and playing children are snowcapped or smouldering views of Etna.

To the south of Via Etnea, on Piazza Federico di Svevia, is **Castello Ursino** ⑬, a restored Swabian castle built on a steep bastion. It commands a view of what was once the harbour: the moat was filled in by the lava flow of 1669, which also left the castle marooned inland, and deposited a large lump of lava outside the walls. Now an art museum and exhibition space, it was the Aragonese seat of government in the 13th century and became a palace under the Spanish viceroys.

The courtyard displays a cavalcade of Sicilian history, featuring fine Hellenistic and Roman sculpture.

The **Museo Civico** (Mon–Sat 9am–1pm, 3–7pm), housed on the upper floors, contains a wide-ranging art gallery.

Fish market

South of the Duomo, sandwiched between the cathedral quarter and the port, is **La Pescheria**, the noisy morning fish market (Mon–Sat). On slabs of marble lie sea bream and swordfish, mussels and sea urchins, squirming eels and lobsters. The area is centred on **Porta Uzeda**, the monumental baroque city gate connecting the port with the public city. Beyond the adjoining park of Villa Pacini, the colourful portside area encircling Via Dusmet is given over to fishermen, traders and the sporadic attentions of *scippi* (bag-snatchers).

Not far away is **Zo** (www.zoculture.it), a futuristic cultural centre housed in an ex-sulphur refinery. As well as theatre spaces, and temporary exhibitions, there are two museums, one focusing on cinema (Wed, Fri & Sun 9am–12.30pm, Tues & Thur 9am–5.30pm; entrance fee), the other on the Allied invasion of Sicily in 1943 (Wed & Fri–Sun 9am–12.30pm, Tues & Thur 9am–12.30pm, 3–5pm; entrance fee).

A visit to the scruffy but appealing **Fera o Luni** market (daily except Sun) on **Piazza Carlo Alberto** ⑭ creates an appetite for Catania's varied cuisine, including *pasta alla Norma* (with aubergine/eggplant), named after Bellini's opera. Framed by two churches and hemmed in by backstreets, the rectangular square is a sea of bright awnings; below lie displays of lemons, garlic and herbs, with clothes, household goods and leatherware on the far side. The Sunday antiques market here sells everything from junk to Sicilian ceramics and country-style furniture. ❏

RESTAURANTS AND BARS

Catania

Catania is renowned for its excellent and diverse restaurants. They display eastern Sicilian seasonal dishes, such as *pasta con il cavolfiore e la ricotta* (pasta with cauliflower and ricotta) and *agnello alla menta* (lamb with bacon, mint and garlic). The more expensive ones require booking.

Antica Marina
Via Pardo 29.
Tel: 095 348 197.
In middle of fish market, so the fish couldn't be fresher. Fish antipasti, pasta dishes with fish sauces and grilled fish. Closed Wed. €€€

La Cantinaccia
Via Calatafimi 1/a.
Tel: 095 537 291.
This upmarket but intimate restaurant is designed in rustic style. Cuisine is international and Sicilian with pizza served in the evening. Closed Mon and Aug. €€

Cantine del Cugno Mezzano
Via Museo Biscari 8.
Tel: 095 715 8710.
In the stables of 16th-century Palazzo Biscari, this *ristorante-enotoca* has a wide selection of top wines (not only Sicilian), wine tasting and a Mediterranean menu. Closed Sun, Mon lunch and 2 weeks Aug. €€

Al Gabbiano
Via Giordano Bruno 128.
Tel: 095 537 842.
Respected trattoria with traditional Sicilian fare. Closed Sun and Aug. €€€

La Marchesana
Via Mazza 4.
Tel: 095 315171.
The menu is particularly strong on fish at this small restaurant, and the friendly owners offer a warm welcome. Eat outside in fine weather, or inside in the elegant vaulted dining room. €€

Menza
Viale Mario Rapisardi 143.
Tel: 095 350 606.
www.menza.it
If you are looking for a typical Sicilian *rosticceria*, this is it. Every kind of snack: try the *arancini* (savoury filled rice balls) or the sweet *crespelle* (pancakes) with honey. Closed Mon. €€

La Paglia
Via Pardo 23.
Tel: 095 346838.
Well placed right by the fish market, this simple trattoria serves the freshest of seafood. Try the spaghetti with clams. Closed Sun. €€

Da Rinaldo
Via Simili 59.
Tel: 095 532 312.
Inexpensive trattoria with a wide selection of Sicilian dishes, not simply dishes from this province. Closed Aug. €

Savia
Via Etnea 302.
Tel: 095 322335.
A historic *pasticceria* that's a favourite with the locals – try the ricotta-stuffed *cannoli*. Closed Mon. €

Sicilia in Bocca
Via Dusmet 35.
Tel: 095 250 0208.
A restaurant with a pleasant terrace set in the sea wall. For a cheaper option, go for the pizza. Closed Mon. €€€

La Siciliana
Viale Marco Polo 52.
Tel: 095 376 400.
www.lasiciliana.it
Sicilian cooking at its best in a charming garden setting. One of Catania's most renowned restaurants, so it is expensive. Specialities include roast lamb, seafood, imaginative vegetable dishes and good red Cerasuolo wine. Closed Sun evening & Mon. Book. €€€

I Tre Bicchieri
Via San Giuseppe al Duomo 31. Tel: 095 715 3540.
www.osteriatrebicchieri.it
Smart, modern establishment praised for its presentation and varied Mediterranean cooking. Known for both meat and fish. Wine bar. Closed Sun and Aug. €€€

PRICE CATEGORIES

Prices for three-course dinner per person with a half-bottle of house wine:
€ = under €15
€€ = €15–30
€€€ = €30–60

RIGHT: seafood dishes in a Catania restaurant.

CATANIA PROVINCE

Although the province embraces a popular coastline crowded with lidos, beaches and quaint fishing villages, at its heart is the glowering volcanic hinterland of Mount Etna

Sicilians are always concerned that one day there may be a "big one", an earthquake or eruption that will reverberate down the centuries. Until then, however, they are happy to live the good life, enjoying the sun, the sea and their country. More than 20 percent of all Sicilians live on the flanks of the volcano. Farmers are enticed there by the fertile soil while wealthy city residents have constructed villas on the mountain's slopes for the views, cooler summer climate and opportunity for skiing in the winter.

Buoyant tourism

Coastal Catania, however, turns away from the volcanic hinterland with atavistic spirit and peasant culture. This is commercial Sicily, profiting from its ancient entrepreneurial roots established when it was a Greek trading colony. From Catania the economic ripples reach the rest of the province, as do the effects of a healthy public administration allied to the native entrepreneurial spirit. To dub it Silicon Valley, as the locals sometimes do, is a wishful overstatement, but the province is thriving – in Sicilian terms, at least. Catania University's noted engineering faculty provides the impetus for Italy's microelectronics and telecommunications industries.

As far as tourism is concerned, there is considerable investment in hotels, thanks partly to the increasing popularity of Etna's natural wonderland. As a result, Catania has budding resorts and significant commercial centres while exercising strict control over its great Etna national park, and curbing rampant building elsewhere.

South of Catania

The southwest of the province is occupied by the **Piana di Catania**,

Map on page 210

LEFT Caltagirone's dramatic Scalazza.
BELOW: contemplating a swim at Aci Trezza.

Welcome at a grocery store, Acireale.

a dullish plain that comes a poor second to Mount Etna's attractions north of **Catania ❶**. The plain was reputedly the abode of the mythological race of man-eating giants, the Laestrygonians, who appear in Homer's *Odyssey,* but until the 19th century it was better known as a malaria-infested region and, as a result, there are few farmhouses. As in Italy, Mussolini was the driving force for eradicating malaria here. However, the orchards, citrus groves and pastures now make the plain a touch more cheerful. **Militello in Val di Catania ❷** is the only significant

centre, with its medieval quarter, ruined castle and baroque churches. Even so, it is a place best visited by accident not design. By contrast, a number of towns in the hilly southern interior have considerable charm, especially Caltagirone, the principal source of Sicily's ceramics.

Grammichele ❸, approached via the SS 417 from Catania, is a bizarre baroque town, a champion of bold town planning after the 1693 earthquake. Within a hexagonal design, roads radiate from the central square like the spokes of a wheel. The Chiesa Madre and town hall person-

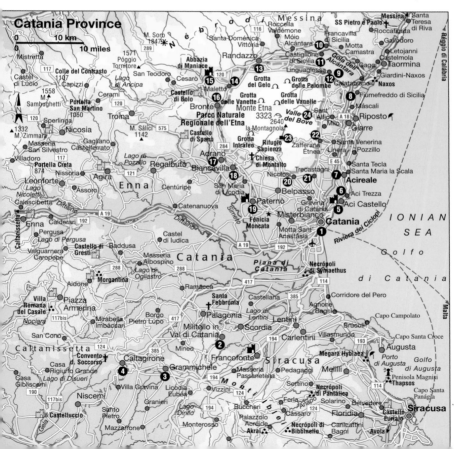

ify the city's cool baroque image and clean geometric design. However, the clinical effect is mocked by the down-at-heel population.

Caltagirone ❹, further along the SS 417, is charming, a town covering three hills. Its name derives from the Arabic words for castle and cave but its history is more ancient; it was settled earlier by the Greeks. The mood is dramatic baroque. Like Acireale and Noto, the old section of hilly Caltagirone feels like a grand theatre, with spacious squares and majestic mansions. Most churches seem truly monumental and contain grand works of art. Yet, more importantly perhaps, Caltagirone is best known as the capital of Sicilian ceramics, delightful ceramic pieces that are instantly recognisable the world over with their vibrant colours and numberless varieties.

The upper town is surprisingly grand for this part of Sicily, with the finest and most imposing public buildings clustered around the **Duomo**, dedicated to San Giuliano. The church, like countless others in Sicily, was initially destroyed by the 1693 earthquake and then rebuilt, but in this instance it was demolished yet again in 1838 because its structure was deemed unsafe. In fact the belltower was attached in 1954 to the 1909 church. The cathedral contains a *Madonna and Child* attributed to the school of Antonello Gagini (1594).

A short distance away is the **Corte Capitaniale**, a dignified mansion decorated by school of Gagini sculptures and, beyond, the **Scalazza**, a staircase of 142 steps leading up to the church of **Santa Maria del Monte**. This stunning staircase links the old and new levels of the town. Each of its 142 lava stone steps is decorated vividly with majolica tiles depicting mythological scenes. On 24–25 July, the feast days of **San Giacomo**, a colourful festival known as "the tapestry of fire" takes place, with a costumed procession and an ingenious carpet of lights to light up each and every step. Every year this ingenious carpet is reinvented in different designs. Nearly 5,000 tiny oil lamps cover the steps to create the effect; these are covered by delicate

Map on page 210

TIP

Two museums in Caltagirone have notable displays of ceramics: **Museo Civico**, Carcere Borbonico, tel: 0933 31590. Located in a former prison. Classical finds and Renaissance ceramics. Open Tues, Fri–Sun 9.30am–12.30pm, 4–7pm, Wed–Thur 9.30am–1.30pm; entrance fee. **Museo della Ceramica**, Via Roma, tel: 0933 58418. Located in the public gardens. Daily 9am–6.30pm; entrance fee.

BELOW: Caltagirone.

paper cylinders called *coppi*.

On the other side of the long piazza, on Via Roma below the cathedral, the **Museo Civico** (Tues, Fri–Sun 9.30am–12.30pm, 4–7pm, Wed–Thur 9.30am–1.30pm; entrance fee) was once a fearsome Bourbon prison and still retains its barbaric, spike-studded metal doors. The museum contains Greek and Roman finds and prized Renaissance ceramics.

Off Via Roma is the church of **San Francesco d'Assisi**, built in 1226 in Gothic form but adapted in the 16th century. Naturally it collapsed in the big earthquake and was then rebuilt in baroque style.

Caltagirone is renowned for its decorative majolica. Signs of the thriving industry are everywhere; not only in the studio-shops selling the items. Ceramic designs occupy tiles, niches, ledges, parapets and balconies. Ceramic flowers even grace the **Ponte San Francesco** (1626–66), the bridge close to San Francesco church. The lovely formal public gardens, the **Giardino Pubblico**, below Piazza Umberto, were designed to emulate English public gardens in the late 1800s. There are balustraded terraces, a charming ceramic-decorated bandstand and a belvedere (1792) among its towering trees. As if to emphasise this ceramics corner, the gardens are home to the **Museo Regionale della Cerámica** (daily 9am–6.30pm; entrance fee), housing a collection of Sicilian ceramic work from prehistoric times to the present; terracotta and glazed ceramics seem to have been produced in Caltagirone since the art was discovered.

The Coast of Cyclops

Heading north from Catania is a welcome release: sea breezes sweep away images of Catania's scruffy outskirts. The province hugs the Ionian coast towards the hillside resort of Taormina, and the Coast of Cyclops, named after the Homeric myth, presents a spectacular seascape. The **Faraglioni dei Ciclopi** (Cyclops) are jagged lumps jutting out of the sea just off the coast at Aci Trezza. Legend has it that these basalt rocks were flung at the fleeing Odysseus by an enraged, blinded one-eyed Cyclops. The scenic rocks are now used as an oceanography station by Catania University.

In summer, the restaurants along this coast are full and flotillas of fishing craft double up as pleasure boats. But essentially the character of the local fishing villages remains unchanged: the daily markets display catches of anchovies and sardines, octopus and small fry for fish soup.

Aci Castello ❺, on the Riviera dei Ciclopi near Catania, is memorable for its dramatic castle perched on a rocky crag overlooking the sea. The crenellated Norman **fortress**, built on a site used for defensive purposes since Byzantine times, is well preserved despite frequent eruptions and a fierce attack by the Aragonese. A charming garden of local plants

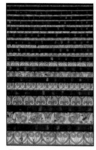

Ceramic adornment for the 142 steps of the Scalazza.

BELOW: Aci Castello's Norman castle.

has recently been created on the roof terrace. From the castle, which houses the **Museo Civico** (Tues–Sun 9am–1pm, 3–5pm) containing trophies found at sea, locals potter on the rocks or wander down to one of several fish restaurants along the gnarled coast.

Aci Trezza ❻, a fishing village hoping to become a resort, is celebrated for its connection with Giovanni Verga, the writer born in Catania *(see margin note, page 214)*, and his novel inspired by this seafaring community, *I Malavoglia* (translated as *Under the Medlar Tree*, 1881). The novel depicts the benighted lives of a fishing family with humour, perception and an intuitive sympathy. Visconti's film *La Terra Trema*, inspired by Verga's novel, was filmed on the same spot. Verga was a master of such lines as: "Unfortunately the boy was conscientiously built, as they still make them at Aci Trezza." More tellingly, he feared the sea: "Property at sea is writ on water."

Close to the harbour is the **Casa del Nespolo** (daily, Apr, June & Sept

9.30am–12.30pm, 4–7pm; July–Aug 9.30am–1pm, 5–9pm; Oct–Mar 9.30am–12.30pm, 4–6pm; entrance fee), a tiny fishing museum linked to Verga's novel.

Acireale ❼, with its population of 52,000, is the most important of the seven towns with the prefix *Aci* on Etna's skirts. Legend has it that Aci (Acis) became the lover of sea-nymph Galatea and when he was killed by a jealous rival she turned him into a river here. (The river, of course, vanished in an earthquake.)

The town is proud of its appellation *Reale* (royal) and stands aloof, both from the over-commercialised resorts and the rural hinterland. As Akis, it was a Greek settlement that fared badly in the face of eruptions and earthquakes. However, thanks to the continuing ravages of Etna and the talent of local craftsmen, today's town is predominantly baroque. Compared with most coastal resorts, even Acireale's modern blocks of flats are respectable As a proper living town rather than a satellite or ugly resort, the city is admired for its sense of balance, quality of life and

Map on page 210

A decorative tile on the Ponte San Francesco.

BELOW: the harbour at Aci Trezza.

Acireale's carnival

A certain number of upper-crust families in Acireale still cultivate a distance, indulging in noblesse oblige charity work and membership of exclusive groups. This snobbish, elitist image helps make Acireale a place for status-seeking Catanese to get married. Only during carnival are social differences put aside, as the town becomes a lively outdoor pleasure dome. Acireale advertises itself as having *il piu bello carnevale della Sicilia*, the best carnival in Sicily. This is borne out by the illuminations, the inventiveness of the decorated floats and the enthusiasm of the crowds. Stalls sell masks, puppets, feathered costumes, nougat, nuts and mushroom pastries.

The novelist and dramatist Giovanni Verga (1840–1922) was born in Catania. His finest works reflect life at the poorer social levels and his story of Cavalleria Rusticana *(1880) was turned ito an opera in 1888 by Pietro Mascagni. D.H. Lawrence translated many of Verga's works, including* Mastro don Gesualdo, *considered a masterpiece, about an ambitious stonemason competing with the local gentry.*

sulphur spas, and shows little sign of searching for tourism.

The **Duomo,** dedicated to the Annunciation and to Santa Vénera, occupies centre stage, its 17th-century grandeur tampered with decades ago by the addition of a pseudogothic facade. However, the grand baroque portal with 17th-century statues of the *Annunciation* and *Santa Vénera e Tecla* make up for the alterations and the peeling vaulted interior is original enough with it *trompe l'oeil* decoration and stucco in musty browns and yellows. The inlaid marble floor contains an appealing 1848 Meridian Line.

The **Palazzo Comunale** represents the first flowering of Catanese baroque with its elegant, graceful facade and delicate wrought-iron balconies. French writer Dominique Fernandez considers this town hall a masterpiece, "full of imagination and rustic ingenuity". On the same square, set among the city *caffès* and grand churches, stands the restored white baroque vision of **Santi Pietro e Paolo**. In Piazza Vigo further down, behind an ornate balustrade

with a dozen 18th-century statues depicting characters in the Old Testament, is the **basilica di San Sebastiano,** such an exuberant baroque feast that the riot of cherubs and fancy carving on the facade threatens to spill into opera.

In the compact historic centre, the grandiose baroque buildings are gathered around Piazza Duomo, typifying the curious contrast between the spacious public squares and the small-scale design of the town beyond the grand *piazze*. Yet the tiny, dark alleys yield rewards in the form of pastry shops and ice-cream parlours. Castorino, a *caffè* in Corso Savoia, is famed for its ice cream, pastries, cassata and *pasta reale* – decorated marzipan confections.

Acireale is surrounded by citrus groves, a source of wealth that continues to sustain the local land-owning class. From the town's public gardens stretches a fine view over the Coast of Cyclops, with the rocky shore riven by coves.

At the south entrance to the town, the **Terme di Santa Vénera,** a spa, exploits the healing properties of Etna's radioactive waters. Hot sulphurous lava mud baths (20°C/68°F) have been considered beneficial here for rheumatism and skin conditions since Roman times.

Just below Acireale, on the road northwards, is the quaint fishing hamlet of **Santa Maria la Scala**, with its lava-stone shore, beached boats, watchtower and handful of simple trattorie. The road, the SS114, follows the coast. It is slow going, passing through **Santa Tecla**, **Pozzillo** and **Riposto**. (The autostrada, A18, is a much faster alternative, cutting through the countryside as it heads to Taormina and Messina.) At Riposto is an efficient, all-year, yacht marina in the flourishing port where fishermen bring their daily catches.

Fiumefreddo di Sicilia ❽, north of Giarre and Riposto, is named after

BELOW: fruit and vegetables for sale.

a cooling river that flows through thick clumps of papyrus. This feudal town has a tumbledown Phoenician tower and two castellated mansions. **Castello degli Schiavi**, the stranger of the two villas, has sculpted stone slaves leaning over an 18th-century parapet. Until the creation of the Etnaland theme park, the town's chief attractions are clear: coastal views and clean beaches. Fiume-freddo is a calming interlude before the volcanic hinterland. Alternatively, it is a springboard to chic Taormina *(see page 229)*.

Mount Etna

Etna is the dramatic volcano where the heart of Catania province should be. The volcano munches Messina and the countryside too, with new lava mouths opening all the time. Locals joke that not even the Mafia can close Etna's myriad mouths. *Mongibello* or *Muncibeddu*, the Sicilian name for Mount Etna, comes from the Latin and Arabic words for mountain (*mons* and *gibel*). It is one of the most active volcanoes in the world.

The sense of appeasing the mountain gods still survives in **Zafferana Etnea**, a hiking village and ski resort that found itself in the path of the 1992 volcanic eruption. Before abandoning his farmhouse to the volcano, Giuseppe Fichera left bread, cheese and wine to satisfy "the tired and hungry mountain". Even gods of destruction need food and rest.

The circular journey around the volcano is a game of light and shade. From the Ionian coast to the fertile Etna foothills is a feast of glistening citrus and olive groves, orchards and nut plantations. But clinging to Etna's flanks are dark volcanic villages and ruined Norman castles. It is a strange trail from green slopes to the moonscape above. From Taormina, a scenic railway runs to Randazzo, travelling along the valley floor, crossing a bridge made of lava blocks and even disappearing inside a lava cutting. But to appreciate Etna's grandeur, drive around the base or follow a similar route on the Circumetnea railway *(see margin note, page 217)*.

Map on page 210

In the 3rd century BC, Theocritus the poet wrote of the vineyards on Etna's slopes. Today more than 600 producers, including Simply Red singer Mick Hucknall, grow vines in the rich but difficult volcanic soil. More details: www.bestofsicily.com/wine

BELOW: the port of Santa Maria la Scala, near Acireale.

The Wrath of Mount Etna

When Sicily's famous volcano erupts, the results are always unpredictable. As local resident Giovanni Giuffrida says: "Lava is like a mole, it takes cover, burrows and reappears where you are not ready to catch it." In terms of duration, an eruption can last 10 minutes or – like the outburst of 1614 – 10 years.

Over centuries, the Catania coastline has receded or advanced in response to Etna's major lava flows. Even the 1908 earthquake, which razed Messina and claimed over 60,000 victims, did not change the coastline. But lava flows from Etna have often redrawn the map, most recently in 1978–79 when lava spilled into the sea, and reached the chapel doors at Fornazzo, a village near Giarre on the coast. A miraculous intervention was claimed after the molten lava was halted by a statue of the Madonna.

Historically, two of the most catastrophic eruptions occurred in 1381 and 1669, with lava flows that engulfed Catania and destroyed Nicolosi. In modern times, lava came close to Trecastagni in 1886 and 1910, while significant eruptions demolished the villages of Gerro and Mascali in the 1920s, and in 1923 narrowly missed Castiglione and Linguaglossa. Randazzo was narrowly spared by an eruption in 1981, which reached the town walls and destroyed surrounding property and vineyards, with repercussions as far east as the Alcántara gorge near Taormina.

The route to Etna Sud, the southern access point, passes lava flows dating from 1984, which destroyed the previous road. Beyond, closer to the volcanic heart, the 1983 eruption destroyed most of the Rifugio Sapienza and neighbouring property, ski lifts and roads.

During the 1992 eruption, the Americans were called in to save the resort of Zafferana Etnea, on Etna's eastern slopes. A US Navy and Marine task force, armed with the world's largest helicopters, made daring forays to the mouth of the crater, dropping blocks of concrete into the seething river of lava and stemming the flow.

The southeastern crater has been responsible for virtually all the eruptions since 1997, including the activity that began in February 1999 and continued into 2000. For much of the time, the glittering red cone was visible from Catania during the day, while tourists in Taormina could see nightly fire-bombs shooting out from a secondary cone. Then, in February 2000 the southeastern crater split into two, with fireballs and eruptive matter being tossed into the air to a height of 600m. An even more violent eruption occurred in 2001, and 2002 saw another state of emergency, with more homes destroyed.

The last few years have seen a flurry of seismic activity. Intense eruptions occurred at the southeast crater from July to December 2006, then, in August 2007, ash exploded from a vent on the eastern side of the Southeast Crater, followed on 4 September by a violent eruption, spewing lava up to 400m into the air for several hours. Subsequent eruptions have been relatively minor, though activity in mid-July 2008 produced loud detonations that could be heard in villages and towns around Etna. ❏

LEFT: firebombs shoot high into the night sky.

Around the volcano

An excellent excursion, if you have time and a car, is a circular tour of Etna, around the **Parco Naturale Regionale dell'Etna**. Leave the coast at Fiumefreddo di Sicilia, before reaching Giardini-Naxos and Taormina, for a foray into the Alcántara Valley starting with **Gola dell'Alcántara** ❾; this is a delightful gorge discovered in the 1950s when a Taormina film director was so enchanted with the prospect of a secret gorge that he had a tortuous path built down to the river. He was the first of many to capture Alcántara on film. Seen from above, the view is of wooded crags descending to a weirdly pitted river canyon. The bed is rocky, the remains of a prehistoric lava flow that created the peninsula of Capo Schiso. The canyon was created not by erosion but by the splintering collision of volcanic magma and the cooling water of the river. The impact threw up lavic prisms in monstrous shapes: these warped black basalt boulders resemble a cross section of a fossil. Today, of course, it is a magnet for the tourist

buses, but it is still worth a visit. You can also get here by public bus from Taormina and Catania. A lift leads down to the grey-green river where waterproof boots are on loan. In summer, low water levels make the initial section accessible to visitors in waders but a waterfall with a sheer drop is a barrier to further exploration of the gorge. Beyond are dangerous whirlpools and fast-flowing currents in ever-narrowing tracts, deceptive rapids that have occasionally claimed lives.

Francavilla di Sicilia ❿, just west along the SS 185, is set in a fertile valley of citrus plantations and prickly pears. Founded by King Roger, Francavilla prospered under Spanish rule. Roger's **ruined castle** occupies a lone mound in the valley and once guarded the route to Randazzo. The other Norman relic is the hermitage of **La Badiazza**, perched atop a rocky platform and victim of the 1693 earthquake. The **Chiesa Madre** has a Gagini *Madonna*, matched by the sculpted Gagini fountain in Piazza San Paolo. The **Matrice Vecchia** has a Renaissance

Map on page 210

TIP

The Circumetnea, in existence since 1894, is the single-track rail route around Etna, a leisurely 114-km (71-mile) journey from Catania, taking in Paternò, Adrano, Bronte, Maletto and Randazzo, returning to the coast at Giarre-Riposto. The trip takes about 5 hours. For more information, tel: 095 541 250; www.circumetnea.it.

BELOW:
almond trees on Etna's fertile slopes.

BELOW:
Castiglione di Sicilia.

door with a vine-leaf motif. The finest sight is the **Convento dei Cappuccini**, a 16th-century monastery on a lovely hillock, protected by Spanish sentry boxes and marble parapets. Inside is a profusion of intarsia work and carving, the handiwork of 17th-century monks.

Castiglione di Sicilia ⑪, set on Etna's northern flank just south of Francavilla, is also a stop on the scenic Circumetnea railway. Perched on a crag, this ancient bastion possesses Greek ramparts but is better known as a Norman fiefdom. Narrow medieval alleys wind to the crumbling lava-stone church of **San Pietro** and the grander **Santa Maria della Catena**. The **Norman castle** dominates the valley, with its jagged lookout tower, walls and roofs. This rocky citadel compels respect, as do the ominous views of rubble and debris trailing from Etna's summit.

Linguaglossa ⑫, at 550 metres (1,800 ft), another stop on the scenic rail route 18 km (11 miles) southeast of Castiglione, is an unsophisticated ski resort and workaday walking and logging centre. The baroque **Chiesa**

Madre pays tribute to the forests, with 18th-century choir stalls and a coffered ceiling, while the village's lava-stone pavements attest to its proximity to Etna. Although not prepossessing, the village makes an acceptable hiking base. Treks lead through pine forests to **Grotta del Gelo**, a lava-stone cave with weird light effects, and also up Etna itself.

Randazzo

West of Castiglione, **Randazzo ⑬** is the most atmospheric and coherent medieval town on the northern slopes of Etna, and the one closest to the volcano craters. Much of the town is built using blocks cut from the dried lava streams. Originally settled by Greeks fleeing from Naxos, it reached its apogee under the Normans. During Swabian rule, Randazzo was a summer court and retreat from the heat of Messina. It remains a self-contained market town with a population of 12,000 and with crenellated churches and sturdy 14th-century walls.

For a town in the jaws of Etna, Randazzo has survived magnificently. The 1981 eruption threatened to engulf the walls and blocked surrounding vineyards, roads and railway lines, leaving a lava flow visible today. But human beings are to blame for damage to the medieval core: Allied bombing in 1943 destroyed much of the enemies' last stronghold in Sicily, including the fortress and finest palazzi.

Until the 16th century, competition for supremacy within the walls was fuelled by the presence of three rival communities talking different dialects. Each parish took its turn as cathedral for a three-year term: the Latins were centred on the church of Santa Maria, the Greeks at San Niccolò and the Lombards at San Martino. The churches were fiercely battlemented and ostentatious. Ultimately, the Catholics tri-

umphed and the church of **Santa Maria** on Piazza Basilica is now the cathedral. Built between 1217 and 1239, it is an elegant grey lava stone church in Norman-Swabian design, with Norman apses and walls and side portals in Catalan-Gothic style. It has been significantly modified since. In fact the bell tower was added around 1860. Its odd interior contrasts Satanic-looking black columns and altar with a pure Gagini font and a 15th-century view of the town.

Porta San Martino, one of two surviving city gates, marks the entrance to the walled medieval town. The elegant Piazza San Martino is the heart of the damaged Lombard quarter, set against the city walls. Appropriately, **Chiesa San Martino** has a 13th-century banded lava and limestone Lombard bell tower matched by an early baroque facade in grey and white stone. Virtually next door is the **Castello-Carcere**, a medieval castle and Bourbon prison, now the **Museo Archeologico Paolo Vagliasindi** (daily 9am–1pm, 4–8pm or 3–7pm in winter; entrance fee), an archeological museum. Beside the lava-stone windows is an inscription to Philip II and bullet holes that attest to the military skirmishes in August 1943. A puppet museum, **Museo dei Pupi Siciliani** (same hours and ticket) is here too.

Via Umberto contains symbols of Randazzo's past role as a royal city, including the **Palazzo Reale**, the severe Swabian summer palace now demoted to a minimarket. Yet surprising signs of wealth remain in the chic jewellery shops, occasionally daubed with anti-Mafia slogans. Via Umberto ends in spacious **Piazza Municipio**, the bustling heart of Randazzo. The square is dominated by **Palazzo Comunale**, the well-restored town hall. But leave the crowds by turning down **Via degli Archi**, a quaint arcaded alley, to Piazza San Niccolò and the Greek quarter. In one corner is Santa Maria della Volta, a 14th-century shell of a bombed church. In the centre of the square is the impressive Greek **San Niccolò**, with its original 14th-century apses and huge early baroque lava-stone facade and tapering campanile. Inside the church are

Map on page 210

Wealthy families in this province often have kid instead of lamb as an Easter treat. Capretto con stracciatella is a slow stew made in an earthenware pot on the stove with the kid, onions, water and seasoning. After an hour, five eggs and grated pecorino cheese are beaten together and poured over the kid, which continues cooking.

LEFT: Randazzo's medieval streets.
BELOW: Basilica di Santa Maria, Randazzo.

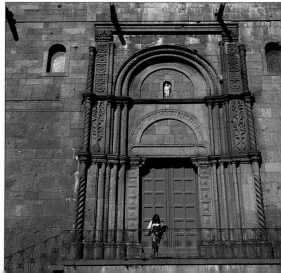

several Gagini sculptures, including, appropriately, a *St Nicholas*.

The Admiral's estate

Between Randazzo and Bronte extends a wooded, volcanic landscape south to **Maletto** , noted for its wine and strawberries. Maletto marks the highest point on the Circumetnea railway line (1,200 metres/ 4,000 ft) and offers views of recent lava flows. From Maletto, take a right fork to Admiral Nelson's castle at Maniace or continue south to Bronte. Following signs to Castello di Nelson leads to the **Abbazia di Maniace**  (daily 9am–1pm, 2.30–7pm, until 5pm in winter; entrance fee), one and the same. Set in a wooded hollow, the fortified abbey was founded by Count Roger, with the chapel commemorating a Saracen defeat in 1040. With Norman help, the Byzantine commander Maniakes routed the Arabs and regained Sicily for Constantinople. But the estate is better known as the fiefdom of Admiral Horatio Nelson, Duke of Bronte.

The title and estates were presented to Nelson by Ferdinand IV in gratitude for the Admiral's part in crushing the 1799 rebellion in Naples. Nelson's descendant, Viscount Bridport, only relinquished his Sicilian seat in 1981, when the 12,500-hectare (30,000-acre) estate was broken up and the orchards, nut plantations and dairy farms sold. Nevertheless, Nelson memorabilia remains, from paintings of sea battles to the Admiral's port decanter.

Inside the castle compound, the best part of the Benedictine abbey owes nothing to Nelson. The late Norman chapel has an original wooden ceiling, doorway and statuary. The original castle is unrecognisable, thanks to the 1693 earthquake and heavy anglicisation. It resembles a gracious Wiltshire manor from outside, an image confirmed by the genteel English cemetery. Even the gardens are home to neat hedges as well as cypresses and palms.

Between Maletto and Bronte are subtle shifts in scenery. Walnut and chestnut groves on the higher hills are dotted with jagged volcanic clumps, including the lava flow of 1823. Around Bronte, the slopes are covered with small nut trees, a reminder that 80 percent of Italy's pistachio crop comes from these well-tended terraces.

Bronte

Bronte , at 760 metres (2,500 ft) and with a population of 20,000, was founded in 1520 by Charles V and is an ill-planned town sandwiched between two lava flows on the western slopes of Mount Etna. Legend says it was founded by the cyclops Brontes, son of Uranus, who was known as The Thunderer and whose forge was in a cavern beneath the mountain. Devastated three times by eruptions, Bronte hangs on as the administrative and agricultural centre of the region.

Pistachio nuts are exported wordwide from here, and each year

As Duke of Bronte, the British sea hero Admiral Lord Nelson never visited his vast Sicilian estate, despite wistful dreams of retiring here with paramour Emma Hamilton. The closest he got was in Emma's nickname for him, "My Lord Thunder" – a reference to Bronte, the mythical giant who forged thunderbolts for Jupiter.

BELOW:
vineyards are a major source of income.

a pistachio festival takes place on the first 10 days of October. Bronte is resolutely shabby, its dingy charm residing in the neglected late Renaissance churches with crenellated towers. It is indeed a pious town: even urchins cross themselves when passing one of the many churches. The church of **l'Annunciata** (1535) has a polychrome marble group attributed to Antonello Gagini that, local lore says, has miraculous powers and on many occasions has been able to stem the flow of molten lava.

South of Bronte, the prosperous air of solid chalets on the alpine plains gives way to ramshackle dwellings and rough scrubland. The pistachio plantations cede to scruffy, cacti-strewn slopes, with lumps of lava interspersed with white lava-coated trees. The makeshift mood reflects a region devastated by the 1985 eruption: everything built in haste but, given Etna's whims, with no time to repent at leisure.

Adrano ⑰, set on Etna's south-western slopes, is a shabby market town with mythical roots. On the outskirts are the remains of a grander past: the Greek city of Adranon was founded here by Dionysius I in the 4th century BC. In antiquity, the city was celebrated for its sanctuary to Adranus, the Sicel god of fire. Still today, during the bizarre August festival, a child dressed as an angel "flies" along a cord linking the old city powers: the castle, town hall and a statue of the god of fire himself. So far, Adranus has kept his city safe from fiery Etna.

Its battered charm lies in the busy **Piazza Umberto**. Like Randazzo, political associations and social welfare clubs are clustered around the main square. Here, too, is the austere **Norman castle** (Mon–Fri 9am–1pm, 4–7pm or 3–6pm in winter; entrance fee), sitting on its squat Saracen base. This powerful bastion was rebuilt by Roger I in the 11th century and remodelled by the Aragonese. The interior, once a Bourbon prison, houses an **archaeological museum** with minor Greek sculptures. On the floor above is Queen Adelaide's chapel, a mysterious room decorated with purplish lava stone capitals by Roger's third wife.

Map on page 210

TIP

One of Sicily's greatest successes is the creation of *granita* (water ices) made from fresh fruit and served in a tall glass accompanied by a brioche – a delightful mixture, especially on a hot day. Flavours change with the season. Watermelon *granita* is a summer favourite, and so are peach, apricot and grape.

BELOW:
harvesting the grapes.

The Norman castle in Adrano was built of black volcanic rock by Roger I. Once a Bourbon prison, it now houses a museum of Greek and Bronze Age artefacts.

BELOW: startling ceramics.

Beside the castle, the **Chiesa Madre** is a Norman church disfigured by clumsy restoration in 1811. The dilapidated interior displays a luridly coloured polyptych and dusty missals. The heavy basalt columns conceivably came from the Greek Temple to Adranon that once occupied the site. Plutarch records a dramatic eve of battle appeal to the gods: in response, a bronze statue of Adranus suddenly quivered into life. A final twinge of nostalgia for ancient Adranon is evoked by the **Greek city walls**, lying at the end of Via Buglio.

Biancavilla ⓲, built on a basalt escarpment 5 km (3 miles) south of Adrano, was founded by Albanian refugees in 1480. Some of the 1991 influx of latter-day Albanians were resettled here but swiftly transferred to Palermo province, and then to wealthier Northern Italy. The sole Albanian link is the *Madonna of the Alms*, an icon brought over by the first refugees and visible in the comically grandiose **Chiesa Madre**.

If Biancavilla is best known for its prickly pears, **Paternò** ⓳, halfway between Biancavilla and Catania, is famous for its oranges, Sicily's juiciest. The town is of baroque inspiration but the Norman **castle** (Mon–Fri 8.30am–11am) on a hilly volcanic site is more striking. Established in 1073 by Count Roger, it was rebuilt later. The severity of the 14th-century lava-stone keep is echoed by the Great Hall and frescoed chapel. Frederick II died here while journeying to his favourite fortress of Enna.

Nearby is the **Chiesa Madre**, a Norman church with a Gothic facelift containing a majestic 17th-century wooden Crucifix, and the ruined Gothic church of **San Francesco**. In World War II, the German forces used this hill as an observation post and drew heavy Allied fire, leading to the death of 4,000 people. Known as **Rocca Normanna**, the castle quarter now enjoys happier associations: in summer, visitors can attend concerts, sample the local stuffed aubergines, or simply drool over terraces glistening with orange groves.

A 10-minute drive from Paternò at Fiumefreddo is **Etnaland** (open end June–early Sept; www.etnaland.eu), Sicily's first theme park worthy of the name, complete with miniature volcanoes and simulations of eruptions, as well as less obviously Etna-related attractions such as the Dinosaur Park and Crocodile Rapids.

Nicolosi

Nicolosi ⓴, east of Paternò, is both a charmless ski resort and the southern gateway to Etna's terraced wine and walking country, covered in oak, pine and chestnut trees. Lying east of the wooded Monti Rossi twin craters, the town has been wiped out by a number of eruptions and has always been re-established. Today it marks the start of bracing treks to Rifugio Sapienza *(see page 224)* and affords a fine view of Etna's active central crater and numerous secondary ones. The helpful tourist office on Piazza

Vittorio Emanuele (tel: 095 914 488; www.aast-nicolosi.it) can advise on hiking routes.

Just east, along the road to **Trecastagni ㉑**, the lava beds of 1886 and 1910 are visible. Once a medieval fiefdom, Trecastagni is noted for the **Chiesa Madre**, a Renaissance church probably designed by Antonello Gagini, as good an architect as he was a sculptor. Nearby, the 15th-century **Chiesa del Bianco** has a quaint, low bell tower while the Lombard-Romanesque **Sant'Antonio di Padova** has 17th-century lava-stone cloisters. Yet more appealing than the sights is the chance to appreciate traditional Etna craftsmanship: these lava-stone streets contain workshops dedicated to producing Sicilian carts and wrought ironwork, basket weaving and painted ceramics, as well as traditional Etna carvings in lava stone or gnarled olive wood. Nor are Trecastagni's almond biscuits, sorbets and red wines to be sniffed at.

From here head for Acireale and follow the autostrade signs to return to Fiumefreddo the quick way.

Ascending the volcano

Circling the volcano is intriguing and safe but an ascent requires caution. Depending on the season and Etna's mood, the menu may include a mere mass of clinker, a spent cone, a smoking cone, or even a seething lava front (*fronte lavica*). When it works, it is wonderful, with suphurous vapours, heat coursing through the soles of your shoes, and sightings of spitting fireballs. But if conditions are misty, wait for a better day.

An organised group trip is the sensible, relatively inexpensive way of experiencing Etna, but for sheer extravagant adventure, a private alpine guide is recommended. Without a guide, suitably clad explorers can clamber about at their own risk up to a certain altitude, currently 3,000 metres (9,850 ft), 323 metres (1,060 ft) short of Etna's great height. Even so, it is essential to get advice on routes and weather conditions from the Refuge personnel. In fact, unless you are extremely fit and appropriately dressed, the best way to make an ascent of Etna is to purchase a cable-car ticket that also

TIP

Tours of the nature reserve and volcano use Linguaglossa as a base. Some excursions feature horse riding, cycling, skiing and canoeing. There is even a difficult cross-Etna orienteering route for fit walkers. Details: Etna Natural Touring, Via Marconi 98, Linguaglossa.
Tel: 095 643 613.
www.naturaltouring.it
info@naturaltouring.it

BELOW: stepping out on Etna's dramatic slopes.

TIP

Below the murmuring summit of Etna is a vast depression, an area created by violent eruptions. Between Monte Rinatu (1,569 metres/5,147 ft) and La Montagnola (2,640 metres/8,660 ft), the **Valle del Bove** has deep lava walls that can reach 1,000 metres/3,280 ft. A desolate, unreal silence fills the valley. One way to see this extraordinary phenomenon on foot is to start at Zafferana Etnea and follow the paths.

BELOW: the cable car from Rifugio Sapienza.

includes a guided drive and walk to the summit. (These trips, available to individuals or groups, are accompanied by guides who often speak basic English, French and German.)

At the cable-car summit, just outside the bar, suitable footwear and warm clothing can be hired. From here, reinforced minibuses take passengers to the correct departure point from which to begin an ascent to the chosen destination, a route and goal which change according to the group and the level of volcanic activity. At this stage, the guides might gently try to deter the elderly and infirm from walking the final stage, but it is entirely an individual decision.

Once driving in the volcanic foothills or national park, follow signs for Etna Sud, the main southern access point, reached via **Zafferana Etnea** ㉒. Set on Etna's eastern slopes, this unprepossessing mountain resort hit the national headlines for a month in 1992 when Etna threatened to engulf the village. The resort had barely recovered from the 1984 earthquake, and a minor eruption in 1986, when the

baroque **Chiesa Madre** became the focus of fervent prayers as the local vineyards and citrus groves were swallowed up. The path of the 1992 eruption has finally been landscaped into a strange cross between a garden memorial and a tourist attraction, signposted *Colata Lavica 1992*, the Lava Flow 1992. Since Zafferana is only 500 metres (1,650 ft) from the crater on Monte Serra Calvarina, landslides and further eruptive activity are still common.

From here, a road leads to the **Rifugio Sapienza** base camp and an ascent of Etna. As one climbs the scenic **Casa Cantoniera** road, citrus groves and wooded slopes give way to a wasteland of lava flows, bare slabs of brown rubble half-covered by snow. Even in deepest winter, snow is unevenly distributed because of heat generated by the volcano.

Route to the top

The base camp of **Rifugio Sapienza** ㉓, situated at 1,800 metres (5,900 ft), includes a refuge and hostel run by the Italian Alpine Club. Like much on Mount Etna, the centre lives dangerously, and has been rebuilt after an eruption recorded on a plaque as 9 April 1983, an event depicted in lurid technicolor inside. Before taking the cable car to the top, glance at the spent cone just in front of the refuge, one of many extinct cones nearby.

A winter **cable car** trip may be made in the company of skiers comparing eyewitness accounts of Etna's most recent devastation. En route are grim views of a burnt-out cable car destroyed in the 1983 eruption, along with ruined access roads, the wreckage of a ski lift and the original mountain refuge, buried by lava in 1971. At the summit, hardy visitors set off by minibus, leaving the less adventurous to simply admire the snowcapped views, usually best in the morning or at sunset, before

sloping off to the mountain bar and videos of the volcano in action.

Torre del Filósofo, Empedocles' so-called observation post, wrecked in a past eruption, currently marks the highest point one can go with a guide, close to the southeast crater. Daring skiers peer into any active cone at their own risk. Empedocles did not live to tell the tale: the Greek philosopher allegedly leapt into the main crater in 433 BC trying to prove that the gases would support his body weight. The charitable interpretation is that it was also a quest for divine consciousness in death. But, as his sandal was found on the edge, perhaps he merely slipped.

The view from the top will depend on volcanic activity and weather conditions, particularly the prevailing winds: it is vital to avoid the gases and burning volcanic matter emitted from active craters. Blue smoke indicates the presence of magma while a *corona*, a halo of sulphurous vapour, is a rare event. At most, you may see an active crater belching out sulphurous fumes or exploding *bombe*, molten "bombs", or the bottom of the misty cone bubbling with incandescent lava. In periods of intense seismic activity, the volcano spits out molten rock or fireballs, a dramatic sight, especially at night, but the guides have to judge a safe distance from which to view the phenomenon.

On the summit, the guides' current gimmick is to let visitors watch a demonstration of the forging of black Etna ashtrays from molten lava. In exceptional circumstances, visitors may be shown a lava front some distance away from the volcano. Usually bathed in mist and emitting a stench of sulphur, the lava front sounds like the clinking of china cups or the hissing of some chained animal.

The descent of Etna may not be an anticlimax if you can visit a lava front, but visitors are strongly discouraged to do this without a guide or local help. In recent eruptions, **Valle del Bove** ❷, best seen from **Milo**, has formed a lava front, hence its eerie, barren surface, devoid of vegetation *(see Tip, opposite page)*. For most people, the descent by cable car will simply mean a return to the tacky bars and souvenir shops. ❑

Map on page 210

Etna's lava-strewn surface.

BELOW: the scorched Silveri crater.

RESTAURANTS AND CAFÉS

Caltagirone

I Marchesi di Santa Barbara
Via San Bonaventura 22.
Tel: 0933 22406.
In a noble old palazzo in the upper town, this popular restaurant serves meat and fish mains, as well as pizza. Closed Mon. €€

La Scala
Scala Santa Maria del Monte 8. Tel: 0933 57781.
Alongside the staircase, two rooms in a 17th-century palazzo, with a charming courtyard and garden for summer. Traditional Sicilian cooking. Closed Wed. €€

Aci Castello

Alioto
Via Mollica 24.
Tel: 0954 94444.

On a terrace by the sea, a popular but expensive fish restaurant. Enjoy the pasta with lobster. Closed Tues. €€€

Barbarossa
Strada Provinciale, the SS 114 road to Aci Castello.
Tel: 095 295 539.
Range of seafood as well as stuffed pancakes and a good list of notable wines. €€€

Aci Trezza

La Cambusa del Capitano
Via Marina 65.
Tel: 095 276 298.
A simple place on the banks of the sea serving only local produce and fish. Welcoming and easy-going. Closed Wed. €€

Galatea
Via Livorno 146a.
Tel: 095 277 913.

Elegant restaurant with a sea view. Wide selection of fish and desserts. Closed Mon. €€€

I Malavoglia
Lungomare dei Ciclopi 167.
Tel: 095 711 6556.
Typical seafront trattoria where fish is naturally the mainstay of the menu. But at good prices. Closed Tues and 23 Dec–23 Jan. €€

Acireale

Nino Castorina
Corso Savoia 109 (closed Mon) and Corso Umberto 63 (closed Tues).
Not restaurants but the place for ice cream, *pasta reale* (marzipan) and pastries. €

Panoramico
Viale Ionico 12, Litoranea.
Tel: 095 885 291.

A panoramic restaurant with a pizzeria and a piano bar. Good seafood. Closed Mon. €€€
● See also Santa Maria la Scala, 2.5 km away.

Cannizaro

Alioto
Via Mollica 24.
Tel: 095 494 444.
The best of Sicilian cooking in a pleasing setting. Pasta dishes with mussels or shrimps are to be recommended. Closed Tues. €€€

Oleandro
Via Musco 8.
Tel: 095 491 522.
www.baiaverde.it
Classic Sicilian cooking, both special meat and fish dishes. Garden setting. Closed Mon. €€€

Santa Maria la Scala

La Grotta
Via Scalo Grande 46.
Tel: 095 764 8153.
A casual, popular place with simple food that, due to demand, extends tables along the water's edge in the summer. Closed Tues and three weeks in Oct. €€

Molino
Via Molino 104.
Tel: 095 764 8116.
In this peaceful sea shore corner, a simple restaurant renowned for its fish. Closed Wed and Jan. €€

LEFT: trattorie offer classic Sicilian cooking.

On Mount Etna

At **Rifugio Sapienza** there are mediocre restaurants and snack bars. The best of a poor choice is **La Cantoniera**, which was destroyed in the lava flow of 1982 and rebuilt.

Belpasso

La Cantina
Strada Provinciale Nicolosi-Belpasso. Tel: 095 912 992.
A rustic restaurant and pizzeria with very different menus. The stars are mushroom or asparagus risotto. Closed Tues and Aug. €€

Nicolosi

Corsaro
Piazza Cantoniera, Etna Sud. Tel: 095 914 122.
www.hotelcorsaro.it
A busy, small hotel (17 rooms) that is a popular inexpensive base for young people exploring Etna. The restaurant offers substantial meals. €€

Etna
Via Etnea 93.
Tel: 095 911 937.
Traditional Etna cuisine in a post-modern restaurant and pizzeria. Specialities include mushroom risotto, *cinghiale alla griglia* (grilled wild boar) and *insalata di funghi crudi* (raw mushroom salad). Pizza in evenings only. Closed Mon. €€

Grotta del Gallo
Via Madonna delle Grazie 40. Tel: 095 911 301.
In a panoramic location,

RIGHT: traditional sweets are part of a typical menu.

the villa has a garden and fine views of both volcano and sea. Farmhouse and classic cooking. Closed Thur. €€

Nero di Cenere
Via Garibaldi 64.
Tel: 095 791 8513.
A well-regarded wine bar and restaurant, with an extensive list of regional wines and a menu of light pasta and vegetarian dishes. Terrace. Closed Mon. €€

Trecastagni

Al Mulino
Via Mulino al Vento 48.
Tel: 095 780 6634.
Set in a grand villa overlooking an old windmill. Specialities include pasta with mushrooms and sausage with herbs. Closed Mon. €€

Villa Taverna
Corso Colombo 42.
Tel: 095 780 6458.
This is 17 km (11 miles) from Catania but popular with the Catanese because it is atmospheric and looks like a film set where good food is served. Family-run and welcoming. Book. €€

Zafferana Etnea

Parco dei Principi
Via delle Ginestre 1.
Tel: 095 708 2335.
www.ristoranteparcodeiprincipe.it
Elegant 18th-century villa serving interesting regional cuisine, with Etna produce and mushrooms. Closed Tues. €€€

Randazzo

Parco Statella
Via Montelaguardia.
Tel: 095 924 036.
www.parcostatella.com.
Between Randazzo and Linguaglossa, this *agriturismo* set in a historic villa, has a charming trattoria, with wild mushrooms a speciality. Closed Wed; open weekends only Oct–May. €€

San Giorgio e Il Drago
Piazza San Giorgio 28.
Tel: 095 923 972.
This attractive restaurant near Santa Maria offers a generous selection of *antipasti* as well as mainly meaty mains. Good value. Closed Tues. €€

Veneziano
Via Nazionale 120, Contrada Arena.
Tel: 0957 991 353.
A restaurant with pretensions but with tasty regional dishes 1 km (½ mile) out of Randazzo. Mushrooms from the slopes of Etna are a speciality. Closed Mon. €€

PRICE CATEGORIES

Prices for three-course dinner per person with a half-bottle of house wine:
€ = under €15
€€ = €15–30
€€€ = €30–60

TAORMINA

As Sicily's foremost international resort, Taormina has a reputation for being a fashionable loafing place, a languorous image it proudly strives to maintain

Taormina is Sicily's most dramatic resort, a stirring place celebrated by poets from Classical times onwards. Goethe waxed lyrical about the majestic setting: "Straight ahead one sees the long ridge of Etna, to the left the coastline as far as Catania or even Siracusa, and the whole panorama is capped by the huge, fuming, fiery mountain, the look of which, tempered by distance and atmosphere, is, however, more friendly than forbidding." D. H. Lawrence was equally enamoured, calling Taormina "the dawn-coast of Europe".

The effects of tourism

Today this elemental site has been domesticated into a safe, sophisticated, unSicilian pocket. A century of tourism has toned down the subversive native spirit, effaced poverty and displaced undesirables. French visitors liken Taormina to a Sicilian St Tropez, stylish but unreal. Still, after Sicily's chaotic major cities, or the wariness of some of the islands' remote mountain villages, who wants reality? May, September and October are the loveliest months in Taormina, when the city enjoys a semblance of solitude combined with the pleasures of a mild climate.

The terraced town was once a wintering place for frustrated northerners and gay exiles. Today, this safe haven appeals to romantic couples, sedate shoppers and the cultured middle classes. As a resort, Cefalù, near Palermo, is Taormina's only serious rival. But Taormina scores by having top-quality hotels and an enlightened, if rampantly commercial, approach to tourism.

Local gossip has it that the town is uncontaminated by corruption because even the Mafia likes a crime-free holiday haunt. Yet despite designer glamour and the hordes of

Map on page 230

LEFT AND BELOW: shopping on Corso Umberto.

Sicilian wine on sale in Taormina.

blasé cruise-liner passengers, the site's majesty is not manufactured. Nor is the heady decadence and timeless charm. Taormina may now have internet cafés, but the locals prefer to pass the time of day chatting from an ancient terrace overlooking the sea.

The town is largely closed to traffic, so parking is expensive and difficult, with access strictly controlled and places limited. As the streets are steep, the hotels scattered around several locations have courtesy buses.

Illustrious past

Taormina started as a Siculi settlement at the foot of Monte Tauro. It was an outpost of Naxos *(see page 252)* until the Greeks fled the first colony for Taoromenion in 403 BC. Under the Romans, the city acquired a garrison and the new name of Tauromenium. The town also prospered in medieval times and became the capital of Byzantine Sicily in the 9th century. It was the last Byzantine stronghold to fall to the Arabs, destroyed in 902. But it was rebuilt almost immediately, and captured in 1078 by the Norman Count Roger d'Altavilla, under whom it enjoyed a long period of prosperity. Aristocratic leanings later drew Taormina into the Aragonese camp and support for the Spanish, with the Catalan legacy reflected in the town's array of richly decorated palazzi.

The main entrance to the town (where the pedestrian zone starts and traffic jams occur) is the medieval gate of **Porta Messina ❶**, close to the bus terminus on Via Pirandello where the cable car *(funivia)* takes you down to the resort beaches of **Mazzarò** on the coast below. Outside the gate is the tiny church of **San Pancrazio**, built over a temple to Isis. On the other side of the arch, the crowds start gathering.

Corso Umberto, the pedestrianised main street, leads through the

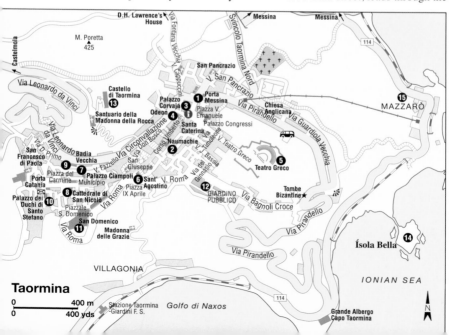

Taormina

town, from Porta Messina to Porta Catania, Taormina's exit gate. It is a feast for shopaholics. The 15th-century palazzi have been converted into craft shops, boutiques and bars. Luxury food emporia display bottled peppers, candied fruit, marzipan animals and fresh kumquats. Majolica tiles, leather goods and traditional puppets vie with elaborate cut-glass chandeliers and reproductions of Classical statuary.

Just off the Corso lies the **Naumachie ❷**, a hybrid construction second only to the Greek theatre in importance. Originally a vaulted cistern connected to the city baths, it evolved into a Hellenic *nymphaeum* and Roman gymnasium. The atmospheric arched buttress walls remain, propping up the Corso. For lunch, the restaurant terraces of the adjoining Via Naumachia beckon.

Palazzo Corvaja

On **Piazza Vittorio Emanuele II**, the main square, is **Palazzo Corvaja ❸**, an historic mansion where the Sicilian Parliament met in 1411. Now a tourist office and exhibition centre, this eclectic building incorporates a crenellated Saracenic tower, a secluded courtyard, sculpted parapet, and Catalan-Gothic decorative details around the doorway and windows. It also contains the small **Museo Siciliano di Arte e Tradizioni Popolari** (Tues–Sun 9am–1pm, 4–8pm; entrance fee) with local costumes, puppets, carts, Christmas cribs, ceramics and other Sicilian memorabilia.

Next to the palazzo is the charming church of **Santa Caterina d'Alessandria**, constructed in the 17th century on part of the remains of the **Odeon Romano ❹**, or Teatrino Romano, a Roman concert auditorium partly hidden by the church.

Now we come to Taormina's *raison d'être* on Via Teatro Greco (just

follow the crowds). This is the **Teatro Greco ❺** (daily 9am–one hour before sunset; entrance fee). It is a setting that is pure drama, with the *cavea* (horseshoe of tiered seats) hewn out of the hillside.

In Greek theatres, sea and sky were the natural backdrop; the Romans preferred proscenium arches. Where the Greeks worshipped nature, the Romans tried to improve on it. The Hellenistic theatre was built under Hieron in the 3rd century BC and enlarged by the Romans in AD 2. Like Tindari's Greek theatre, Taormina's was turned into an arena for gladiatorial combat. Roman theatrical conventions caused the view to be obscured by arches. By adding a double portico and colonnades behind the stage, they showed insensitivity to the natural setting.

Romantics side with the Olympian gods in seeing Roman grandiosity as no match for the timeless character of Greek art. However, Roman erudition is evidenced in the well-preserved *scena* (the construction behind the stage that served as a backdrop and

Map on page 230

TIP

Many visitors may need to use taxis to go out of Taormina. Fleecing tourists is a local art so establish the taxi fare before setting out: there are fixed rates for many journeys but you'll need to find this out from your hotel, and make sure the driver knows you know.

BELOW:
on the Corso, a street artist draws a crowd.

also storage area). But in the 19th century, the granite columns and Corinthian capitals were wrongly repositioned on the site. Still, Greek purists are delighted to see the Roman *scena* crumble, the better to appreciate the Greek atmosphere.

Not that the cats sunning themselves on the ruins distinguish between Greek marble and pinkish Roman brickwork. In high season, the theatre is best explored early in the morning or near closing time, to avoid the crowds. Views from the terraces above the *cavea* and *parascenia* (wings) reveal a perfect fusion of the elements. The writer Vincent Cronin likened the theatre to a seagull suspended between sky and sea. The scene is shrouded in mystery by a smouldering volcano or snowcapped peak. Citrus groves carpet the slopes while the cliff face is a tangle of cacti and orchids. Below stretches a craggy coastline and the romantic islet of Isola Bella.

The theatre is still used today, not just for performances of Classical plays, as at Siracusa, but also as the venue for an international arts festival, Taormina Arte, which presents drama, cinema, ballet and music from June to August (tickets and information from the tourist office in Palazzo Corvaja, Piazza Santa Caterina; www.taormina-arte.com).

Halfway down the Corso, **Piazza IX Aprile** ❻ offers glittering views of Etna and close-ups of preening poseurs at chic cafés: the expensive Caffè Wunderbar attracts unsuspecting tourists. **Sant'Agostino**, the forbidding 15th-century church on the square, has been converted into a cosy library and art gallery. The other church feels more like a social than a spiritual centre: **San Giuseppe**'s rococo interior overflows after a Sunday service; after much hand-shaking, the congregation spills into the *caffès*.

The Corso continues beyond the Porta di Mezzo, a clock tower marking the city's medieval quarter. Steps lead to the Catalan-Gothic **Palazzo Ciampoli** ❼, now Hotel Palazzo Vecchio. After admiring its Aragonese battlemented facade and mullioned windows, call in for a sweet Sicilian pastry at Bar Saint Honoré

At play in Piazza Duomo.

BELOW: the Wunderbar in Taormina is a honey-pot for tourists.

before climbing Via Venezia, a charming alley by the Corso, or strolling further to the cathedral.

Piazza del Duomo is a central meeting place. At sunset, or at the first sign of spring sun, children fetch their footballs, the *jeunesse dorée* pose, and Taormina's perma-tanned lounge lizards, not a dying breed, search for foreign prey. Matrons still swan around in weighty furs: in Taormina, the fur coat parade lasts until March.

The Duomo itself, the **Cattedrale di San Niccolò ❽** (daily, 8am–noon, 3.30–6.30pm) draws crowds to its winter cycle of classical concerts. The crenellated stone facade has a severity that survived Renaissance remodelling but is softened by the baroque fountain on the square, which sports sea horses, cherubs and a podgy female centaur. This weird mythological creature is the city symbol, confirmed by a stone centaur unearthed on the Greek site.

Badia Vecchia

Opposite the fountain, steps lead to Piazza del Carmine and the **Badia Vecchia ❾**, a battlemented 15th-century abbey (Mon–Sat 9am–1pm, 3–7pm). Although over-restored, the abbey still has Trecento flourishes, Gothic arched windows, fretwork and friezes. Set on a lower level, **Palazzo dei Duchi di Santo Stefano ❿** is a gracious ducal palace and Taormina's loveliest medieval building. Highlights are the Norman-Gothic windows, delicate lava stone cornices, and the lacy frieze of *intarsia* work (decorative wood inlay), a Saracenic legacy. Exhibitions are presented here.

From here, Via del Ghetto winds down to **San Domenico ⓫**, a 15th-century monastery converted into a *de luxe* hotel. During World War II, it was Marshal Kesselring's headquarters and suffered bomb damage, although the cells and cloisters were spared. The cells are now distinctly unspartan bedrooms. The Corso ends at **Porta Catania**, the archway that matches the Porta Messina gate that greets visitors to the town. The Post Office and a collection of restaurants and small hotels are outside this gate.

English connection

It is a short stroll to the **Giardino Pubblico ⓬**, a lush park on Via Roma bequeathed to the town by an eccentric Englishwoman in the 1920s. Florence Trevelyan adorned her hanging gardens with pagoda-style follies and observation towers for bird-spotting (she was a keen amateur ornithologist). The tiered gardens are linked by mosaic paths and wind past tropical plants, from spiky cacti and lilies to dull English hedges.

St George's Anglican Church also dates from Trevelyan's time. Her contemporary, D. H. Lawrence, lived for a few years in a villa in Via Fontana Vecchia, part of which has been renamed Via David Herbert Lawrence. When King George V

Map on page 230

Taormina's Duomo.

BELOW: the church of San Giuseppe overlooks Piazza IX Aprile.

Map on page 230

The sun designs on modern ceramics can be traced back to the late Greek period.

BELOW:
shopping in Taormina.

visited, Lawrence was the only British resident to ignore him. Undeterred, the King called on the writer and helped water his garden. In Taormina, the sickly Lawrence chose to live a solitary life, writing of sensuality. His former home is still a private house, marked by a plaque: "D. H. Lawrence, English author, lived here 1920–23".

On the north side of town, perched on **Monte Táuro**, is a tumbledown medieval **Castello** ⓭. It can be reached by a half-hour ascent up a steep, winding path that passes by the clifftop **Santuario della Madonna della Rocca**. It is a strenuous climb, which should not be attempted in the middle of a summer's day, but the panoramas from the top are worth the effort.

Via Leonardo da Vinci climbs circuitously from Taormina to **Castelmola** above, a hamlet perched on a limestone peak (there is a bus service). From this natural balcony over the sea, there is a sense of what Taormina used to be. Out of season it is home to old craftsmen and part-time potters, but in summer it resembles a tourist trap, with trinket shops and bars. **Caffè San Giorgio** is the place for celebrity autographs, a reminder of (separate) visits by Churchill and Kesselring. Once Churchill's local, it is now patronised by hearty German drinkers.

Below Taormina, sheer cliffs drop to the tempting islet of **Isola Bella** ⓮. From Via Pirandello, the cable car links the city to the pebbled beach at **Mazzarò** ⓯. Nearby are entrances to underwater caves, where scuba divers spot shrimps, red starfish, perch, scorpion fish and sea urchins. If you prefer your fish on a plate, leave the sea for the grey and pink cliffs above Taormina. For details of beaches close to Taormina, see Giardini-Naxos *(page 252)*.

Chic living

As Sicily's glitziest resort, Taormina is sophisticated fun, from the summer cultural season to the Sunday posers. The chic crowd wears whatever is in fashion. If the summer colours are white for men and orange for women, then the local crowd wears it and the shop windows will echo the mood. The backdrop is equally vivid: balconies hung with geraniums and bougainvillea; inner courtyards with sculpted cornices, grape-carved motifs, and miniature lemon trees.

Taormina by night is charming. The Catalan-Gothic facades are illuminated, the shops glow and the squares seem tinged pink in the moonlight. From the belvedere, Etna's fiery cone glitters before dissolving into the sea, stars and smoky peaks. Solitary walkers climb Salita Ibrahim to the piazza, alongside the church of Carmine that is now a gallery, a tranquil monastic spot with a tower and wild garden behind. Dreamers take Via Caruso to the Badia Vecchia and bay views, a reminder that Taormina is a setting in search of a city. ❑

Gay Taormina

When Harold Acton pronounced Sicily "a polite synonym for Sodom", he was really referring to Taormina. The town was founded during a period of Greek decadence and has always lived down to its debauched reputation. In this, it has been helped by its theatrical foreign residents. From the Belle Epoque to Edwardian times, Taormina was, along with Capri, the quintessential homosexual haunt.

The gay resort was first publicised by a trio of Germans: a poet, a painter and a photographer. Goethe pronounced Taormina a "patch of paradise on earth" in 1787. Otto Geleng, a landscape artist, settled there nearly a century later. The Prussian's paintings of the scenery drew gasps when they were exhibited in Paris salons. Although married to a Sicilian, he was a firm believer in the dictum of girls for procreation, boys for pleasure.

His younger friend, Wilhelm von Gloeden, arrived in 1880 and stayed until his death 50 years later. The exiled blond baron photographed nude Sicilian shepherd boys whose beauty elevated them to the status of Greek gods. His lithe peasants, draped in panther skins or photographed against sunsets, soon entranced jaded Berliner high society.

Oscar Wilde often helped in the compositions, crowning the boy models with laurels or posing with pan pipes. Von Gloeden swooned over Wilde, declaring the poet "beautiful as a Greek god". Wilde returned the compliment, at least artistically, but preferred his "marvellous boys" as companions.

A later voluptuary with showbiz connections was the Bavarian Gayelord Hauser, the Hollywood dietician to the stars. In the 1940s, such luminaries as Gloria Vanderbilt, Marlene Dietrich, Rita Hayworth and Joan Crawford danced until dawn at his parties. But while most of Taormina's male population ogled the screen goddesses, Hauser was more enamoured of the local gods.

Truman Capote and Tennessee Williams were regular guests at the wild parties at Villa Hauser. Both worked in Taormina before alcohol and drugs wreaked havoc with their writing. Capote accused Williams of "hiring boys for the afternoon" but both were often picked up drunk in bars on the Corso. Drunk or sober, Williams singularly failed to live up to his "lone wolf" reputation in Taormina.

Somerset Maugham and Anatole France were familiar figures on the Taormina scene, indulging in "the Disneyland of sin". Inspired by gossip about gay Taormina, the poet Jean Cocteau also came to see "the boys with almond eyes".

All this was seemingly at odds with Taormina's air of twee Edwardian gentility, not to mention the mores of the English expatriate community. Douglas Sladen's book on fin-de-siècle Sicily confessed: "Nobody goes about naked, as might be imagined from the photographs." Thus reassured or disappointed, the British turned Taormina into a cosy hillside resort.

When showing Evelyn Waugh around Taormina in the 1950s, a downcast Harold Acton pointed out a placard inscribed "Nice Cuppa Tea" and complained that Taormina was now "quite as respectable as Bournemouth". Outwardly at least, nothing has changed much since then. ❏

RIGHT: a shepherd boy poses for von Gloeden.

RESTAURANTS AND BARS

Taormina
Taormina has a huge choice of eating places, from international style to regional specialities. The hilltop village of Castelmola offers in-expensive alternatives to dining in Taormina itself, while at the foot of the cliffs, reached by cable car, the coastal area of Mazzarò has lively and good-value trattorie specialising in seafood.

In Taormina, try to avoid most restaurants in Corso Umberto, which cater to indiscriminate tourists and tend to be bland and expensive. In general, dining in Taormina is more elegant and select than eating out in Mazzarò or Castelmola.

'A Zammara
Via Fratelli Bandiera 15.
Tel: 0942 24408.
www.zammara.it
Pleasant garden setting for traditional Sicilian dishes and some unusual variations based on fresh, seasonal produce. Closed end Jan. €€€

L'Arco dei Cappuchini
Via Cappucini 1.
Tel: 0942 24893.
Near Porta Messina. A crowded, welcoming place where the smart set gather. Excellent Sicilian cooking with an emphasis on fresh fish as well as meat. Good Sicilian wines and liqueurs. Book. Closed Wed and 10 days in Nov. €€€

Il Baccanale
Piazzetta Filea 1.
Tel: 0942 625 390.

Simple trattoria with many tables on the small piazza. Popular with tourists. Closed Jan. €€

La Botte
Piazza Santa Domenica 4.
Tel: 0942 24198.
www.labotte1972.it
Simple trattoria with large terrace. Easy-going, casual and welcoming with traditional Sicilian cooking. Closed Wed. €€

Casa Grugno
Via Santa Maria de'Greci.
Tel: 0942 21208.
www.casagrugno.it
Popular, expensive establishment with menu containing inter-national dishes as well as Sicilian. Dinner only. Closed Nov–Apr Sun eve & Mon; Jan–Feb. €€€€

Al Duomo
Vico Ebrei 11.
Tel: 0942 625 656.
www.ristorantealduomo.it
In the centre, with sim-ple outdoor facilities and good traditional Sicilian fare. Closed Wed except Easter–Oct. €€€

Gambero Rosso
Via Naumachia 11.
Tel: 0942 23011.
Family-run and welcom-ing, with good Sicilian cuisine. Closed Thur. €€

Al Giardino
Via Bagnoli Croci 84.
Tel: 0942 23453.
www.algiardino.net
Another friendly, family-run restaurant specialis-ing in traditional Sicilian food, with a seasonal menu. Closed Tues. €€

Granduca
Corso Umberto 170.
Tel: 0942 24983.
www.granducataormina.com
This chic, old-fashioned and rather grand restaur-ant offers lovely views over the bay. The price covers the view as much as the food. Closed Tues. €€€

La Giara
Vico la Floresta 1.
Tel: 0942 23360.
www.lagiara-taormina.com
Highly respected restau-rant and piano bar. Ele-gant dining, on roof or terraces with traditional menu and service. Dress: smart. Book. Closed Mon and Nov, Feb, Mar. €€€€

Licchio's
Via Patricio 10.
Tel: 0942 625 327.
Charming garden setting only seconds' walk from Porta Messina. Both popular and fashionable. Excellent fresh fish including fish *carpaccio*. Pasta dishes include lin-guine with sea urchins when in season. Book. Pizza and Thai curry too. Closed Thur. €€€

Da Lorenzo
Via Roma 4.
Tel: 0942 23480.
Prohibitive prices and a standard menu but a glorious setting. Closed Wed and mid-Dec–mid-Jan. €€€€

Maffei's
Via San Domenico de Guz-man 1. Tel: 0942 24055.
Elegant garden setting.

Proud of their fish. Book. Closed Tues in winter, and most of Feb. €€€€

Mamma Rosa
Via Naumachia 10.
Tel: 0942 24361.
With tables lining the lively alley in the summer months, this restaurant serves up crispy pizzas, cooked in a wood-fired oven, as well as standard Italian fare. Closed Tues in winter. €€€

Da Nino
Via Luigi Pirandello 37.
Tel: 0942 21265.
An excellent, untouristy restaurant serving Sicilian specialities; try the *gnocchi*. Fairly priced for well-heeled Taormina. €€

Siciliana
Salita Ospedale 9.
Tel: 0942 24780.
Surprisingly good value for Taormina, this trattoria has its own little terrace. Try the smoked swordfish. Closed Wed. €€€

Vecchia Taormina
Vico Ebrei 3.
Tel: 0942 625 589.
www.vecchiataormina.com.
An excellent pizzeria in the heart of town, with a wood-burning oven and courtyard seating. Closed Wed and lunch July–Aug. €

Villa Zuccaro
Piazza Carmine 5.
Tel: 0942 628 018.
A pizzeria in a simple setting; large garden open in fine weather. Unusual pizza choices. Closed Tues. €

Castelmola

In season, this tiny village above Taormina represents a boisterous alternative to the town – and the steep climb is one way of working up an appetite. The village specialises in inexpensive bars and *paninoteche* (sandwich places) which are popular with younger visitors.

Ciccino's
Piazza Duomo 3.
Tel: 0942 28081.
A rustic pizzeria near the cathedral, excellent for thin pizza cooked in a wood-fired oven. €€

Il Maniero
Via Salita Castello.
Tel: 0942 28180.
Great sea views from this restaurant in a tower that was once part of a castle. Booking essential. Closed Wed. €€€

Giardini-Naxos

Although this resort comes under the province of Messina, it is only 5 km (3 miles) from Taormina and 54 km (34 miles) to Messina.

Sea Sound
Via Jannuzzo 37.
Tel: 0942 54330.
Fish a speciality served on a garden terrace overlooking the sea. Simple menu, large portions. Open May–Oct. €€€

Caffè Cavallaro
Via Umberto 165.
Tel: 0942 51259.
Caffè serving delicious pastries such as *sfoglie*

all ricotta, traditional Sicilian almond confections and *cassatelle* (ice cream cakes). €

Mazzarò

Visit the coast by cable car (*funivia*) from Via Pirandello, outside Porta Messina.

La Conchiglia
Piazzale Funivia (near the cable car). Tel: 0942 24739.
Serves very good pizza at weekends in low season and all week in summer. Closed Tues and 15–20 days in Oct or Nov. €€

Delfino
Via Nazionale.
Tel: 0942 23004.
Serves traditional dishes from the Messina region on a pretty terrace with bay views. Try the fish. Open summer only. €€

Il Gabbiano
Via Nazionale 115.
Tel: 0942 625 128.
Locals go for the *risotto alla marinara* (seafood

risotto). Closed Tues. €€€

Da Giovanni
Via Nazionale 115.
Tel: 0942 23531.
Classic water's-edge restaurant with traditional sea fare. Closed Mon and Jan–Feb. €€

Da Giorgio
Vico Sant'Andrea 7.
Tel: 0942 625 502.
On the Isola Bella beach. Excellent for fish. Closed Mon. €€

Oliviero
Via Nazionale 137.
Tel: 0942 625 837.
www.grandhoteltimeo.com
At Mazzarò beach. Excellent restaurant. Also has a piano bar. €€€€

PRICE CATEGORIES
Three-course dinner and half-bottle of house wine:
€ = under €15
€€ = €15–30
€€€ = €30–60
€€€€ = over €60

MESSINA PROVINCE

Where Sicily meets Italy, the province offers popular coastal resorts, a seemingly remote, mountainous hinterland waiting to be explored and seaways to the Aeolian Islands and further

T he province of Messina's official slogan is *Monte e Mare*, mountains and seas, a promise, as the people from Messina see it, of a glorious gateway into Sicily. Certainly, the province delivers rugged mountain ranges and contrasting coastlines. The Tyrrhenian coast, the northern coastline leading to Palermo, is one of rocky inlets, saltwater lakes, sand dunes and dry gravel-beds; citrus groves are fringed by myrtle, broom and prickly pear. The Ionian coast is a gentler but equally exotic coastline as far south as Taormina, with sandy shores and resorts. Both coasts offer Classical sites, stumpy castles, seafood dishes and an enticing hinterland.

A history of disasters

Messina, which thrived for centuries as a seafaring power, was a Phoenician-Punic colony settled by the Greeks in 730 BC. Its decline set in with the outbreak of plague in 1743, followed by earthquakes and, in the 1800s, by a naval bombardment and cholera epidemic. But the greatest calamity was the 1908 earthquake, which killed 84,000 people in 30 seconds. In 1943, in World War II, the port of Messina represented the Germans' last stand: the city was devastated and 5,000 people died during Allied bombing.

The ensuing fresh start favoured economic enterprise. Today, the *provincia* has pockets of industry at Messina and Milazzo, with oil, tyres, terracotta and cement replacing the dependence on fruit production. Tourism is important too and hotels in the province abound. However, the province's long-term prosperity, like Sicily's, could depend on better communications, symbolised by the building of a suspension bridge over the Straits to the mainland near Villa San Giovanni in Calabria.

Map:
pages
240–1

LEFT: a cruise ship squeezes into Messina's harbour.
BELOW:
at home in Messina.

TIP

Messina's port is linked to Villa San Giovanni in Calabria by a continuous service of passenger, car and cargo ferries run by various lines. With so many ferries, you can just turn up and buy a ticket. For car ferries to Salerno, outside Naples, the link is Caronte & Tourist, tel: 800 627 414, www.carontetourist.it. The nearest hydrofoil link to the Isole Eolie is from Milazzo, with Siremar, tel: 892 123, www.siremar.it.

BELOW:
Messina's Duomo.

Messina, the city

The wide boulevards, grid system, austere public buildings and matter-of-factness don't make **Messina ①** instantly appealing. But with its bustling port, stream of car and cargo ferries and population of 260,000, it does conceal a few sunken treasures and lively *caffès*. As a touring base, Taormina or a Tyrrhenean coastal resort are infinitely preferable.

The port's protectress is the *Madonna della Lettera*, the tall statue on a column built on the ancient harbour walls of the 16th-century fort, **Forte San Salvatore**, erected to protect the inner harbour. Curved around the sickle-shaped harbour is the neglected **Cittadella**, the remains of the 16th-century Spanish bastion and the naval base. The harbour welcomes grey NATO warships docked in deep water and long-prowed feluccas in pursuit of swordfish. Ever present are the boats of the Guardia di Finanza, the efficient

coastguard protecting the Straits who are alert for illegal immigrants and drug smugglers. Despite the bustle, the overwhelming feeling is of space and sweeping views; the townward side of the harbour has no walls.

Just above the port, the **Cattedrale** (Mon–Sat 7am–7pm, Sun 7.30am–1pm, 4am–7.30pm) symbolises the stubbornness of the natives: in its own way this Norman cathedral has survived medieval fires, earthquakes and wartime American firebombing (1943). It is set on a lower level than the surrounding streets that were redeveloped after the 1908 earthquake, when the cathedral was shattered, its 26 granite columns reduced to rubble and its ceiling collapsed.

The sculpted main portal and much of the Gothic facade are original, including the vivid farming scenes. The designer pink and grey interior impresses with its pleasing proportions. Restored treasures

Messina Province

TYRRHENIAN SEA

include a painted wooden ceiling, 14th-century mosaics in the semi-circular apses, glittering Renaissance altars and a Gagini statue of *St John the Baptist*. The high altar boasts a copy of the venerated Byzantine *Madonna della Lettera* (the original was destroyed during World War II), a vision of Sicilian literalism adorned with a silver crown and Byzantine gold background.

An amusing curiosity is the free-standing **campanile** outside, rebuilt in 1933. It houses the largest astronomical clock in the world; at midday mechanical figures from religious and mythological scenes appear accompanied by a cockerel flapping his wings, Dina and Clarenza, two popular heroines of the Sicilian Vespers, who ring the bells to the roaring sound of a lion that is waving a flag. There is even Jesus coming out of a tomb and the Madonna presenting a letter to the burghers of Messina to sounds of

Schubert's *Ave Maria*. The Treasury (daily 9am–1.30pm, some afternoons; entrance fee) contains church valuables including silver, reliquaries, paintings and a 14th-century work of the Madonna surrounded by saints and archangels.

Celebrating water

The **Orion fountain** (1547) in Piazza del Duomo, is a Renaissance masterpiece by Giovanni Montorsoli and Domenico Vanello that has survived in its original form. It is a tribute to Orion, a mythical city founder, and also a celebration of the first aqueduct to supply the city with water. Human figures represent the rivers Tiber, Nile, Ebro and Camaro.

Piazza Antonello, the next square north, houses a cluster of Art Nouveau public buildings leading to the vaulted Vittorio Emanuele gallery, an elegant Art Nouveau concoction. In a neighbouring square is the small **Chiesa Annunziata dei Catalani**

Map: pages 240–1

The Orion fountain and Torre dell' Orologio in Piazza del Duomo.

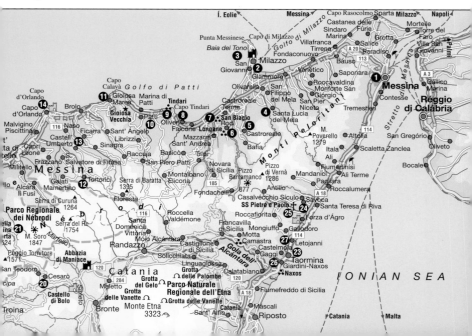

(Mon–Sat 9.30–11am), a sunken Arab-Norman church with Byzantine echoes. Built on the site of a Temple to Neptune, this eclectic church has Norman arches, blind arcading, 13th-century portals and honeycomb apses. The mellow stonework is often festooned with flowers: as Messina University chapel, it is much in demand for academic weddings.

Due to the earthquakes and war damage the city churches are a wayward mixture of restoration and invention. However, **Santa Maria degli Alemanni**, a few blocks south of the cathedral, is an authentic roofless Gothic ruin, founded by the Order of Teutonic Knights.

Behind it is the severe 17th-century **Sant'Elia** church, named after a patron saint who failed to save the city from the 1743 plague.

Messina's magpie approach to architecture is illustrated by the neoclassical Town Hall, mock-Renaissance Chamber of Commerce, Fascistic Tribunal and Art Deco Prefecture. Contemporary churches can be Rhenish, Bavarian, Spanish or, like San Giuliano, a Byzantine pastiche. Even genuine relics are given a contemporary twist by an incongruous setting: San Francesco, a Gothic fortress of a church, overlooks a frothy ice-cream parlour.

In Piazza Unità is Montorsoli's **Fountain of Neptune**, but the original Renaissance sculpture lies in the **Museo Regionale** (Wed & Fri 9am–2pm, Tues, Thur & Sat 9am–2pm, 3–6pm, Sun 9am–1pm; entrance fee), on Via della Libertà. The museum is noted for its works by artists connected to the city. Antonello da Messina (1430–78) is Sicily's master painter and southern Italy's greatest Renaissance artist. His moving polyptych of the *Madonna with Saints Gregory and Benedict* blends Flemish technique with Italian delicacy and a Sicilian sense of light. The best-preserved panel is the *Madonna and Child*.

Messina by night

Writer Rodolfo de Mattei likened the city to "a sailing ship, low in the water, ready for a night cruise". Indeed, mercantile Messina looks romantic at night, its lights glittering along the harbour front. Summer strollers take a *passeggiata* from the seafront to the lively *caffès* on Piazza Cairoli. After dinner, under-age lovers enjoy the scenic drive up Viale Umberto to the botanical gardens.

In summer, city life shifts to **Lido di Mortelle**, a youthful resort 10 km (6 miles) north of Messina. En route, the coastal road passes the **Ganzirri** lake, once famed for its mussel beds, now a popular place for dinner in summer, and the lighthouse of **Torre del Faro** on Capo Pelaro, at the entrance of the **Stretto di Messina**, the narrow Straits of Messina separating Sicily from Italy's toe. This peninsula was once graced by a Temple of Neptune whose columns ended up, shattered, in Messina Cathedral. Today's view is sadly of gigantic pylons and power cables

Caravaggio worked in Messina and his theatricality imbues Sicilian art. His familiar dramatic poses and gloomy shadows can be seen here in The Adoration of the Shepherds *and* The Raising of Lazarus, *on show at the Museo Regionale (Viale della Libertà 465).*

BELOW:
Messina's Fontana del Nettuno.

that supply Sicily with electricity.

Lido di Mortelle, just around the cape, offers sandy beaches, restaurants, open-air films and pop concerts. This stretch of coast is devoted to popular summer tourism and fishing. As a result, the air is heavy with a peculiar combination of petrol fumes and grilled swordfish.

The Tyrrhenian coast

From Messina to Milazzo 41 km (26 miles) away – where ferries sail to Stromboli and Lipari – and to the Tyrrhenian coast, you could take the fast route on the autostrada A20, but follow the SS 113, the old Roman road, for the best scenery. The first stretch climbs the **Monti Peloritani**, winding past pine groves, broom, oleanders and geraniums. But even from the motorway are dazzling glimpses of azure inlets through the pines. On the way out of town are views of three ruined forts and apricot-coloured churches in the hills.

Just before the SS 113 passes under the motorway, take the rough road on the right to the **Badiazza** (always open). This fortified Benedictine convent is set in an overgrown gully. Local lore has it that these 12th-century ruins were converted from a Byzantine granary. What is not in dispute is that the abbey was the meeting place of Eleanor of Anjou and her future husband, Frederick of Aragon.

The SS 113 allows panoramic views of pine forests and the Straits, particularly from Portella San Rizzo, the road leading along the crest of the Peloritani range to Monte Antennamare. The coastline from Messina to Palermo has been heavily fortified since Aragonese times. The headlands are still dotted with defensive towers built by the Spanish and exploited by the French. The Napoleonic forces boasted of being able to transmit a message to Naples in under two hours by lighting a string of fires in the coastal towers.

Tunnels thread through pine and olive groves to **Milazzo ❷**. The vision of this verdant peninsula is slightly marred by the presence of an oil refinery. Compensations lie in the welcoming breezes and dramatic castle, with views of the jagged

Map:
pages
240–1

Waiting for the ferry in Milazzo.

BELOW:
Torre del Faro, the tip of Messina province.

On 20 July 1860 Giuseppe Garibaldi led his Redshirts against the Bourbon troops garrisoned in Milazzo castle. His victory freed Sicily from Spanish rule.

BELOW:
Milazzo, crowned by its Norman citadel.

green spit stretching towards the Aeolian Islands (Isole Eolie). This is the place to while away the time waiting for a ferry by sampling swordfish or *bottarga* (tuna roe).

Traces of ancient civilisations around the port of Milazzo include a Bronze Age settlement north of the castle and a Greek necropolis in Piazza Roma. From the Norman era onwards, the citadel of Milazzo was regularly besieged; the victors could then control the Tyrrhenean Sea.

The unprepossessing commercial centre lies at the foot of the castle, clustered around the isthmus, but the historic nucleus is the walled city. Palazzi with baroque balconies and elegant stonework embellish the lower town, particularly along Via Umberto I. Here too, the **Duomo Nuovo**, the new cathedral, is memorable for its Renaissance paintings in the apse. But the most satisfying churches are the 15th-century **San Giacomo Apostolo** (1432) and the **Chiesa del Carmine**, a 16th-century church and Carmelite convent.

Salita San Francesco, a steep stairway, climbs through the Spanish

quarter to the impressive medieval citadel, its flanks encrusted with churches. The 17th-century **San Salvatore** belonged to a Benedictine abbey whereas **San Rocco** represents an older, fortified church. **San Francesco di Paola** is a frescoed 15th-century shell with a baroque facelift.

Facing the castle is the **Chiesa del Rosario**, once a seat of the Spanish Inquisition. This Dominican church is studded with stucco, an oddly fluffy vision for the rigorous interrogators.

The Castello's finest hour

The **Castello** (hourly guided tours Tues–Sun: Mar–May 9.30–11.30am, 5.30–7pm; June–Aug 9.30–11.30am, 5–7pm; Sept 9.30–11.30am, 4–6pm; Oct–Feb 9.30–11.30am, 2.30–3.30pm; entrance fee), perched beside a rocky precipice, occupies the site of the Greek acropolis. Erected between 1237 and 1240 and originally Arab-Norman, the citadel later fell into Hohenstaufen, Aragonese and Spanish hands. The castle's finest hour was in July 1860 when its seizure by Garibaldi's forces spelt the rout of the Royalists and the Republican conquest of Sicily. The surviving fortress is of 13th-century Hohenstaufen dynastic design with Aragonese walls. A Gothic gateway leads to the keep and parliamentary Great Hall. Also within the castle walls is the **Duomo Vecchio**, one of the few examples of 17th-century Sicilian baroque, and the ruins of the 14th-century Palazzo dei Giurati.

Boat trips to the **Baia del Tono** ❸ visit reefs, coves and grottoes, including favoured swimming spots such as the Baia San Antonio or Baia la Renella. Near the Baia del Tono is **Grotta di Polifemo**, Polyphemus' cave, where Odysseus blinded the Cyclops. The 7-km (4-mile) boat trip around the peninsula from **Al Faro** (the lighthouse) to Baia del Tono affords views of Sicily's two active

volcanoes, Etna and Stromboli. Alternatively, a stroll along the Al Faro promontory from the lighthouse to Capo di Milazzo leads through lush vegetation to the cape. For the energetic, a climb to the heights of Monte Trinita provides a view towards the Aeolian Islands.

Inland excursions

If the hinterland beckons, then **Santa Lucia del Mela ❹**, 20 km (12 miles) inland from Milazzo along a winding rural road, is a Saracen village with a Norman castle. It rose to prosperity in the 16th century as a trading post on the Lombard silk route. The churches are well endowed with works of art, thanks to the wealth generated by the local silver mine.

The Norman **cathedral**, revamped in 1607, contains a Gothic portal and 16th-century treasures including an Antonello Gagini statuette of *St Lucy*. The church attached to the castle seminary contains a Gagini *Madonna* while the library has a collection of illuminated manuscripts. Garibaldi stayed in the monastery of San Francesco before he fought his decisive battle against the Bourbons the following day.

Castroreale

Back on the SS 113, take the turning south signposted Castroreale for another foray into the hinterland. **Castroreale ❺**, a shabby upland village dominating the Micazzo valley, was founded by the Siculi in the 8th century BC. Although the settlement flourished as a medieval barony, a ruined tower is all that remains of Frederick II's summer home. If trapped overnight in this medieval time warp, male visitors may consider staying or dining with the lonely abbot at the crumbling **Collegio dei Redentori**, a depopulated monastery. Many churches in the region were damaged by the 1978 earthquake, but they retain their original treasures.

The fertile coastal plain is rich in vineyards, olive plantations and orange groves, not to mention money-making spas. Bland **Castroreale Terme**, Castroreale's coastal counterpart, appeals to enthusiasts of water cures *(see margin note)*.

From here, an inland road leads to the archaeological site of **Longane ❻** (9am–one hour before sunset), near **Rodi**. Set on the edge of the Peloritani mountains, this megalithic and Sikel settlement was razed by Messina in the 5th century BC. The remains of a turreted fort are visible and there are Bronze Age cavity tombs in the nearby necropolis. From Rodi, join the SS 185 as if returning to the coast.

Just before Castroreale Terme lies the Roman site of **San Biagio ❼**, a Roman villa built in the 1st century (daily 9am–one hour before sunset; entrance fee). The baths feature a black and white mosaic of fishermen and dancing dolphins.

The SS 113 takes you westwards to **Oliveri ❽** and a chance to exchange churches for seafood and excellent beaches. Between here and

Map: pages 240–1

Castroreale Terme, a noted spa centre, faces the Aeolian archipelago and claims cures for liver congestion, gastritis, constipation and genital diseases, with treatments including mud baths and the drinking of sulphurous waters.

BELOW: one of the crumbling towers at Capo Milazzo.

BELOW: Oliveri lagoon, seen from Tindari.

Cefalù is arguably the cleanest stretch of coastline on the island. Oliveri itself is a standard Sicilian resort with a Norman-Arab feudal castle and sandy beaches. On the seafront is a converted *tonnara*, the traditional tuna-processing plant, a reminder of life before tourism.

Oliveri is on the **Golfo di Patti**, a wilder spot than the Gulf of Milazzo, stretching west to the rocky ridges of Capo Calavà. Its bays are framed by the moody Nebrodi mountains. The coastal road crosses *fiumare*, wide, dry torrent-beds, and overlooks World War II pillbox defences.

Tindari

Dominating the Capo Tindari headland is **Tindari 9**, formerly Tyndaris, one of the last Greek colonies established in Sicily, founded by Dionysius in 396 BC. Pliny records that in AD 70 much of the city slipped into the sea. Despite subsidence and earthquake, the Greco-Roman city prospered until razed by the Arabs in 836.

The **Santuario della Madonna Nera** (Mon–Sat 6.45am–12.30pm, 2.30–7pm, Sun 6.45am–12.45pm, 2.30–8pm; closes one hour earlier in winter), built on to an old chapel in 1957, stands on the site of an ancient acropolis. This glittering church is a contemporary effusion of kitsch beloved by Sicilians who make pilgrimages throughout the year, particularly on the Madonna's feast day, 8 September. The A20 autostrada exit is just 8 km (5 miles) away, and Messina only 65 km (40 miles). The sanctuary is revered all over southern Italy as a shrine to a black-faced Byzantine icon with miraculous powers. The seated 16th-century *Madonna Nera* bears the motto: *Nigra sum, sed hermosa* ("I am black, but beautiful"). Among other miracles, she is credited with causing the sea to withdraw to provide a magic mattress of sand to cushion a child's fall over the cliff.

The **archaeological park** (daily 9am–two hours before sunset; entrance fee) is pleasingly wild. Italian visitors, of course, are more impressed by the sacred *Black Madonna* housed in the church bordering the park. The Greek city cov-

ers a Bronze Age site and has left its mark in impressive boundary **walls** (3rd century BC) and assorted public buildings. The Greco-Roman **theatre** cannot compare with Taormina's but enjoys a superb natural setting overhanging the bay. Classical drama, concerts and opera are now performed here in summer. A wide thoroughfare, one of three original *decumani*, links the theatre to the vaulted **basilica**. This Augustan basilica was once a grand entrance to the *agora*, a ceremonial space for meetings and festivals. Nearby are the remains of Roman baths, villas, workshops and taverns. One villa is adorned with geometrical mosaics while the thermal baths enclose mosaics of dolphins, bulls, warriors and the *Trinacria*, the symbol of Sicily. The on-site **antiquarium** displays sculptures, ceramics, a tragic mask and a bust of Augustus.

Below Cape Tindari is the **Oliveri lagoon**, one of Sicily's loveliest natural havens. Migratory birds, including grebes, coots and egrets, are drawn to the pale green saltwater pools and wide beaches of translucent grey pebbles. The lagoon's capricious sands are a sublime spot, yet also the place for a picnic of fresh bread and local *caciocavallo* cheese.

Patti ⑩, set on a low hill facing the sea and overlooking a cultivated plain, was damaged in the earthquake of 1978 but the medieval quarter, linking Via Ceraolo and the 18th-century cathedral, has a quiet charm and several art-filled churches. San Niccolò and San Michele contain works by Gagini while the 15th-century Sant'Antonio Abate has Corinthian capitals supporting delicately rounded arches.

The remodelled **cathedral** is home to remarkable treasures: a subtle *Madonna* by Antonello da Saliba and the Renaissance **sarcophagus** of Queen Adelasia, Roger I's wife, complete with the original Norman effigy.

Sadly, this historic hill town is ringed by a jagged necklace of new development. Even so, Patti has recently unearthed its greatest attraction, a **Roman villa** (daily 9am–one hour before sunset; entrance fee) at **Marina di Patti**. Its fate is indeed curious. This sumptuous late-Imperial villa was destroyed by an earthquake in AD4 but restored and then occupied until Byzantine times. After centuries of oblivion, it was rediscovered during the construction of the motorway in 1973. The gracious rooms lead off a porticoed peristyle, looking incongruous beside the motorway flyover. The mosaics display geometric, animal, figurative and floral motifs, often of African inspiration. But Patti suffers from periodic waterlogging and wilful neglect.

After a surfeit of art and architecture, picnic among the poppies, as the Roman aristocracy did, or retreat to the beaches of Marina di Patti.

Seaside and mountains

On the road from Patti to the agricultural and commercial centre of

Map: pages 240–1

The Trinacria, the symbol of Sicily, represents the three capes of the island (which was once called Trinacria). The Medusa denotes the protection of Athena, Sicily's patron goddess.

BELOW: the remains of the basilica at Tindari.

Village life.

Capo d'Orlando are a cluster of resorts fighting a battle against coastal ribbon development and Mafia influence, currently losing the former but winning the latter. On the Capo's promontory, reached by a hard climb, are the remains of a mediaeval castle and the sanctuary of **Santa Maria di Capo d'Orlando**, erected in 1598.

From the sandy resort of **Gioiosa Marea** , one can walk up to the ghost town of **Gioiosa Vecchia**, abandoned after an 18th-century landslide. **Brolo**, just west, has a crenellated Saracen tower, crumbling city walls and several grand palazzi. But food is the real incentive: fish soups and squid dishes, as well as strong-tasting salami from the hills behind Brolo.

From Brolo, a rural foray inland visits Raccuja, Tortorici and Castell'Umberto, a case of the journey being more pleasurable than the destination. Citrus groves give way to pine forests and steep ridges, with stunning views from the hill-top villages to the Aeolian Islands.

From Brolo, a tortuous inland road leads to **Raccuja** via Sinagra. In winter, you can continue south along the SS 116 to the ski resort of **Floresta**. Heading back to the coast from Floresta, turn off left to visit a couple of villages before returning to the coast at Capo d'Orlando. **Tortorici**, the first significant village, is traditionally associated with the Mafia but has several fine churches and school of Gagini sculptures.

About 10 km (6 miles) north along switchback roads is **Castell'Umberto**, a former feudal domain with a long Dominican tradition. Constant landslides persuaded the citizens to abandon the historic centre for a new home. Nonetheless, the *centro stórico* still has a whimsical, rustic charm, with its ruined castle and vine-hung churches.

Back on the coast

Capo d'Orlando is a windswept headland subject to sudden storms. Set on the edge of a fertile plain, the town is geared to tourism and citrus farming. There is little of interest in this sprawling resort save a sandy beach strewn with whale-shaped boulders or a climb to the ruined medieval castle and church perched on the cape.

Sant'Agata di Militello, the first significant seaside resort west of Capo d'Orlando, is known for its summer promenades and its popular pebbled beach. Sant'Agata is dedicated to fun and seafood, with the local castle turned into a restaurant.

For those wishing to remain on the coast, the SS 113 leads west through **Acquedolci** to **Santo Stéfano di Camastra**, a main centre of pottery production. The rows of vivid streetside wares make purchase a mere formality.

At this point you could turn from the coast. The enchanting SS 117 road leads 16 km (10 miles) inland across the Nebrodi range to **Mistretta**, a rust-coloured town

commanding a ridge. The mellow stone town is noted for power controlling the region rather than piety, despite its churches, most of which were rebuilt during the 17th century.

With its ruined feudal castle, sculpted **Chiesa Madre** (1630), red-tiled houses and cobbled streets, the town has a faded charm. Its **Museo Civico** (Tues–Fri & Sun 8am–2pm, 4–7pm, Sat 8am–2pm) contains archaeological and church pieces.

Castel di Tusa ⑱, which marks Messina's provincial border with neighbouring Palermo, is noted for its ruined castle, rocky beach and eclectic avant-garde hotel, the Atelier sul Mare (tel: 0921 334 295; www.ateliersulmare.it).

Inland is the pretty little town of **Tusa**, with a road leading to the site of **Halaesa** (9am–one hour before sunset), a Greek city founded in 5 BC. Remains include the agora, boundary walls, theatre and temple.

Monti Nebrodi

A rural drive through the wooded hinterland of the **Nebrodi** mountains takes you into remote, rugged hill-walking country. The rounded silhouettes of the Nebrodi offer vistas of rocky outcrops or rolling hills covered in oak and beech woods or rough pasture. Apart from grazing sheep, the terrain is home to falcons, hawks, eagles and wild fowl. Compared with the Madonie range extension that is the background to Cefalù and Palermo, the Nebrodi are less accessible: transport within the range is necessarily slow since the lack of east–west roads frequently means retracing one's steps to the coast.

But if you have a car and fancy an adventure trail, a circuit around the **Parco Regionale dei Nebrodi** is yet another way to see this extraordinary countryside. You could start anywhere between Patti and Sant'Agata di Militello where road signs point to the Parco and to San Fratello.

San Fratello ⑲, 18 km (11 miles) from the coast, at an altitude of 675 metres (2,215 ft) and with a population nearing 5,000, is one of the most characteristic villages and particularly colourful during its famous demonic Easter festival, the Feast of the Jews, **Festa dei Giudei**,

Map: pages 240–1

TIP

Milazzo is the Sicilian link to the Aeolian Islands. For ferries and hydrofoils contact: Siremar, tel: 892 123, www.siremar.it
The larger ferries are run by Navigazione General Italiana, tel: 800 250 000, www.ngi-spa.it.

LEFT: on guard at Mistretta.
BELOW: the Feast of the Jews at San Fratello.

The Festa dei Giudei is a unique annual Easter event at San Fratello. Men and women dress up as Giudei (Jews) in bright red jackets and hose, covered with Arab ornament. They carry trumpets and wear grotesque masks. This is by no means anti-Semitic. It is assumed the tradition started in order to poke fun at the Jewish role in the Catholic ritual of the Easter Passion but now it is just an occasion for making merry.

BELOW:
Lago Biviere di Cesarò.

a shrieking costumed chase through the village. It is not so much anti-Semitic as Sicilian, hence a sacrifice of subtlety to spectacle. This scenic mountain village has a Norman church and a 15th-century Franciscan monastery. Horses and horse breeding have always played a big part in community life here and each September there are display events when the horses, mostly Arabs, are put through their paces.

Further along, the SS 289 road then snakes through rugged terrain to **Cesarò ㉑**, where on 15 August they too celebrate the horse with the magnificent local horses in the **Palio dei Nebrodi**.

But, before Cesarò, as you climb the range, **Portella Fèmmina Morta ㉑** offers a detour on foot or with an off-road vehicle to **Monte Soro**, the highest point in the Nebrodi at 1,847 metres (6,060 ft), with fabulous views, thick woods and wildlife that includes falcons, herons, wild cats and wolves. The **Lago Biviere di Cesarò** also here is an ancient lake that turns bright pink with algae in the hotter months and is visited by

migratory storks. Further on the SS289 is Cesarò itself with its population of only 3,000, most of whom farm the land or are shepherds. The village shows signs of having been part of a battle between feuding dynasties in 1334 with the ruins of a castle. In the **Chiesa Madre** (1623) is a **Crocifisso** painted on board.

At this point you could take a detour 20 km (12 miles) along the SS120 to **Troina ㉒**, at 1,120 metres (3,675 ft) the highest town in Sicily. The views are superb: panoramas of hills, valleys and trees. Prehistoric man lived here. Still visible are the remains of ancient Greek walls, while the **Chiesa Madre** has a fine 16th-century campanile and has some 15th-century paintings on board, including a *Madonna and Child* and a painting highlighted with gold of *San Michele* (1512).

To complete the circuit of the parco, from Cesarò the SS120 leads to **Abbazia di Maniace**, Admiral Nelson's 18th-century home *(see page 220)* and on to **Randazzo** (really in the province of Catania), where the Sunday morning market has stalls selling artefacts made from wood grown in the region, then to **Floresta**, and after some breath-taking bends, back down to **Patti** and the coast. The complete circuit is about 230 km (143 miles).

Messina's Ionian coast

This narrow coastal strip is characterised by a contrast between the barren slopes of the **Monti Peloritani** (highest point 1,374 metres/4,500 ft) facing the shore and the wooded slopes facing inland. As you travel south, there are architectural contrasts between the baroque or modern coastal towns and the medieval settlements in the hilly hinterland.

From Messina, the motorway hugs the shore south for 52 km (32 miles) from the narrow Straits of Messina to **Taormina ㉓** *(see page*

229), hemmed in by mountains. The exotic coastal vegetation, ravaged by development, is wilder further south. From the old coastal road south, tracks explore the hinterland.

If you are travelling on the A18 motorway, at **Santa Teresa di Riva** leave the coastal crowds for mountain air and curious hamlets. Despite the proximity of Taormina, this is timeless Sicily, as remote as anywhere on the island. The scenery is stark: skeletal peaks and brooding ravines; mountains gouged by winter torrents and scorched brown in summer. Such fierceness is softened by sweet-scented scrub and the curves of Moorish monasteries.

Sávoca

Just inland is the battered mountain village of **Sávoca** ㉔, best known for its macabre mummies, embalmed in a crypt by local monks. The monastery was in use until 1970.

The catacombs of the **Cappuccini** monastery (Apr–Sept Tues–Sat 9am–1pm, 4–7pm; Sun 11am–1pm, 4–7pm; Oct–Mar Tues–Sat 9am–noon, 4–7pm, Sun 11am–noon,

4–7pm; donation) contain 32 ghoulish mummified corpses dating from the 17th century. At a time when corpses were thrown into the communal ditch, genteel mummification was a tradition among noble families. The bodies were drained, sprinkled with salt and left to dry for a year before being washed in vinegar, aired and then dressed in their original clothes. These gruesome, wizened faces and shrunken puppet-like forms are mummified abbots, lawyers, noblemen and priests.

After this macabre scene, leave the monastery for the evocative medieval village, a former Saracen stronghold. Sávoca's name derives from sambuca, not the famed Italian liqueur, but the elder trees that still perfume the hills. A paved path climbs cacti-dotted terraces and olive groves to the village. The roads were repaved with the proceeds of *The Godfather*, filmed on location here. Francis Ford Coppola found his perfect setting in the dusty piazza, the windswept church, the shots of Etna smouldering in the distance, and the shimmer of the Ionian Sea.

Map: pages 240–1

Robert de Niro, who starred in The Godfather II, *said of Sicilians: "Ultimately, everyone else is a foreigner. Suspicion runs high. And although they are very cordial to you as a tourist, you are still aware of this. Sicilians have a way of watching without watching; they'll scrutinize you thoroughly and you won't even know it."*

BELOW: mummified remains in the catacombs of the Cappuchin Convent, Sávoca.

Map:
pages
240–1

←	≡	bar Turrisi
←	≡	bar Duomo
←	↖	hotel Panorama di Sicilia
←	✕	bar trattoria 777
←	✕	Le Mimose PIZZERIA
←	✕	da Pippo
←	✕	La Campagnola
←	✕	PIZZERIA Valle dell' Etna
←	≡	bar S. Giorgio

A surfeit of signs in Giardini-Naxos.

BELOW:
Giardini-Naxos, with
Mount Etna looming
in the background.

Equally atmospheric are the churches overgrown with prickly pear, the tumbledown dovecote, abandoned houses and the terraces slipping into the sea. The church of San Niccolò lost its choir in a landslide but kept its dignity, while the Chiesa Madre retains the charm that caught Coppola's eye. This solitary church, on a narrow ridge overlooking the sea, was renovated with film money. The scruffy Bar Vitelli, immortalised in Michael Corleone's wedding banquet, comfortably hosts peasants and *borghesi*, united in their thirst for a cool *granita di limone* (lemon sorbet).

Casalvécchio Sículo, charmingly set above Sávoca, is a livelier but less complex village. Its Chiesa Madre has a gilded interior. Nearby are windswept views over terraces. On the outskirts of the village, take the first turning left, a steep road signposted to the monastery of **SS Pietro e Paolo d'Agro** ㉕, a monastic church down in the Val d'Agro. Despite its desolate location on the bank of the dry Agro river, SS Pietro e Paolo is the most significant Nor-

man church in eastern Sicily. The twin-domed exterior is reminiscent of a Turkish mosque. A banded facade combines red brick, black lava, cool limestone and grey granite. Restored in 1171, the church is a synthesis of Byzantine and Norman styles. Moorish roundness and decorative flourishes compete with Norman verticality and austerity.

Giardini-Naxos

Before ascending to Taormina, consider visiting neighbouring **Giardini-Naxos** ㉖, Sicily's first Greek colony. It was founded (as Naxos) on an ancient lava flow by Euboeans in 735 BC and became a springboard for colonisation of Catania and the east coast. But after supporting Athens against Siracusa, the colony was destroyed by Dionysius in 403 BC.

The archaeological site (daily 9am–one hour before sunset; entrance fee) occupies the promontory of Capo Schiso (follow signs for *scavi*, excavations). A stretch of Greek lava-stone city walls remains but the elusive **Temple of Aphrodite** is still being excavated, as are some noble houses. The small museum contains Greek, Roman and Byzantine exhibits, including a head of Silenus, god of fertility and wine.

Lemon groves are giving way to ribbon development, for Giardini-Naxos is Sicily's fastest-growing beach resort. Still, for the young crowd there are compensations: cheap and cheerful trattorie, wide beaches fringed by volcanic rocks and a riotous nightlife that Silenus might have enjoyed. Moreover, unlike Catania province, this stretch of coast offers sandy, rocky or pebbled shores, with a wide variety of free and private beaches.

Letojanni, ㉗ a humble fishing village until the 1960s, is now a bustling resort with facilities for horse riding, water sports and sub-aqua photography. ❏

RESTAURANTS

Messina

Da Bacco
Via Cernaia 15.
Tel: 090 771 420.
Hostaria with a good range of seafood. Closed Sun. €€

Davai
Via XXVII Luglio 36.
Tel: 090 293 4865.
Welcoming restaurant based on the old Teatro Savoia serving *cucina messinese*, the best of local dishes. Closed Mon. €€€

Le Due Sorelle
Piazza Municipio 4.
Tel: 090 44720.
A long established but modernised trattoria. Good wines and simple cooking. Book. Closed Sat lunch and Sun. €€

Osteria del Campanile
Via Loggia dei Mercanti 7.
Tel: 090 711 418.
Behind the Duomo, this simple restaurant has a good range of pasta dishes, as well as crispy pizzas. Closed Sun except summer. €€

Al Padrino
Via Santa Cecilia 54.
Tel: 090 292 1000.
This inexpensive trattoria is a good place to sample regional specialities; try the house dish, *melanzane al Padrino* (aubergine stuffed with pasta and ricotta). Closed Sat dinner and Sun. €€

Gambero Rosso
Via Consolare Pompea.
Tel: 090 393 873.
Good, inexpensive. Fish, mostly. Closed Tues. €€

Shawarma
Via M.Giurba 8.
Tel: 090 712 213.
A welcome break from Italian cuisine, this restaurant serves up North African specialities such as tagines and couscous. Closed Mon. €

Trattoria del Popolo
Piazza Lo Sardo.
Tel: 090 671 148.
An appealing restaurant with outside tables and seafood specialities such as squid in breadcrumbs. Closed Sun. €€

Milazzo

La Casalinga
Via D'Amico 13.
Tel: 090 922 2697.
A fish specialist; the house dish is spaghetti with crab sauce. Closed Sun dinner Oct–June. €€

Al Castello
Via Federico di Svevia 20.
Tel: 090 928 2175.
A charming place to be in the summer season when tables are outside, lit by the floodlights on the walls of the Castello. Sicilian cooking. (Annual closure varies each year.) Closed Tues. €€€

Covo del Pirata
Via San Francesco 2.
Tel: 090 928 4437.
Cucina Messinese (dishes famed in Messina) served in rooms decorated with a marine theme. Closed Wed. €€€

Al Pescatore
Via Marina Garibaldi 176.
Tel: 090 928 6595.
Popular trattoria known for its seafood served at reasonable prices. Decorated to match its passion for fish. Closed Thur. €€

Piccolo Casale
Via Riccardo d'Amico 12.
Tel: 090 922 4479.
www.piccolocasale.it
Discreet trattoria, elegant and with flowery terrace. A favourite with locals. Dinner only. Closed Jan and Aug. €€€

Letojanni

Da Nino
Via Rizzo 29.
Tel: 0942 36147.
www.danino.it
Warm and welcoming hotel/restaurant in a charming location. Lots of fresh fish dishes on the menu. €€€

Peppe
Via Vittorio Emanuele 346.
Tel: 0942 36159.
Old-style trattoria, part of 45-room hotel. Simple fare. Sicilian dishes. Closed Nov–Feb. €€

PRICE CATEGORIES

Three-course dinner and half-bottle of house wine:
€ = under €15
€€ = €15–€30
€€€ = €30–60
€€€€ = over €60

RIGHT: Sicilians have a sweet tooth.

THE AEOLIAN ISLANDS

Although two of the Isole Eolie still have active
volcanoes, the archipelago is characterised by
a sleepy charm that is barely affected
by the recent growth in tourism

A rching out from the north coast
of Sicily lies an underwater
volcanic ridge 200 km (125
miles) long, from which rise the
rocky islands of the Aeolian chain.
Seven of them are inhabited today,
as they have been since before the
Bronze Age; there are fragments of
Iron Age villages and Roman buildings to be seen, and Greek graves
within the Spanish walls of the
island of Lípari's citadel.

The mineral-rich volcanic rocks
of the Aeolians provided the basis of
their early wealth: obsidian, a black,
glass-like rock used to make cutting
tools, was mined in Lípari and traded
all over the Mediterranean more than
5,000 years ago, and pumice works
are still active on the island.

The decline in the traditional
sources of income shrank the
islands' population from over 20,000
in 1911 to around 12,600 today.
Many relocated to Australia in the
1950s and you will hear returned
émigrés with a Queensland tang in
their voices. There is even a *Miss
Eolie* competition in Sydney. Now,
with the fast development of tourism
a major new source of income has
been created. But the strict controls
on building, the declaration of nature
reserves and the relative remoteness
of the islands ensure that even in
high summer you can find an empty

beach or a quiet house. Only Lípari
has not been declared a nature
reserve. Strómboli and Vulcano are
still active volcanoes, though the last
eruptions – as opposed to continuous
emissions of steam or smoke – were
in the 1880s.

Map
on page
256

Lípari

The largest of the islands and home
to just over 11,000 of the total Aeolian population, Lípari is the lively
hub of the archipelago, and its mineral wealth and thermal waters lead

LEFT: the hydrofoil
arrives at Marina Corta.
BELOW:
pumice and obsidian
for sale to tourists.

the fortunes of the whole region. As the boat approaches, the crowded roofs of **Lípari Town ❶** come into view, dominated by a citadel, the Castello, set on a small hill, its massive Spanish walls enclosing the cathedral and the 17th-century bishop's palace.

Hydrofoils dock at **Marina Corta** on the southern side of the citadel, ferries on the north side at **Marina Lunga**. The two are linked by the main shopping street, Corso Vittorio Emanuele. The main sights are all within a short stroll of the harbour within the **Castello** walls. These include the cathedral, museums and archaeological park. From the Castello you can look down on the whole town, a cool vantage point among the pines. This also provides the best views of the other two main classical sites, the **Parco Archeologico Diana** and the **necropolis**, both to the west of Corso Vittorio, sadly neglected and overgrown. The

maze of backstreets off Via Garibaldi which rings the landward side of the Castello are picturesque, with some elegant stonework and lush potted plants decorating the tall facades.

Dedicated to San Bartolomeo, the **cattedrale** was established in Norman times but destroyed in 1544 by Barbarossa the pirate and then rebuilt again around 1654. Its baroque facade was added in 1761. Only the glorious **cloisters** of the San Bartolomeo monastery of the Norman period remain but, for anyone with a taste for the macabre, there is also a silver statue of San Bartlomeo to examine. The islands' patron saint was martyred by being flayed alive: for the statue he is carrying his skin over his arm.

The excavations opposite the cathedral provide a striking illustration of the layers of building on the site over 2,000 years up to Roman times, each culture stamping its authority by further development of

Lípari's old town, rich in archaeology.

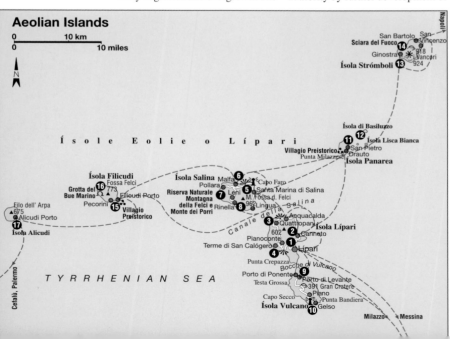

Aeolian Islands

0   10 km
0   10 miles

N

Napoli

San Bartolo   San
Sciara del Fuoco   ●Vincenzo
Ginostra●   ❶❹ ●918
   ✳Vancori
Ísola Strómboli   ❶❸ ●924

Ísola di Basiluzzo

Í s o l e   E o l i e   o   L í p a r i
        ❶❶ ❶❷ ●Ísola Lisca Bianca
Villagio Preistorico●   ●San Pietro
   Punta Milazzese●   ●Drauto
        Ísola Panarea

Ísola Filicudi
  Fossa Felci
Grotta del ❶❻773   **Ísola Salina** Malfa● ❻
Bue Marino▲   Pollara●   ✳Capo Faro
   Filicudi Porto   Riserva Naturale ❺●Santa Marina di Salina
Pecorini●   Leni ❼ M. Fossa d. Felci
   ❶❺●Villagio   Montagna   ●962
Filo dell' Arpa   **Preistorico**   della Felci e   Lingua▲Salina
▲675   Rinella● ❽ Monte dei Porri
●Alicudi Porto   Monte dei Porri   Canale della Salina
❶❼   ❸●   Anquacalda
Ísola Alicudi   ●Quattropani
              ●602   ❷●Canneto **Ísola Lípari**
          Pianoconte●   ❶ ●Lipari
      Terme di San Calógero●   ❹
         Punta Crepazza●
      Porto di Ponente●   Bocche di Vulcano
T Y R R H E N I A N   S E A   Testa Grossa●   ❾ ●Porto di Levante
            ▲391 Gran Cratere
         Capo Secco●   ●Piano
        Ísola Vulcano   ❶❿ ●Punta Bandiera
            ●Gelso

Cefalù, Palermo

Milazzo ▲Messina

Map on page 256

the stronghold. This archaeological evidence is unique in Europe and has enabled the dating of other sites. The superb **Museo Archeologico Regionale Eoliano** (daily 9am–1pm, 3–6pm; entrance fee), housed partly in the 18th-century bishop's palace, contains a wealth of material from across the archipelago, including impressive items from the islands' Neolithic period, the Copper and Bronze ages as well as the oldest and most complete set of Greek theatrical masks in existence (*see box in margin*).

Canneto

A good road rings Lípari, linking the eight main villages, and a taxi tour often provides enthusiastic commentary and plenty of stops for photographs. **Canneto ❷**, 4 km (2½ miles) north of Lípari town, has a long pebble and black sand beach and a range of small bars and trattorie. About 1 km (1,100 yards) further you can take a winding path down to **Spiaggia della Papesca**, a sandy beach whitened by pumice dust. It is this dust that turns the sea an extra-

ordinary turquoise all along to **Porticello**, about 2 km (1 mile) to the north. Pumice is still quarried here, and sold for a wide range of products including building blocks, cosmetics and fertiliser. You can buy chunks and carvings from roadside stalls or pick up small pumice stones all along the beaches.

Continuing the circuit of the island for 2 km (1 mile) or so, you come to the northernmost village, **Acquacalda**, on the slopes of **Monte Chirica**, at 602 metres (1,806 ft) Lípari's tallest mountain. A few bars and a small trattoria along the stony beach look out to Salina across a narrow strait. From Acquacalda the road winds up past the **Puntazze** rocks, with wide views right across from Stròmboli to Alicudi, and on through fields and green countryside for 5 km (3 miles) to **Quattropani ❸**. Here there is a pretty church and views across the fertile westerly side of the island. Another 6 km (4 miles) on, past several small hamlets, is **Pianoconte**, home to Lípari's largest vineyards and three restaurants. Just outside the

In Lípari's museum is a remarkable collection of more than 100 theatrical masks made in terracotta found on the island, dating from the early 4th century to the latter part of the 3rd century BC.
They depict old men, slaves, handsome youths and young girls. Every character seen in the Greek plays is here. It is an extraordinarily rich collection.

BELOW: the Cattedrale on Lípari.

Transport on the islands

L ípari and Salina have a network of roads but, as space is limited and the islands small, visitors should leave their cars on the mainland. Both these islands have reasonable bus services (for timetables, visit the port tourist offices). Or you can hire a scooter to get around. The other islands have a very basic road network.

There are regular ferries and hydrofoils to the Aeolians from Milazzo, near Messina: the ferry is cheaper and provides better views of each island you pass. Their volcanic origins are immediately apparent. Each has at least one crater and the black rivers of rock bear witness to past lava flows.

● Transport contacts: page 266.

BELOW:
an outdoor café
in Lípari town.

village, down a narrow road towards the coast, are the thermal baths of **San Calógero** ❹. The modern spa hotel is closed, but you can explore the ancient site and splash yourself with the hot therapeutic waters that come out of the ground in a domed chamber dating from the Mycenean period. Back on the main road, the circular route winds back down another 4 km (2½ miles) to Lípari Town, passing **Quattrocchi** where the **belvedere** provides a resting place and views across to Vulcano.

Salina

In lush green contrast to Vulcano's searing colours, the second largest Aeolian Island, Salina, has two extinct volcanic peaks (Monte Fossa delle Felci, 962 metres/3,156 ft and Monte dei Porri, 860 metres/2,822 ft) that are thickly wooded with conifer, sweet chestnut and oak, and the island's small towns and quiet beaches offer a peaceful relaxing stay. Salina is the richest island in agricultural terms, with 2,300 inhabitants living in three separate communities: Santa Marina Salina,

Malfa and Leni, linked by 20 km (12 miles) of road.

Boats arrive at **Santa Marina di Salina** ❺, halfway along the island's east coast. Here there is a small main street and a couple of bars and trattorie where you can watch the comings and goings on the quay. About 2 km (1 mile) along the rocky palm-lined coast lies **Lingua**, its tiny lighthouse marking the southern tip of the island, and behind it a lagoon previously used for salt extraction, which gave the island its name.

The main town of **Malfa** ❻ is 7 km (4½ miles) from Santa Marina, its small harbour backed by a steep jumble of picturesque old boatsheds and crumbling fishermen's houses. In the town, and indeed all over the island, you will see signs advertising Malvasia, a sweet golden dessert wine made from sun-dried grapes and still produced and exported by small growers on the island. Excellent local organic red wine can also be found. Another great export is packaged capers; like the excellent grapes, capers grow here in abundance. Bus services run from Malfa all over the island. Beware of missing the last bus back; finding a taxi can be difficult.

From Malfa, the road winds steeply for about 6 km (4 miles) to the small village of **Pollara** ❼, perched on one side of a half-submerged crater. There are two beautiful beaches, reached by a small path 20 minutes' walk from the bus stop by the church. To the right is a tiny beach ringed with boathouses hacked into the cliff. To the left the path leads down to a black sandy beach backed by huge white cliffs. In the summer canoes and pedaloes can be hired for exploring the dozens of coves and inlets.

Between the two peaks, from which the ancient name for the island, Didyme (twin) was derived, the road runs directly south through the **Val di Chiesa** past the **Santuario**

della Madonna del Terzito (1630). This convent and church have been the object of pilgrimages for many years and the first pages of the visitors' book make interesting reading. A party of young children, accompanied by their priest, noted their pious thoughts on the visit: no mean feat when travel was by rowing boat.

Behind the church is the path up to **Monte Fossa delle Felci**, the easterly peak that is the highest point on the islands at 962 metres (3,156 ft). The ascent is shaded by mixed woodland, and well signposted, culminating in a rocky scramble and fabulous views. Depending on the route you take, the walk is between four and six hours. The steep path down to Santa Marina is very slippery and has to be taken slowly.

From Val di Chiesa, the road descends steeply through the small village of **Leni** and twists 3 km (2 miles) down to **Rinella ⑧**, a pretty fishing port where most of the ferries and hydrofoils make a second stop. There is a small beach below low cliffs in which you can see a row of caves now used for storage, but once used for isolating smallpox victims.

The island is now designated the **Riserva Naturale Montagna delle Felci e Monte dei Porri,** which means its wild habitat, flora and fauna are protected. A large colony of falcons from Madagascar nest here in the spring.

Vulcano

As you approach the third largest island, only 1 km (1,100 yards) from Lípari across the Bocche di Vulcano channel, the steaming crater (**Gran Cratere**) of the great volcano on the island of Vulcano rises behind its smaller cousin, **Monte Vulcanello** (123 metres/404 ft), perched on the north of the island, which erupted from the sea in 183 BC. In fact the island is made up of four volcanoes, the grumbling Gran Cratere and the

old pensioners, Vulcanello, Saraceno and Aria. As the ferry arrives in **Porto di Levante ⑨** you can smell the sulphur fumes, and the lime green, yellow and red rocks add to the extraordinary experience. Porto di Levante's **beach** is popular despite the smell, and immediately to the south of it, behind a huge multi-coloured rock, are the famous mud baths *(fanghi)*. The therapeutic qualities of the mud for the treatment of arthritis, rheumatism and skin disorders have been praised for centuries. After your mud bath you can wash off in the thermally heated sea, taking care to test the water, as some areas are scaldingly hot. *Fumarole* (fissures of escaping volcanic gases) cause the sea to bubble.

Ten minutes' walk across the island's isthmus is the beautiful curve of black sand at **Porto di Ponente**, on the western coast, where pleasure boats await visitors; in the evening there are westerly views to the sunset and the jagged forms of the rocks Pietralunga and Pietra Menalda off the coast. To the north the road leads to Monte Vulcanello and, about 2 km

Map on page 256

TIP

A trip around Vulcano by boat views the island at its dramatic best and the passage through the narrow Bocche di Vulcano channel that separates Vulcano from Lípari is exhilarating. Fishermen will offer a trip in summer.

BELOW: taking a mud bath on Vulcano.

(1 mile) away on the northeastern extreme of the island, to the **Valle dei Mostri** (Valley of the Monsters), a bizarre collection of sculptures created by lava eruptions in 1888 and erosion since; they are particularly evocative in early morning or evening when shadows create the impression of wild beasts.

Although it is claimed that the influx of visitors is now degrading the tender habitat to the extent that it will never recover, any visit to Vulcano would be incomplete without a study of the volcano itself. Environmentalists suggest a boat tour of the island is sufficient but, if you wish, you can still climb to the active crater, **Gran Cratere** (or **Fossa di Vulcano**). Although only 391 metres high (1,125 ft), the ascent takes about an hour and, though it's hot and exposed, can be undertaken by anyone who is reasonably fit. Take water and wear stout shoes. The smell of sulphur intensifies as the path zigzags up the slope, over black sand and crusty volcanic rock, and past deep furrows cut by previous eruptions. At the top you are rewarded by the extraordinary unworldly sight of the massive bowl of the crater, hissing and steaming and crusted with crystals of yellow and red. A walk round the crater takes about half an hour and there are excellent views of the other islands and the flat southern plain.

The crater and the views of the archipelago can also be seen from **Capo Grillo**, about 10 km (6 miles) from Porto di Levante. The hamlet of **Gelso** on the south coast is named after the mulberries that are grown in the area *(see margin tip)*.

TIP

Gelso is about 15 km (9 miles) from Porto di Levante but bus services on the island's one road are extremely limited. The easiest way to get there is to negotiate a boat trip with a local fisherman, ensuring enough time for lunch at one of Gelso's excellent trattorie.

Panarea

Northeast of Lípari is the smallest, prettiest and most fashionable island of the Aeolians, Panarea. It's also known locally as the island of flowers, with its holiday villas awash with bougainvillea and hibiscus. It was declared a nature reserve in 1997.

Decidedly chic compared with its rugged neighbours, Panarea's tiny harbour fills up in the summer with a well-heeled crowd and a flotilla of elegant yachts. This is where many of Italy's wealthiest families have their holiday homes. The three villages of **Ditella**, **San Pietro** and **Drauto**, form a continuous huddle of pretty, neat houses and tiny lanes along the eastern coast. The ferries dock at **San Pietro** .

From Drauto it is an easy 1-km (1,100-yard) walk past steps to the sandy beach to **Punta Milazzese**, a beautiful rocky headland where the remains of a *villagio preistorico* (Bronze Age village) can be seen. The artefacts found there in 1948 are on display in the museum in Lípari. A path from Drauto also leads up to the highest point on Panarea, **Timpone del Corvo** (382 metres/ 1,254ft), with a wonderful view of Strómboli and its smoking volcano.

Just past the headland is the tiny bay of **Cala Junco**, with excellent swimming. By boat it is also possible

BELOW: Panarea

to see the caves and other tiny coves along the cliffs.

A steep signposted path leads from Cala Junco up into the high western side of the island, and back down to San Pietro, a fairly stiff but enjoyable three-hour walk. To the north of Ditella is **Calcara** beach, where a *fumarole* emits jets of gas and steam from fissures in the rock, coating the surface with yellow, white and green minerals and causing patches of sea to be decidedly warm.

From San Pietro you can get a boat trip out to **Basiluzzo** , now uninhabited though a Roman jetty lies submerged and scraps of mosaic can be seen on its rocky heights, and to the tiny islets of **Datillo, Bottaro** and **Lisca Bianca**, where the swimming is superb.

Strómboli

Even those who have never heard of the Aeolian Islands have heard of Strómboli. The climb to its crater, blasting rod hot rock into the sky, is an unforgettable reminder of the power below the earth's crust. **Strómboli** town, officially made up of three villages, Strómboli, San Vincenzo and San Bartolo, but usually grouped together simply as Strómboli, is a lively little place, busy with hikers of all shapes and sizes, and offering a good range of restaurants and bars where you can sit to plan your ascent of 924 metres (3,000 ft). For days of relaxing, there are long flat beaches, black sand to the north of the jetty, stone and shingley sand to the south.

Tiny **Ginostra** on the southwest side of the island is accessible only by sea, and the ferry has to weigh anchor and wait while passengers and assorted packages are brought out in small boats. Boat trips are also possible to **Strombolicchio**, a tiny island of dramatic coloured craggy rock topped with a lighthouse, and round to the base of

Sciara del Fuoco , the fiery slope where lava from the craters flows down to the sea. This is particularly exciting at night when the explosions above and the glowing lava can be seen brightly against the dark sky.

The craters erupt every 20 minutes or so with varying intensity, when huge roars and booms echo all around with each cloud of rock, dust and gas thrown up. There are fabulous views of the distant islands of Filicudi and Alicudi, and from the high ridge of **i Vancori** opposite, you can look down on the craters and across the whole archipelago.

Filicudi

Four hours by ferry westwards from Lípari, or an hour on the speeding hydrofoil, Filicudi's smooth humped shape, reminiscent of a whale, lies quietly in the clear water. **Filicudi porto** , with its modern buildings and hotel development, is the port where ferries and hydrofoils land their cargos and passengers. From here the island's rugged beauty can be explored along the narrow paths and tracks that cross the island. From

Map on page 256

TIP

The ascent to Strómboli's summit and its four active craters is officially forbidden without a guide, but you can book to join a group at a number of agencies in the village. You should not attempt the climb if it is raining or there is heavy cloud on the summit. You will need to allow seven hours, and time your start to allow you to get down before dark.

BELOW: Strómboli's cloud-capped volcano.

Traditional means of transport on Alicudi.

BELOW: the Grotta del Bue Marino on Filicudi.

Val di Chiesa you can also climb the tallest of the island's three peaks, **Fossa delle Felci**, 773 metres (2,319 ft), although it is advisable to ask for a guide as it is an unsignposted climb. A boat trip gives views of the sheer northern side, the **Grotta del Bue Marino** , a cave where Mediterranean monk seals used to live, and **La Canna**, a natural obelisk towering 70 metres (230 ft) out of the sea.

The much-reduced population, around 300, has left many houses empty and their ruins are being taken over by giant *fichi d'India* (prickly pear cactus). On **Capo Graziano**, the tail of the island, less than 1 km (1,100 yards) along from the port, are the remains of the oldest settlement on the Aeolians, a Bronze Age village dating from the 18th century BC. Also on this southern coast is the seaside village of **Pecorini**, linked to the port by the only road on the island. It is a good place to hire a boat for a tour of the island.

Filicudi is popular with divers due to the excellent quality of the water and the variety of marine life, and there are a few restaurants, a bar and a couple of hotels (open only in summer). Locals used to survive financially by diving for coral but since coral is now protected, sponges are collected instead.

Alicudi

At the western end of the chain is the least visited island of the Isole Eolie, **Alicudi**, a near-perfect green cone, scattered with pink-and-white homes and terraced fields right up to its peak at **Filo dell'Arpa** (675 metres/2,025 ft); here are the remains of the old settlements, secure from maurauding pirates, nestling among the gorse and carpet of heather. All the 200 or so residents live on the eastern side of the island, in a scattered settlement around the port, **Alicudi Porto** . (This population shrinks to around 30 out of season.) The western side of the island, too steep for houses, is a nature reserve, the **Riserva Naturale**.

For the energetic visitor it is possible to circumnavigate the whole island on foot, but the 7 km (4 miles) entails a scramble in some places and two short swims around impassably steep sections. Allow six or seven hours and take water and a picnic. A boat trip round to see the twisted colourful strata and black lava flows offers a less strenuous option. There are two small shops and a hotel (summer only). Otherwise, although Alicudi has had mains electricity since 1991, this is Sicilian life as it was for centuries.

The tiny 17th-century church of **San Bartolo** perches high above the sea, looking down the steep slopes of **Scorbio** to the small plain of **Bassina** round the coast to the east. The island has no driveable roads, and donkeys carry their burdens up the ancient stepped paths. The quiet lapping of the water on the rocky beaches and the sound of birdsong amongst the old olive trees are the only sounds to be heard. ❏

Map on page 256

RESTAURANTS

Lípari

Filippino
Piazza Municipio.
Tel: 0909 811 002.
www.filippino.it
A local favourite, pricey
but good. Delicacies
include fish risotto and
complicated main
courses. Garden. Book.
Closed Mon in winter and
10 Nov–26 Dec. €€€€

Kasbah
Via Maurolico 25.
Tel: 090 981 1075.
Popular restaurant with a
pleasant garden setting.
Known for its creative
fish dishes. Closed Mon
and Oct–Mar. €€€

La Nassa
Via Franza 36.
Tel: 0909 811 319.
www.lanassavacanze.it
Typical Aeolian cooking
in welcoming surround-
ings. Open Mar–Nov. €€

E Pulera
Via Diana.
Tel: 090 981 1158.
www.bernardigroup.it
Attractive setting with
traditional local cuisine.
Dinner only. Booking rec-
ommended. Open
Apr–Oct. €€€€

Subba
Corso Vittorio Emanuele 92.
Tel: 090 981 2522.
The island's most historic
café, with shady terrace,
is also a restaurant, serving up pizzas with a huge
range of toppings. €€

Salina

Il Delfino
Piazza Marina Garibaldi 5,
Lingua. Tel: 0909 843 024.
Trattoria with good sea-
food at low prices. €€

Da Franco
Via Belvedere 8, Santa
Marina di Salina.
Tel: 0909 843 287.
Great views of sea and
Lípari from a veranda.
Simple local cooking with
the emphasis on local
produce. Closed Dec. €€

Nni Lausta
Via Risorgimento 188,
Santa Marina Salina.
Tel: 0909 843 486.
www.isolasalina.com
Eccentric establishment.
The owner says: "This is
what I am cooking" – so
stay or go. It's worth stay-
ing. Open Apr–Oct. €€€

Porto Bello
Via Bianchi 1, Santa Marina
Salina. Tel: 0909 984 3125.
Three simple terraces
with good home-cooking
based on traditional
Aeolian dishes. Closed
Wed in low season and
Dec–Feb. €€

Vulcano

Maniaci
Gelso. Tel: 0909 852 242.
You are offered only
what the chef feels like
cooking that day. But it is
good. Open Easter–end
Oct. €€

Maria Tindara
Via Provinciale 38.
Tel: 0909 853 004.
Homemade pasta with
special sauces. Excel-
lent meats and fresh
fish. Popular, inexpen-
sive. Open Mar–Oct. €€

Da Vincenzino
Via Porto Levante 25.
Tel: 0909 852 016.
Simple and inexpensive.
Open Mar–Oct. €

Panarea

Restaurants on this
wealthy island are pricey.

Cincotta
Via San Pietro.
Tel: 0909 83014.
www.hotelcincotta.it
Smart hotel with smart,
restaurant where people
dress down expensively
and eat costly fish. Open
Apr–Oct. €€€€

Paolino
Via Ditella. Tel: 0909 83008.
Fresh fish at its best as
the place is owned by a
fisherman. Open Apr–
Dec. €€

La Sirena
Via Drauto 4.
Tel: 0909 83012.
www.hotelsirena-panarea .it
Simple but pleasing food
with daily specials worth
consideration. Open
Easter–Oct. €€

Strómboli

Barbablù
Via Vittorio Emanuele 17.
Tel: 0909 86118.
www.barbablu.it
Restaurant in hotel gar-
den. The food is cooked
by the owner who imagi-
natively combines Sicilian
and Neapolitan recipes.
Closed Nov–Feb. €€€

Punta Lena
Via Marina, Ficogrande.
Tel: 0909 86204.
With a view over the tiny
island of Strombolicchio,
a charming fish restau-
rant. Open Apr–Oct. €€€

Da Zurro
Via Picone 18, Scari.
Tel: 0909 86283.
Considered modestly
better than rival places.
Fish, of course. Open
Easter–Oct. €€€

Filicudi

La Canna
Via Rosa 43.
Tel: 0909 889 956.
www.lacannahotel.it
The pleasing restaurant
is in a small hotel (14
rooms) with panoramic
views and good food.
Closed Nov. €€

La Sirena
Pecorini Mare.
Tel: 0909 889 997.
www.pensionelasirena.it
Charming trattoria with
guestrooms. Dinner on a
terrace with a fine view.
Closed 15 Dec–15 Jan
and 2 weeks in Nov. €€

Alicudi

Ericusa
Via Regina Elena.
Tel: 0909 889 902.
www.alicudihotel.it
This is the only place to
stay on the island and it
has a reasonable tratto-
ria. Closed Oct–May. €€

PRICE CATEGORIES

Three-course dinner and
half-bottle of house wine:
    € = under €15
    €€ = €15–30
    €€€ = €30–60
    €€€€ = over €60

T RANSPORT

GETTING THERE AND GETTING AROUND

GETTING THERE

By Air

Sicily has two international airports: **Palermo** (Punta Raisi) and **Catania** (Fontanarossa). There is also a small domestic airport at **Trápani**. Travellers for **Messina** use the Reggio di Calabria airport on the Italian mainland, just across the Straits of Messina.

Lampedusa and **Pantelleria**, two of the small islands with their own airports, are linked by services from Palermo or Trápani.

Scheduled flights for Alitalia, the national airline, as well as all major international airlines are usually routed, with transfers, through Milan, Rome or Naples. These major airlines include British Airways, Lufthansa, Air Malta, Meridiana, KLM and Air France. A number of low cost airlines also run regular services into Sicily.

Flight schedules and fares can be obtained from airlines or travel agencies.

Palermo

All major airlines use Palermo's Falcone-Borsellino airport, 30km (19 miles) from the city at **Punta Raisi**. (The small Aeroporto Boccadifalco on the city outskirts

handles only private aircraft.)

Bus services run every 30 mins, linking the airport with **Stazione Centrale** and with the general bus terminal at **Piazza Ruggero Settimo** (Teatro Politeama Garibaldi). Timetables vary according to the season and are displayed at both the airport and the station. The first journey to the airport departs at 5am, and the last leaves at 10.45pm. From the airport, the first bus is

BETWEEN AIRPORTS

Should you need to transfer, i.e. arrive and depart from different airports (Palermo, Trápani, Catania or Messina), this can be done by pre-booked mini-bus.

For the journey between Palermo and Catania airports, a taxi will charge about €50. An airport shuttle mini-bus service will charge €30 for 2 passengers plus €5 for each additional passenger. Add €8 if it is between 10pm and 6am. Baggage is free. This service must be pre-booked.

Similar rates apply for transfers between other airports, tel: 091 685 9723 or mail@airporteasyshuttle.it

at 7.30am, and the last leaves at around midnight. The journey takes about an hour. The last bus usually waits for the final flight of the day.

The airport is also linked by trains every 30 mins to and from **Stazione Centrale**, 4.30am to 11pm. Allow an hour for the journey. €5.

A taxi will charge about €50 for the trip. A pre-booked airport shuttle mini-bus service charges €30 for 2 passengers, and €5 for each additional passenger, plus €8 if it is between 10pm and 6am. Baggage is free. It must be pre-booked.
Tel: 091 685 9723 or
mail@airporteasyshuttle.it.
Flight information: tel: 091 702 0111 for international and domestic flights – or call toll-free 800 541 880, a line which occasionally functions. See also the Palermo airport website:
www.gesap.it.

Catania

All international, domestic and charter flights arrive and depart from Catania's chaotic but developing airport, **Fontanarossa**, just 5km (3 miles) south of the city. There is an Alibus service into town, 5am to midnight, departing every 20 mins for **Stazione Centrale** (railway station). Tickets can be bought from tobacconists.

A metered taxi costs about €25. Fontanarossa Airport enquiries: www.aeroporto.catania.it.

Messina

Air travellers coming to or passing through Messina usually use the **Reggio di Calabria** airport on mainland Italy or make arrangements to arrive via Catania or Palermo. There is a hydrofoil shuttle service that links Messina and Villa San Giovanni, a short distance away from Reggio di Calabria's airport. Hotels and travel agents usually arrange a taxi or coach link.
Airport information, Reggio di Calabria, tel: 0965 640 517: www.sogas.it.

By Sea

If you wish to avoid air travel, a long car drive or, indeed, the train journey through Italy, ferries *(traghetti)* are an excellent alternative. They link Sicily with **Naples**, **Genova** (Genoa), **Salerno** and **Civitavecchia** in Italy, with **Cagliari** in Sardegna, and with **Ustica** and the **Isole Eolie** (Aeolian Islands). There is also a link with **Tunis**, Tunisia, and **Malta**. Hydrofoils *(aliscafi)* also link Sicily to its smaller islands.

All ferries can be booked through a local travel agent or an Italian hotel, but personal booking is also possible direct through the shipping lines' Italian offices. For advance reservations, use the Internet, either booking directly with the ferry company or using one of the several websites that take bookings for all the ferry companies. The advantage of these is that you can compare prices easily. There are cabins on the longer routes, and these must be booked well in advance for high summer. Italians make great use of the ferries in the holiday periods.

Ferry prices tend to be low. Where more than one company runs ferries or hydrofoils on a particular route, they normally work in competition, not collabo-

ration, i.e. your ticket will only be valid on the ships of the carrier from which you bought it. This sometimes makes single tickets a better bet than return ones.

Remember that sailing schedules are prone to change, especially in winter months when the seas can turn rough. The small islands are often cut off during bad weather.

Palermo

Palermo's port is central, on the eastern periphery road, Via Francesco Crispi. No matter which shipping line, all cruise ships, ferries and hydrofoils embark and disembark passengers on one of the busy quays of the **Stazione Marittima**. Taxis are on hand to greet arrivals.

Ferries link Palermo with **Cagliari** in Sardegna, with **Naples**, **Genova** (Genoa) and **Civitavecchia** on the Italian mainland, with **Ustica** and the **Isole Eolie** (Aeolian Islands) and with **Tunis**, Tunisia. All travel agents and hotels can arrange ticketing. Sailing schedules are prone to change.
Cagliari Weekly. Tirrenia: tel: 081 017 1998 or 892 123 (in Italy only). www.tirrenia.it
Civitavecchia Tues and Thur 8pm; Sun 6.30pm. SNAV: tel: 091 631 7900. www.snav.it
Genova Mon–Sat 10pm. Grandi Navi Veloci: tel: 899 199 069. www.gnv.it
Naples Daily 8pm. SNAV: tel: 091 631 7900. www.snav.it
Also daily 8.15pm. Tirrenia: tel: 081 017 1998 or 892 123 (in Italy only). www.tirrenia.it
Tunis (Tunisia) Twice weekly. Grimaldi: tel: 091 587 404. www.grimaldi-ferries.com
Ustica and **Isole Eolie** Daily 8am. Also daily June–Sept only by *aliscafo* (hydrofoil) 8.15am and 5.30pm. Siremar: tel: 091 582 403. www.siremar.it

Messina

All ferries and the train link to mainland Italy go through the Porto. The quay is on Via Rizzo.

By Rail

The Italian mainland is linked to Sicily by an efficient train service, the best stations to join the route being Milan, Rome and Naples. You should book a seat for any long-distance travel. There are overnight sleeper cars available.

Credit card booking can be made online (www.trenitalia.com). Train tickets are valid for three months.

Timetables change twice a year, so for up-to-date information, contact the Italian tourist office or a travel agent, who can arrange reservations – easier than the endless queues at railway stations.

For anyone under 26, the purchase of youth and student rail cards will give unlimited use of the European rail system for a month; it's best to arrange these before arriving in Italy as most local travel agents deal only with Italian travellers, not tourists, so will deny any knowledge of them. Often there are also a number of special deals available. For these enquire at Italian stations or travel agents for details of current offers.

There is a daily *rapido* service between Rome and Palermo, Catania and Siracusa.

The crossing from Villa San Giovanni to Messina is an experience in itself: the train carriages are literally (and time-consumingly) shunted into the ferry, and then shunted off again at Messina. If you arrive on an overnight train, your first view of Sicily from the ship's deck may be of early morning sunlight on the sea and the mountains.

Palermo

The main station is **Statione Centrale**. Toll-free information tel: 892 021. All principal destinations are linked to Palermo with daily services to and from Rome, Naples, Florence and Genova.

By Coach

Palermo

Autolinee (coaches) run by various companies leave Piazza Ruggero Settimo daily. There are services not only to Sicily's main towns but also to Bologna, Florence, Parma, Modena, Rome and Siena. Timetables change, summer and winter, and coaches may not run on public holidays, New Year's Day and Easter.

GETTING TO THE ISLANDS

Aeolian Islands

Ferries and hydrofoils run frequently from Milazzo (near Messina), which is reached by train from Messina and Palermo, and by bus from Messina and Catania airport.

In the summer, there are up to 11 hydrofoils a day to **Lípari** and **Vulcano**, and 6 a day to **Salina**. There are direct ferries to the islands several times a week, but all can best be reached through Lípari. The ferry takes about 2 hours to Lípari and the hydrofoil about 45 minutes.
Ferry details: Daily. Siremar: tel: 892 123 in Italy, +39 081 017 1998 from mobile phones or from abroad. Call centre open daily except public hols 9am–8pm. www.siremar.it

Egadi Islands, Pantelleria

Ferries and hydrofoils from Trápani (which can be reached by train or by bus from Palermo) run several times a day to Favignana, Lévanzo and Maréttimo. To Favignana the ferry takes 45 minutes, to Pantelleria the daily ferry is about 6 hours.
Ferry details: Siremar: tel: 892 123 in Italy, +39 081 017 1998 from mobile phones or from abroad. www.siremar.it

Ustica

In summer both ferries and hydrofoils run daily between Palermo and Ustica. In the low season, there are ferries only.
Ferry details: Daily. Siremar, *as above.*

Pelagie Islands

● BY AIR
Most air traffic from these airports is domestic, within Sicily. Flights to these islands via
Trápani Birgi (open daily dawn–dusk). Information, tel: 0923 842 502.
Lampedusa Daily flights, to and from Palermo, Milan and Rome. Information, AirOne, tel: 199 207 080; www.flyairone.it.
Pantelleria Daily flights to and from Trápani. Information, Meridiana, tel: 0923 911 398; www.meridiana.it.
● BY FERRY
Ferries run once a day (overnight) in summer from Porto Empedocle (a town bus runs about every 30 minutes from Agrigento) to Lampedusa, stopping at Linosa on the way. In winter, there are ferries six times a week. It's worth taking a cabin. The ferries carry cars, but in summer can be fully booked. There is also a summer hydrofoil service between the two islands.
Lampedusa ferries:
Siremar, *as above.*
Linosa ferries:
Siremar, *as above.*

GETTING AROUND

By Car

A car in Sicily is not essential but it is a great help exploring, even though the island is well served by coaches and the many excellent tour companies that arrange visits to distant sites. In cities like Palermo or Siracusa where the traffic is so hectic and the sights so close to each other, it is easier to use public transport or taxis.

If you intend bringing your car to Sicily, the fastest crossing from the mainland is the 20-minute shuttle ferry service to and from Messina from Villa San Giovanni, in Calabria.

Throughout Italy, you will need a current driving licence (with an Italian translation unless it is the standard EU licence) and valid insurance. You must carry your driving licence, car registration and insurance documents with you at all times when driving.

Fuel and **autostrada tolls** can be paid with cash or credit card (which you simply push into the machine; no paperwork). Many Italians and Sicilians have *TelePass* cards which enable them to drive through specially marked toll gates, the charge being deducted directly from their bank accounts.

Autostrada charges vary, with long-haul trucks, campers, caravans and towed boats paying the highest rates. In Italy, the Autostrada del Sole south of Salerno leading to the Reggio di Calabria crossing point is free.
Car hire: Major hire companies include: Avis, Europcar, Hertz and Sixt.

By Taxi

In cities, taxis may be hailed, telephoned or found at taxi ranks. Licensed taxis are white, with a Taxi sign on the roof, and have a meter which should be turned on at the start of a journey. Remind the driver if he or she "forgets".

There are many ranks in the big cities and outside airports (where unofficial taxi drivers tout for business illegally and then overcharge their passengers). Prices start at €3.81 and there are surcharges for large pieces of luggage, on Sundays and holidays, to or from an airport and on journeys after 10pm.

Hotels will often arrange for private hire car companies to provide a chauffeur-driven car. This service will be better but expect to pay more. (Agree the price with the hotel before setting out.)

Palermo: To phone for a taxi: Autoradio Taxi: tel: 091 513 311, 091 513 198. Radio Taxi: tel: 091 682 5441. **Catania:** Radio Taxi: tel: 095 333 216 or 095 330 966.

By Rail

Catania

Catania is well linked with the major cities. Trains depart and arrive at **Stazione Centrale**, Piazza Papa Giovanni XXIII.

The narrow-gauge train, Ferrovia Circumetnea, that calls at all villages around Mount Etna on a circular route *(see page 217)* leaves from **Corso delle Provincie**.

Messina

Messina is well linked to both Palermo and Catania, and all trains to Italy pass through its port in order to cross the Straits of Messina by ferry. Trains depart and arrive at **Stazione Centrale**, Piazza Repubblica; the boat trains at neighbouring **Stazione Marittima**.

By Bus

Fast buses link Sicily's main towns and are a good way of getting around the island, particularly the interior and the south. Generally speaking, buses are more reliable and quicker than trains, but they cost more. The main exception where the train is generally better is the Palermo–Messina route.

The following lists the most important and popular routes on the island and the bus company which runs them.

From Palermo

SAIS, Via Balsamo 16.
Tel: 091 616 6028/617 1141.
Buses go to Rome, Caltanissetta, Catania, Caltagirone, Enna, Piazza Armerina, Gela, Sciacca, Messina, Cafalù.
Cuffaro, Via P. Balsamo 13.
Tel: 091 616 1510.
Buses go to Agrigento, Favara,

BUS AND TRAIN TICKETS

When travelling on trains, buses and the metro, you must have your ticket validated by machine on departure. There are yellow franking machines at the entrance to each platform and on every bus or tram. Tickets are valid for 75 minutes, including changes of bus routes and metro lines. Anyone caught without a validated ticket can be fined €50 on the spot plus the price of the ticket.

Bus tickets (€1) are sold from newspaper kiosks, bars, tobacconists, and from machines at bus terminals and metro stations. Rail stations have ticket desks and automated machines.

Racalmuto, Grotte, Castrofilippo, Comitini.
Interbus, Via P. Balsamo 26.
Tel: 091 616 7919.
Buses go to Catania and Siracusa.
Segesta. Via P. Balsamo 26.
Tel: 091 616 9039.
Buses go to Rome and Trápani.
Salemi, Piazza Marina.
Tel: 091 617 5411.
Buses go to Castelvetrano (near Selinunte), Marsala, Mazara del Vallo and Salemi.

From Trápani

City buses and those for the rest of Trápani province leave from Piazza Umberto.
AST, Piazza Malta.
Tel: 0923 23222.
For Palermo and Agrigento, buses start from Piazza Garibaldi.

From Agrigento

City buses leave from outside the station in Piazza Marconi. The main bus station for the rest of Sicily is in Piazza Roselli, near the Post Office. Main bus companies:
SAIS, Via Ragazzi del 99 12.
Tel: 0922 595 933.
S. Lumia, Via F. Crispi 87.
Tel: 0922 20414.

From Caltanissetta

Buses leave from Via Catania.
SAIS, Via Colejanni 20.
Tel: 0934 564 072.
Buses go to Palermo, Catania, Agrigento, Enna.

From Enna

SAIS, Viale Diaz.
Tel: 0935 500 902.
Buses leave from Piazza Scelfo in the lower town and connect with Piazza Armerina, Catania, Palermo, Caltagirone.

From Ragusa

All buses stop outside the railway station. Destinations include Rome, Catania, Messina, Siracusa, Caltagirone and Piazza Armerina.

From Siracusa

AST, Piazza delle Poste.
Tel: 0931 462 711.
Buses go to Lentini, Catania, Comiso, Ispica, Módica, Noto, Pachino, and Ragusa.
Interbus. Tel: 0931 66710.
Destinations include Catania, Noto, Pachino, Palermo and Taormina.

From Catania

The bus terminal is in front of the central station.
AST, Via Sturzo 220.
Tel: 095 746 1096.
Buses connect with Acireale, Etna Rifugio Sapienza and Caltagirone.
SAIS, Via d'Amico 181.
Tel: 095 536 168.
Buses go to Messina, Taormina, Enna, Agrigento, Caltanissetta, Palermo, Nicosia, Siracusa, Noto, Pachino.

From Messina

Giuntabus
Via Terranova 8, Milazzo.
Tel: 090 673 782.
SAIS
Piazza della Repubblica 6.
Tel: 090 771 914.
Buses connect with Taormina, Catania and Palermo.

TRANSPORT

ACCOMMODATION

ACTIVITIES

A – Z

LANGUAGE

A CCOMMODATION

WHERE TO STAY

Choosing a Hotel

Sicily has more than 500 hotels of various grades. Outside the main resorts, hotel standards are generally not as high as in northern or central Italy. With a few notable 5-star de luxe exceptions, hotel accommodation is reasonably priced. But it may prove difficult to find away from the thriving cities of Syracuse, Catania, Messina and Taormina, so book ahead.

Although many hotels are now rapidly upgrading, it is sometimes advisable to choose a higher grade hotel than you might normally. One and 2-star hotels may be inexpensive but their facilities are modest. Stipulate if you want single beds or a double bed *(letto matrimoniale)*. Also, if arriving by car, ensure the hotel has overnight garaging. Most hotels have rigid No Smoking rules.

Hotel categories: Hotels are classified according to a star rating system: 5-star de luxe; 4-star which are first class and exceptionally comfortable; 3-star are comfortable and economical; 2-star are hotels with fairly basic accommodation; and 1-star hotels range from simple to frugal.

Bed & breakfast accommodation is now fairly common in Sicily. These are based on their British counterpart: a clean room with bed/s and breakfast at a competitive price in a private house or apartment. Most are very good value indeed, but ask to see the room before taking it. When visiting smaller towns, the bed & breakfast establishments are in the historic centres, while modern hotels are in the new town or industrial zone that surrounds it.

Expect to find considerable differences in quality between hotels of the same grade in "tourist" and "non-tourist" towns. Off the beaten track, hotels can be basic but conceivably cost the same as in better resorts. There are also price differences between high and low season.

The local tourist offices have up-to-date lists which include prices. Hotels are not allowed to charge more than the price written on the rate card – usually located on the inside of the door of each room – but that doesn't mean they won't try.

A number of hotels are open only in the high season (around Easter to October). Some resort hotels may insist on guests taking either half or full board (i.e. dinner or lunch and dinner). Conversely, in the low season, ask prospective hotels what their best price is, that way you might be able to get reduced rates. Request a *sconto* (discount) because it is *bassa stagione* (low season).

Remember that there is a gulf between urban and rural Sicily. In the mountainous hinterland, advise the hotel if you expect to check in late at night.

Agriturismo: As distances in Sicily are great, this may be the solution for touring travellers who find themselves stranded with nowhere to stay. These are farmhouses in the countryside that often offer good value either on a bed & breakast or weekly basis. Much thought has been given to making this a viable way to increase farm revenue and many *agriturismi* are exceptionally well-appointed. For further information, *see page 282*.

Hotel safety: In general, the higher grade hotels are in safer and more salubrious areas. Take particular care in choosing hotels in the old quarters of Catania or Palermo – parts of historic Palermo and Catania can be deserted or slightly intimidating at night, with a greater risk of *scippatori* (street thieves). Families or women travelling alone should choose a hotel on a main street or in a modern quarter.

PALERMO CITY

Palermo

There is a large concentration of hotels at the southern ends of Via Roma and Via Maqueda, between the station, Stazione Centrale, and Corso Vittorio Emanuele. On the Corso, the hotels are more expensive. The modern Viale della Libertà quarter, within walking distance of the historic centre, is a good choice from many points of view, offering safety, convenience and fashionable neighbourhood bars.

It is worth noting that there are an increasing number of bed & breakfast establishments in Palermo. These offer a clean room with bed/s and breakfast at a competitive price in a private house or apartment. Ask to see the room before taking it.

5-star

Grand Hotel Federico II
Via Principe Granatelli 60.
Tel: 091 749 5052.
www.grandhotelfedericoii.it
Converted in 2003 into an efficient luxury hotel, its ambiance reflects earlier epoques. Roof terrace. €€€€

Grand Hotel Villa Igiea
Salita Belmonte 43.
Tel: 091 631 2111
www.villa-igiea-palermo.com
To the north, away from the city centre, it was originally a villa built by one of the great entrepreneurial and political families of the 19th century and has been carefully restored to early 20th-century glory. This is Palermo's prestige hotel where heads of state and official visitors stay. From its position in Acquasanta, on a cliff above the bay, the view over palms stretches across the Gulf of Palermo as well as inland over the plains of the Conca d'Oro. Pool. Garage. Facilities include a piano bar and La Terrazza restaurant with gourmet dishes. €€€€€

4-star

Astoria Palace
Via Montepellegrino 62.
Tel: 091 628 1111.
www.ghshotels.it
A luxury hotel known for its modern, elegant restaurant. 320 rooms, 14 suites. Due to its size, popular for conferences. Garage. €€€

Centrale Palace
Corso Vittorio Emanuele 327.
Tel: 091 336 666.
www.centralepalacehotel.it
A luxury hotel, restored in 1997. 104 rooms with a 1930s charm near Quattro Canti crossroads. Breakfast served on the terrace with panoramic view over the old town roofs. Garage. €€€€

Excelsior Palace
Via Marchese Ugo 3.
Tel: 091 625 6176
www.excelsiorpalermo.it
Extremely comfortable. Refurbished in the original 19th-century style. Rooms vary considerably so you may wish to see the room before booking. A good location opposite a park in the chic part of Palermo. Friendly staff. Excellent restaurants. €€€€

Grand Hotel et des Palmes
Via Roma 398.
Tel: 091 602 8111.
www.grandhoteldespalmes.com
Considered the smart place to stay even though for years it lay neglected. Excellently situated at the city centre and retaining elegant traces of its 1900s Belle Epoque origins. Now undergoing welcome stylish renovation to restore its ageing facilities. The original Art Nouveau lobby is delightful. Wagner completed Parsifal here in 1882. €€€€€

Principe di Villafranca
Via G.Turrisi Colonna 4.
Tel: 091 611 8523.
www.principedivillafranca.it
Away from the centre, close to the Gallery of Modern Art, the hotel was created in 1998. 34 elegant rooms are decorated with Sicilian antiques. Restaurant too has impeccable style. Garage. Fitness centre. Business facilities. €€€

Massimo Plaza
Via Maqueda 437.
Tel: 091 325 657.
www.massimoplazahotel.com
Pleasing hotel in a restored building close to Teatro Massimo. Comfortable, good service. €€€

Politeama Palace
Piazza Ruggero Settimo 15.
Tel: 091 322 777
www.hotelpoliteama.it
Modern, in the central area near Teatro Politeama and major shopping streets. Popular with large tour groups. €€€

3-star

Cristal Palace
Via Roma 477.
Tel: 091 611 2580.
www.cristalpalacehotelsicily.com
Modern, highly rated hotel, just across the street from the Grand Hotel et des Palmes. Centrally located for the historic quarter. Good service, comfortable. Garage facilities available. €€

Joli
Via Michele Amari 11.
Tel: 091 611 1765.
www.hoteljoli.it
Just off Via Roma,

TRANSPORT

ACCOMMODATION

ACTIVITIES

A – Z

LANGUAGE

centrally situated, quiet, unpretentious hotel. Very attractive, cosy rooms, some with frescoed ceilings. Good facilities and service. Parking available. **€€€**

Mediterraneo
Via Rosolino Pilo 43.
Tel: 091 581 133.
www.abmedpa.com
Unattractive modern frontage masks a functional hotel in central location. Efficient service. Garage arrangements available. **€€€**

Tonic
Via Stabile 126.
Tel: 091 581 754.
www.hoteltonic.it
Recently restored with elegant style. Comfortable and centrally located. **€€**

Villa D'Amato
Via Messina Marine 180.
Tel: 091 621 2767.
www.hotelvilladamato.it
Small hotel located outside city between autostrada and sea. Large rooms, garden, restaurant. **€€**

2-star

Posta
Via Antonio Gagini 77.
Tel: 091 587 338.
www.hotelpostapalermo.it
Centrally located and comfortable hotel. 30 rooms. Family-run. Favoured by touring actors appearing in local theatres. **€**

B&Bs

Alla Kala
Corso Vittorio Emanuele 71.
Tel: 091 743 4763.
www.allakala.it
A stylish B&B with five individually designed rooms, all with views of the port. Friendly and helpful staff. **€€**

BB22
Largo Cavalieri di Malta 22.
Tel: 091 611 1610.
www.bb22.it.
With an excellent location, tucked behind San Domenico, this boutique B&B has refined, relaxing decor and excellent service. **€€**

Budget

Casa Marconi
Via Monfenera 140.

Tel: 091 657 0611.
www.casamarconi.it
The city's youth hostel. Well run. Book but confirm reservation.**€**

Orientale
Via Maqueda 26.
Tel: 091 616 5727.
www.albergoorientale.191.it
Basic 1-star hotel. Half of the rooms are en-suite. Former palazzo with marble courtyard and plenty of atmosphere. **€**

Mondello

For families with young children or anyone seeking a beach with a busy nightlife, Mondello makes a better summer base than Palermo. During the hot months, much of fashionable Palermo society moves to the resort, so book early. The best hotels have private beaches. Elsewhere, beaches tend to charge a fee.

Mondello Palace
Viale Principe di Scalea.
Tel: 091 450 001.
www.mondellopalacehotel.it

Modern, luxury hotel on the seafront. 83 rooms. Private beach, pool, restaurant and bar. **€€€**

Splendid La Torre
Via Piano Gallo 11.
Tel: 091 450 222.
www.latorre.com
Very modern hotel built on the rocky point of the bay at the quieter end of Mondello Lido. Own beach, pool and tennis courts. Many of the 169 rooms overlook the sea or garden. **€€**

Addaura Residence
Lungomare Colombo 4452.
Tel: 091 684 2222.
www.addaurahotel.it
A stylish business-class hotel with garden, pool, private beach. **€€**

Conchiglia d'Oro
Viale Cloe 9.
Tel/fax: 091 450 359.
www.hotelconchigliadoro.com
Cosy rooms. Pool and beach. **€**

Villa Esperia
Via Margherita di Savoia 53.
Tel/fax: 091 684 0717.
www.hotelvillaesperia.it
An elegant hotel, recently refurbished, on the beach. **€€**

PALERMO PROVINCE

Castelbuono

Relais Santa Anastasia
Contrada Santa Anastasia.
Tel 0921 672 233
www.santa-anastasia-relais.it
Luxury in a converted grand house. Pool.
€€€€

Milocca
Contrada Piano Castagna.
Tel: 091 671 944.
www.albergomilocca.com
Pleasant, well serviced hotel located in the middle of an oak wood within the Parco delle Madonie. A car is

essential here. Swimming pool. Tennis. **€€**

Baita del Faggio
Acque del Faggio.
Tel: 0921 662 194
www.baitadelfaggio.com
Popular, all season, resort hotel. **€€€**

Piano Torre Park
Piano Torre, near Piano Zucchi.
Tel: 0921 662 671
www.pianotorreparkhotel.com
At the heart of the reserve with 27 charming rooms, pool and tennis courts. Excellent restaurant. Conference

facilities for 300. **€€**

Cefalù

An ideal choice for families or elderly people and popular with groups. The beaches are more accessible here than at Taormina. There is a wide range of accommodation. It is worth noting that out of season the beaches may not be cleaned and the sea may be rough.

Gli Alberi del Paradiso
Via dei Mulini 18.
Tel: 0921 423 9000.

www.alberidelparadiso.it
Typical beach hotel with pools, tennis, restaurant. **€€€€**

Baia del Capitano
Contrada Mazzaforno.
Tel: 0921 420 005.
www.baiadelcapitano.it
About 5 km (3 miles) west of Cefalù. Modern

but set in an olive grove. Pool, tennis, and nearby beach. €€€€
Carlton Riviera
Località Capo Plaia.
Tel: 0921 420 200.
www.carltonhotelriviera.it
About 5 km (3 miles) west of Cefalù, a large modern hotel on the cliffs. Tennis, pool. Open Apr–1 Oct. €€€
Kalura
Via Vincenzo Cavallaro 13, Caldura. Tel: 0921 421 354.
www.hotel-kalura.com
3 km (2 miles) east of Cefalù. Slightly worn, but most rooms have a sea view. Terrace, beach. €€€
Riva del Sole
Lungomare Columbo 25.
Tel: 0921 421 230.
www.rivadelsole.com
Modern, functional. 28 rooms, some with sea view. Closed Nov. €€
Tourist
Via Lungomare Giardina 4.
Tel: 0921 421 750.
www.touristhotel.it
Friendly hotel with a reasonable restaurant. €
Al Pescatore
Località Caldura.
Tel/fax: 0921 421 572.
www.hotelpescatore.it
Two-star comfort. €€

Monreale

Carrubella Park
Via Umberto 233.
Tel: 091 640 2188.
www.carrubellaparkhotel.com

About 1 km (½ mile) outside Monreale with wonderful views across Conca d'Oro. €€

Montelepre

Castello di Giuliano
Via Pietro Merra 1.
Tel: 091 8941 006.
www.castellodigiuliano.it
Basic comfort with pleasant service. €
Rose Garden
Via Circonvallazione 120.
Tel: 091 878 4360, fax: 091 878 4192.
Typical 2-star hotel. €

Termine Imerese

Grand Hotel delle Terme
Piazza Terme.
Tel: 091 811 3557.
www.grandhoteldelleterme.it
Garden setting. Panoramic views, pool and mineral springs. Good restaurant. €€
Il Gabbiano
Via Libertà 221.
Tel: 091 811 3262.
www.hotelgabbiano.it
On the outskirts, business hotel. No restaurant. 24 rooms. €

Ustica

In the traditional summer months, June to September, hotels tend to fill up fast. But there are many opportunities to rent rooms: call in at

the Bar Centrale in Piazza Umberto.
Grotta Azzurra
Contrada San Ferlicchio.
Tel: 091 844 9048.
www.framonhotels.com
51 rooms with terraces cut into the rocks, private beach and pool. Good restaurant. Open June–Sept. €€
Clelia
Via Sindaco 29.
Tel: 091 844 9039.
www.hotelclelia.it
Located on the main square, Clelia is the oldest pensione in town. Good value. Good restaurant. If you enjoy lentils try their *lenticchie all'Usticese*, an island speciality. €€
Punta Spalmatore
Località Spalmatore. Tel: 091 844 9388, fax: 091 844 9482. Holiday village with bungalows and rooms. Open June–Sept (prices vary widely). €€–€€€
Ariston
Via della Vittoria 5–7. Tel: 091 844 9042, fax: 091 844 9335. Inexpensive base. €
Diana
Contrada San Paolo.
Tel/fax: 091 844 9109.
www.hoteldiana-ustica.com
Good position, with beach. €
Locanda Castelli
Via San Francesco 16.
Tel: 091 844 9007.
Three apartments for two people. Minimum stay one week. €

Pelagie Islands

Alba d'Amore
Via Favorolo 1, Lampedusa.
Tel: 0922 970 272, fax: 0922 970 786.
Comfortable. €€
Guitgia Tommasino
Via Lido Azzurro 13, Lampedusa.
Tel: 0922 970 879.
hotelguitgiatommasino@lampedusa.to
Two comfortable buildings with 35 rooms leading directly to the beach. €€
Residence la Posta
Via Alfieri, Linosa.
Tel: 393 498 2649.
www.linosaresidencelaposta.it.
Attractive, air-conditioned accommodation in the centre of the village. €€
Martello
Salita Medusa 1, Lampedusa.
Tel: 0922 970 025.
www.hotelmartello.it
Comfortable. €€€
Medusa
Piazza Medusa 3, Lampedusa.
Tel: 0922 970 126.
www.medusahotels.it
20 modern rooms in Moorish style. €€€€

PRICE CATEGORIES

For a double room in high season:
€ = less than €100
€€ = €100–180
€€€ = €180–250
€€€€ = €250–400
€€€€€ = over €400

TRÁPANI PROVINCE

Trápani

Crystal
Piazza Umberto 1.
Tel: 0923 20000.
www.nh-hotels.com
Central, modern hotel with 68 rooms, good

restaurant. €€€
Baia dei Mulini
Lungomare Dante Alighieri, San Cusumano.
Tel: 0923 584 111.
www.baiadeimulini.it
On waterfront towards Erice, comfortable with

restaurant, bar, tennis, pool and private beach. €€€
Vittoria
Via Francesco Crispi 4.
Tel: 0923 873 044.
www.hotelvittoriatrapani.it
Central, 65 rooms,

some with sea view. Comfortable. Mostly business clientele. €€

Cavallino Bianco
Lungomare Dante Alighieri 5.
Tel: 0923 21549.
www.hotelcavallinobianco.eu
By the sea. Functional. €

Moderno
Via Tenente Genovese 20.
Tel: 0923 21247.
www.hotelmodernotrapani.it
Centrally located, with 13 rooms. €€

Castellammare del Golfo

This charming fishing port is a small resort, an ideal base for families or independent travellers, especially those with a car, who want to be close to Palermo yet in a quieter, more manageable location. It also appeals to those wishing to swim in clean waters near the nature reserve of Lo Zíngaro. Some regular visitors rent villas here.

Al Madarig
Piazza Petrolo 7.
Tel: 0924 33533.
www.almadarig.com
Pleasant modern hotel with 33 rooms overlooking the port. €

Punta Nord Est
Viale Leonardo da Vinci 67.
Tel: 0924 30511.
www.puntanordest.com
A holiday hotel with a private beach. €€

Erice

Erice is an ideal base and an extremely attractive village. In summer its hilltop position makes it far more comfortable than Trápani. However, in high season it can be crowded and accommodation is in

great demand. Early booking is recommended.

Elimo
Via Vittorio Emanuele 75.
Tel: 0923 869 377.
www.hotelelimo.it
A small hotel, 21 charming rooms, in the old town with a pleasant restaurant and bar. Views from rooms and roof terrace. €€

La Pineta
Viale Nunzio Nasi.
Tel: 0923 860 127.
www.lapinetaerice.com
A hotel made up of a number of small bungalows among the pine trees. Pleasant service. Good restaurant. €€

Moderno
Via Vittorio Emanuele 67.
Tel: 0923 869 300.
www.hotelmodernoerice.it
In the old town. Renovated, but it feels fairly intimate, with 40 rooms. It has an excellent roof terrace and a good restaurant known for its fish couscous. €€

Ermione
Via Pineta Comunale 43.
Tel: 0923 869 138, fax: 0923 869 587.
Set in a pine grove just outside the walls, it looks unattractive but has large rooms, great views, a pool and an average restaurant. €

Edelweiss
Cortile Padre Vincenzo 5.
Tel: 0923 869 420.
www.edelweisserice.com
This basic but quiet pensione has a distinctly Alpine feel. 13 rooms. €

Marinella

Marinella di Selinunte has a number of standard beach hotels on its seafront.

Paradise Beach
Contrada Belice di Mare. Tel: 0924 46333, fax: 0924 46477.
Set beside the sea 6 km (4 miles) from Marinella centre. An impressive hotel-club with sports facilities, a pool and tennis courts, 250 rooms. Closed Nov–Feb. €€€

Alceste
Via Alceste 23.
Tel: 0924 46184.
www.hotelalceste.it
1 km (½ mile) away from town, close to the sea. 26 simple but comfortable rooms. Terrace, garden and solarium. Closed 16 Nov–14 Dec; 16 Jan– 14 Feb. €€

Garzia
Via Antonio Pigafetta 6–8.
Tel. 0924 46024.
www.hotelgarzia.com
Modern, on the seafront, in walking distance of sites. 68 rooms. €€

Lido Azzurro
Via Marco Polo 98.
Tel: 0924 46256.
lazzurro@freemail.it
Small, friendly 2-star villa in the centre but close to beach. Some rooms with sea views. Restaurant. €

Marsala

New Hotel Palace
Longomare Mediterraneo 57.
Tel: 0923 719 492.
www.newhotelpalace.com
Charming five-star hotel with sea-view rooms. Swimming pool, good restaurant. €€€

President
Via Nino Bixio 1.
Tel: 0923 999 333.
www.hotelpresidentmarsala.com
128 rooms. Popular hotel for conferences. Swimming pool and tennis courts. €€

Delfino Beach
Lungomare Mediterraneo 672.
Tel: 0923 751 076.
www.delfinobeach.com
Some 4 km (2½ miles) south of the centre, with 91 rooms, conference facilities, pool, tennis, restaurant. €€

Villa Favorita
Via Favorita 27.
Tel: 0923 989 100.
www.villafavorita.com
A 19th-century villa set in extensive garden with great views. Comfortable with large rooms. €€

Garden
Via Gambini 36.
Tel/fax: 0923 982 320.
Two-star comfort near the railway station. €

Mazara del Vallo

Hopps
Via G. Hopps 29.
Tel: 0923 946 133.
www.hoppshotel.it
Relatively expensive with 188 rooms. On the waterfront with traditional service; recommended for its hospitality and cuisine. Garden, covered pool; private beach reached by shuttle bus. €€

San Vito Lo Capo

This is an up-and-coming resort near Castellammare with something of a Wild West feel about it. It is pleasant and safe, though, with many hotels to choose from, and a good choice for families or those on a limited budget, even though prices here have risen recently due to the increasing presence of tourists during July and August. The most popular hotels are around Via Savoia and Via Mulino.

TRANSPORT

Capo San Vito
Via Principe Tommaso 29.
Tel: 0923 972 122.
www.caposanvito.it
Hotel with 35 rooms,
10 km (6 miles) south
of Capo San Vito but on
the beach. Private lido
for guests; gardens and
tennis courts. €€€

Riva del Sole
Via Generale Arimondi 11.
Tel: 0923 972 629.
www.hotelrivadelsole.it
Only 9 rooms and run
by a welcoming family.
Excellent restaurant
with gastronomic aspi-
rations. Open Apr–Sept.
€€

Villaggio Cala Mancina
Via Eboli 29. Tel: 0923 621 611.
www.calamancina.it
On the beach, with pool.
60 rooms. Family hotel.
€€
Egitarso
Via Lungomare 54.
Tel: 0923 972 111.
www.hotelegitaso.it

Basic, with 42 rooms,
but on the seafront. €€
Vecchio Mulino
Via Mulino 49.
Tel: 0923 972 518.
www.hotelvecchiomulino.com
13 rooms plus
panoramic terrace
views and good restaur-
ant. €€

EGADI ISLANDS

Favignana

In July and August
accommodation can
be hard to find: booking
is essential for this
period. However, the
ferries tend to be met
by locals offering
rooms.
Aegusa
Via Garibaldi 11.
Tel: 0923 922 430
www.aegusahotel.it
Simple conversion
of a palazzo at the
centre of the island.
28 comfortable rooms.
Dining in the garden.
Closed Jan–Feb.
€€

Approdo di Ulisse
Cala Grande.
Tel: 0923 925 000.
www.aurumhotels.it
Comfortable resort
hotel. 131 rooms.
Beach, pool, tennis.
Open Easter–Oct. €€€
Egadi
Via Cristofero Colombo 17.
Tel: 0923 921 232.
www.albergoegadi.it
Stylish hotel with 9
rooms and the island's
most highly regarded
restaurant. Open Mar–
Oct. €€€
Bouganville
Via Cimabue 10.
Tel: 0923 922 033.
www.albergobouganville.it

Simple and quiet.
Open Apr–Oct. €€

Levanzo
Paradiso
Via Lungomare 8.
Tel: 0923 924 080.
www.albergoparadisolevanzo.it
15 rooms. Simple
restaurant on terrace
overlooking sea. €
Pensione dei Fenici
Via Calvario 18.
Tel/fax: 0923 924 083.
Family-run. 10 pleasant
rooms with a terrace
restaurant. €

Pantelleria
Club Village
Punta Fram
at Punta Fram. Tel: 0923 918
075, fax: 0923 918 244.
On the western coast.
Pool, tennis, restaurant.
€€
Cossyra
At Musia. Tel: 0923 911 154.
info@cossyrahotel.it
About 3 km (2 miles)
from Pantelleria port, in
pleasant grounds with
pool, tennis courts and
a private beach. €€
Mursia
At Mursia. Tel: 0923 911 217.
info@mursiahotel.it
Not far from airport. On
its own beach with
pools, tennis. Under
same ownership as
Cossyra. €€

Papuscia
At Tracino. Contrada Sopra
Portella 28.
Tel: 0923 915 463
www.papuscia.it
Only 11 spacious and
simple rooms but in
a typical *dammusi*
setting; lots of lava.
Tranquil location
outside Tracino. €€€
(Dinner only, with deli-
cious fare. €€)
Port'Hotel
Lungomare Borgo Italia 6.
Tel: 0923 911 299.
porthotel@pantelleria.it
40 rooms in a modern
building. €€
Miryam
Corso Umberto 1.
Tel: 0923 911 374.
www.miryamhotel.it
Traditional, comfortable
hotel. €€

PRICE CATEGORIES
For a double room in
high season:
€ = less than €100
€€ = €100–180
€€€ = €180–250
€€€€ = €250–400
€€€€€ = over €400

BELOW: a vital ingredient of Sicilian holidays.

ACCOMMODATION
ACTIVITIES
A – Z
LANGUAGE

AGRIGENTO CITY AND PROVINCE

Agrigento

Unlike the rest of the province, the city is well provided with good-quality hotels. This section also includes the Valley of the Temples.

Atenea 191
Villa Atenea 191.
Tel: 0922 595 594.
www.atenea191.com
On Agrigento's main street, this appealing B&B has large rooms with sea views. There's a roof terrace too. No credit cards. €

Camere a Sud
Via Ficani 6.
Tel: 349 638 4424.
www.camereasud.it.
A lovely boutique B&B off Via Atenea, with just three stylish rooms. Breakfst is served on the roof terrace in summer. No credit cards. €

Colleverde Park
Passeggiata Archeologica.
Tel: 0922 29555.
www.topsicilia.it
Further up the slope from Villa Athena, at the start of Strada Panoramica. 48 rooms. Lovely temple views. Reasonable restaurant. €€

Letto e Latte
Via Cannatello 101.
Tel: 0922 651 945.
www.lettolatte.it
This attractive, family-run B&B has just six rooms with private bathroom and balconies with temple views. Great value. No credit cards. €

Villa Athena
Via Passeggiata Archeologica 33. Tel: 0922 596 288.
www.athenahotels.com
This fairly expensive 18th-century villa with 40 comfortable rooms is set in an attractive

garden with lovely views of Tempio della Concordia. It is worth making the most of the spot for lunch or dinner, graced by serene views. €€€

Tre Torri
Viale Cannatello 7.
Tel: 0922 606 733.
www.hoteltretorri.eu
Large hotel just east of the temples. Restaurant, bar, indoor and outdoor swimming pools, sauna. €€

Pirandello
Via Giovanni XXIII 5.
Tel: 0922 595 666.
www.hotelpirandello.it
Comfortable 3-star hotel. €

Cammarata

Rio Platani
Via Scalo Ferroviario.
Tel: 0922 909 051.
Functional. €

Canicattì

To Italians, Canicattì is rather like Timbuktu – an emergency stop only.

Belvedere
Via Resistenza 22.
Tel: 0922 851 860.
www.hotel-belvedere.org
Functional. €

Licata

This historic but down-at-heel town is a possible overnight stop if Agrigento hotels are full.

Piccadilly
Via Panoramica.
Tel/fax: 0922 893 626.
Basic. €

Baia d'Oro
Località Mallarella.
Tel: 0922 774 666.
www.baiadoro.com
Basic with 72 rooms, views and beach. €

Al Faro
Via Dogana 6. Tel: 0922 773 5503, fax: 0922 773 087.
25 rooms. Basic. €

Porto Empedocle

Not recommended as a base but the town makes a sensible overnight stop if you are catching a ferry to the Pelagie Islands.

Dei Pini
On SS 115, Località Vincenzella. Tel: 0922 634 844.
hdeipini@virgilio.it
Renovated, with garden and beach. €€

Tiziana Residence
Località Durueli. Tel: 0922 637 202, fax: 0922 637 363.
With beach and pool. €

San Leone

Pirandello Mare
Via Giorgio de Chirico 17.
Tel: 0922 412 333, fax: 0922 413 693.
Unattractive but very comfortable. Restaurant and bar. €

Akragas
Via Emporium 16 (between the

sea and the town). Tel/fax: 0922 414 082.
On the coast with restaurant and bar. Ideal location for families. €

Sciacca

Sciacca is a possible base in Agrigento province. While rather scruffy, it is popular as a spa town.

Delle Terme
Via delle Nuove Terme.
Tel: 0925 23133.
info@termehotel.com
72 rooms, covered and outdoor pools and reserved beach, with a thermal treatment centre and spa. €

Paloma Bianca
Via Figuli 5. Tel: 0925 25130.
Basic amenities. €

BELOW: the Valley of the Temples, Agrigento.

TRANSPORT

ACCOMMODATION

ACTIVITIES

A – Z

LANGUAGE

CALTANISSETTA PROVINCE

The province has limited accommodation and, while the hinterland is lovely, Caltanissetta itself is dull and does not provide a satisfactory base for touring. Those who wish to stay in the mountains would do better going to Enna.

Caltanissetta

San Michele
Via Fasci Siciliani.
Tel: 0934 553 750.
www.hotelsanmichelesicilia.it
New, stylish hotel short distance from centre, with 122 rooms, pool, good views from the garden over the valley. Restaurant. €€€

Butera

Stella del Mediterraneo
SS 115, Località Falconara.
Tel: 0934 349 004.
www.stelladelmediterraneo.it
Comfortable. €

Gela

Gela is a sensible stopping place only if you have to do business there. The town has a large oil refinery and a high rate of petty crime.
Sole
Via Mare 32.
Tel: 0933 925 292.
g.vitale_hotelsole@alice.it
Adequate. 18 rooms. €

ABOVE: Caltanissetta's church of San Sebastiano.

ENNA PROVINCE

Enna

Enna itself has very few hotels so reservations are advisable. Because of Enna's altitude, take warmer clothes and expect to find views from your hotel window swathed in mist.
Bristol
Piazza Grisleri.
Tel: 0935 24 415.
www.hotelbristolenna.it
Rooms here are simple and comfortable, if a little bland. €€
Grand Albergo Sicilia
Piazza Colaianni 7.
Tel: 0935 500 850.
www.hotelsiciliaenna.it
This is a centrally located, comfortable and reasonably efficient 3-star hotel. Some of the 76 rooms have fine views. €€

Nicosia

This untouristy inland town is a refreshing base for exploring Enna's hilly interior.
Baglio San Pietro
Contrada San Pietro.
Tel: 0935 640 529.
www.bagliosanpietro.com
Charming converted farmhouse with garden, pool and only 10 rooms. Closed Mar. Restaurant serves own produce. €
Vineta
Contrada San Basile.
Tel: 0935 646 074.
7 km (4 miles) north of Nicosia, this is a modern, comfortable hotel. €

Piazza Armerina

This appealing town makes a good stop for visitors wishing to see its famous Villa Romana, the Roman villa.
Ostello del Borgo
Largo San Giovanni 6.
Tel: 0935 687 019.
www.ostellodelborgo.it
A B&B in an old convent in the centre of Piazza Armerina. Simple, dormitory-style rooms, formerly the nuns' quarters. There are more comfortable private rooms upstairs. Closed Dec–Feb. €
Park Hotel Paradiso
Contrada Ramalda.
Tel: 0935 680 841.
www.parkhotelparadiso.it
95 rooms, pool, tennis. €€
Villa Romana
Via Alcide De Gasperi 18.
Tel/fax: 0935 682 911.
Popular with tour groups. 55 rooms. €

Mosaici da Battiato
Contrada Paratore 11.
Tel/fax: 0935 685 453.
www.hotelmosaici.com
Very close to the Villa Romana and with a renowned restaurant. 23 rooms. Tennis and riding. Closed Nov. €

Troina

Quiet town; good alternative to Nicosia.
Costellazioni
Contrada San Michele.
Tel: 0935 653 966,
fax: 0935 653 660.
Pool, riding, squash. €€

RAGUSA PROVINCE

The province is easily accessible on day trips from Ragusa city, but you'll probably find a stay in the old town of Ragusa itself a more memorable experience. As a whole, the province is appealingly un-touristy, its people extending a warm welcome to foreign visitors.

Ragusa

Ragusa Ibla (the medieval "lower" town) is a lovely place to stay the night: though some small hotels and B&Bs have opened in recent years, the atmosphere is still appealingly low-key. Ragusa Alta (the baroque and modern "upper" town) holds a few characterless business-class places. Parking can be tricky (though hotels can usually help out with this) and the town's sign-posting and one-way system confusing.

Eremo della Giubiliana
Contrada Giubiliana, Km 75.
Tel: 0932 669 119.
www.eremodellagiubiliana.it
Outside Ragusa, near Marina di Ragusa, this fortified 15th-century hermitage, converted into one of Sicily's most delightful hotels, is both charming and austere. Pool, garden, reserved beach. **€€€€**

Locanda Don Serafino
Via XI Febbraio 15.
Tel: 0932 222 0065.
www.locandadonserafino.it
A boutique hotel in Ragusa Ibla with 10 beautifully decorated rooms. There's an excellent restaurant too. **€€€**

Mediterraneo Palace
Via Roma 189.
Tel: 0932 621 944.
www.mediterraneopalace.it
Modern, central hotel with power-shower bathrooms. 89 rooms. **€€**

Montreal
Via San Giuseppe 6.
Tel: 0932 621 133.
montreal@sicily-hotels.net
Centrally located near

the Duomo. Restaurant. Parking. **€€€**

Palazzo Castro al Duomo
Piazza del Duomo 2.
Tel: 0932 621887.
www.palazzocastro.it.
With an excellent location on the cathedral square, this is an atmospheric place to stay. There's a tranquil garden too. **€**

Risveglio Ibleo
Largo Camerina 3.
Tel: 0932 247811.
www.risveglioibleo.com
Stylish self-catering suites in a lovely town-house in Ragusa Ibla. Excellent breakfasts too. **€**

Módica

Módica is an appealing provincial town and would make an acceptable, if less convenient, alternative to Ragusa if its selection of hotels were better.

Bristol
Via Risorgimento 8b.
Tel: 0932 762 890.

www.hotelbristol.it
Functional, impersonal, modern hotel for business travellers. Hard to find in back streets. **€€**

Il Cavaliere
Corso Umberto I 259.
Tel: 0932 947219.
www.bbilcavalieremodica.it.
A lovely B&B with friendly owners in an elegant palazzo, with tastefully furnished rooms and a breakfast room with a frescoed ceiling. **€**

Pozzallo

Villa Ada
Corso Vittorio Veneto 3.
Tel: 0932 954 022.
www.hotelvillaada.it
Functional hotel used by ferry port passengers. Simple restaurant. **€€**

SIRACUSA CITY AND PROVINCE

Siracusa

Compared with much of Sicily, hotels here are more international and efficient if, occasionally, a little characterless. Many also

tend to be some distance from the archaeological sites and the island of Ortigia.

Grand
Via Mazzini 12.
Tel: 0931 464 600.
www.grandhotelortigia.it
The best hotel in town and "the most romantic" beds in Ortigia. An Art Nouveau-style building overlooking the Porto Grande and yacht marina. 40 rooms. Roof garden with panoramic views. **€€€€**

Bella Vista
Via Diodoro Siculo 4.
Tel: 0931 411 437, fax: 0931 37927.
Central, comfortable and efficient. **€€**

Domus Mariae
Via Vittoria Veneto 76.
Tel: 0931 24854.
www.sistemia.it/domusmariae
A restored ancient building in the historic centre, this small hotel with 13 rooms is run by Ursoline nuns, who offer a warm welcome and good service. **€€€**

Como
Piazza Stazione 13.
Tel: 0931 464 055.
www.hotelcomosiracusa.com
Conveniently located midway between the archaeological park and Ortigia. Good restaurant. **€**

Gutowski
Lungomare Vittorini 26.
Tel: 0931 465 861.
www.guthotel.it
Small but comfortable.
13 rooms plus small
sunny terrace with
panoramic views. €€

Augusta

This is an emergency
overnight stop for those
catching an early ferry
the next day. In the
vicinity there is the
touristy resort village of
Brucoli.
Villa dei Cesari
Località Monte Tauro.

Tel: 0931 983 311.
www.hotelvilladeicesari.com
24 rooms, garden,
private beach. Simple
but comfortable. €€

Noto

Centro Storico
Corso Vittorio Emanuele 64.
Tel: 0931 573 967.
www.centro-storico.com
A quaint B&B in the cen-
tre of historic Noto, with
en-suite rooms. Closed
Feb and Nov. No credit
cards. €
La Fontanella
Via Rosalino Pilo 3.
Tel: 0931 894 724.

www.albergolafontanella.it
The only hotel in the
centre of town is this
tasteful, attractive
three-star hotel. €
Villa Favorita
C. da Falconara.
Tel: 0931 812 912.
www.villafavoritanoto.it
Retreat in countryside
south of Noto. Charm-
ing rooms and service.
Pool. Rooms for
conferences. €€€
Villa Mediterranea
Viale Lido, at Lido di Noto.
Tel: 0931 812330.
www.villamediterranea.it
Small, unassuming villa
converted into 2-star

hotel, 15 cosy rooms,
across road from
beach. €€€

Portopalo di Capo Passero

Jonic
Viale Vittorio Emanuele 19.
Tel/fax: 0931 842 723.
www.jonichotel.com
An inexpensive, 12
room hotel in the south-
ernmost resort facing
the sea. €
El Condor
Via Vittorio Emanuele 38.
Tel: 0931 842 016.
16 rooms in basic hotel
overlooking sea. Open
mid-June–Sept. €

CATANIA CITY AND PROVINCE

Catania

Many of the hotels are
geared to business
travellers and so can
seem somewhat
charmless, if efficient.
Bellini
Piazza Trento 13.
Tel: 095 316 933.
www.nh-hotels.com
Recently modernised
hotel in city centre. 130
rooms. €€
Etnea 316
Via Etnea 316.
Tel: 095 2503076.
www.hoteletnea316.it
This recently refurbished
B&B makes a lovely
home-from-home,
with spacious, beauti-
fully decorated rooms
and a relaxed, welcom-
ing atmosphere. €
Excelsior
Piazza G. Verga 39.
Tel: 095 747 6111.
www.amthotels.com
Expensive and impos-
ing, with 176 com-
fortable rooms and a
reputable restaurant.
€€€

Jolly Ognina
Via Messina 628.
Tel: 095 752 8111.
www.nh-hotels.com
Modernised and
updated business-style
hotel on the seafront.
Some of 56 rooms have
sea views. €€
Nettuno
Viale Ruggero di Lauria 121.
Tel: 095 712 2006.
www.hotel-nettuno.it
With pool and restaur-
ant. €€
Una Hotel Palace
Via Etnea 218.
Tel: 095 250 5111.
www.unahotels.it
Luxurious, recently
refurbished and
situated on the main
shopping street. €€€€
La Vecchia Palma
Via Etnea 668.
Tel: 095 432 025.
www.lavecchiapalma.com
Charming Art Nouveau
villa in the centre with
12 rooms. €
San Domenico
Via Cifali 76. Tel: 095 438 480.
Well-situated but
modest. €

Villa Mater Sanctitatis
Via Bottego. Tel: 095 580 532,
fax: 095 580 032.
Comfortable economy
option. €

Aci Castello

President Park
Via Litteri 88.
Tel: 095 711 6111.
www.presidentparkhotel.com
Modern, on a small hill
with garden, covered
pool and private beach.
96 rooms. Good restau-
rant. €€

Aci Trezza

Faraglioni
Lungomare dei Ciclopi 115.
Tel: 095 093 0464.
www.grandhotelfaraglioni.com
Set in a fishing village
with its own private lido
and a good regional
restaurant. €€

Acireale

Orizzonte Acireale
Via C. Colombo.
Tel: 095 886 006.

www.hotelorizzonte.it
Large comfortable
hotel, 125 rooms, with
swimming pool and
panoramic terrace view.
€€
Santa Tecla Palace
Via Balestrate 100 at Santa
Tecla. Tel: 095 763 4015.
www.santatecla.it
Holiday hotel in excel-
lent, panoramic location
3 km (2 miles) from
Acireale. Garden, swim-
ming pool, restaurant.
€€€
La Perla Ionica
Via Unni 10, Capomulini.
Tel: 095 766 1111.
www.laperlaionica.com
Large hotel with 300
rooms, plus suites and
apartments. Two pools,
tennis, gym, solarium,
2 restaurants and piano
bar. €€

Caltagirone

La Pilozza Infiorata
Via Santissimo Salvatore 97.
Tel: 0933 22162.
www.lapilozzainfiorata.com
Stylish, Art Nouveau-style B&B, in the historic centre of Caltagirone, with a handful of comfortable, tastefully decorated rooms and a terrace. €
Tre Metri Sopra il Cielo
Via Bongiovanni 72.
Tel: 0933 193 5106.
www.bbtremetrisoprailcielo.it.
A small, but friendly B&B overlooking the Santa Maria del Monte steps, with just two rooms (one en-suite) and a lovely breakfast terrace with stunning views. €
Villa San Mauro
Via Porto Salvo 14.
Tel: 0933 26500.
www.nh-hotels.com
Good base in the hills with a swimming pool. Decor a bit corporate, but rooms are comfortable and all have balconies overlooking Caltagirone. €€

Cannizzaro

Sheraton Catania
Via A da Messina 45.
7 km (4 miles) from Catania.
Tel: 095 711 4111.
www.sheratoncatania.com
Comfortable with a pool, suites and renowned restaurant, Il Timo. Popular for congresses. €€
Baia Verde
Via Angelo Musco 8. Tel: 095 491 522, fax: 095 494 464.
www.baiaverde.it
Right on water's edge, with modern rooms and good services. €€€

Castelmola

Villa Sonia
Via Porta Mola 9.5 km (3 miles) outside Taormina.
Tel: 0942 28082.
www.hotelvillasonia.com
Charming villa converted into hotel with 40 rooms. Pool, garden and view of Mount Etna. Closed Nov–end Feb, but open for the Christmas season during this period when early booking essential. €€€€

Linguaglossa

On the northern slopes of Etna, so accommodation tends to be fully booked during the skiing season.
Happy Day
Via Mareneve 9.
Tel: 095 643 484.
Basic hotel. Open in winter only. €

Nicolosi

If you plan to stay during winter, book early, especially if it is predicted to be a snowy winter. There are mountain walks from Nicolosi, organised by the local tourist office, year round.
Biancaneve
Via Etnea 163.
Tel: 095 911 176.
www.hotelbiancaneve.com
Family-friendly hotel open all year, with swimming pool, wellness centre and view of Mount Etna, refurbished rooms. €€
Gemmellaro
Via Etnea 160.

Tel: 095 911 060.
www.hotelgemmellaro.it
Quiet, modern and popular. €

Paternò

Sicilia
Via Vittorio Emanuele 391.
Tel: 095 853 604.
www.hotelsiciliapaterno.com
Often full as it is the only hotel here. €

Zafferana Etnea

On southern slopes of Etna. Good skiing base.
Airone
Via Cassone 67.
Tel: 095 708 1819.
www.hotel-airone.it
Views reaching coast. 60 rooms, garden. €€€
Primavera dell'Etna
Via Cassone 86.
Tel: 095 708 2348.
www.hotel-primavera.it
With 55 rooms, terrace with panoramic views and meeting rooms. €
Del Bosco Emmaus
Via Cassone 75.
Tel: 095 708 1888.
www.albergoemmaus.it
Basic hotel. €

TAORMINA

During the peak season (Apr–Oct) and around Christmas, many hotels insist on half-board. Some have beach concessions on the coast below the town and can provide transport with their own mini-buses.
San Pietro
Via Pirandello 50.
Tel: 0942 620 711.
www.grandhotelsanpietro.net
Charming hotel that opened in 2005. Superb views, comfort, terraces, pool and delightful garden. €€€

San Domenico Palace
Piazza San Domenico 5.
Tel: 0942 613 111.
www.thi.it
A beautiful former Dominican monastery turned into a hotel. Not to everyone's taste because some rooms remain cell-sized. But fashionable and expensive, and at the centre of Taormina. Magnificent views from many rooms and from the terrace towards Etna and the sea. Well appointed. Fine

restaurant. €€€€€
Timeo
Via Teatro Greco 59.
Tel: 0942 625 837.
www.grandhoteltimeo.com
For some this is Taormina's grandest hotel. Certainly there is a feel of luxury. It is comfortable, spacious, with panoramic views, well located in town, and with transport to a private beach. €€€€€
Excelsior
Via Toselli 8. Tel: 0942 23975.
www.excelsiorpalacetaormina.it
Dullish revamped hotel,

but it commands a promontory and enjoys lovely grounds and a spectacularly sited pool. €€€€

Villa Diodoro
Via Bagnoli Croci 75. Tel: 0942 23312, fax: 0942 23391.
www.gaishotels.com
Favoured because both its pool and restaurant have wonderful panoramic views that include Etna and the coastline. 100 rooms. Shuttle bus to sister hotel on beach. A few minutes' easy stroll into the centre. €€€€

Miramare
Via Guardiola Vecchia 27. Tel: 0942 23401.
www.miramaretaormina.it
Elegant building with 68 rooms, pool, parking, tennis, gardens and views. Closed mid-Nov–mid-Dec. €€€€

Villa Paradiso
Via Roma 2. Tel: 0942 23922.
www.hotelvillaparadisotaormina.com
Family hotel. All rooms with fine views and a private beach. €€€

Villa Belvedere
Via Croce Bagnoli 79. Tel: 0942 23791.
www.villabelvedere.it
Comfortable, with covered pool, garden and parking. 47 rooms. Open Mar–Nov. €€€

Isabella
Corso Umberto 58. Tel: 0942 23153.
www.gaishotels.com
Small but charming hotel in the centre of the pedestrianised Corso. €€€

Villa Fiorita
Via Pirandello 39. Tel: 0942 24122.
www.villafioritahotel.com
On the hillside edging the town. 25 pleasant rooms, many with wonderful views. Garden. €€

Condor
Via Dietro Cappuccini 25. Tel: 0942 23124.
www.condorhotel.com
Friendly, only 12 rooms, and with beach concession. Open Mar–Oct. €

La Campanella
Via Circonvallazione 3. Tel: 0942 23381, fax: 0942 625 248.
Pleasant, but hillside location not suitable for the disabled. €

Palazzo Vecchio
Salita Ciampoli 9. Tel: 0942 23033, fax: 0942 625 104.
Charming and quaint medieval mansion in the town centre. Sea views. Closed Nov–Feb. €

Victoria
Corso Umberto 81. Tel: 0942 23372.
www.albergovictoria.it
On the pedestrianised Corso in the centre of town. Simple but charming rooms. Roof terrace breakfasts. €€

Villa Greta
Via Leonardo da Vinci 46. Tel: 0942 28286.
www.villagreta.it
A small, family-run hotel which is surprisingly affordable, considering most rooms come with a balcony and incredible views. It's a 15-minute walk from Taormina on the Castelmola road. €€

Villa Kristina
Via Leonardo da Vinci 3. Tel: 0942 28366
www.hvle.it
Can be rather noisy in the height of the season, but it is good value for money. €€

Villa Schuler
Piazzetta Bastione 16. Tel: 0942 23481.
www.hotelvillaschuler.com
Lots of charm. Comfortable with beach concession arrangements. Closed Dec–Feb. €€

Villa Taormina
Via Fazzello 49. Tel: 0942 620 072.
www.hotelvillataormina.com
A charming boutique hotel, with rooms full of antiques, a lovely terrace, parking and a shuttle service to the beach. €€€€

Mazzarò

Mazzarò is the beach resort below Taormina. A cable car connects the two. Mazzarò's popularity is confirmed by a variety of lively restaurants and clubs which tend to be less expensive than those in Taormina.

Mazzarò Sea Palace
Via Nazionale 147. Tel: 0942 612 111.
www.mazzaroseapalace.it
Splendidly appointed, luxurious, holiday hotel over the small bay. Open Apr–Oct. €€€€€

Capotaormina
Via Nazionale 105. Tel: 0942 572 111.
www.atahotels.it
Sleek hotel perched above the beautiful bay of Mazzarò. Saltwater pool built into the cliff. All rooms have private terraces. Private beach. €€€€

Villa Sant'Andrea
Via Nazionale 137. Tel: 0942 625 837.
www.hotelvillasantandrea.com
Comfortable beach hotel described as in English-style. Garden, parking and covered pool. €€€€

Baia Azzurra
Via Nazionale 240. Tel: 0942 23249.
www.hotelbaiaazzurra.it
Three-star comfort. €€

Villa Esperia
Via Nazionale 244. Tel: 0942 23377, fax: 0942 211 05.
Simple but comfortable. Closed Oct–Nov. €€

BELOW: much of life is lived outdoors in Taormina.

MESSINA PROVINCE

Messina

Grand Hotel Liberty
Via I Settembre 15.
Tel: 090 640 9436.
www.nh-hotels.it
An Art Nouveau-style
hotel conveniently
situated opposite the
station, geared towards
business travellers.
€€€

Royal Palace
Via Tommaso Cannizzaro 224.
Tel: 090 6503.
www.nh-hotels.com
A comfortable but
unremarkable hotel
in the heart of the
commercial district.
€€€

Paradis
Via Consolare Pompea 335.
Tel: 090 310 682.
www.hotelparadis.it
Modern hotel over-
looking the Straits of
Messina. €

Capo d'Orlando

Il Mulino
Via Andrea Doria 46.
Tel: 0941 902 431.
www.hotelilmulino.it
92 rooms, some with
views. Restaurant with
Sicilian specialities. €€

La Tartaruga
Via Consolare Antica 70,
at Lido San Gregorio.
Tel: 0941 955 012.
www.hoteltartaruga.it
Comfortable with

private beach and highly
regarded Tartaruga
restaurant known for
Messina specialities. €

Amato
Via Consolare Antica 150.
Tel: 0941 911 476.
www.hotelamato.it
Functional hotel with
garden and swimming
pool. €€

Giardini-Naxos

A lively, if downmarket,
resort, popular with
families and young
holidaymakers. Accom-
modation is cheaper in
winter.

Arathena Rocks
Via Calcide Eubea 55.
Tel: 0942 51349, fax: 0942
51690.
Set on the rocks a little
out of town (free bus
available). Very tranquil.
Garden, pool, tennis.
Rooms are sea-facing or
air-conditioned. Closed
Nov–Easter. €€

Hellenia Yachting
Via Jannuzzo 41.
Tel: 0942 51737.
www.hotel-hellenia.it
Large hotel with private
sandy beach and with
pool and restaurant.
€€€

Naxos Beach
Via Recanati 26.
Tel: 0942 6611.
www.atahotels.it
Resort hotel with 189

rooms, four swimming
pools, beach, sports
facilities, entertain-
ment. €€€

Nike
Via Calcide Eubea 27.
Tel: 0942 51207.
www.hotelnike.it
36 simple rooms in
hotel with prime posi-
tion with terrace over-
looking the sea, private
beach, garden. €€

Russott
Via Jannuzzo 47.
Tel: 0942 51931.
www.russotthotels.it
Large modern complex
with 300 rooms, private
beach, swimming pool,
tennis. €€€€

La Sirenetta
Via Naxos 177.
Tel/fax: 0942 53637.
www.hotelsirenetta.com
Basic but friendly.
Closed Nov–Feb. €

Letojanni

Da Peppe
Via Vittorio Emanuele 345.
Tel: 0942 36159.
www.hoteldapeppe.it
Typical two-star hotel.
€€

Olimpo
Loc. Poggio Mastropietro.
Tel: 0942 6400, fax: 0942
642 020.
Great views. 323
rooms, garden, pool.
Not suitable for dis-
abled or older guests
due to its position.
€€€€

San Pietro
Via L. Rizzo.
Tel: 0942 36081, fax: 0942
37012.
Comfortable and with
private beach. Open
Easter–end Oct. €€

Silemi Park
Via Silemi 1.
Tel: 0942 36228.
www.parkhotelsilemi.com

Holiday hotel. Private
beach, pool, garden.
Open Easter–end Oct.
€€

Milazzo

This is the port for the
Aeolian Islands connec-
tions. Milazzo is not a
particularly panoramic
or interesting town, but
it is convenient for an
overnight stop if you
plan to cross to the
islands.

Petit
Via dei Mille 37.
Tel: 090 9286 784.
www.petithotel.it
A friendly, attractive
hotel opposite the
harbour, with an eco-
friendly outlook: recent
renovation work used
only natural materials in
the refurbishing of the
nine rooms. Good
restaurant using
organic ingredients.
€€€

Riviera Lido
Via Panoramica.
Tel: 0909 283 457.
www.hotelrivieralido.it
Garden, private beach,
parking. Some rooms
offer a sea view. €€€

PRICE CATEGORIES

For a double room in
high season:
€ = less than €100
€€ = €100–180
€€€ = €180–250
€€€€ = €250–400
€€€€€ = over €400

BELOW: Messina, looking towards Torre Faro.

AEOLIAN ISLANDS (ISOLE EOLIE)

The islands have a number of *pensioni/locande* but you should expect to have full board – this is the custom here. The islanders are keen to let rooms to tourists and will greet each ferry.

Alicudi

Ericusa
Via Regina Elena. Tel: 0909 889 902. www.alicudihotel.it
Basic but fine accommodation on water's edge. 21 rooms. Half- or full-board only during peak season. Closed Oct–May. €

Filicudi

Phenicusa
Via Porto. Tel: 0909 889 9946. www.hotelphenicusa.com
The 34 rooms are a bit run down but those facing the sea have a superb view. Breakfast not included. Open May–end Sept. €
La Canna
Contrada Rosa 43. Tel: 0909 889 956. www.la cannahotel.it
Located above the harbour, the best position in Filicudi with fine views. The rooms are cosy and stylish, all overlooking the sea. Reservation is recommended. Closed mid-Nov–Dec. €€

Lípari

Villa Meligunis
Via Marte 7. Tel: 0909 812 426. www.villameligunis.it
Villa near the sea and the centre of Lípari. 32 rooms. Panoramic terrace. €€€
Augustus
Via Ausonia 16. Tel: 0909 811 232. www.villaaugustus.it
Classic villa with garden. Comfortable. €€€
Carasco
Porto delle Genti. Tel: 0909 811 605. www.carasco.it
Popular hotel with its own private rocky beach and excellent views. 89 rooms. Open Easter–end Oct. €€
Diana Brown
Vico Himera 3.
Tel: 090 981 2584. www.dianabrown.it
Run by a Sicilian-South African couple, this friendly B&B has seven rooms with self-catering facilities and a lovely roof terrace. €
Gattopardo Park
Viale Diana.
Tel: 0909 811 035. www.gattopardoparkhotel.it
Near the centre of Lípari, an 18th-century villa and bungalows. 53 rooms. Open Mar–Oct. €€€
Giardino sul Mare
Via Maddalena 65.
Tel: 0909 811 004. www.giardinosulmare.it
On the sea and not far from the centre of Lípari. With swimming pool and direct access to sea. €€€
Oriente
Via Marconi 35.
Tel: 0909 811 493. www.hotelorientelipari.it
Lots of character. 32 rooms. Garden setting. €€
La Filadelfia
Via M.F. Profilio.
Tel: 0909 812 795. www.lafiladelfia.it
Basic 3-star hotel with simple rooms; pool. €€
Poseidon
Via Ausonia 7.
Tel: 0909 812 876. www.hotelposeidonlipari.com
Small rooms but welcoming service. €€

Panarea

Cincotta
Via San Pietro. Tel: 0909 83014. www.hotelcincotta.it
On water's edge with fine terraces and pool. €€€€
Lisca Bianca
Via Lani 1. Tel: 0909 83004. www.liscabianca.it
With 25 rooms, beach and pool. Large garden and balconies to each room. Open Apr–end Oct. €€€
Hycesia
Via San Pietro. Tel: 0909 83041. www.hycesia.it
With 8 rooms and garden. €€€
Tesoriero
Via Lani-San Pietro. Tel: 0909 83098. www.hoteltesoriero.it
Overlooks the sea. €€€

Salina

Bellavista
Via Risorgimento 8, Santa Marina Salina. Tel: 0909 843 009. www.hotelbellavista.me.it
On the sea with verandas and views. Open Apr–Oct. €€€
Signum
Via Scalo 15, at Malfa. Tel: 0909 844 222. www.hotelsignum.it
Sited near beautiful cliffs. €€€€
Mamma Santina
Via Sanità 40, S. Marina Salina. Tel: 0909 843 054. www.mammasantina.it
Luxurious hotel in the centre of Salina. Pool. Open end Mar–mid-Sept. €€€

Strómboli

La Sirenetta
Via Marina 33.
Tel: 0909 86025.

www.lasirenetta.it
Elegant with its own nightclub and pool. 55 rooms. Open Mar–Oct. €€€
La Sciara Residence
Via Soldato Cincotta.
Tel: 0909 86004. www.lasciara.it
A comfortable hotel, one of Strómboli's best. 62 rooms, friendly service. Open May–end Oct. €€€€
Miramare
Via Nunziante 3.
Tel: 0909 86047. www.miramarestromboli.it
Basic but smart. Open Apr–Oct. €€
Petrusa
Via Vittorio Emanuele 13.
Tel: 0909 86045. www.hotelvillapetrusa.it
Some distance from the port, with pleasant garden. €€

Vulcano

Les Sables Noirs
Località Porto Ponente.
Tel: 0909 850.
Luxury seafront hotel near the black-sand beach. Restaurant. Open Easter–end Oct. €€€€
Garden Vulcano
Località Porto Ponente.
Tel: 0909 985 3265. www.hotelgardenvulcano.com
Old-fashioned hotel in exotic gardens, owned by a retired sea-captain who has decorated the rooms with his "treasures". Open Apr–Oct. €€

OTHER PLACES TO STAY

VILLAS

Villas are a popular alternative to hotels in Cefalù, Taormina, Mondello, Castellammare del Golfo and the more salubrious coastal and mountain resorts. As an independent traveller, it is difficult to book villas on the spot since most are reserved well in advance or have tie-ins with foreign agents. As a result, holiday villas tend to be booked as packages through travel agencies and holiday companies in your country of origin.

RURAL HOLIDAYS

Agriturismo describes a holiday stay in the countryside on a working farm whose cuisine is locally produced. (This is distinct from "rural tourism" – which can mean a bungalow or an apartment in a rural location.) It can offer an interesting alternative to a hotel-based holiday and provides a real opportunity for contact with Sicilians and a traditional way of life. You can stay a night or two or, on some of the larger farmsteads where they offer small apartments, stay much longer and use the place for a self-catering holiday. This alternative is popular for families with children.

Most *agriturismo* locations are, naturally enough, in small villages or out in the country. Some can be booked through internet websites, others simply by following the signs and driving up to the door. The following three websites offer illustrated choices:
www.agriturismo-sicilia.com
www.agriturist.it
www.agriturismoonline.com

The *agriturismo* sector isn't yet sophisticated or internationally minded, and it can be hard to make bookings unless you have a certain knowledge of Italian. It also helps to know some basic Italian when staying at these places, although some families speak a little English (certainly the children do) and all are so welcoming that sign-language becomes part of the enjoyment.

CAMPING

There are around 100 official campsites in Sicily, the majority on the coast. The sites are ranked from 1- to 4-star according to the facilities they offer: 1-star sites are basic, 4-star luxurious. Hot water may not always be available. Some sites cram in large numbers at the height of the season. Many sites will also provide sleeping bag space for those without tents.

Prices are reasonable and vary from €10 to €20 per night per person plus a contribution for all utilities that varies according to the standard of the site. Prices may vary greatly between the different provinces. In the summer, sites may be full – or closed if trade is slack.

Camping rough is frowned upon, and is illegal in the national parks. In summer, beware of starting fires which can be dangerous and destructive.

YOUTH HOSTELS

Youth hostels in Sicily have a tendency to be closed except at the height of season when they are full of school parties. The private hostel in Siracusa is the most reliable and generally the most pleasant. There are backpackers' hostels in the main towns. After booking, be sure to confirm by fax.

Lípari

Baia Unci
Via Castello 17.
Tel: 090 981 1540.
www.liparicasevacanze.it
No reservations during Aug. Midnight curfew. Lock-out system operates during the day. Closed Nov–Mar.

Nicolosi

Ostello della Gioventù Etna
Via della Quercia 15.
Tel/fax: 095 791 4686.
Only suitable for Etna excursions.

Siracusa

Lol Hostel
Via Francesco Crispi 92.
Tel: 0931 465 088.
www.lolhostel.com
Clean and relaxed; four beds per room.

BELOW: rural areas are ideal for family holidays.

A CTIVITIES

THE ARTS, NIGHTLIFE, FESTIVALS, SHOPPING AND SPORT

THE ARTS

Theatre and Music

There is a wealth of artistic activity in Sicily. Most of the provincial capitals have their own theatre or opera house where touring companies appear. Catania and Palermo have their own companies and present complete seasons of opera and ballet in their major theatres as well as musical and theatrical events. In both Palermo and Catania opera tickets are hard to find.

In summer virtually every province stages some form of cultural event, from film festivals to opera and ballet, classical music and theatre to art exhibitions. Many include internationally known companies and artistes. All theatrical performances are in Italian.

Palermo

Teatro Massimo Piazza Giuseppe Verdi. Tel: 091 605 3111; www.teatromassimo.it. The city opera house. Opera and ballet.
Teatro al Massimo Piazza Verdi 9. Tel: 091 589 575; www.teatro almassimo.it. Drama, comedy.
Teatro Metropolitan Viale Strasburgo 356. Tel: 091 688 6532; www.teatrometropolitan.it. Drama,

ballet, classical music.

Catania

Teatro Massimo Bellini Via Perrotta 12. Tel: 095 730 6111; www.teatromassimobellini.it. Opera, classical music and ballet.
Villa Bellini Concerts and other open-air events in the gardens.

Erice

Erice stages the summer Settimana di Musica Medievale e Rinascimentale (Medieval and Renaissance music festival) in its lovely churches. For details, contact Erice tourist office, Via T. Guarrisi, tel: 0923 869 388.

Classical Drama

Sicily's classical theatres often return to their original function as great settings for ancient Greek drama. The season runs during May and June, with different dramatic cycles performed in the traditional Greek amphitheatres.
Siracusa is home to the Istituto Nazionale del Drama Antico (Institute of Classical Drama) so has home-grown talent to display in the great Greek tragedies. The dramas are produced in the Teatro Greco in May and June in alternate years.
Segesta stages classical and contemporary dramas in its Greek Theatre in odd-numbered

years, alternating with Siracusa. **Taormina**'s Greco-Roman theatre is the venue for an annual festival in July and August which includes classical drama as well as opera, dance and music.

Puppet Theatre

Traditional plays featuring puppets can be seen in Acireale, Catania, Palermo and Siracusa.

Palermo

Associazione Figli d'Arte Cuticchio Via Bara all'Olivella 95. Tel: 091 323 400. Perhaps the last generation of an old puppeteering family. They put on modernised, shortened versions of traditional puppet theatre. Mimmo Cuticchio is one of the few remaining amazing recitors of the *cuntastorie*.
Opera dei Pupi Via Collegio di Maria 17. Tel: 091 814 6971. Two or three shows weekly at 5.30pm.
Museo delle Marionette Via Butera 1. Tel: 091 328 060; www.museomarionettepalermo.it. Free shows in summer: check with museum for details.

Monreale

Munna Via Kennedy 10. Puppet performances on Sun in summer.

TRANSPORT

ACCOMMODATION

ACTIVITIES

A – Z

LANGUAGE

Acireale

Cooperativa E. Magri Corso Umberto 113. Tel: 095 604 521; www.teatropupimacri.it.
Turi Grasso Via Nazionale 95. Tel: 095 764 8035.

Siracusa

Piccolo Teatro dei Pupi Via della Giudecca 17. Tel: 0931 465 540; www.pupari.com.
Traditional puppet shows are staged here several times a week. Check the website for details.

NIGHTLIFE

Compared with much of Italy, Sicilian nightlife is somewhat introverted, centred on restaurants and private parties rather than mass discos. Even so, the advent of tourism has led to an explosion of bars and clubs on the coastal resorts. Cefalù and Taormina are the main centres for nightlife in summer, revolving around piano bars and the more sophisticated night-clubs.

Why not Palermo, Catania or Siracusa? This has a lot to do with the special status of inter-national tourism that Cefalù and Taormina have achieved, both offering visitors a certain level of security from the activities of petty criminals at night.

An active and interesting cul-tural life in the big cities like Catania and Palermo has taken shape, bringing people back to concerts, cinemas and theatres, and thereby encouraging the opening of new pubs, caffès, piano bars and restaurants. On summer evenings there is a wide choice of events of all kinds. Some events are free or at a token fee.

Although there are no major rock venues, open-air concerts take place in Catania and other cities. Evening entertainment often ties in with local cultural festivals.

Passeggiata

The passeggiata (stroll) is an Italian institution that finds favour in Sicily. Mondello and Taormina are the places to see a nightly parade of this year's Italian fashion. If white is the summer colour, then everyone is in white. If it is orange, then...

On summer nights, the off-shore islands come alive. In particular, Ustica, the Egadi Islands (especially Lévanzo) and the Aeolian Islands (especially Lípari) are awash with strollers.

Young Nightlife

The small coastal resorts in Palermo and Messina provinces have lots of clubs catering to the young. Rough and ready video bars and short-lived clubs come and go in Giardini-Naxos (near Taormina) and on most of the north coast towns. In most towns, the neighbourhood pizze-ria or gelateria is the focus of attention – and a motorbike-riding crowd. When a disco is popular, do not expect sophistication.

Sophisticated Nightlife

For sophistication, try the piano bars in all the main resorts. In order to fit in, it is best to dress elegantly. Even here, there is a wide range of wealth and style. The resort of Mondello and, par-ticularly, the Aeolian island of Panarea, offer spots for the ostentatious jet set.

City Nightspots

Palermo

High society in Palermo is relatively closed. Much social-ising takes place at private functions, often taking over a nightclub or restaurant for the night. Even so, in the early evening, the upmarket quarter around Viale della Libertà wit-nesses a passeggiata and chic caffès are busy. In summer, city bars, however, tend to close early and by 11pm the city can seem dead.

CLUBS AND DISCOS
There are several in Viale Strasburgo, a middle-class residential quarter.
Kandinsky-Florio Discesa Ton-nara 4 (on the coast at Arenella, near the Hotel Villa Igiea).
Calembour Via Gerbasi. Disco-dance and Latin American.
Biergarten Viale Regione Sicil-iana 6469. Techno music and theme nights.
Gorky Club Via Ugo La Malfa 95.
Kursaal Kalhesa Foro Italico 21. An elegant café, restaurant, wine bar and club in a beautiful set-ting, within ancient stone walls. Attracts a lively young crowd.

PIANO BARS
Palermo's many piano bars include:
Drive Bar Via del Bersagliere 70. Blumix Via Venezia 62. Live music every night.
Grand Hotel et des Palmes Via Roma 396.
Malaluna Via Resurrezione.
Villa Igiea Salita Belmonte 43. Out of town but the undoubted star.

Mondello

Some socialising is a question of private parties in summer villas. However, **Villa Boscogrande** (Via Tommaso Natale 91, tel: 091 244 022) is public, a club set in a dreamy palazzo where Visconti filmed scenes for The Leopard. Mondello is also an inexpensive youth hang-out.

Three popular piano bars are:
Mondello Palace Viale Principe di Scalea 2.
Thula Club Viale M di Savoia 102.
Villa Verde Via Piano Gallo 36.

Catania

Catania's nightlife is fairly diverse, revolving around bars and clubs.

Popular young locations are:
Gelaterie del Duomo, Piazza del Duomo; **Bar Centrale**, Via Etna

121; and **Pasticceria Caprice**, Via Etnea 30. These are the places for *gelati* (ice-creams) and *granite* (sorbets).

CLUBS

Some worth investigating are:
Empire Via Milazzo. Tel: 095 375 684.
Divina Via Carnazza 53. Tel: 095 399 631.
Il Banacher Via Vampolieri 66 (on the SS 114 near Aci Castello). One of the best-known open-air discos.
Medea Club Via Medea 2.
Villa Romeo Via Platemone 20. Latin American music.

Cefalù

Like Taormina, Cefalù's favoured clubs tend to come and go. Piano bars like **Kentia** are popular (Via Nicola Botta 4, tel: 0921 423 801).

Erice

Despite its tiny size, Erice has a number of piano bars and nightclubs, such as **Blu Notte**, in Via San Rocco, while **Boccaccio**, in Via dei Misteri, is more of a disco.

Siracusa

Much of Siracusa's nightlife is really *caffè* life on the island of Ortigia. Most *caffès* are on Fontana Aretusa, Porta Marina and around the Duomo. Lungomare Alfeo has some lively bars. For magical live entertainment, the Greek theatre is the stage for classical drama *(see page 283)*. Contact the tourist office.

Taormina

A sophisticated evening is guaranteed in the bars and restaurants of Taormina's hotels. To see more, check the latest clubs locally; clubs change hands at an amazing rate. Among the more enduring are:
Panasia Beach Via Nazionale, Contrada Spisone. www.panasia beach.it.
Re di Bastoni Corso Umberto I 120. Tel: 0942 23037.
Wunderbar Caffè Piazza IX Aprile. Tel: 0942 625302.

CALENDAR OF EVENTS

January/February

Agrigento: Almond Fair (runs January to March).
Agrigento: International Folklore Festival (February).
Palermo: Opera Season continues, Teatro Massimo.

March/April

Catania: Etna Bicycle Race (April).
Catania: Drama, classical music and jazz season.
Palermo: Drama, opera and classical season continues.

May

Caltanissetta: Livestock and Crafts Fair.
Catania: Sicilian Theatre in the World.
Palermo: Panormus Veteran Car Rally
Palermo: Trade Fair (held between May and June)
Siracusa and **Segesta**: Classical comedies and tragedies in the Greek theatres. The season runs May–June. (Siracusa in even-numbered years, Segesta in odd years.)
Taormina: Folk festival and display of Sicilian carts.

June

Catania: Musica Estate. Concert, dance and theatre season lasts until October.
Erice: Estate Ericina. Summer season, including competitions for the most flowery courtyards.
Siracusa and **Segesta**: Classical comedies and tragedies in Greek theatres.
Taormina: June–mid-September. Taormina Arte, an international festival of cinema, music, opera, ballet and theatre held in the Greek theatre.

July

Palermo: Palermo di scena. Music, theatre, cinema, ballet through the whole summer.

Agrigento: Settimana Pirandelliana. A week celebrating Pirandello's plays in drama, film and debate.
Catania: Estate a Catania. Music, theatre and cinema in summer.
Cefalù: Estate Cefaludese. Music and summer puppet shows.
Enna: Estate Ennese. Summer in Enna, including recitals and concerts in the city castle. Also the Grand Prix del Mediterraneo at Lake Pergusa.
Erice: Festival of Medieval Music, held in town churches.
Palermo: Targa Florio, International Sicily Rally.
Siracusa: Summer season of opera, music and ballet.
Taormina: Prestigious International Film Festival.

August

Agrigento: Persephone Festival.
Enna: Summer festival continues.
Siracusa: Summer season continues, with music and ballet.
Taormina: Taormina Arte continues.
Palermo: Palermo di Scena continues.
Catania: Estate a Catania continues.

September

Catania: Bellini International Music Prize. Teatro Massimo.
Milo: Table Grapes and Etna Wine Fair.
Palermo: Sicily International Tennis Championships.
Taormina: the last month of the Taormina Arte season.
Palermo: Festival di Palermo sul Novecento. A month of theatre, music, video and cinema.

October/November

Catania: Concert season starts in the Teatro Massimo Bellini.
Catania: Classical concert seasons of the Associazione Musicale Etnea and Lyceum Club start, until June.
Catania: Jazz concert season of Associazione Catania Jazz e del Brass starts, runs till June.

Catania: Italian theatre season opens in the Teatro Verga, Teatro Musco and in the Metropolitan, Ambasciatori, Piccolo Teatro and Nuovo Teatro.
Palermo: Festival di Palermo sul novecento continues.
Monreale: Sacred organ music in the cathedral.

December

Caltagirone: Biennale of Sicilian Ceramics.
Palermo: Fiera del Mediterraneo (Trade Fair).
Palermo: Opera season (Teatro Massimo), runs until May.
Zafferana Etnea: Award of the Brancati literature prize.

SHOPPING

Sicily is not as sophisticated as mainland Italy, nor as wealthy. Major Italian fashion designers are represented in some of the boutiques, but few designers have opened their own premises. However, the major Italian fashion chains are here (that is, not international brands), so good quality Italian clothes and shoes are readily available at reasonable prices.

Pottery, puppets and papyrus represent the best of traditional Sicilian handicrafts, along with jewellery made with coral. Like some of the food and drink (cheeses, chocolates and liqueurs, for example), these make excellent gifts or souvenirs.

Shopping Hours

Normal weekday hours are 9am–1pm and 4–7.30pm. All shops except those selling food are normally closed on Monday mornings, some may be closed all day. Many food shops (except supermarkets) close on Wednesday afternoons. In tourist resorts like Taormina the shops are open seven days a week.

Antiques

Siracusa is renowned for its reproductions of Classical Greek coins. Palermo has a daily antiques market near the Cappucini Catacombs. There are some real treasures here, but also plenty of fakes and rubbish. In Palermo a number of shops around Corso Umberto sell a mixture of antiques and bric-a-brac.

Books

For second-hand books (including lavish books on art and history), try the Quattro Canti area in Palermo, especially the university quarter and Via Roma.

Sellerio publish beautiful books on the island's culture, literature, history and art, available from **Libreria Sellerio** di Sellerio Olivia, Viale Regina Elena 59, Palermo, tel: 091 684 1612. **Novecento**, also a respected Palermitan publisher, is based at Via Siracusa 7/a, tel: 091 625 6814.

The classic **Feltrinelli** bookshop, one of a successful chain, is in Palermo at Via Maqueda 395, tel: 091 587 785. It offers a small selection of recent best-selling books in foreign languages, as do a few smaller bookshops in Catania, Siracusa and Taormina.

Clothes

For fashionable clothes, the best bets are Viale della Libertà and Via Ruggero Settimo in Palermo, Via Etnea in Catania, and Corso Umberto in Taormina. Here you will find designer clothes from Valentino, Coveri, Gucci and Armani. For cheaper shopping in Palermo try Via Maqueda (the continuation of Viale della Libertà) or Via Roma. In Catania try the side streets off Via Etnea.

Jewellery

Coral and gold jewellery is made and sold on the island. The best is obtainable from jewellers in Palermo, Catania or Taormina's main shopping areas. Fairly expensive craft jewellery is sold in Cefalù, in shops off Corso Ruggero. Cheaper coral pieces can be bought from tourist shops and stalls in resorts. Coral is a protected marine substance, its use covered by international law.

Around Etna necklaces and bracelets made from lava are a tourist novelty not to all tastes.

Painted Carts

Models of traditional Sicilian carts (see pages 198–9) are sold all over the island. In Aci Sant'Antonio (Catania Province) craftsmen will make specially commissioned carts.

Papyrus

Papermaking and writing and drawing on papyrus are traditional crafts around Siracusa. Stalls and shops sell inexpensive examples, ranging from copies of Egyptian designs to portraits of you while you wait.

Pottery and Ceramics

Pottery, one of Sicily's glories, has been around for a long time. Kilns from the 3rd century BC have been found around Gela, Siracusa and Catania as well as on Mozia. When the Arabs arrived in Sicily in 827, they introduced glazing techniques used in Persia, Syria and Egypt. Tin-glazed pottery, or majolica, appeared in the Trápani area in 1309.

The devastating 1693 earthquake destroyed much of eastern Sicily as well as razing the ceramics workshops of Caltagirone to the ground. As market demands still had to be satisfied, quality gave way to quantity.

At the end of the 19th century the Sicilian market, led by the Bourbons, became flooded with imported Neapolitan wares. To stem the flow, a pottery factory was set up in San Stefano di Camastra.

Caltagirone ceramics have always been famous for their instantly recognisable animal and floral designs in dark blue and copper green with touches of yellow. Look out for the tall *alberelli*, jars with nipped-in waists once used for storing dry drugs, and the vast selection of heads depicting characters from Sicilian history that are used as ornaments of flower pots. Also consider acquiring painted tiles, sturdy vases and chunky little stoups. Some of the newer and more individualistic styles are also highly attractive.

San Stefano ceramics As a ceramics centre, San Stefano di Camastra comes into sight behind a jumble of crockery on the Messina–Palermo road. Tiers of dishes, soup tureens and fruit bowls rise at ever increasing heights on each bend in the road, while cracked platters along the roadside testify to cars that have come a cropper among the cauldrons and cake stands.

High-quality local clay and fine workmanship have ensured the town's fame. Styles are very mixed but the authentic ware has a rustic look and feel. Look out, too, for lovely wall tiles decorated with smiling suns and local saints.

Puppets *(Pupi)*

Puppetry's main traditions are in Palermo and some of the best models are still made there.

Vincenzo Argento (Corso Vittorio Emanuele 445, Palermo, tel: 091 611 3680) continues a 160-year-old family tradition. He will make you a *paladino* (paladin or knight) to order in his tiny workshop. After carving the wooden body, he solders on the copper armour and creates the costume with the help of his wife. Open 7.30am–8pm. Argento also organises puppet shows in Palazzo Asmundo, Via Pietro Novelli.

In Taormina, **Francesco and Sabatino del Popolo Lampuri** (Via Luigi Pirandello 51, tel: 0942 626 043) sell inexpensive

puppets, with finishing touches added by the family.

Rugs

Erice has a tradition of hand-woven rugs which can be bought in many of the shops there.

Straw and Cane

Monreale produces traditional straw and cane goods which are sold by the artisans themselves.

Wine

It is possible to visit the following wine growers and to buy directly from them. Not all speak English, but most do. It is advisable to telephone to arrange a visit beforehand. They will explain how to find them.

Az. Agr. Vecchio Samperi, Marco De Bartoli, C/da Fornara Samperi 292, Marsala. Tel: 0923 962 093.

Cantine Piero Colosi, Via Militare Ritiro 23, Messina. Tel: 090 53852.

Casa Vin, Duca di Salaparuta, Via Nazionale SS 113, Casteldaccia (Palermo Province). Tel: 091 945 201.

COS, Giusto Occhipinti, Piazza del Popolo 34, 97019 Vittoria. Tel: 0932 876 145.

Loc. Malfa, Isola di Salina. (The island of Salina). Especially for Malvasia.

Tenuta di Donnafugata, Loc. Marzaporro, Contessa Entellina (Palermo Province). Tel: 0923 724 245.

Tenuta San Michele, Barone Scammacca del Murgo, Via Zafferana 13 (Catania Province). Tel: 095 950 520.

Terre di Ginestra, Piano Piraino, 90040 San Cipirello (Palermo Province). Tel: 091 857 6767.

Marsala: Florio (now owned by Martini) and Pellegrino lead the market in terms of sales. Wine-tasting (including a film and a short guided tour of the cellars) is possible at the bigger producers *(stabilmenti)*.

● **Pellegrino**, 39 Via Fante, Marsala. Tel: 0923 719 911.
● **Stabilmento Florio**, V. Vincenzo Florio 1. Tel: 0923 781 111. The Florio staff are particularly amenable to visits and offer an interesting and enjoyable tour of the cellars (closed Fri pm). Their Vergine Marsala is best.

SPORT

Spectator sports

Cycling

The round Etna bicycle race is held in April. It is an interesting event to take part in, but perhaps more fun is to be had standing on the sidelines watching and enjoying the scenery.

Motor Racing

Lago Pergusa at Enna. It does not host Formula One events, but races are normally held there at least once a month.

Participant sports

Diving

Sicily's coasts are rich in flora and fauna. Both snorkelling and scuba diving are popular. The island of Ustica is the haunt of scuba fans. Its coastline is protected and offers spectacular diving in deep water. There are the remains of a wreck visible in one spot. The Egadi islands, particularly Marettimo, are also a favourite with divers: they have crystal clear, clean, deep water. Tanks can be filled on most islands, and several, including Ustica, also have decompression chambers available.

Snorkelling can be enjoyed by anyone who can swim, and it is well worth mastering the art since along Sicily's coasts it gives instant access to an exciting and different world. It is particularly worthwhile wherever there are rocky shorelines, which

TRANSPORT   ACCOMMODATION   A – Z   ACTIVITIES   A – Z   LANGUAGE means the north and the islands. The area around Isola Bella, Taormina, is good for snorkellers.

Golf

Il Picciolo Golf Club is an 18-hole, par 72 course on the slopes of the ever-present Mount Etna. The clubhouse used to be a family farmhouse. www.ilpicciolo golfclub.com

Le Madonie Golf Club, near Cefalù, is an 18-hole, par 72 course overlooking the Tyrrhenean Sea on one side and the Madonie Hills nature reserve on the other. Villas can be rented. www.lemadoniegolfclub.com

Facilities at both courses include a driving range, pitching and chipping green. For more information: www.sicilygolf.com

Gyms

There are a surprising number of gyms in Sicily; it has become part of the lifestyle here as it has everywhere. Most gyms will accept guest visitors. Many larger hotels also have a gym facility, though these may be limited. Ask your hotel or tourist office for additional information.

Hiking

Walks range from peaceful coastal strolls through the nature reserve of Lo Zingaro on Capo San Vito (Palermo Province) to treks in the Nebrodi and Madonie mountains. Walks through Sicily's volcanic landscapes are always popular. The Aeolian Islands offer magnificent unspoilt coastal walks.

The excitement of walking on Etna exerts an obvious pull, but it is not wise to do so without a guide *(see page 223)*. Etna Trekking, Via Roma 334, Linguaglossa (tel: 095 647 877; www.etnatrekking.com) is an agency that organises hikes, or call the information office in Linguaglossa, tel: 095 643 094.

Riding

Horse-riding is not really a traditional sport in Sicily: mules rather than horses have always been used to carry loads across the mountains. Nevertheless, riding is catching on and there are several stables from which horses can be hired, particularly in the Nebrodi and Madonie mountains, where trekking over longer distances is growing in popularity. The following are some of the stables in Palermo province:

Balestrate: Fattoria Manostalla, C. da Manostalla, tel: 091 878 7033.

Gratteri: Fattoria Pianetti, C. da Pianetti, tel: 0921 421 890.

Montelepre: Don Vito, Piano Aranci, tel: 091 878 4111.

Sailing

Palermo province has lovely beaches not too far from the city of Palermo. Many have exclusive yacht clubs as well as a sophisticated nightlife. West of Palermo, the stretch of coast from Mondello and Capo Gallo to Isole delle Femmine is a standard yacht excursion. East of Palermo, the stretch of coast from Romagnolo to Capo Zafferano makes a pleasant boat trip.

The wild stretch of northern coastline from Capo d'Orlando to Cefalù is one of the loveliest in Sicily, particularly near the lagoons below Tindari.

Skiing

Ski on Etna, on black snow with a view of orange trees? Not quite. You would need a very strong telescope to see the orange trees, but they are there. Etna is frequently snow-capped all summer, and the skiing season normally runs from December to March. The snow really is black, at least in patches, where ash, dust and lava from minor eruptions have blown across it. In places, "hot" rocks, those which are still cooling, melt the snow and then stand out through it like lumps of coal.

The views are spectacular, and perhaps there is an element of bravado in the idea of skiing on a live volcano. Every now and then, Etna really does come to life again, and the skiing areas have to close because of the danger from ash or lava flows. Check that your insurance covers you for this risk.

MAIN SKI RESORTS:

Linguaglossa is on the northern side of Etna. The *Autobus della Neve* (snow bus) runs every Sunday between January and April from Piano Provenzano, organised by the *Ferrovia Circumetnea (see page 217)*. General information from the Pro Loco, Piazza Annunziata, tel: 095 643 094.

Nicolosi (Rifugio Sapienza) is on the southern side of Etna, above Zafferana Etnea; the altitude is slightly higher than the northern side. For information on the pistes, *Etna Guide*, tel: 095 791 4755.

Both resorts are suitable for intermediate and expert skiers; Linguaglossa is the better choice for beginners.

Swimming

It is not a problem to find somewhere to swim, whether in the sea, lakes or rivers. The smaller islands offer the cleanest and clearest water *(see Diving, above)*. There may be plenty of sea but patches of it are severely polluted (the coasts around Augusta, Gela, Termini Imerese are nobody's choice).

Tennis

Where there are tennis clubs (and there are not many) they are open only to members and their guests. However, many hotels have well-kept tennis courts.

Windsurfing

Surf boards can be hired locally. The south coast is the best place for surfing because of the strong dry wind, but conditions in Mondello's bay are also adequate.

A - Z

A HANDY SUMMARY OF PRACTICAL INFORMATION, ARRANGED ALPHABETICALLY

A dmission Charges

Museum and gallery charges vary, but the average is between €6 and €8. Minor exhibitions may charge less or, when sponsored, be free. Most state and civic galleries offer free entrance or special rates to EU citizens under 18 or over 65. A document of proof of age may be asked for.

B udgeting for a Trip

Prices generally match those in Italy; the island is not much cheaper except, perhaps, when eating out and shopping in vegetable markets. The move to the euro from the lira gave just about every commercial enterprise the opportunity to raise its profit margins. However, when compared with many other European countries some items seem inexpensive, and certainly many products are very good value – clothes, for example, and wine.

Mid-range hotels charge around €130 a night for a double room, and you can pay more than €400 at a luxury hotel. But there are good bed & breakfast establishments, and the spread of *agriturismo* provides inexpensive farmhouses for people exploring with a car.

Restaurant prices have risen too. In touristy areas you'll find a three-course dinner with wine will set you back €40 a head, but explore the neighbourhood streets, where simple trattorie with equally delicious food and wine charge much less.

Fuel costs have risen in line with rising costs across Europe but public transport remains comfortably inexpensive. Single tickets on the bus and metro, for example, cost €1 for 75 minutes, including any changes you need to make. There are also passes which give unlimited travel.

Business Hours

Shops are generally open 9am–1pm and 4–7.30pm. Except for those in tourist resorts, shops are closed on Sundays. Food shops and fuel stations may also close on Wednesday afternoons. In cities, other shops are closed on Monday mornings.
Bars and restaurants are legally obliged to close one day a week: a notice indicates which day.
Banks are open Mon–Fri 8.30am–1.30pm. Some also open in the afternoon 2.30–4pm or 3–4.30pm. Changing money

TRANSPORT
ACCOMMODATION
ACTIVITIES
A – Z
LANGUAGE

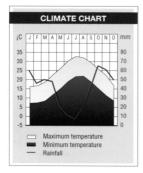

CLIMATE CHART

☐ Maximum temperature
■ Minimum temperature
Rainfall

can be a slow operation. Allow plenty of time and ideally visit in the morning. Banks may close early the day before a public holiday. If the holiday falls on a Tuesday or a Thursday, many offices may also close on the preceding Monday or the following Friday. This is known as a *ponte*, bridging the gap. ATMs are widespread, but may not be available in the smallest villages.

C limate

Sicily is renowned for its sunshine. The hottest months are July and August (averaging 28°C/85°F) when high temperatures are intensified by a rise in humidity and lack of rain. The coldest month is February (10°C/50°F).

Along the coasts, winters are short and generally mild. The Etna ski resorts are usually open December to March. Temperatures remain comfortable into May or June, but the landscape begins to brown.

C lothes to Bring

You will need light clothing during the hot summer months. But remember that many churches and cathedrals will not admit visitors with bare legs (i.e. no short skirts or shorts) or bare shoulders (you may be required to cover them with a scarf or shawl). In spring (April and May) and autumn (October and Novem-

ber), you will need light clothes but also a summer jacket or sweater for evenings.

Between December and March, it is advisable to bring warmer clothes since winter, particularly in the mountainous central areas, can be cold. Hotels and houses tend to be less well heated than is usual in northern climates: indoors is sometimes chillier than out. Mount Etna is often snow-covered in winter, and its lava-based rock requires strong footwear in any season.

Crime and Safety

The main problem for tourists is petty crime: pick-pocketing and bag-snatching (by young criminals known as *scippatori* or *scippi*) together with theft from cars in Palermo, Catania and the historic centre of Siracusa. Most tourist resorts require caution, but Taormina and Cefalù are normally extremely safe. Use common sense and don't flaunt valuables.

Expect the police to have a casual attitude to petty crime and a slightly suspect attitude to a woman on her own. Expect, also, to have to prove who you are and where you are staying before even beginning to embark on your tale of woe. In the event of a serious crime, contact your country's consulate or embassy as well as the Carabinieri. Following that, try the Sicilian approach: summon the most influential Sicilian you know on the island and request advice. Having friends in the right places helps.

If you are robbed: Report it as soon as possible to the local police. You will need a copy of the declaration in order to claim on your insurance. Even more importantly, it is highly likely that part of your property will be returned, often very rapidly. There is apparently an unspoken agreement between police and thieves: provided documents and credit cards are returned and no violence is used, the police apply minimum effort to arresting

those responsible. So although your camera, cash and traveller's cheques have gone for good, the thieves may call the police within hours to report the whereabouts of your passport, credit cards, exposed film and possibly even your empty wallet.

Danger Zones: Palermo, Catania and Ortigia in Siracusa are the most likely places for *scippi*. Avoid the station areas of Palermo and Catania, and also the myriad unlit back streets of Palermo's historic centre after dark. La Kalsa in Palermo is fairly safe during the day, but should be avoided by night. Also avoid the San Cristoforo area of Catania (behind the castle) at all times and be wary in the portside fish markets. In Siracusa, by all means visit the characteristic restaurants, but steer clear of the Via Nizza port area late at night unless there are plenty of people about. In Mazara del Vallo, explore the Moorish Casbah but ideally in company.

Car Crime: In Catania and Palermo, some *scippatori* specialise in what could be called mobile crime: stealing from "moving" cars. It works like this: you are crawling in a traffic jam. Suddenly a motorbike swerves in front of you. You brake. A youth approaches the car, pulls open the door, grabs whatever is reachable, leaps on the back of the motorbike and is gone. The moral: lock car doors when driving and keep valuables hidden.

Customs Regulations

For European Union citizens: provided goods obtained in the EU are for your personal use there is no further tax to be paid.

For non-EU citizens: the duty-free allowances are 200 cigarettes, 50 cigars, or 3 lb (1,360g) of tobacco; 1 US quart of alcoholic beverages and duty-free gifts worth up to $175.

If you plan to import or export large quantities of goods, or goods of exceptionally high value, contact the Italian Consulate and your own customs authorities beforehand to check on any special regulations which may apply.

The customs authorities are quite active in Sicily, partly to combat smuggling from North Africa, and partly because of the level of Mafia activity and the associated movements of goods and money. But this is unlikely to affect the ordinary tourist.

D isabled Facilities

Like many other countries, Sicily believes it caters for people with disabilities but, in reality, it remains a difficult holiday destination. Most churches, museums and sites have steps, inside and out. Little has been done to create wheelchair access.

Some trains have access arrangements (but check first), as do many city buses. Some have seats reserved for disabled passengers, others have ramps and central areas reserved for wheelchairs. These buses carry the international sign for Accessibility on their front and sides.

A Rome-based association, COIN, offers general information about hotels, galleries, museums, etc. Freephone (in Italy): 800 810 810.

E lectricity

Standard: 220 volts AC, 50 cycles. Connections are either two or three round-pins. Adaptors can be found locally, but it is wiser to carry an international adaptor.

E mbassies & Consulates

IN ROME:
Australian Embassy
Via A. Bosio 5
Tel: 06 852 721
www.italy.embassy.gov.au
Open Mon–Fri 9am–5pm.
Canadian Embassy
Via Zara 30
Tel: 06 0544 43937
www.canada.it
Open Mon–Fri 8.30am–12.30pm
and 1.30–4pm.

Irish Embassy
Piazza Campitelli 3
Tel: 06 697 9121
www.ambasciata-irlanda.it
Open Mon–Fri 10am–12.30pm
and 3–4.30pm.
New Zealand Embassy
Via Clitunno 44
Tel: 06 853 7501
Open Mon–Fri 8.30am– 12.45pm
and 1.45–5pm.
www.nzembassy.com
UK Embassy
Via XX Settembre 80a
Tel: 06 4220 0001
www.britain.it
Open Mon–Fri 9.30am–1.30pm.
US Embassy
Via Vittorio Veneto 119
Tel: 06 46741
www.usembassy.it
Open Mon–Fri 8.30am–noon.

IN NAPLES:
UK Consulate
Via dei Mille 40, Naples
Tel: 081 423 8911.
Open Mon–Fri 9.30am–12.30pm
and 2–4.30pm.
US Consulate
Piazza della Repubblica
Naples; tel: 081 583 8111.
Open Mon–Fri 8am–noon
(8–10am for visas).

Emergency Numbers

Police: 113
Carabinieri: 112
Fire: (Vigili del fuoco is the fire brigade): 115
Ambulance: 115

Entry Requirements

Visas are not required by visitors from EU countries A current passport or valid Identification Card is sufficient documentation for entry. For visitors from the US, Canada, Australia or New Zealand a visa is not required, but a valid passport is essential for entry to be granted for a stay of up to three months. Nationals of most other countries require a visa. This must be obtained in advance from an Italian Embassy or Consulate.

Animal Quarantine: If you want to take a pet you need to have a Pet Passport, or the pet must be micro-chipped and have a vaccination certificate for rabies and an official document stating that the pet is healthy. For further information, contact the Italian Consulate in your country.

G ays and Lesbians

There is little of an organised gay scene in Sicily but attitudes are fairly relaxed and gay magazines are sold at most newsstands.

Taormina is still the focus for the native and foreign gay community. It has several gay clubs and bars, which come and go.
Le Perroquet (Piazza San Domenico. tel: 0942 25311) is currently popular.

For more information, contact **Arci-Gay**, a gay organisation in Palermo, tel: 349 884 5809; email: palermo@arcigay.it.

H ealth and Medical Care

European Union residents are entitled to the same medical treatment as Italians as long as they obtain a European Health Insurance Card (EHIC) before they travel. This covers medical treatment and medicines, although you will have to pay a percentage of the costs. Note that the EHIC does not provide for repatriation in case of illness.

In many areas in summer, there is a Guardia Medica Turistica (tourist emergency medical service) which functions 24 hours a day. Telephone numbers are available from hotels, chemists, tourist offices and local papers.

The Guardia Medica or Pronto Soccorso (first aid) for the area can also help in an emergency.

Lists of duty pharmacists are published in the daily papers (Giornale di Sicilia for Palermo and the west or La Sicilia for Catania and the east). In Palermo and Catania some are open late at night. The duty

TRANSPORT

ACCOMMODATION

ACTIVITIES

A – Z

LANGUAGE

pharmacists will often speak some English.

General emergencies: Dial 113.

Mosquitoes: There are a lot in Sicily, as you will quickly discover if you leave your light on and the window open for any length of time. Slow-burning mosquito repellent rings can be bought cheaply at supermarkets. As effective and less intrusive are the small electrical devices which plug into a standard socket.

Mosquito repellents are available in supermarkets.

Thermal spas: Many islands and resorts offer the chance to wallow in mud baths or take water cures. These are available at Sciacca (Agrigento Province), Castellammare del Golfo (Trápani Province) or on the Egadi and Aeolian Islands.

Water supply: Tap water is safe to drink in most places, but Italians generally prefer to drink mineral water, and this will usually be offered in restaurants. In some places the water supply becomes erratic in summer.

In a few places, particularly in the south of the island, the ground water has become polluted by industrial effluent, and the water from village pumps may not be good to drink. If in doubt, ask the locals. Water supplies marked *Non Potabile* should never be used for drinking.

I nternet

Internet cafés are now opening up everywhere. Ask in a shop selling computers for the nearest link. Their rates vary, but some are cheaper in the late evening. Many local municipal offices have internet rooms alongside their libraries, with modest fees.

L ost Property ·

Items lost in the street are never recovered. But, if you should lose something on a train, it may be handed in. Go to the terminus station left-luggage office and enquire there.

M aps

The Sicilian tourist offices can supply maps which may be adequate if you are staying in one place. If touring, you will certainly need a better map. Very detailed maps are produced by the Touring Club Italia (TCI). One of their maps covers the whole of Sicily together with the islands. The scale is 1:200,000, 1 cm to 2 km. For general purposes, *Insight Flex-iMap Sicily* is laminated for ease of use and durability and contains useful facts and travel information as well as clear cartography.

Magazines

The following are Sicilian publications that may interest visitors.
Sicilia Magazine – a glossy, highly illustrated magazine in Italian and English. It includes articles on art, culture and personalities. It is published in Catania four times a year.
Sicilia Illustrata – this glossy monthly covers Sicilian current affairs, politics and culture.
Kalos – this is a highly illustrated bi-monthly on art and history.
Sikelia – this is an academically oriented journal on Sicilian art, history and culture. It appears in black and white, and is published bi-monthly.
Sicilia Tempo – an economic and political monthly.

Money

The currency in Italy is the euro, written as €. A euro is divided into 100 cents with 1, 2, 5, 20 and 50 cent coins. The euro notes are €5, €10, €20, €50, €100, €200 and €500.

Credit cards: Except in the smaller villages, major credit cards are accepted by shops, hotels and restaurants. They can also be used to pay autostrada tolls. ATMs, the automated cash dispensers (known here as Bancomat), can be found on the outer walls of most banks and are an excellent alternative to the

endless queues that accompany any transaction in a bank.

Changing money: If you have traveller's cheques to cash, look for one of the larger banks. The paperwork is considerable and many smaller banks may even refuse to cash them.

N ewspapers

The main Italian papers *(Corriere della Sera, La Repubblica)* publish southern editions, but the local dailies are more popular.

Il Giornale di Sicilia, Palermo's morning paper, covers the western part of the island and provides a supplement for each of the eastern provinces. It offers the most complete practical listings (timetables, etc).

La Sicilia, Catania's main paper, also has provincial supplements for Siracusa, Ragusa and Enna. It is identified with right of centre politics.

La Gazzetta del Sud is not strictly a Sicilian paper: it is based in Messina and Reggio di Calabria. It is the highest circulation daily in Messina province and is somewhat less parochial than the purely island papers.

P ostal Services

Post Offices are generally open Mon–Fri 8.30am–6pm, with offices in smaller towns closing at 2pm. In Palermo, the main post office in Via Roma (near Piazza Domenico) is open Mon–Sat 8am–6.30pm.

Stamps *(francobolli)* are also available from tobacconists *(tabacchi)* and bars that also sell cigarettes.

The postal service is not renowned for its speed. If you need to send an urgent letter, send it by Posta Prioritaria (ask for the special stamps at the tobacconists and the mail should be posted in the blue pillar boxes not the red ones).

It is possible to have mail sent Posta Restante to main post offices. Letters should be marked *fermo posta*.

Public Holidays

Banks and most shops are closed on the following holidays:
1 January: New Year's Day *(Capodanno)*
6 January: Epiphany *(Befana)*
Easter Monday *(Lunedì di Pasqua)*: variable
25 April: Liberation Day *(Anniversario della Liberazione)*
1 May: May Day *(Festa del Lavoro)*
2 June: Republic Day *(Giorno della Repubblica)*
15 August: August holiday *(Ferragosto)*
1 November: All Saints' Day *(Ognissanti)*
8 December: Feast of the Immaculate Conception *(Immacolata Concezione)*
25 December: Christmas Day *(Natale)*
26 December: Boxing Day *(Santo Stefano)*

R eligious Services

Italy is a Catholic country. The hours of Mass and services vary from city to country village, but Masses are usually held on Saturday afternoon and Sunday. Each church has its own Mass timetable pinned inside its main door. Other denominations may practice their faith without hindrance and have their own services in Palermo and Catania.

T elephones

Telephone boxes take phone cards *(scheda telefonica)*, which you can buy at bars, newspaper kiosks and post offices; some telephone boxes still take coins and those at airports will take credit cards. It is not uncommon to find telephone boxes out of order, particularly in the large cities. More reliable are the public telephones available in many bars and other commercial premises.

For calls within Italy, telephone numbers must be preceded by the area code even if the call is made within the same district.

Mobile telephones work well in Sicily. Remember that if you are using a "home" cellphone to call a number within Sicily you will need to dial the international access code number followed by the local area code (including the initial zero), then the number itself, and that you will be charged an international rate by your provider.
Enquiries:
12 for directory assistance for all of Italy
4176 for international directory enquiries
170 for operator assisted calls
International dialling codes:
To make international calls, dial 00, then the country code
Australia: 61
Canada and US: 1
Ireland: 353
UK: 44
Telephone offices:
In Palermo
Piazza Giulio Cesare: 24 hours.
Via P. Belmonte 92: 8am–8pm.
At the port: 8am–8pm.
At the airport: 8am–10pm.
In Catania
Via A. Longo: 24 hours.
Piazza Giovanni XXIII: 8am–8pm.
At the airport: 8am–8pm.

T elevision and Radio

There are dozens of private radio and TV stations, most of them awful. The commercial radio stations provide a mix of pop and phone-ins. The national radio stations (RAI) include news, current affairs and documentaries, and also, particularly on RAI 3, some classical music.

Reception of the BBC World Service is only possible in the short wave band and not usually good in southern Italy.

National TV stations (which include RAI, with four channels, and seven others) broadcast some local news programmes. Occasionally a local travelogue or documentary makes it onto the local television stations. On the whole, however, the local television is bad to appalling.

If you have children, be aware that Italian private television sometimes, during the night, fills its schedules with pornographic films of a type that would be encoded or banned elsewhere.

Time Zones

Italy and Sicily follow Central European Time (GMT + 1) but, from the last Sunday in March to the last Sunday in October, the clocks advance one addition hour to become GMT + 2. This means in summer when it is noon in Sicily it will be 11am in London, 6am in New York, and 8pm in Sydney.

Toilets

Bars, cafés, restaurants and autostrada service stations have toilet facilities; they must provide them by law. The condition of some may leave much to be desired. In a bar you do not have to consume something first before heading for a toilet, but it helps, especially when it is one where you have to ask at the *cassa* (cash desk) for the key *(chiave)*.

Many major sites now have toilet facilities. Most are well maintained so expect to pay a small fee to use them.

Tourist Information

Most tourist offices in Sicily have some staff who speak English, French or German. Availability of these staff varies however, as does their ability.

Many offices have a wealth of information on their province, including detailed brochures, maps and books. The best are excellent; the worst appear to dislike their work and see visitors as a tiresome distraction from reading the newspaper and drinking coffee.

If writing for information, be prepared for a long wait: the postal service is not speedy. Alternatively, use the Internet, where you will find a wealth of information on Sicily.

The provincial tourist offices are now all called AAPIT (*Azienda Autonoma Provinciale per l'Incremento Turistico*), and are often abbreviated to APT. The local offices are usually called *Azienda Autonoma di Soggiorno e Turismo* (AAST). In small places they are sometimes called Pro Loco, and may have limited opening hours. When looking for the office, ask for *l'ufficio informazioni turistiche*.

Palermo Province and city are covered by: AAPIT, Piazza Castelnuovo 34; tel: 091 605 8111; info@palermotourism.com; www.aapit.pa.it; open Mon–Fri 8.30am–2pm and 3–6pm, Sat 9am–1pm (summer only).

Information offices are also located at the airport (tel: 091 605 8351) and the station (tel: 091 616 9969) as well as at the airport (tel: 091 616 9969).

Tipping

In restaurants, a service charge is included in the bill unless the menu indicates otherwise. It is customary to leave a few euros (€3–5), rather than a percentage of the total bill, if the service has been good. In hotels, leaving a tip *(una mancia)* in your room for the maids is no longer the custom unless they have been visible and given good service.

Taxi drivers will expect a passenger to round up the fare for a short journey or tip around 10 percent of the fare for a long trip.

Tips to local guides and coach drivers depend on their ability and the length of the trip: around €5 per person is normal.

In many small towns and villages, churches and other monuments may appear to be permanently closed for lunch: there is usually a custodian (or elderly "helper") nearby who will be pleased to open the door. A tip of around €5 per person and many *grazie* are then appropriate.

Generally speaking, €5 is considered an appropriate tip,

neither too generous, nor mean – unless the service has been exceptional.

U seful Addresses

For tourist information outside Sicily:
Canada: Office National Italien de Tourisme, 175 Bloor Street East, South Tower, Suite 907, Toronto. Tel: 416 925 4882.
Ireland: Italian State Tourist Office, 47 Merrion Square, Dublin 2. Tel: 01 766397.
UK: Italian State Tourist Board, 1 Princes Street, London W1B 2AY. Tel: 020 7399 3562.
USA: Italian Government Tourist Office, 630 5th Avenue, Suite 1565, New York, NY 10111. Tel: 212 245 5618.
The official website is www.enit.it

W eights and Measures

All weights and measurements are in the metric system. As a rough but approximate guide:
A kilometre (1 km) is five-eighths of a mile. That is, 80 km equals 50 miles.
2.5cm = 1 inch
1 metre = approximately 1 yard
100 grams = 4oz
1 kilo = 2lb 2oz.

What to Read

HISTORY AND CULTURE
Luigi Barzini: *The Italians*, Penguin. A classic study.
Antonino Buttitta: *Easter in Sicily*, Sicilian Tourist Service, Palermo. An introduction to Sicilian festivals.
David Gilmour: *The Last Leopard: A Life of Giuseppe di Lampedusa*, Quartet.
Giuseppe di Lampedusa: *The Leopard*, Vintage
John Julius Norwich: *The Normans in Sicily*, Penguin
Regione Sicilia. *Archaeology in Sicily*, D'Agostini, Italy.
Finley and Mack Smith: *History of Sicily*, Chatto & Windus. The best overall Sicilian history.

CRIME AND SOCIETY
Anton Blok: *The Mafia of a Sicilian Village*, Harper & Row.
Andrea Camilleri: *The Shape of Water, The Terracotta Dog, The Voice of the Violin, The Snack Thief*. Four detective stories written in Sicilian vernacular language have become best-sellers in Italy. English paperback editions. Picador.
Giovanni Falcone: *Men of Honour, the Truth about the Mafia*, Little, Brown. Judge Falcone's testament.
Norman Lewis: *The Honoured Society*, Eland Press. A colourful if exaggerated account of the wartime Mafia.
Clare Longrigg: *Mafia Women*, Vintage. The changing role of women in *la Cosa Nostra*.
Gavin Maxwell: *Ten Pains of Death*, Alan Sutton. Account of the people Maxwell met while living in Scopello in the 1950s.
Mario Puzo: *The Sicilian*, Bantam Books.
Peter Robb: *Midnight in Sicily*, Panther. Insights on art, food, history, travel and the Mafia.
Gaia Servadio: *To a Different World*, Hamish Hamilton.
Clare Sterling: *The Mafia*, Grafton. Analysis of the "Pizza Connection".

TRAVEL AND GENERAL
Vincent Cronin: *The Golden Honeycomb*, Granada.
Paul Duncan: *Sicily*, John Murray.
Giuseppe Fava: *I Siciliani*, Cappelli Editore.
J.W. Goethe: *Italian Journey 1786–1788*, Penguin.
Norman Lewis: *In Sicily*, Picador.
Theresa Maggio: *The Stone Boudoir*, Headline.
Daphne Phelps: *A House in Sicily*, Virago Press
Mary Taylor Simeti: *On Persephone's Island*, Penguin.
Mary Taylor Simeti: *Sicilian Food*, Random Century.

L ANGUAGE

UNDERSTANDING THE SICILIANS

The language of Sicily is Italian, supplemented by Sicilian dialects. Dialects may differ enormously within a few villages, and are an essential part of Sicilian culture.

In large cities and tourist centres you will find many people who speak English, French or German. In fact, given the number of returning immigrants – descendants of the families that were part of the massive emigration over the past 100 years – you may meet fluent speakers of these languages, often with a New York, Melbourne, Brussels or Bavarian accent.

One dialect with a difference is that Piana degli Albanesi in Palermo province: here Albanian is spoken. The population is descended from Albanians who arrived in the 15th century.

Pronunciation:

A few important rules for English speakers: c before e or i is pronounced ch, e.g. *ciao* ("chow"), *mi dispiace* ("mee dispyache"). Then ch before i or e is pronounced as k, e.g. *la chiesa* ("la kyesa"). Z is pronounced as ts, e.g. *la coincidenza* ("la coinchidentsa"), and gli is pronounced ly, e.g. *biglietto* ("bilyetto").

The stress is usually on the penultimate syllable of a word. In this book, where the stress falls elsewhere, we have indicated this with an accent (e.g. Trápani, Cefalù), although Italians often do not bother to use one (and, if they do, they may disagree about their direction).

Nouns are either masculine (il, plural i) or feminine (la, plural le). Plurals of nouns are most often formed by changing an o to an i and an a to an e, e.g. *il panino – i panini; la chiesa – le chiese*.

To supplement the phrases below, we recommend the handy and inexpensive *Berlitz Italian Phrasebook & Dictionary*.

Numbers

1 Uno	**16** Sedici
2 Due	**17** Diciassette
3 Tre	**18** Diciotto
4 Quattro	**19** Diciannove
5 Cinque	**20** Venti
6 Sei	**30** Trenta
7 Sette	**40** Quaranta
8 Otto	**50** Cinquanta
9 Nove	**60** Sessanta
10 Dieci	**70** Settanta
11 Undici	**80** Ottanta
12 Dodici	**90** Novanta
13 Tredici	**100** Cento
14 Quattordici	**200** Duecento
15 Quindici	**1,000** Mille

Basic Phrases

Hello (Good day) Buon giorno
  Good evening Buona sera
  Good night Buona notte
Goodbye Arrivederci
Hi/Goodbye (familiar) Ciao
Yes Sì
No No
Thank you Grazie
You're welcome Prego
Alright (OK) Va bene
Please Per favore/per piacere.
Excuse me (to get attention) Scusi (singular)/Scusate (plural)
Excuse me (in a crowd) Permesso
Can you show me...? Puo indicarmi..?
Can you help me, please? Puo aiutarmi, per piacere?
I'm lost Mi sono perso
Sorry Mi dispiace
I don't understand Non capisco
I am English/American Sono inglese/americano
Do you speak English? Parla inglese?
Do you like Sicily? (you will often be asked) Le piace la Sicilia?
I love it Mi piace moltissimo (correct answer)

Questions And Answers

I would like... Vorrei...
I would like that one, please Vorrei quello li, per favore

Is there ...? C'è (un) ...?
Do you have ...? Avete ...?
Yes, of course Si, certo/Ma certo
No, we don't No, non c'è (also used to mean: S/he is not here)
Where is the lavatory? Dov'è il bagno?
Gentlemen Signori or Uomini
Ladies Signore or Donne

Transport

airport l'aeroporto
aeroplane l'aereo
arrivals arrivi
boat la barca
bus il autobus
bus station autostazione
connection la coincidenza
departures le partenze
ferry il traghetto
ferry terminal stazione marittima
flight il volo
hydrofoil l'aliscafo
left luggage il deposito bagaglio
no smoking vietato fumare
platform il binario
port il porto
station la stazione
railway station stazione ferrovia
return ticket un biglietto di andata e ritorno
single ticket un biglietto di andata sola
stop la fermata
train il treno
What time does the train leave? Quando parte il treno?
What time does the train arrive? Quando arriva il treno?
What time does the bus leave for Monreale? Quando parte l'autobus per Monreale?
How long will it take to get there? Quanto tempo ci vuole per arrivare?
Can you tell me when to get off? Mi può dire di scendere alla fermata giusta?
The train is late Il treno è in ritardo

Directions

right a destra
left a sinistra
straight on sempre diritto
far away lontano

nearby vicino
opposite di fronte
next to accanto a
traffic lights il semaforo
junction l'incrocio, il bivio
Turn left Gira a sinistra
Where is ...? Dov'è ...?
Where are ...? Dove sono...?
Where is the nearest bank/petrol station/bus stop/hotel/garage? Dov'è la banca/il benzinaio/la fermata di autobus/l'albergo/ l'officina più vicino?
Can you show me where I am on the map? Potrebbe indicarmi sulla cartina dove mi trovo?
How do I get there? Come si può andare?
You're on the wrong road. E sulla strada sbagliata.

Road Signs

Alt **Stop**
Attenzione **Caution**
Caduta massi **Danger of falling rocks**
Deviazione **Diversion**
Divieto di campeggio **No camping allowed**
Divieto di passaggio **No entry**
Divieto di sosta, Sosta vietata **No parking**
Galleria **Tunnel**
Incrocio **Crossroads**
Limite di velocità **Speed limit**
Passaggio a livello **Railway crossing**
Parcheggio **Parking**
Pericolo **Danger**
Pericolo di incendio **Danger of fire**
Rallentare **Slow down**
Rimozione forzata **Parked cars will be towed away (Tow Zone)**
Semaforo **Traffic lights**
Senso unico **One way street**
Sentiero **Footpath**
Strada interrotta **Road blocked**
Strada senza uscita **Dead end**
Vietato il sorpasso **No overtaking**

Shopping

How much does it cost? Quanto costa?
(half) a kilo un (mezzo) kilo
100 grams un etto

200 grams due etti
a little un pochino
That's enough Basta così
That's too expensive E troppo caro
It's too small E troppo piccolo
It's too big E troppo grande
I like it Mi piace
I don't like it Non mi piace
I'll take it Lo prendo

In the Hotel

I would like Vorrei
a single/double room (with a double bed) una camera singola/doppia (con letto matrimoniale)
with bath/shower con bagno/doccia
for one night per una notte
How much is it? Quanto costa?
Is breakfast included? E compresa la colazione?
half/full board mezza pensione/pensione completa
key la chiave
towel un asciugamano
toilet paper la carta igienica
Do you have a room with a balcony/view of the sea? C'è una camera con balcone/una vista del mare?
Can I see the room? Posso vedere la camera?
Is it a quiet room? E una stanza tranquilla?
We have one with a double bed Ne abbiamo una matrimoniale.
Can I have the bill, please? Posso avere il conto, per favore?

Finding the Sights

Custode **Custodian**
Suonare il campanello **Ring the bell**
Abbazia **Abbey**
Aperto **Open**
Chiuso **Closed**
Chiesa **Church**
Entrata **Entrance**
Museo **Museum**
Ruderi **Ruins**
Scavi **Excavations/ archaeological site**
Spiaggia **Beach**
Tempio **Temple**

ART & PHOTO CREDITS

AKG London 28, 33, 85T
**Saffo Alessandro/SIME/
4Corners** 75
The Art Archive 244T
**Adriano Bacchella/
CuboImages srl/Alamy** 107
Jenny Bennathan 44
Carlo Chinca 109T, 110
Marco Di Lauro/Getty Images
140, 152
Lise Dumont/Alamy 31
**Robert Francis/Robert
Harding Picture Library** 7CL
**Alessandro Fucarini/AP/
Empics** 38
Christopher Gannon/Alamy
112, 132T, 132
**Alfio Garozzo/Robert Harding
Picture Library** 247, 249R,
250, 259, 262
Glyn Genin 7B, 8B, 9CL, 62, 64L,
65T, 72, 74T, 86, 89, 94T, 95,
96, 97, 100, 101, 101T, 102,
103T, 104T, 114, 115, 117, 120,
121, 122, 122T, 125, 128, 130,
148T, 156, 166T, 170, 175, 176,
177, 178, 178T, 179, 181, 185T,
186, 189, 190, 191, 204, 204T,
205, 206, 209, 212, 213, 214,
215, 220, 223, 224, 225T, 234T,
251, 252T, 255, 256T, 258, 273
F. Giaccone/Marka 45, 65, 196T
**Corrado Giambalvo/AP/
Empics** 84
Ronald Grant Archive 39
Lyle Lawson 1, 6T, 6B, 10/11,
12/13, 14, 16, 17, 19, 20, 21,
22, 23, 24, 25, 26, 27, 29, 32,
40, 41, 42, 46, 48/49, 50/51,
52, 67, 71, 73T, 74, 83, 85T,
90T, 92, 93, 96T, 98, 99, 102T,
104, 106, 108, 108T, 109, 109T,
111, 119, 124, 126T, 128T, 131,
136, 138T, 139, 143, 143T, 144,

146, 149, 150, 150T, 151T,
152T, 154, 154T, 155, 158, 161,
163T, 172, 172T, 179T, 180,
182, 182T, 183, 184, 188, 195,
196, 200, 202T, 210T, 216, 217,
222, 222T, 225, 233, 239, 243,
243T, 244, 246, 248, 248T, 254,
260, 261, 262T
**Riccardo Lombardo/Cubo
Images srl/Alamy** 168R
**Riccardo Lombardo/Robert
Harding Picture Library** 249L,
257
John Heseltine 5B
Michael Jenner 4, 47
Magnum 36, 37
**Museo Internazionale della
Marionette** 3
Axel Poignant Archive 4B
**Herber Scholpp/Westend61/
Alamy** 18, 66
**Enzo Signorelli/Robert
Harding Picture Library** 129,
245
Stock Italia/Alamy 231
Salvo Veneziano 90
Wilhelm von Gloeden/AKG 235
Gregory Wrona 59, 118, 118T,
127, 167, 168L, 169, 171
Gregory Wrona/Apa 7T, 8T, 9T,
43, 58, 60T, 61, 61T, 63, 64R,
67T, 68, 69, 70, 73, 80, 81, 82T,
85, 86T, 87, 87T, 88, 88T, 91,
113, 116T, 137, 141, 142, 147,
151, 153T, 159, 161T, 162,
162T, 163, 164, 165, 166, 173,
176T, 185, 187, 192, 193, 193T,
194, 194T, 195T, 197, 201, 203,
203T, 207, 208, 211, 212T,
213T, 218, 219L, 219R, 221,
226, 227, 228, 229, 230T, 232,
232T, 233T, 234, 236, 237, 238,
240, 241T, 242, 252, 253, 274,
275, 279, 280, 282

Pages 34/35:
Top row, left to right:
M. Cristofori/Marka; M.
Capovilla/Marka.
Middle row: John Heseltine, Glyn
Genin.
Bottom row: M. Capovilla/Marka,
Glyn Genin, John Heseltine, M.
Capovilla/Marka.
Pages 78/79:
Top row left to right: John
Heseltine, F. Lovino/Marka, John
Heseltine.
Bottom row: John Heseltine, John
Heseltine, F. Giaconne/Marka,
M. Mazzola/Marka.
Pages 134/135:
Top row: Axel Poignant Archive.
Centre row: F. Giaccone/Marka,
Bottom row: Axel Poignant
Archive, F. Giaccone/Marka, P.
Ongaro/Marka,
F. Giaccone/Marka.
Pages 198/199:
Top row left to right: Axel Poignant
Archive, F. Pizzochero/Marka.
Centre: L. Fioroni/Marka.
Bottom row: Axel Poignant
Archive, F. Giaccone/Marka,
Museo Internazionale della
Marionette, Glyn Genin.

Touring map credits: cover, Jon
Arnold Images/Alamy, Intro, Drives
3 & 5: Lyle Lawson, Drives 4 & 6:
Glyn Genin, Drives 1 & 2: Gregory
Wrona/Apa

Map Production:
Dave Priestley, James Macdonald
and Mike Adams
©2009 Apa Publications GmbH & Co.
Verlag KG, Singapore Branch

INDEX

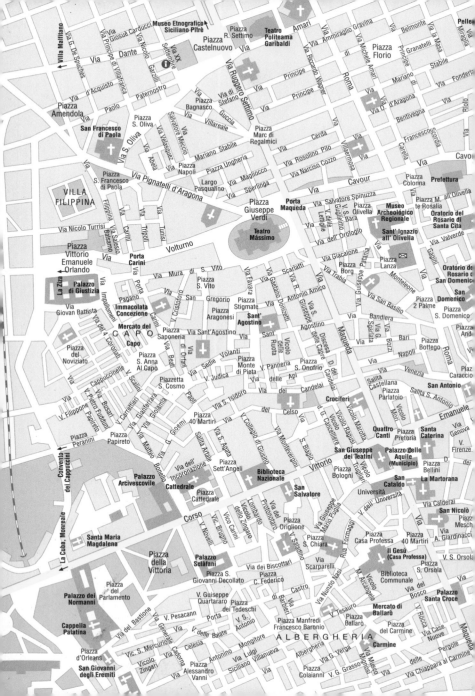